Datsun Owners Workshop Manual

Alec J Jones
BSc Eng, C Eng

Models covered

Datsun Sunny Saloon, Coupe, Fastback Estate & Estate/Van with
1171 cc, 1397 cc & 1488 cc engines

Covers automatic and four- & five-speed manual transmissions

ISBN 1 85010 095 0

Printed in England   *(525–11K1)*

ABCDE
FGHIJ
K

Haynes Publishing Group
Sparkford Nr Yeovil
Somerset BA22 7JJ England

Haynes Publications, Inc
861 Lawrence Drive
Newbury Park
California 91320 USA

British Library Cataloguing in Publication Data

Jones, A.J.
   Datsun Sunny '78 to '82 owners workshop manual. –
(Haynes Owners Workshop Manual)
   1. Sunny automobile
   I. Title
629.28'722   TL215.5/–
ISBN 1–85010–095–0

Acknowledgements

Thanks are due to the Nissan Motor Company Limited for the supply of technical information and certain illustrations. The Champion Sparking Plug Company supplied the illustrations showing the various spark plug conditions, Castrol Limited provided lubrication data and many of the workshop tools came from Sykes-Pickavant.

Lastly, special thanks are due to all of those people at Sparkford who helped in the production of this manual.

About this manual

Its aim

The aim of this manual is to help you get the best value from your vehicle. It can do so in several ways. It can help you decide what work must be done (even should you choose to get it done by a garage), provide information on routine maintenance and servicing, and give a logical course of action and diagnosis when random faults occur. However, it is hoped that you will use the manual by tackling the work yourself. On simpler jobs it may even be quicker than booking the car into a garage and going there twice, to leave and collect it. Perhaps most important, a lot of money can be saved by avoiding the costs a garage must charge to cover its labour and overheads.

The manual has drawings and descriptions to show the function of the various components so that their layout can be understood. Then the tasks are described and photographed in a step-by-step sequence so that even a novice can do the work.

Its arrangement

The manual is divided into thirteen Chapters, each covering a logical sub-division of the vehicle. The Chapters are each divided into Sections, numbered with single figures, eg 5; and the Sections into paragraphs (or sub-sections), with decimal numbers following on from the Section they are in, eg 5.1, 5.2, 5.3 etc.

It is freely illustrated, especially in those parts where there is a detailed sequence of operations to be carried out. There are two forms of illustration; figures and photographs. The figures are numbered in sequence with decimal numbers, according to their position in the Chapter – eg Fig. 6.4 is the fourth drawing/illustration in Chapter 6. Photographs carry the same number (either individually or in related groups) as the Section or sub-section to which they relate.

There is an alphabetical index at the back of the manual as well as a contents list at the front. Each Chapter is also preceded by its own individual contents list.

References to the 'left' or 'right' of the vehicle are in the sense of a person in the driver's seat facing forwards.

Unless otherwise stated, nuts and bolts are removed by turning anti-clockwise, and tightened by turning clockwise.

Valve manufacturers continually make changes to specifications and recommendations, and these, when notified, are incorporated into our manuals at the earliest opportunity.

Whilst every care is taken to ensure that the information in this manual is correct, no liability can be accepted by the authors or publishers for loss, damage or injury caused by any errors in, or omissions from, the information given.

Introduction to the Datsun B310 series

The Datsun New Sunny (B310) and the 210 (North America) retains many features of the B210 or 120Y which it replaced, but has an improved body style and includes as standard equipment some features which were extras on the earlier models. The principal change is that the front suspension includes an anti-roll bar and the rear suspension is of the coil spring type on some models.

The model is available in four main body versions: Saloon (2- or 4-door), Coupe, Fastback Estate and Estate/Van. In an attempt to avoid too much confusion Fastback Estate models are referred to as 'Estates' and Estate/Van models are called 'Vans'. The 1200 cc engine is fitted to the manual saloon models and the 1400 cc engine is fitted to the automatic saloon models for the European market and the 1400 cc to the corresponding US models. The Coupe/Hatchback version has the 1400 cc engine and the Estate version has the 1200 cc engine for territories outside North America and either a 1400 or 1500 cc engine in North America.

The general design of the models is conventional, they are fully equipped, reliable and easy to service. Standard models outside North America have a four-speed manual gearbox, except for the Coupe/Hatchback which has a five-speed gearbox, but the five-speed gearbox is available as an option on all North American models. Automatic transmission is available except on the Coupe.

Contents

4

The Datsun Sunny GLS Saloon

The Datsun Sunny Fastback Estate

The Datsun 210 Sedan

The Datsun 210 Hatchback

Capacities, dimensions and weights

For modifications, and information applicable to later models, see Supplement at end of manual

Refill capacities	US	Imperial	Metric
Fuel tank	$13\frac{1}{4}$ gal	11 gal	50 litres
Cooling system – A12 engine (UK)			
With heater			
Manual transmission	5 qt	$4\frac{1}{8}$ qt	4·7 litres
Automatic transmission	$5\frac{1}{4}$ qt	$4\frac{3}{8}$ qt	5·0 litres
Without heater			
Manual transmission	$4\frac{3}{8}$ qt	$3\frac{5}{8}$ qt	4·1 litres
Automatic transmission	$4\frac{5}{8}$ qt	$3\frac{7}{8}$ qt	4·4 litres
Cooling system – A14 and A15 engines (UK)			
With heater			
Manual transmission	$5\frac{1}{8}$ qt	$4\frac{1}{4}$ qt	4·8 litres
Automatic transmission	$5\frac{1}{8}$ qt	$4\frac{3}{8}$ qt	4·9 litres
Without heater			
Manual transmission	$4\frac{1}{2}$ qt	$3\frac{3}{4}$ qt	4·2 litres
Automatic transmission	$4\frac{1}{2}$ qt	$3\frac{3}{4}$ qt	4·3 litres
Cooling system – 210 (USA and Canada)			
With heater			
Manual transmission	$6\frac{1}{4}$ qt	$5\frac{1}{4}$ qt	5·9 litres
Automatic transmission	6 qt	5 qt	5·7 litres
Without heater			
Manual transmission	$5\frac{1}{2}$ qt	$4\frac{5}{8}$ qt	5·2 litres
Automatic transmission	$5\frac{1}{4}$ qt	$4\frac{3}{8}$ qt	5·0 litres
Engine oil			
With filter – A12, A14 and UK A15 engines	$3\frac{3}{8}$ qt	$2\frac{7}{8}$ qt	3·2 litres
Without filter – A12, A14 and UK A15 engines	$2\frac{7}{8}$ qt	$2\frac{3}{8}$ qt	2·7 litres
With filter – USA A15 engine	$3\frac{1}{4}$ qt	$2\frac{3}{4}$ qt	3·1 litres
Without filter – USA A15 engine	$2\frac{3}{4}$ qt	$2\frac{1}{4}$ qt	2·6 litres
Manual transmission			
4-speed with A12 engine	$2\frac{1}{2}$ pint	$2\frac{1}{8}$ pint	1·2 litres
4-speed with A14, A15 engines	$2\frac{3}{4}$ pint	$2\frac{1}{4}$ pint	1·3 litres
5-speed	$2\frac{1}{2}$ pint	$2\frac{1}{8}$ pint	1·2 litres
Automatic transmission	$5\frac{5}{8}$ qt	$4\frac{5}{8}$ qt	5·3 litres
Differential carrier	$1\frac{7}{8}$ pint	$1\frac{5}{8}$ pint	0·9 litres
Steering gear	$\frac{1}{2}$ pint	$\frac{1}{2}$ pint	0·25 litres
Air conditioning system			
Compressor oil	8·1 fl. oz	8·4 fl. oz	0·24 litres

Overall dimensions

Length
Saloon
  Normal bumper . . . . 155·1 in (3940 mm)
  Larger bumper . . . . 157·3 in (3995 mm)
Coupe
  Normal bumper . . . . 155·1 in (3940 mm)
  Larger bumper . . . . 157·3 in (3995 mm)
Estate . . . . 163·8 in (4160 mm)
Sedan (North America) . . . . 165·0 in (4190 mm)
Hatchback (North America) . . . . 165·0 in (4190 mm)
Wagon (North America) . . . . 167·3 in (4250 mm)

Width
Saloon and Estate . . . . 62·2 in (1580 mm)
Coupe . . . . 62·8 in (1595 mm)
All models (North America) . . . . 62·2 in (1580 mm)

Height
Saloon . . . . 53·7 in (1365 mm)
Coupe . . . . 52·6 in (1335 mm)
Estate . . . . 52·8 in (1340 mm)
Sedan (North America) . . . . 53·7 in (1365 mm)
Hatchback (North America) . . . . 52·6 in (1335 mm)
Wagon (North America) . . . . 52·6 in (1335 mm)

Ground clearance
Saloon, Coupe and Estate . . . . 7·5 in (190 mm)
Sedan (North America)
  Without catalytic converter . . . . 7·7 in (195 mm)
  With catalytic converter . . . . 6·5 in (165 mm)
Hatchback (North America)
  Without catalytic converter . . . . 7·5 in (190 mm)
  With catalytic converter . . . . 6·3 in (160 mm)
Wagon (North America)
  Without catalytic converter . . . . 7·7 in (195 mm)
  With catalytic converter . . . . 6·7 in (170 mm)

Kerb weight
4-door Saloon
  120Y . . . . 1850 lb (840 kg)
  140Y . . . . 1930 lb (875 kg)
2-door Saloon
  120Y . . . . 1830 lb (830 kg)
  140Y . . . . 1905 lb (865 kg)
Coupe . . . . 1930 lb (875 kg)
Estate . . . . 2020 lb (915 kg)
Sedan (North America) . . . . 2775 lb (1260 kg)
Hatchback (North America) . . . . 2800 lb (1270 kg)
Wagon (North America) . . . . 2855 lb (1295 kg)

Use of English

As this book has been written in England, it uses the appropriate English component names, phrases, and spelling. Some of these differ from those used in America. Normally, these cause no difficulty, but to make sure, a glossary is printed below. In ordering spare parts remember the parts list may use some of these words:

English	American	English	American
Accelerator	Gas pedal	Leading shoe (of brake)	Primary shoe
Aerial	Antenna	Locks	Latches
Anti-roll bar	Stabiliser or sway bar	Methylated spirit	Denatured alcohol
Big-end bearing	Rod bearing	Motorway	Freeway, turnpike etc
Bonnet (engine cover)	Hood	Number plate	License plate
Boot (luggage compartment)	Trunk	Paraffin	Kerosene
Bulkhead	Firewall	Petrol	Gasoline (gas)
Bush	Bushing	Petrol tank	Gas tank
Cam follower or tappet	Valve lifter or tappet	'Pinking'	'Pinging'
Carburettor	Carburetor	Prise (force apart)	Pry
Catch	Latch	Propeller shaft	Driveshaft
Choke/venturi	Barrel	Quarterlight	Quarter window
Circlip	Snap-ring	Retread	Recap
Clearance	Lash	Reverse	Back-up
Crownwheel	Ring gear (of differential)	Rocker cover	Valve cover
Damper	Shock absorber, shock	Saloon	Sedan
Disc (brake)	Rotor/disk	Seized	Frozen
Distance piece	Spacer	Sidelight	Parking light
Drop arm	Pitman arm	Silencer	Muffler
Drop head coupe	Convertible	Sill panel (beneath doors)	Rocker panel
Dynamo	Generator (DC)	Small end, little end	Piston pin or wrist pin
Earth (electrical)	Ground	Spanner	Wrench
Engineer's blue	Prussian blue	Split cotter (for valve spring cap)	Lock (for valve spring retainer)
Estate car	Station wagon	Split pin	Cotter pin
Exhaust manifold	Header	Steering arm	Spindle arm
Fault finding/diagnosis	Troubleshooting	Sump	Oil pan
Float chamber	Float bowl	Swarf	Metal chips or debris
Free-play	Lash	Tab washer	Tang or lock
Freewheel	Coast	Tappet	Valve lifter
Gearbox	Transmission	Thrust bearing	Throw-out bearing
Gearchange	Shift	Top gear	High
Grub screw	Setscrew, Allen screw	Trackrod (of steering)	Tie-rod (or connecting rod)
Gudgeon pin	Piston pin or wrist pin	Trailing shoe (of brake)	Secondary shoe
Halfshaft	Axleshaft	Transmission	Whole drive line
Handbrake	Parking brake	Tyre	Tire
Hood	Soft top	Van	Panel wagon/van
Hot spot	Heat riser	Vice	Vise
Indicator	Turn signal	Wheel nut	Lug nut
Interior light	Dome lamp	Windscreen	Windshield
Layshaft (of gearbox)	Countershaft	Wing/mudguard	Fender

Buying spare parts
and vehicle identification numbers

Buying spare parts

Spare parts are available from many sources, for example Datsun garages, other garages and accessory shops and motor factors. Our advice regarding spare parts is as follows:

Officially appointed Datsun garages – This is the best source of parts which are peculiar to your car and otherwise not generally available (eg, complete cylinder heads, internal gearbox components, badges, interior trim etc). It is also the only place at which you should buy parts if your car is still under warranty; non-Datsun components may invalidate the warranty. To be sure of obtaining the correct parts, it will always be necessary to give the storeman your car's engine and chassis number and if possible, to take the old part along for identification. Remember that many parts are available on a factory exchange scheme – any parts returned should always be clean! It obviously makes good sense to go to the specialists on your car for this type of part, for they are best equipped to supply you.

Other garages and accessory shops – These are often very good places to buy material and components needed for the maintenance of your car (eg, oil filters, spark plugs, bulbs, fan belts, oils and grease, touch-up paint, filler paste etc). They also sell general accessories, usually have convenient opening hours, charge lower prices and can often be found not far from home.

Motor factors – Good factors will stock all of the more important components which wear out relatively quickly (eg, clutch components, pistons, valves, exhaust systems, brake cylinders/pipes/hoses/seals/shoes and pads etc). Motor factors will often provide new or reconditioned components on a part exchange basis. This can save a considerable amount of money.

Vehicle identification numbers

Modifications are a continuing and unpublicised process in vehicle manufacture, quite apart from major model changes. Spare parts manuals and lists are compiled upon a numerical basis, the individual vehicle number being essential for correct identification of the component required.

The vehicle identification number – is located on the top surface of the instrument panel cowl and it is visible through the windscreen on vehicles manufactured for and operating in North America. Vehicles operating in other territories have the identification (chassis) number stamped on the engine compartment rear bulkhead (photo).

The car identification plate giving the model number is on a plate attached to the front bulkhead in the engine compartment (photo).

The car serial (chassis) number on North American models is stamped on to the front bulkhead below the identification plate.

The body colour coding is shown on a plate attached to the upper surface of the radiator crossmember.

The emission control information, for vehicles fitted with this equipment, is on the underside of the bonnet lid, on the right-hand side when viewed from the front.

The engine type number is cast into the right-hand side of the cylinder block and the engine serial number is stamped on to the block alongside it.

The MVSS or FMVSS (Motor Vehicle Safety Standard or Federal Motor Vehicle Safety Standard) certification label is fixed to the centre pillar on the driver's side.

The manual transmission number is stamped on to the top of the transmission bellhousing case.

The serial number of the automatic transmission is stamped on the plate on the right-hand side of the transmission casing.

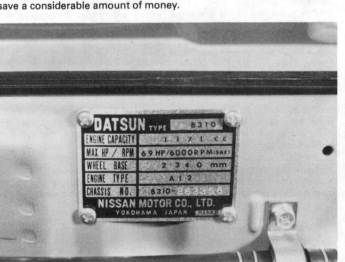

Car identification plate

Car serial number

Tools and working facilities

Introduction

A selection of good tools is a fundamental requirement for anyone contemplating the maintenance and repair of a motor vehicle. For the owner who does not possess any, their purchase will prove a considerable expense, offsetting some of the savings made by doing-it-yourself. However, provided that the tools purchased are of good quality, they will last for many years and prove an extremely worthwhile investment.

To help the average owner to decide which tools are needed to carry out the various tasks detailed in this manual, we have compiled three lists of tools under the following headings: *Maintenance and minor repair, Repair and overhaul,* and *Special.* The newcomer to practical mechanics should start off with the *Maintenance and minor repair* tool kit and confine himself to the simpler jobs around the vehicle. Then, as his confidence and experience grows, he can undertake more difficult tasks, buying extra tools as, and when, they are needed. In this way, a *Maintenance and minor repair* tool kit can be built-up into a *Repair and overhaul* tool kit over a considerable period of time without any major cash outlays. The experienced do-it-yourselfer will have a tool kit good enough for most repair and overhaul procedures and will add tools from the *Special* category when he feels the expense is justified by the amount of use to which these tools will be put.

It is obviously not possible to cover the subject of tools fully here. For those who wish to learn more about tools and their use there is a book entitled *How to Choose and Use Car Tools* available from the publishers of this manual.

Maintenance and minor repair tool kit

The tools given in this list should be considered as a minimum requirement if routine maintenance, servicing and minor repair operations are to be undertaken. We recommend the purchase of combination spanners (ring one end, open-ended the other); although more expensive than open-ended ones, they do give the advantages of both types of spanner.

> Combination spanners - 6, 7, 8, 9, 10, 11, 13, 14 & 17 mm
> Adjustable spanner - 9 inch
> Engine sump/gearbox/rear axle drain plug key (where applicable)
> Spark plug spanner (with rubber insert)
> Spark plug gap adjustment tool
> Set of feeler gauges
> Brake bleed nipple spanner
> Screwdriver - 4 in long x $\frac{1}{4}$ in dia (flat blade)
> Screwdriver - 4 in long x $\frac{1}{4}$ in dia (cross blade)
> Combination pliers - 6 inch
> Hacksaw, junior
> Tyre pump
> Tyre pressure gauge
> Oil can
> Fine emery cloth (1 sheet)
> Wire brush (small)
> Funnel (medium size)

Repair and overhaul tool kit

These tools are virtually essential for anyone undertaking any major repairs to a motor vehicle, and are additional to those given in the *Maintenance and minor repair* list. Included in this list is a comprehensive set of sockets. Although these are expensive they will be found invaluable as they are so versatile - particularly if various drives are included in the set. We recommend the $\frac{1}{2}$ in square-drive type, as this can be used with most proprietary torque wrenches. If you cannot

afford a socket set, even bought piecemeal, then inexpensive tubular box spanners are a useful alternative.

The tools in this list will occasionally need to be supplemented by tools from the *Special* list.

> Sockets (or box spanners) to cover range in previous list
> Reversible ratchet drive (for use with sockets)
> Extension piece, 10 inch (for use with sockets)
> Universal joint (for use with sockets)
> Torque wrench (for use with sockets)
> 'Mole' wrench - 8 inch
> Ball pein hammer
> Soft-faced hammer, plastic or rubber
> Screwdriver - 6 in long x $\frac{5}{16}$ in dia (flat blade)
> Screwdriver - 2 in long x $\frac{5}{16}$ in square (flat blade)
> Screwdriver - 1 $\frac{1}{2}$ in long x $\frac{1}{4}$ in dia (cross blade)
> Screwdriver - 3 in long x $\frac{1}{8}$ in dia (electricians)
> Pliers - electricians side cutters
> Pliers - needle nosed
> Pliers - circlip (internal and external)
> Cold chisel - $\frac{1}{2}$ inch
> Scriber (this can be made by grinding the end of a broken hacksaw blade)
> Scraper (this can be made by flattening and sharpening one end of a piece of copper pipe)
> Centre punch
> Pin punch
> Hacksaw
> Valve grinding tool
> Steel rule/straight edge
> Allen keys
> Selection of files
> Wire brush (large)
> Axle-stands
> Jack (strong scissor or hydraulic type)

Special tools

The tools in this list are those which are not used regularly, are expensive to buy, or which need to be used in accordance with their manufacturers' instructions. Unless relatively difficult mechanical jobs are undertaken frequently, it will not be economic to buy many of these tools. Where this is the case, you could consider clubbing together with friends (or a motorists' club) to make a joint purchase, or borrowing the tools against a deposit from a local garage or tool hire specialist.

The following list contains only those tools and instruments freely available to the public, and not those special tools produced by the vehicle manufacturer specifically for its dealer network. You will find occasional references to these manufacturers' special tools in the text of this manual. Generally, an alternative method of doing the job without the vehicle manufacturer's special tool is given. However, sometimes, there is no alternative to using them. Where this is the case and the relevant tool cannot be bought or borrowed you will have to entrust the work to a franchised garage.

> Valve spring compressor
> Piston ring compressor
> Balljoint separator
> Universal hub/bearing puller
> Impact screwdriver
> Micrometer and/or vernier gauge
> Dial gauge

Stroboscopic timing light
Dwell angle meter/tachometer
Universal electrical multi-meter
Cylinder compression gauge
Lifting tackle
Trolley jack
Light with extension lead

Buying tools

For practically all tools, a tool factor is the best source since he will have a very comprehensive range compared with the average garage or accessory shop. Having said that, accessory shops often offer excellent quality tools at discount prices, so it pays to shop around.

Remember, you don't have to buy the most expensive items on the shelf, but it is always advisable to steer clear of the very cheap tools. There are plenty of good tools around at reasonable prices, so ask the proprietor or manager of the shop for advice before making a purchase.

Care and maintenance of tools

Having purchased a reasonable tool kit, it is necessary to keep the tools in a clean serviceable condition. After use, always wipe off any dirt, grease and metal particles using a clean, dry cloth, before putting the tools away. Never leave them lying around after they have been used. A simple tool rack on the garage or workshop wall, for items such as screwdrivers and pliers is a good idea. Store all normal spanners and sockets in a metal box. Any measuring instruments, gauges, meters, etc, must be carefully stored where they cannot be damaged or become rusty.

Take a little care when tools are used. Hammer heads inevitably become marked and screwdrivers lose the keen edge on their blades from time to time. A little timely attention with emery cloth or a file will soon restore items like this to a good serviceable finish.

Working facilities

Not to be forgotten when discussing tools, is the workshop itself. If anything more than routine maintenance is to be carried out, some form of suitable working area becomes essential.

It is appreciated that many an owner mechanic is forced by circumstances to remove an engine or similar item, without the benefit of a garage or workshop. Having done this, any repairs should always be done under the cover of a roof.

Wherever possible, any dismantling should be done on a clean flat workbench or table at a suitable working height.

Any workbench needs a vice: one with a jaw opening of 4 in (100 mm) is suitable for most jobs. As mentioned previously, some clean dry storage space is also required for tools, as well as the lubricants, cleaning fluids, touch-up paints and so on which become necessary.

Another item which may be required, and which has a much more general usage, is an electric drill with a chuck capacity of at least $\frac{5}{16}$ in (8 mm). This, together with a good range of twist drills, is virtually essential for fitting accessories such as wing mirrors and reversing lights.

Last, but not least, always keep a supply of old newspapers and clean, lint-free rags available, and try to keep any working area as clean as possible.

Spanner jaw gap comparison table

Jaw gap (in)	Spanner size
0·250	$\frac{1}{4}$ in AF
0·276	7 mm
0·313	$\frac{5}{16}$ in AF

Jaw gap (in)	Spanner size
0·315	8 mm
0·344	$\frac{11}{32}$ in AF; $\frac{1}{8}$ in Whitworth
0·354	9 mm
0·375	$\frac{3}{8}$ in AF
0·394	10 mm
0·433	11 mm
0·438	$\frac{7}{16}$ in AF
0·445	$\frac{3}{16}$ in Whitworth; $\frac{1}{4}$ in BSF
0·472	12 mm
0·500	$\frac{1}{2}$ in AF
0·512	13 mm
0·525	$\frac{1}{4}$ in Whitworth; $\frac{5}{16}$ in BSF
0·551	14 mm
0·563	$\frac{9}{16}$ in AF
0·591	15 mm
0·600	$\frac{5}{16}$ in Whitworth; $\frac{3}{8}$ in BSF
0·625	$\frac{5}{8}$ in AF
0·630	16 mm
0·669	17 mm
0·686	$\frac{11}{16}$ in AF
0·709	18 mm
0·710	$\frac{3}{8}$ in Whitworth; $\frac{7}{16}$ in BSF
0·748	19 mm
0·750	$\frac{3}{4}$ in AF
0·813	$\frac{13}{16}$ in AF
0·820	$\frac{7}{16}$ in Whitworth; $\frac{1}{2}$ in BSF
0·866	22 mm
0·875	$\frac{7}{8}$ in AF
0·920	$\frac{1}{2}$ in Whitworth; $\frac{9}{16}$ in BSF
0·938	$\frac{15}{16}$ in AF
0·945	24 mm
1·000	1 in AF
1·010	$\frac{9}{16}$ in Whitworth; $\frac{5}{8}$ in BSF
1·024	26 mm
1·063	$1\frac{1}{16}$ in AF; 27 mm
1·100	$\frac{5}{8}$ in Whitworth; $\frac{11}{16}$ in BSF
1·125	$1\frac{1}{8}$ in AF
1·181	30 mm
1·200	$\frac{11}{16}$ in Whitworth; $\frac{3}{4}$ in BSF
1·250	$1\frac{1}{4}$ in AF
1·260	32 mm
1·300	$\frac{3}{4}$ in Whitworth; $\frac{7}{8}$ in BSF
1·313	$1\frac{5}{16}$ in AF
1·390	$\frac{13}{16}$ in Whitworth; $\frac{15}{16}$ in BSF
1·417	36 mm
1·438	$1\frac{7}{16}$ in AF
1·480	$\frac{7}{8}$ in Whitworth; 1 in BSF
1·500	$1\frac{1}{2}$ in AF
1·575	40 mm; $\frac{15}{16}$ in Whitworth
1·614	41 mm
1·625	$1\frac{5}{8}$ in AF
1·670	1 in Whitworth; $1\frac{1}{8}$ in BSF
1·688	$1\frac{11}{16}$ in AF
1·811	46 mm
1·813	$1\frac{13}{16}$ in AF
1·860	$1\frac{1}{8}$ in Whitworth; $1\frac{1}{4}$ in BSF
1·875	$1\frac{7}{8}$ in AF
1·969	50 mm
2·000	2 in AF
2·050	$1\frac{1}{4}$ in Whitworth; $1\frac{3}{8}$ in BSF
2·165	55 mm
2·362	60 mm

Jacking and towing

Towing points

If the vehicle has to be towed, any rope or cable should be connected to the eye attached to the front sidemember (photo). On vehicles equipped with automatic transmission, the towing speed should not exceed 20 mph (30 km/h) nor the towing distance 6 miles (10 km) otherwise the transmission may be damaged due to lack of lubrication. If towing distances are excessive, disconnect the propeller shaft from the rear axle pinion flange and tie the shaft up out of the way.

Where another vehicle is being towed, always attach the rope or cable to the rear towing eye (photo).

Jacking points

The pantograph type jack supplied with the vehicle must only be used at the positions below the body sills (photos). Other types of jack should be located below the front crossmember or rear axle differential casing. If axle-stands are to be used, then they must be positioned under the bodyframe sidemembers or rear axle casing. No other positions should be used for jacking or support.

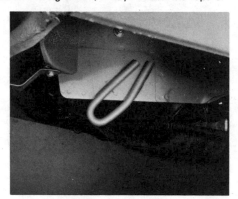

Front towing eye

Rear towing eye

Jack in position with notch on sill

Jack in correct position for lifting

Wheel chocks in position

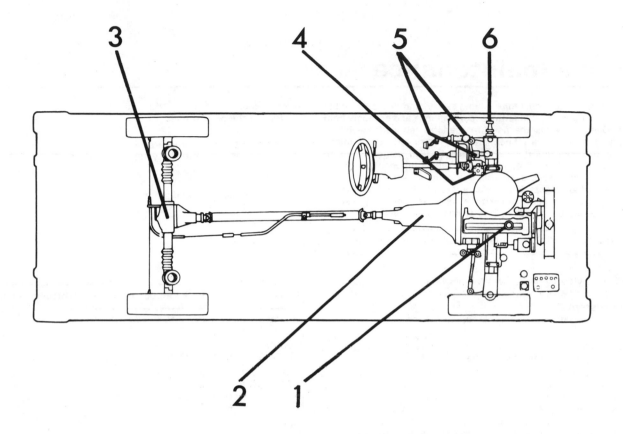

Recommended lubricants and fluids

Component or system	Lubricant type or specification
Engine (1)	Multi-grade engine oil
Gearbox (2)	
Manual	90 EP hypoid gear oil
Automatic	Dexron type automatic transmission fluid
Rear axle (3)	90 EP hypoid gear oil (MIL-L-2105B)
Steering gearbox (4)	90 EP hypoid gear oil
Brake and clutch fluid (5)	Hydraulic fluid (SAE J1703C)
Front wheel bearings (6)	Multi-purpose grease

Note: The above recommendations are general: lubrication requirements vary from territory-to-territory. Consult the operators handbook supplied with your car.

Routine maintenance

Maintenance is essential for ensuring safety, and desirable for the purpose of getting the best in terms of performance and economy from your car. Over the years the need for periodic lubrication – oiling, greasing and so on – has been drastically reduced, if not totally eliminated. This has unfortunately tended to lead some owners to think that because no such action is required, components either no longer exist, or will last forever. This is a serious delusion. It follows therefore that the largest initial element of maintenance is visual examination and a general sense of awareness. This may lead to repairs or renewals, but should help to avoid roadside breakdowns.

Every 250 miles (400 km) or weekly – whichever comes first

Engine
Check the sump oil level. Top up if necessary

Cooling system
Check the radiator coolant level. Top-up if necessary

Braking system
Check and, if necessary, top-up the reservoir fluid level
Check the efficiency of the braking system

Electrical system
Check and, if necessary, top-up the battery electrolyte level
Check for correct operation of all lights, and the horn
Check the windscreen washer reservoir fluid level. Top-up if necessary

Wheels
Check the tyre pressures
Examine the tyres for wear and damage

Every 3000 miles (4800 km) or three months – whichever comes first

Engine (severe operating conditions eg dusty environment, mainly short trips or long high speed journeys)
Renew the oil and filter

Braking system (in areas using salt or other corrosive materials)
Check and lubricate the system components

Body (dusty environment)
Lubricate all locks and hinges

Every 6000 miles (9600 km) or six months – whichever comes first

In addition to, or instead of, the 250 mile (400 km) checks

Engine
Renew the oil and filter

Fuel system
Clean, check and, if necessary, adjust the carburettor
Clean the fuel pump

Ignition system
Check and, if necessary, adjust the distributor points gap
Check and, if necessary, adjust the timing
Check and, if necessary, adjust the spark plug electrode gap

Clutch
Check and, if necessary, top-up the fluid level
Check pedal free movement

Transmission
Check and, if necessary, top-up the fluid level in the manual gearbox, automatic transmission and rear axle (as applicable)

Checking oil level

Oil sump drain plug

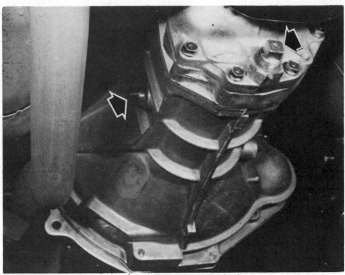

Manual gearbox filler and level plug (at side) and drain plug (at rear)

Oil filter assembly

Braking system
Check the brake pads for wear. Renew if necessary

General
Check all systems for operation, wear, security and lubrication (where necessary)

Every 12 000 miles (19 000 km) or twelve months – whichever comes first

---

In addition to, or instead of, the 6000 mile (9600 km) checks

Engine
Check and, if necessary, adjust the valve clearances

Cooling system
Check the fanbelt for wear and tension. Adjust or renew as necessary

Fuel system
Clean the positive crankcase ventilation (PCV) hoses and check the valve for correct operation
Renew the air cleaner element (dusty conditions)

Clutch
Renew master and slave cylinder seals
Renew hydraulic fluid

Ignition system
Renew the distributor contact breaker assembly
Renew the spark plugs

Propeller shaft
Check all components for adequate lubrication

Braking system
Check the brake shoes for wear. Renew if necessary
Renew all cylinder seals
Renew the brake fluid

Suspension and steering
Check all components for adequate lubrication
Check wheel alignment. Adjust if necessary
Check and rebalance the steering, if necessary

Every 24 000 miles (38 000 km) or two years – whichever comes first

---

In addition to, or instead of, the 12 000 mile (19 000 km) checks

Cooling system
Change the engine coolant

Fuel system
Renew the fuel filter
Renew the air cleaner element

Transmission
Renew the oil in the manual gearbox and rear axle (as applicable)

Braking system
Check the Nissan Proportioning (NP) valve for operation

Suspension and steering
Remove, clean, repack (with grease) and adjust the front hub bearings
Grease the balljoints

Every three years

Fuel system
Renew the positive crankcase ventilation valve and filter

Additionally the following items should be attended to as time can be spared

---

Cleaning
Examination of components requires that they be cleaned. The same applies to the body of the car, inside and out, in order that deterioration due to rust or unknown damage may be detected. Certain parts of the body frame, if rusted badly, can result in the vehicle being declared unsafe and it will not pass the annual test for roadworthiness.

Exhaust system
An exhaust system must be leakproof, and the noise level below a certain level. Excessive leaks may cause carbon monoxide fumes to enter the passenger compartment. Excessive noise constitutes a public nuisance. Both these faults may cause the vehicle to be kept off the road. Repair or renew defective sections when symptoms are apparent.

Chapter 1 Engine

For modifications, and information applicable to later models, see Supplement at end of manual

Contents

Specifications

Engine (general)

Type	Water cooled, 4 cylinder, in-line ohv		
Firing order	1 – 3 – 4 – 2		
	A12	**A14**	**A15**
Capacity	1171 cc (71·45 cu in)	1397 cc (85·24 cu in)	1488 cc (90·80 cu in)
Compression ratio	9·0 : 1	9·0 : 1	8·9 : 1 (California and 5-speed non-California models) 8·5 : 1 (Canada and US except 5-speed non-California and California models)
Bore	2·874 in (73·0 mm)	2·992 in (76·0 mm)	2·992 in (76·0 mm)
Stroke	2·756 in (70·0 mm)	3·031 in (77·0 mm)	3·228 in (82·0 mm)
Idle speed			
Manual transmission	600 rpm	650 rpm	700 rpm
Automatic transmission	700 rpm in N	750 rpm in N	650 rpm in D
Oil capacity			
With filter	2$\frac{7}{8}$ Imp qt, 3$\frac{3}{8}$ US qt, 3·2 litres	2$\frac{7}{8}$ Imp qt, 3$\frac{3}{8}$ US qt, 3·2 litres	2$\frac{3}{4}$ Imp qt, 3$\frac{1}{4}$ US qt. 3·1 litres
Without filter	2$\frac{3}{8}$ Imp qt, 2$\frac{7}{8}$ US qt. 2·7 litres	2$\frac{3}{8}$ Imp qt. 2$\frac{7}{8}$ US qt. 2·7 litres	2$\frac{1}{4}$ Imp qt, 2$\frac{3}{4}$ US qt, 2·6 litres

Valves

Valve clearances:	
Inlet and Exhaust (cold)	0·010 in (0·25 mm)
Inlet and Exhaust (hot)	0·014 in (0·35 mm)
Valve length:	
Valve length – A12 engine	4·030 to 4·041 in (102·35 to 102·65 mm)
Valve length – A 14, A15 engines	4·079 to 4·094 in (103·6 to 104·0 mm)
Seat angle	45° 30'

Valve lift:
  Inlet .... 0·3114 in (7·91 mm)
  Exhaust .... 0·3236 in (8·22 mm)
Valve head diameter:
  Inlet .... 1·457 to 1·465 in (37·0 to 37·2 mm)
  Exhaust .... 1·181 to 1·189 in (30·0 to 30·2 mm)
Valve stem diameter:
  Inlet .... 0·3138 to 0·3144 in (7·970 to 7·985 mm)
  Exhaust .... 0·3128 to 0·3134 in (7·945 to 7·960 mm)
Valve spring free length .... 1·831 in (46·5 mm)
Valve guides:
  Length .... 1·929 in (49·0 mm) 2·09 in (53·0 mm) California
  Height from head surface .... 0·709 in (18·0 mm)
  Inside diameter .... 0·3150 to 0·3156 in (8·000 to 8·015 mm)
Stem clearance:
  Inlet .... 0·0006 to 0·0018 in (0·015 to 0·045 mm)
  Exhaust .... 0·0016 to 0·0028 in (0·040 to 0·070 mm)
Valve seat width – A12 engine:
  Inlet .... 0·051 in (1·3 mm)
  Exhaust .... 0·071 in (1·8 mm)
Valve seat width – A14, A15 engines:
  Inlet .... 0·071 in (1·8 mm)
  Exhaust .... 0·087 in (2·2 mm)

Cylinder block
Top face warp limit .... 0·004 in (0·10 mm)
Bore wear limit .... 0·0079 in (0·20 mm)
Maximum ovality in bores .... 0·0006 in (0·015 mm)
Maximum taper in bores .... 0·0006 in (0·015 mm)

Camshaft
Endfloat .... 0·0004 to 0·0020 in (0·01 to 0·05 mm)
Lobe lift:
  Inlet .... 0·2224 in (5·65 mm)
  Exhaust .... 0·2331 in (5·92 mm)
Camshaft journal diameters:
  No 1 .... 1·7237 to 1·7242 in (43·783 to 43·796 mm)
  No 2 .... 1·7041 to 1·7046 in (43·283 to 43·296 mm)
  No 3 .... 1·6844 to 1·6849 in (42·783 to 42·796 mm)
  No 4 .... 1·6647 to 1·6652 in (42·283 to 42·296 mm)
  No 5 .... 1·6224 to 1·6229 in (41·208 to 41·221 mm)
Camshaft distortion (max) .... 0·0006 in (0·015 mm)
Camshaft bearing to journal clearances:
  No 1 .... 0·0015 to 0·0024 in (0·037 to 0·060 mm)
  No 2 .... 0·0011 to 0·0020 in (0·027 to 0·050 mm)
  No 3 .... 0·0016 to 0·0025 in (0·040 to 0·063 mm)
  No 4 .... 0·0011 to 0·0020 in (0·027 to 0·050 mm)
  No 5 .... 0·0015 to 0·0024 in (0·037 to 0·060 mm)
Camshaft bearing inside diameter:
  No 1 .... 1·7257 to 1·7261 in (43·833 to 43·843 mm)
  No 2 .... 1·7056 to 1·7060 in (43·323 to 43·333 mm)
  No 3 .... 1·6865 to 1·6868 in (42·836 to 42·846 mm)
  No 4 .... 1·6663 to 1·6667 in (42·323 to 42·333 mm)
  No 5 .... 1·6243 to 1·6247 in (41·258 to 41·268 mm)

Connecting rods and bearings
Bearing clearance .... 0·0004 to 0·0024 in (0·010 to 0·060 mm)
Wear allowanace (max) .... 0·0039 in (0·10 mm)
Big-end endplay .... 0·004 to 0·008 in (0·1 to 0·2 mm)

Piston and piston rings
Diameter – A12 engine:
  Standard .... 2·8735 to 2·8755 in (72·987 to 73·037 mm)
  0·50 Oversize .... 2·8924 to 2·8944 in (73·467 to 73·517 mm)
  1·00 Oversize .... 2·9121 to 2·9149 in (73·967 to 74·017 mm)
  1·50 Oversize .... 2·9318 to 2·9337 in (74·467 to 74·517 mm)
Piston ring side clearances – A12 engine:
  Top .... 0·0016 to 0·0028 in (0·04 to 0·07 mm)
  2nd .... 0·0016 to 0·0028 in (0·04 to 0·07 mm)
  Oil .... 0·0016 to 0·0032 in (0·04 to 0·08 mm)
Ring gap – A12 engine:
  Top .... 0·0079 to 0·0138 in (0·20 to 0·35 mm)
  2nd .... 0·0079 to 0·0138 in (0·20 to 0·35 mm)
  Oil .... 0·0118 to 0·0354 in (0·30 to 0·90 mm)

Diameter – A14, A15 engines:
Standard .... 2·9908 to 2·9927 in (75·967 to 76·017 mm)
0·50 Oversize .... 3·0105 to 3·0125 in (76·467 to 76·517 mm)
1·00 Oversize .... 3·0302 to 3·0322 in (76·967 to 77·017 mm)
Piston ring side clearances – A14, A15 engines:
Top .... 0·0016 to 0·0028 in (0·04 to 0·07 mm)
2nd .... 0·0012 to 0·0024 in (0·03 to 0·06 mm)
Oil ring .... Combined
Ring gap – A14, A15 engines:
Top .... 0·0079 to 0·0138 in (0·20 to 0·35 mm)
2nd .... 0·0059 to 0·0118 in (0·15 to 0·30 mm)
Oil .... 0·0118 to 0·0354 in (0·30 to 0·90 mm)

Crankshaft and main bearings
Journal diameter:
A12 engine .... 1·9666 to 1·9675 in (49·951 to 49·974 mm)
A14, A15 engines .... 1·9666 to 1·9671 in (49·951 to 49·964 mm)
Journal taper and ovality (Max):
A12 engine .... – 0·0004 in (–0·01 m)
A14, A15 engine .... – 0·0002 in (– 0·005 mm)
Endfloat .... 0·0020 to 0·0059 in (0·05 to 0·15 mm)
Maximum endfloat .... 0·0118 in (0·30 mm)
Crankpin diameter .... 1·7701 to 1·7706 in (44·961 to 44·974 mm)
Crankpin taper and ovality (Max):
A12 engine .... 0·0004 in (0·01 mm)
A14, A15 engines .... 0·0002 in (0·005 mm)
Crankpin clearance .... 0·0008 to 0·0024 in (0·020 to 0·062 mm)
Crankpin wear limit .... 0·0039 in (0·10 mm)

Lubrication
Oil pump type .... Externally mounted, bi-rotor, driven by camshaft

Torque wrench settings

	lbf ft	kgf m
Cylinder head bolts	51 to 54	7·0 to 7·5
Rocker shaft bracket bolts	14 to 18	2·0 to 2·5
Main bearing cap bolts	36 to 43	5·0 to 6·0
Flywheel fixing bolts – A12 engine	47 to 54	6·5 to 7·5
Flywheel fixing bolts – A14, A15 engines	58 to 65	8·0 to 9·0
Driveplate fixing bolts		
A14 engine	58 to 65	8·0 to 9·0
A15 engines	61 to 69	8·5 to 9·5
Connecting rod cap nuts	23 to 27	3·2 to 3·8
Camshaft sprocket bolt	29 to 35	4·0 to 4·8
Locating plate bolts	3·6 to 5·8	0·5 to 0·8
Valve rocker adjusting nuts	12 to 16	1·6 to 2·2
Oil strainer bolts	6·5 to 10·1	0·9 to 1·4
Sump bolts	2·9 to 4·3	0·4 to 0·6
Sump drain plug	14 to 22	2·0 to 3·0
Timing chain cover bolts	3·6 to 5·1	0·5 to 0·7
Crankshaft pulley bolt	108 to 145	15 to 20
Water pump bolts	6·5 to 10·1	0·9 to 1·4
Spark plugs	11 to 14	1·5 to 2·0
Engine mounting bolts	14 to 18	1·9 to 2·5

1 General description

The engines are of the four cylinder in-line type with overhead valves operated from the camshaft via pushrods and a rocker arm assembly.

The cast iron cylinder block has integral cylinders and waterways.

The crankshaft is located in five main bearings and has drilled oilways to provide the necessary lubrication to the respective main bearings and connecting rod big-end journals.

The H-section connecting rods have oil jets to supply a splash feed lubrication to the cylinder walls.

Aluminium alloy cast pistons are used and are located on the connecting rods by a gudgeon pin which is an interference fit in the small-end.

The camshaft is located in five bearings which are lubricated via holes intersecting the main oil gallery in the cylinder block. Each cam lobe is lubricated via a hole in its base from the integral passages.

The cylinder head is manufactured in aluminium alloy and is of conventional layout having the inlet and exhaust valves in line, with the respective inlet and exhaust ports and manifolds on the left-hand side.

The pushrod operated valve system uses single valve springs and the valves to rocker arm clearances are fully adjustable via a ball head stud and locknut. The tappets are located within the cylinder block and can only be withdrawn with the camshaft removed, as they cannot be extracted or inserted from the top of the block.

The camshaft is driven from a double row chain which is automatically adjusted between the crankshaft and camshaft sprockets by a spring loaded chain tensioner.

The engine oil pump unit is externally mounted and the housing incorporates the oil filter location. The pump, which is a trochoid type, is driven by a shaft from the camshaft, and distributes oil to the various engine components via the respective internal oilways.

The inlet manifold is aluminium and the exhaust manifold is cast iron and incorporates a quick warm up valve.

2 Major operations possible with engine fitted

1 Removal and refitting the cylinder head assembly.
2 Removal and refitting the timing case, timing chain and sprockets (after removal of sump).
3 Removal and refitting the oil pump unit.

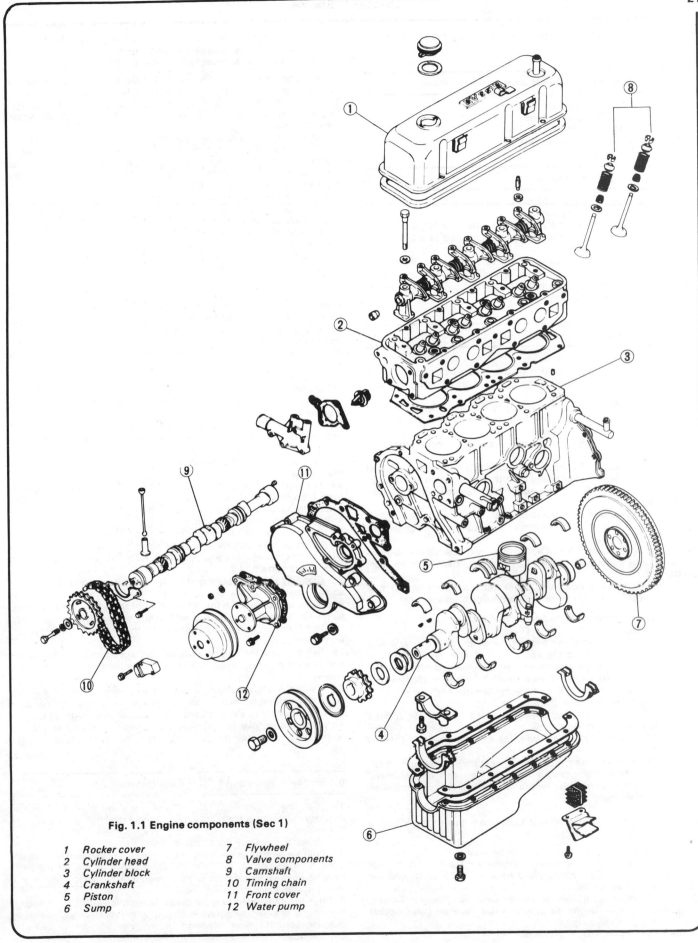

Fig. 1.1 Engine components (Sec 1)

1	Rocker cover	7	Flywheel
2	Cylinder head	8	Valve components
3	Cylinder block	9	Camshaft
4	Crankshaft	10	Timing chain
5	Piston	11	Front cover
6	Sump	12	Water pump

4   Removal and refitting the pistons, connecting rods, and big-end bearings.

3   Major operations only possible with engine removed

1   Removal and refitting the crankshaft.
2   Removal and refitting the flywheel.
3   Renewal of the crankshaft rear oil seal.
4   Removal and refitting the camshaft.

4   Engine – method of removal

1   The engine can be removed from the vehicle either on its own or as a combined unit with the gearbox.
2   Although depending on the work to be carried out, it is usually preferable to remove the engine/transmission combined as it is easier to separate them out of the car.
3   Lifting tackle of suitable capacity will be required and if removing both engine and transmission combined, allow for sufficient height when at full lift as they must be tilted to clear the bulkhead tunnel and front radiator attachment panel.

5   Engine and transmission – removal

1   Disconnect the battery cables.
2   Mark the bonnet hinge location on the underside using a soft lead pencil. This will assist in correctly realigning it on assembly. Remove the bonnet.
3   Drain the radiator coolant, referring to Chapter 2 if necessary. If the engine is to be dismantled, the engine oil must be drained at this stage.
4   Disconnect the upper and lower coolant hoses from the engine/radiator connections.
5   On automatic transmission models, detach the lower splash panel and disconnect the oil cooler hoses from their installation at the lower end of the radiator. Drain the automatic transmission fluid (see Chapter 6).
6   Where applicable remove the radiator shroud.
7   Disconnect and carefully remove the radiator and grille (see Chapter 2).
8   Detach the air cleaner hoses and withdraw the air cleaner. Detach the accelerator cable and choke cable (where fitted) from the carburettor.
9   The following wires must be disconnected but make a note of their respective locations so that there is no confusion on reassembly:

(a)   *Starter motor wires and cable from the battery*
(b)   *Ignition coil to distributor HT lead*
(c)   *Distributor lead at the body terminal, and also the earth wire to the terminal on the vacuum diaphragm retaining screw. The wires are the same colour so label them to differentiate*
(d)   *The oil pressure switch wire which is located on the filter unit*
(e)   *The alternator wires, and the carburettor choke wire (when fitted) and fuel cut solenoid.*
(f)   *The temperature gauge wire from the front of the cylinder head at the right-hand side*
(g)   *The engine earth cable from the front bolt retaining the oil filter unit*
(h)   *From underneath the car, disconnect the reverse light switch wire from the transmission terminal, and on automatic transmission models, detach the inhibitor switch and downshift solenoid wires.*

10   On models fitted with Emission Control equipment the following items must also be disconnected:

(a)   *Detach the automatic choke heater wire*
(b)   *On air conditioned models disconnect the fast idle control device (FICD) magnet valve hose at the dashpot and the three way connector*
(c)   *Detach the combined air control (CAC) valve hose on California models, or the air control valve hose on other models (except Canada)*
(d)   *The air pump air cleaner hose*
(e)   *The boost controlled deceleration device (BCDD) vacuum control valve hose on California models*
(f)   *The carbon canister hose on the engine connection*

11   Disconnect the heater hoses, (inlet and outlet), and the Master-Vac vacuum hose from the inlet manifold (where applicable).
12   Disconnect the fuel hose from the fuel pump and plug or clamp it to prevent spillage or the ingress of dirt. Tie back out of the way to prevent damage.
13   Detach and withdraw the accelerator linkage from its bracket.
14   On models fitted with a mechanically operated clutch, disconnect the cable from the withdrawal lever at the clutch housing. On models fitted with a hydraulically operated clutch, disconnect the slave cylinder (operating cylinder) from the clutch housing. Further information on both systems is given in Chapter 5.
15   On models fitted with air conditioning equipment, slacken the compressor drivebelt idler pulley nut and bolt and with the tension released, remove the drivebelt. Unscrew and remove the compressor securing bolts and relocate the compressor away from the engine so that it will not get in the way during engine withdrawal. Do *not* under any circumstances detach the hoses or allow the gas to discharge from the system.
16   The following operations are carried out underneath the car and therefore it must be over a work pit or raised sufficiently clear of the ground to enable the respective components to be disconnected. Do not rely purely on the jack supplied with the car – supplement with axle-stands and/or suitable blocks to make secure.
17   Unscrew and detach the speedometer cable from its location in the transmission.
18   Detach the manual or automatic transmission control lever or linkage as applicable, refer to Chapter 6 if necessary.
19   Unscrew the exhaust pipe to manifold flange nuts and detach the pipe, secure it safely to one side using a piece of wire.
20   Scribe a mating mark across the flange faces of the propeller shaft and companion flange joints to ensure correct alignment on reassembly.
21   Now detach the propeller shaft from the differential carrier companion flange.
22   Lower the propeller shaft at the rear and withdraw it rearwards from the gearbox extension housing to remove. Plug the end of the extension housing or locate a plastic bag over the end to prevent oil spillage, especially during removal.
23   Position a jack under the transmission and raise to just support it.
24   Unscrew and remove the bolts/nuts securing the transmission supporting crossmember and remove it. Note the respective bolt positions and lengths.
25   Carefully locate the lifting sling around the engine and arrange it so that the front of the engine can be tilted upwards to provide the necessary angle required for the removal of the engine and transmission unit. Raise the engine just sufficiently to allow the weight to be relieved from the engine mountings and then remove the nuts/bolts from the insulators.
26   Before lifting the engine/transmission unit check that all adjacent and interconnecting fittings and attachments are free and clear of the engine.
27   Raise the engine slowly and tilt it to enable the front end and sump to clear the radiator crossmember and the transmission to clear the bulkhead tunnel. When clear of the car, lower the engine/transmission unit and remove to a workbench or clean floor area so that the respective ancillary components can be removed as necessary.

6   Engine – separation from manual transmission

1   With the engine and transmission removed from the vehicle, unscrew and remove the bolts which connect the clutch bellhousing to the engine block.
2   Unbolt and remove the starter motor.
3   Pull the transmission from the engine in a straight line, at the same time supporting the transmission so that its weight does not hang up on the primary shaft, even momentarily, whilst the shaft is still engaged with the clutch mechanism.
4   It is recommended that the clutch is removed also at this stage if the engine is undergoing repair. This is to prevent contamination by cleaning solvents when cleaning the engine (Section 8). Refer to Chapter 5 for further information on clutch removal.

7 Engine – separation from automatic transmission

1   Remove the rubber plug from the lower part of the engine rear plate.

2   Unscrew and remove the bolts which secure the driveplate to the torque converter. The crankshaft will have to be turned by means of the pulley bolt so that each driveplate bolt comes into view in turn.

3   With all the driveplate bolts removed, mark the relative position of the driveplate to the torque converter. This is best achieved by placing a dab of coloured paint around one bolt hole in the driveplate and also on the torque converter hole top threads.

4   Remove the starter motor and the fluid filler tube support bolt.

5   Unscrew and remove the bolts which secure the torque converter housing to the engine.

6   Withdraw the automatic transmission in a straight line; expect some loss of fluid as the torque converter moves away from the driveplate and position a drip tray to catch it.

8 Engine dismantling – general

1   It is best to mount the engine on a dismantling stand but if one is not available, stand the engine on a strong bench so as to be at a comfortable working height. Failing this, the engine can be stripped down on the floor.

2   During the dismantling process, the greatest care should be taken to keep the exposed parts free from dirt. As an aid to achieving this, it is a sound scheme to thoroughly clean down the outside of the engine removing all traces of oil and congealed dirt.

3   Use paraffin, or a good grease solvent. The latter compound will make the job much easier, as, after the solvent has been applied and allowed to stand for a time, a vigorous jet of water will wash off the solvent and all the grease and filth. If the dirt is thick and deeply embedded, work the solvent into it with a wire brush.

4   Finally wipe down the exterior of the engine with a rag and only then, when it is quite clean should the dismantling process begin. As the engine is stripped, clean each part in a bath of paraffin.

5   Never immerse parts with oilways in paraffin (eg the crankshaft) but to clean, wipe down carefully with a paraffin dampened rag. Oilways can be cleaned out with wire. If an air-line is present all parts can be blown dry and the oilways blown through as an added precaution.

6   Re-use of old engine gaskets is false economy and can give rise to oil and water leaks, if nothing worse. To avoid the possibility of trouble after the engine has been reassembled, always use new gaskets throughout.

7   Do not throw old gaskets away as it sometimes happens that an immediate replacement cannot be found and the old gasket is then very useful as a template for making up a replacement. Hang up the old gaskets as they are removed on a suitable hook or nail.

8   To strip the engine, it is best to work from the top down. The oil sump provides a firm base on which the engine can be supported in an upright position. When the stage where the sump must be removed is reached, the engine can be turned on its side and all other work carried out with it in this position.

9   Wherever possible, refit nuts, bolts and washers fingertight from wherever they were removed. This helps avoid later loss and muddle. If they cannot be refitted lay them out in such a fashion that it is clear from where they came.

10   Even though the engine may not have to be completely dismantled, it is a good system to clean it thoroughly, whilst removed from the car.

9 Ancillary components – removal

1   If you are stripping the engine completely or preparing to fit a reconditioned unit, all the ancillaries must be removed first. If you are going to obtain a reconditioned 'short' motor (block, crankshaft, pistons and connecting rods), the cylinder head and associated parts will need retention for fitting to the new engine. It is advisable to check just what you will get with a reconditioned unit, as changes are made from time to time.

2   Remove the fan assembly, noting that the shallow recess of the fan boss faces the radiator. Remove the alternator.

3   Remove the right-hand engine mounting bracket.

4   Unscrew and remove the oil filter and discard it. The use of a chain wrench or similar tool will probably be required to remove the filter. Unbolt and remove the oil pump housing and gasket.

5   Unscrew and remove the oil pressure switch.

6   Withdraw the engine oil dipstick.

7   Unscrew the crankshaft pulley bolt. To prevent the engine turning during this operation, jam the flywheel starter ring gear by passing a sharp cold chisel or large screwdriver through the starter motor aperture in the engine rearplate.

8   Withdraw the crankshaft pulley. The insertion of two tyre levers behind the pulley will usually extract the pulley, but if it is exceptionally tight, use an extractor but take care not to distort the rims of the pulley.

9   Disconnect the HT leads from the spark plugs then remove the distributor cap complete with leads.

10   Unscrew and remove the spark plugs.

11   The next step is to detach the fuel, water, air and suction hoses. These vary considerably on the different engines and the only satisfactory way of doing the job is to attach identity labels so that refitting can be readily carried out. The connections will typically be:

(a)   Crankcase PCV hoses
(b)   Fuel pump-to-carburettor hose
(c)   Rocker cover-to-air cleaner hose
(d)   Intake manifold water hoses
(e)   Vacuum tube to carburettor hoses
(f)   Air control valve hoses
(g)   EGR valve vacuum hose
(h)   EGR tube
(i)   Anti-backfire valve hose

12   Having removed the hoses, the associated emission control or engine ancillary items can be removed. Typically these will be:

(a)   EGR valve, tube and passage
(b)   Fuel pump
(c)   Air pump and idler pulley
(d)   PCV valve
(e)   Dashpot bracket
(f)   Check valve
(g)   Air control valve

13   Remove the thermostat housing.

14   Unbolt and remove the manifold assemblies complete with carburettor.

15   Remove the engine left-hand mounting bracket.

16   Remove the water pump.

17   Unscrew and remove the distributor clamp plate bolt from the crankcase and withdraw the distributor from its recess. Refer to Chapter 4 for further information.

18   Remove the rocker cover.

19   The engine should now be stripped of its ancillary components, and dismantling proper may be carried out as described in Section 10 onwards.

10 Cylinder head – removal

1   If the cylinder head is to be removed with the engine in the car, then the following procedures must first be carried out:

(a)   Disconnect the battery
(b)   Drain the radiator
(c)   Remove all HT leads from the rocker cover
(d)   Remove all connections to the carburettor and remove the air cleaner assembly
(e)   Remove the exhaust downpipe from the exhaust manifold
(f)   Remove all hoses connected to the cylinder head
(g)   Remove the crankcase ventilation hose from the inlet manifold
(h)   Remove the rocker cover
(i)   Remove the two bolts which secure the cylinder head to the timing chain cover

2   With the rocker cover removed, progressively loosen the respective valve rocker shaft bracket bolts. Lift the rocker shaft assembly clear when free. Note that the end bolts retain the rocker arms and springs on the shaft and therefore unless the shaft assembly is to be dismantled, leave the bolts in their locations in the brackets.

Fig. 1.2 Removing the rocker shaft assembly (Sec 10)

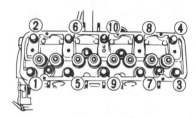

Fig. 1.3 Cylinder head bolt loosening sequence (Sec 10)

3   Withdraw the pushrods keeping them in order so that they can be refitted to their respe locations on re-assembly. A piece of wood or thick cardboard with two rows of holes drilled in it and numbered accordingly will provide a suitable rack for the pushrods.
4   Progressively loosen the cylinder head bolts as shown in Fig. 1.3.
5   Carefully lift the cylinder head clear. If it appears to be stuck do not attempt to prise it free but tap it lightly all round using a soft head mallet or wooden block. Remove the cylinder head gasket.

11 Valves – removal

1   The valves can be removed from the cylinder head by the following method. Compress each spring in turn with a valve spring compressor until the two halves of the collets can be removed. Release the compressor, and remove the spring and spring retainer.
2   If, when the valve spring compressor is screwed down, the valve spring retaining cap fails to free from the split collet, do not continue to screw down on the compressor as there is a likelihood of damaging it.
3   Gently tap the top of the tool directly over the cap with a light hammer. This will free the cap. To avoid the compressor jumping off the valve spring retaining cap when it is tapped, hold the compressor firmly in position with one hand.
4   Slide the rubber oil control seal off the top of each valve stem and then drop out each valve through the combustion chamber.
5   It is essential that the valves are kept in their correct sequence unless they are so badly worn that they are to be renewed.

12 Rocker assembly – dismantling

1   Withdraw the end bolts from the rocker brackets and simply slide the brackets, springs, and rocker arms off the shaft, keeping them in order of sequence.

13 Sump and oil pipe – removal

1   Unscrew in a progressive manner the respective sump securing bolts and remove the oil sump and gasket. **Note**: *If the engine is in the car it will be necessary to disconnect the front mountings and lift the engine approximately 3 in (76.2 mm) in order to remove the sump.*
2   Unscrew the two retaining bolts from the oil pipe and remove it (photo).

14 Timing chain cover, chain and gears – removal

1   Remove the bolts from the timing chain cover, then take off the cover and gasket.
2   Remove the oil thrower disc from the crankshaft, noting which way round it is fitted.
3   Unbolt and remove the chain tensioner.
4   Unscrew and remove the bolt and washers retaining the camshaft sprocket in position. Jam the flywheel to prevent the engine from turning when applying pressure to loosen the bolt.
5   Remove the camshaft and crankshaft gearwheels simultaneously, complete with double roller chain. Use tyre levers behind each gear, and lever them equally a little at a time. If they are stuck on their shafts, the use of a puller may be required (photo).
6   When the gearwheels and chain are removed, extract the two Woodruff keys from the crankshaft. Take care not to damage any shims fitted between the crankshaft sprocket and flange (if fitted).

15 Flywheel – removal

1   If the clutch has not been removed refer to Chapter 5 and detach it from the flywheel.
2   Unscrew the six special bolts retaining the flywheel to the crankshaft. To prevent the crankshaft from turning, block a crankshaft web. Lift the flywheel clear taking care not to drop it.
3   If the engine is being completely stripped, remove the rear plate and gasket at this stage.

16 Camshaft and tappets – removal

1   Unscrew and remove the two camshaft retaining plate bolts and remove with washers. Note which way round the plate faces.
2   Lay the engine on its side and carefully withdraw the camshaft. Special care is needed during removal, to avoid damaging the camshaft journals with the corners of the lobes.
3   The respective tappets can now be extracted from inside the block. If stuck, poke them down from above using a screwdriver, but on

13.2 Oil feed pipe and strainer

14.5 Timing sprockets and chain ready for removal

17.3 Cylinder number markings on connecting rod and cap

removal, keep them in sequence, so that they can be refitted into their respective positions.

17 Pistons and connecting rods – removal

1   With the cylinder head and sump removed, undo the connecting rod (big-end) retaining bolts.
2   The connecting rods and pistons must only be lifted out from the top of the cylinder block.
3   Remove the big-end caps one at a time, taking care to keep them in the right order and the correct way round. Also ensure that the shell bearings are kept with their correct connecting rods and caps unless they are to be renewed. Normally, the numbers 1 to 4 are stamped on adjacent sides of the big-end caps and connecting rods, indicating which cap is fitted on which rod, and which way round the cap is fitted (photo). If no numbers or lines can be found, then, with a sharp screwdriver or file, scratch mating marks across the joint from the rod to the cap. One line for connecting rod No. 1, two for connecting rod No. 2 and so on. This will ensure there is no confusion later, as it is most important that the caps go back in the correct position on the connecting rods from which they were removed.
4   If the big-end caps are difficult to remove they may be gently tapped with a soft hammer.
5   To remove the shell bearings, press the bearings opposite the groove in both the connecting rod, and the connecting rod caps and the bearings will slide out easily.
6   Withdraw the pistons and connecting rods upwards and ensure they are kept in the correct order so that they can be refitted in the same bore. Reassemble the connecting rod, caps and bearings to the rods if the bearings do not require renewal, to minimise the risk of getting the caps and rods mixed up.

18 Crankshaft and main bearings – removal

1   Unscrew and remove the securing bolts from the main bearing caps. The caps are numbered 1 to 5 starting from the timing cover end of the engine and arrows are marked on the caps. These point towards the timing cover to ensure correct orientation of the caps when refitting. If arrows are not visible, dot punch the caps on the side nearer the camshaft. Unscrew the securing bolts in the sequence shown (Fig. 1.4).
2   Withdraw the bearing caps complete with the lower halves of the shell bearings.
3   Remove the rear oil seal.
4   Lift the crankshaft from the crankcase and then remove each of the upper halves of the shell bearings.
5   Unscrew the baffle plate retaining screws and remove the plate. Extract the wire gauze from its recess in the crankcase to complete its dismantling.

19 Piston rings – removal

1   Each ring should be sprung open only just sufficiently to permit it to ride over the lands of the piston body.
2   Once a ring is out of its groove, it is helpful to cut three $\frac{1}{4}$ in (6 mm) wide strips of tin and slip them under the ring at equidistant points.
3   Using a twisting motion this method of removal will prevent the ring dropping into an empty groove as it is being removed from the piston.

20 Gudgeon pin – removal

1   The gudgeon pins are a finger pressure fit (at room temperature) in the pistons, but are an interference fit in the connecting rod small-end.
2   It is recommended that the removal of the gudgeon pins is left to a local dealer having a suitable press.
3   Where such facilities are available to the home mechanic, the body of the piston must be supported on a suitably shaped distance piece into which the gudgeon pin may be ejected. Ensure that each gudgeon pin remains with its correct piston.

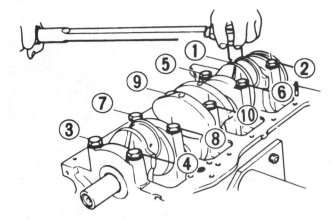

Fig. 1.4 Main bearing cap bolt loosening sequence (Sec 18)

21 Lubrication system – description

1   A force-feed system of lubrication is fitted with oil circulated around the engine from the sump below the cylinder block (Fig. 1.5). The level of engine oil in the sump is indicated by the dipstick which is fitted on the right-hand side of the engine.
2   The oil pump is mounted on the side of the crankcase and is driven by a helical gear and spindle from the camshaft. Oil is drawn from the sump through a gauze screen in the oil strainer, and is sucked up the pick-up pipe and drawn into the trochoid type oil pump. From the pump it is forced under pressure along a gallery on the right-hand side of the engine, and through drillings to the big-end, main and camshaft bearings. A small hole in each connecting rod allows a jet of oil to lubricate the cylinder wall with each revolution.
3   From the camshaft central bearing, oil is fed through drilled passages in the cylinder block and head to the rocker bracket where it enters the hollow rocker shaft. Holes drilled in the hollow rocker shaft allow for lubrication of the rocker arms, the valve stems and pushrod ends. Oil from the front camshaft bearing also lubricates the timing gears and timing chain.
4   Oil returns to the sump by various passages, the tappets being lubricated by oil returning via the pushrod drillings in the block.
5   A full flow cartridge type filter is fitted and oil passes through this filter before it reaches the main oil gallery. The oil is passed directly from the oil pump to the filter.
6   An oil pressure relief valve and warning switch are located in the pump unit body (photos).

21.6 Oil filter and oil pressure switch

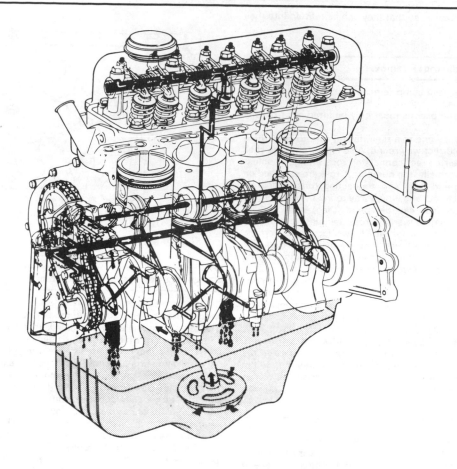

Fig. 1.5 Engine lubrication system (Sec 21)

22 Examination and renovation – general

1   With the engine stripped, and all components thoroughly cleaned, examine everything for wear and damage.
2   Individual parts and assemblies should be checked and, where possible, renovated or otherwise renewed, as described in the following Sections.

23 Crankshaft and main bearings – examination and renovation

1   Examine the crankpin and main journal surfaces for signs of scoring or scratches. Check the ovality of the crankpins at different positions with a micrometer. If out-of-round by more than the specified amount, the crankpin will have to be reground. It will also have to be reground if there are any scores or scratches present. Also check the journals in the same fashion.
2   If it is necessary to regrind the crankshaft and fit new bearings your local Datsun garage or engineering works will be able to decide how much metal to grind off and the size of the new bearing shells required.
3   Full details of crankshaft regrinding tolerances and bearing undersizes are given in the Specifications.
4   The main bearing clearances may be established by using a strip of Plastigage between the crankshaft journals and the main bearing/shell caps. Tighten the bearing cap bolts to the specified torque. Remove the cap and compare the flattened Plastigage strip with the index provided. The clearance should be compared with the tolerances in the Specifications.
5   Temporarily refit the crankshaft to the crankcase having positioned the other halves of the shell main bearings in their locations. Refit the centre main bearing cap only, complete with shell bearing and tighten the securing bolts to the specified torque. Using a feeler gauge, check the endplay by pushing and pulling the crankshaft. Where the endplay is outside the specified tolerance, the centre bearing shells will have to be renewed (photo).
6   Finally examine the clutch pilot bearing (bush) which is located in the centre of the flywheel mounting flange at the rear end of the crankshaft. If it is worn, renew it by tapping a thread in it and screwing in a bolt. Carefully press in the new bush so that its endface will lie below the crankshaft flange surface by 0.110 in (2.8 mm). Lubrication of the bush is not required.

23.5 Measuring crankshaft endfloat

24.2 Shell bearing identification marks on rear face

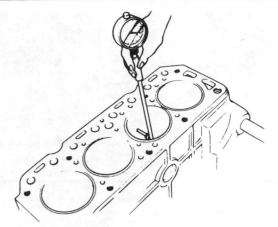

Fig. 1.6 Measuring cylinder bore wear (Sec 25)

24 Connecting rods – examination and renovation

1   Big-end bearing failure is indicated by a knocking from within the crankcase and a slight drop in oil pressure.

2   Examine the bearing surfaces for pitting and scoring. Renew the shells in accordance with the sizes specified in the Specifications (photo). Where the crankshaft has been reground, the correct undersize shell bearings will be supplied by the repairer.

3   Should there be any suspicion that a connecting rod is bent or twisted or the small-end bush no longer provides an interference fit for the gudgeon pin, the complete connecting rod assembly should be exchanged for a reconditioned one. Ensure that the weight of all rods is equal within 0.176 oz (5 grm).

4   Measurement of the big-end bearing clearances may be carried out in a similar manner to that described for the main bearings in the previous Section. The running clearances are given in the Specifications.

5   Finally check the big-end thrust clearance, which should be within the limits given in the Specification.

25 Cylinder bores – examination and renovation

1   The cylinder bores must be examined for taper, ovality, scoring and scratches. Start by carefully examining the top of the cylinder bores. If they are at all worn, a very slight ridge will be found on the thrust side. This marks the top of the piston ring travel. The owner will have a good indication of the bore wear prior to dismantling the engine, or removing the cylinder head. Excessive oil consumption accompanied by blue smoke from the exhaust is a sure sign of worn cylinder bores and piston rings.

2   Measure the bore diameter just under the ridge with a micrometer and compare it with the diameter at the bottom of the bore, which is not subject to wear. If the difference between the two measurements is more than 0.008 in (0.20 mm) then it will be necessary to fit special pistons and rings, or to have the cylinders rebored and fit oversize pistons.

3   The standard clearance between a piston and the cylinder walls is given in the Specification. The easiest way to check this is to insert the piston into its bore with a feeler gauge 0.001 in (0.03 mm) thick, inserted between it and the cylinder wall. Attach the feeler gauge to a spring balance and note the force required to extract the gauge while pulling vertically upwards. This should be between 0.020 and 0.059 lb (0.5 and 1.5 kg). The ambient temperature during this test should be around 68°F (20°C).

4   Where less than the specified force is required to withdraw the feeler gauge, then remedial action must be taken. Oversize pistons are available as listed in the Specifications.

5   These are accurately machined to just below the indicated measurements so as to provide correct running clearances in bores bored out to the exact oversize dimensions.

6   If the bores are slightly worn but not so badly worn as to justify reboring them, special oil control rings and pistons can be fitted which will restore compression and stop the engine burning oil. Several different types are available and the manufacturer's instructions concerning their installation must be followed closely.

7   If new pistons are being fitted and the bores have not been reground, it is essential to slightly roughen the hard glaze on the sides of the bores with fine glass paper so that the new piston rings will have a chance to bed in properly.

26 Crankcase, and cylinder block – examination and renovation

1   Examination of the cylinder block and crankcase should be carried out in conjunction with examination of the cylinder bores. If any faults or damage are visible, it will be a waste of money having the block rebored.

2   Check for cracks especially between the cylinder bores. Repair of cast iron is a specialized job and it may be more economical to purchase a new assembly or one in good condition from a car breaker.

3   Examine stud and bolt holes for stripped threads. New spiral type thread inserts can often be used to overcome this problem, but the manufacturer's fitting instructions must be strictly observed.

4   Probe all oil and water passages with a piece of wire to ensure freedom from obstruction.

5   Examine the engine mountings. Although the mountings can be renewed with the engine in position in the vehicle by taking its weight on a hoist, if they are suspect it is preferable to renew them when the engine has been removed.

27 Pistons and piston rings – examination and renovation

1   Where new pistons have been supplied to match the rebore diameter, new sets of piston rings will also be provided but it is worthwhile checking the ring clearances, as described in the following paragraphs (photo).

2   If the original pistons are being used, carefully remove the piston rings as described in Section 19.

3   Clean the grooves and rings free from carbon, taking care not to scratch the aluminium surfaces of the pistons.

4   If new rings are being fitted to old pistons and the cylinders are not being rebored, obtain a set of new rings which has the top ring stepped, to avoid the ridge at the top of the bore.

5   Before refitting the rings to the pistons, push each ring in turn down its cylinder bore (use an inverted piston to do this to keep the ring square) and then measure the ring endgap. The gaps must be as given in the Specification and should be measured with a feeler blade.

6   Piston ring endgaps can be increased by rubbing them carefully with carborundum stone.

7   The piston rings should now be tested in their respective grooves for side clearance. The clearances must be as listed in the Specifications.

27.1 Measuring ring to piston clearance with a feeler gauge

28.1 Check that the camshaft oilways are clear

8   Where necessary, a piston ring which is slightly tight in its groove may be rubbed down holding it perfectly squarely on a carborundum or a sheet of fine emery cloth laid on a piece of plate glass. Excessive tightness can only be rectified by having the grooves machined out.
9   The piston pin should be a push fit into the piston at room temperature. If it appears slack, then both the piston and piston pin should be renewed.

28 Camshaft and bearings – examination and renovation

1   Carefully examine the camshaft bearings for wear. If the bearings are obviously worn or pitted then they must be renewed. This is an operation for your local Datsun dealer or local engineering works as it demands the use of specialized equipment. The bearings are removed with a special drift after which new bearings are pressed in, and line-bored, care being taken to ensure the oil holes in the bearings line-up with those in the cylinder block and that the holes are clear (photo).
2   The camshaft itself should show no signs of wear, but, if very slight scoring on the cams is noticed, the score marks can be removed by very gently rubbing down with very fine emery cloth. The greatest care should be taken to keep the cam profiles smooth.
3   Check the camshaft sprocket for hooked teeth or distortion and renew if evident.
4   When refitting, the camshaft endplay must not exceed the specified amount. If above the maximum, the locating plate must be renewed.

29 Timing chain, gears and tensioner – examination and renovation

1   Examine the teeth on both the crankshaft gear wheel and the camshaft gearwheel for wear. Each tooth forms an inverted 'V' with the gearwheel periphery and if worn, the side of each tooth under tension will be slightly concave in shape when compared with the other side of the tooth (ie, one side of the inverted 'V' will be concave when compared with the other). If any sign of wear is present, the gearwheels must be renewed.
2   Examine the links of the chain for side slackness and renew the chain if any is noticeable when compared with a new chain. It is a sensible precaution to renew the chain at about 30 000 miles (48 000 km) and at a lesser mileage if the engine is stripped down for a major overhaul. The actual rollers on a very badly worn chain may be slightly grooved.
3   Examine the chain tensioner for wear and ensure that the slipper pad and plunger move smoothly under the action of the spring. Renew as necessary.

30 Cylinder head and valves – servicing and decarbonising

1   With the cylinder head removed, use a blunt scraper to remove all traces of carbon and deposits from the combustion spaces and ports. Remember that the cylinder head is aluminium alloy and can be damaged easily during the decarbonising operations. Scrape the cylinder head free from scale, old pieces of gasket and jointing compound. Clean the cylinder head by washing it in paraffin and take particular care to pull a piece of rag through the ports and cylinder head bolt holes. Any dirt remaining in these recesses may well drop onto the gasket and cylinder block mating surface as the cylinder head is lowered into position and could lead to a gasket leak after reassembly is complete.
2   With the cylinder head clean, test for distortion, especially if a history of coolant leakage has been apparent. Carry out this test using a straight edge and feeler gauges or a piece of plate glass. If the surface shows any warping in excess of 0.0039 in (0.1 mm) the cylinder head will have to be resurfaced which is a job for a specialist engineering company.
3   Clean the pistons and top of the cylinder bores. If the pistons are still in the block then it is essential that great care is taken to ensure that no carbon gets into the cylinder bores as this could scratch the cylinder walls or cause damage to the piston and rings. To ensure this does not happen, first turn the crankshaft so that two of the pistons are at the top of their bores. Stuff rag into the other two bores and seal them off with paper and masking tape. The waterways should also be covered with small pieces of masking tape to prevent particles of carbon entering the cooling system and damaging the water pump.
4   Before scraping the carbon from the piston crowns, press grease into the gap between the cylinder walls and the two pistons which are to be worked on. With a blunt scraper carefully scrape away the carbon from the piston crown, taking great care not to scratch the aluminium. Also scrape away the carbon from the surrounding lip of the cylinder wall. When all carbon has been removed, scrape away the grease which will be contaminated with carbon particles, taking care not to press any into the bores. To assist prevention of carbon build-up the piston crown can be polished with a metal polish. Remove the rags or masking tape from the other two cylinders and turn the crankshaft so that the two pistons which were at the bottom are now at the top. Place rag or masking tape in the cylinders which have been decarbonised and proceed as just described.
5   The valves can be removed from the cylinder head by the following method. Compress each spring in turn with a valve spring compressor until the two halves of the collets can be removed. Release the compressor and remove the spring and spring retainer.
6   If, when the valve spring compressor is screwed down, the valve spring retaining cap fails to free from the split collets, do not continue to screw down the compressor as there is a likelihood of damaging it.
7   Gently tap the top of the tool directly over the cap with a light

hammer. This will free the cap. To avoid the compressor jumping off the valve spring retaining cap when it is tapped, hold the compressor firmly in position with one hand.

8 Slide the rubber oil control seal off the top of each valve stem and then drop out each valve through the combustion chamber.

9 It is essential that the valves are kept in their correct sequence unless they are so badly worn that they are to be renewed.

10 Examine the heads of the valves for pitting and burning, especially the heads of the exhaust valves. The valve seatings should be examined at the same time. If the pitting on valve and seat is very slight the marks can be removed by grinding the seats and valve together with coarse and then fine, valve grinding paste.

11 Where bad pitting has occurred to the valve seats it will be necessary to recut them and fit new valves. If the valve seats are so worn that they cannot be recut, it will be necessary to fit new valve seat inserts. These latter two jobs should be entrusted to the local Datsun agent or engineering works. In practice it is very seldom that the seats are so badly worn that they require renewal. Normally, it is the valve that is too badly worn to be refitted, and the owner can easily purchase a new set of valves and match them to the seats by valve grinding.

12 Valve grinding is carried out as follows: Smear a trace of coarse carborundum paste on the seat face and apply a suction grinder tool to the valve head. With a semi-rotary motion, grind the valve head to its seat, lifting the valve occasionally to redistribute the grinding paste. When a dull matt even surface finish is produced on both the valve seat and the valve, wipe off the paste and repeat the process with fine carborundum paste, lifting and turning the valve to redistribute the paste as before. A light spring placed under the valve head will greatly ease this operation. When a smooth unbroken ring of light grey matt finish is produced, on both valve and valve seat faces, the grinding operation is complete.

13 Scrape away all carbon from the valve head and the valve stem. Carefully clean away every trace of grinding compound, taking great care to leave none in the ports or in the valve guides. Clean the valves and the valve seats with a paraffin soaked rag then with a clean rag, and finally, if an air-line is available, blow the valves, valve guides and valve ports clean.

14 Test each valve in its guides for wear. After a considerable mileage, the valve guide bore may wear oval. This can best be tested by inserting a new valve in the guide and moving it from side to side. If the tip of the valve stem deflects by about 0.0080 in (0.2 mm) then it must be assumed that the tolerance between the stem and guide is greater than the permitted maximum.

15 New valve guides (oversize available) may be pressed or driven into the cylinder head after the worn ones have been removed in a similar manner. The cylinder head must be heated to 392°F (200°C) before carrying out these operations and although this can be done in a domestic oven, it must be remembered that the new guide will have to be reamed after installation and it may therefore be preferable to leave this work to your Datsun dealer.

16 Finally check the free-length of the valve springs and renew them if they are much less than specified or if they have been in operation for 30 000 miles (48 000 km) or more.

31 Valve operating gear – examination and renovation

1 Thoroughly clean the rocker shaft and then check the shaft for straightness by rolling it on plate glass. It is most unlikely that it will deviate from normal, but if it does, purchase a new shaft. The surface of the shaft should be free from any worn ridges caused by the rocker arms. If any wear is present, renew the shaft.

2 Check the rocker arms for wear of the rocker bushes, for wear at the rocker arm face which bears on the valve stem, and for wear of the adjusting ball ended screws. Wear in the rocker arm bush can be checked by gripping the rocker arm tip and holding the rocker arm in place on the shaft, noting if there is any lateral rocker arm shake. If shake is present, and the arm is very loose on the shaft, a new bush or rocker arm must be fitted.

3 Check the tip of the rocker arm where it bears on the valve head for cracking or serious wear of the case hardening. If none is present re-use the rocker arm. Check the lower half of the ball on the end of the rocker arm adjusting screw.

4 Check the pushrods for straightness by rolling them on the bench. Renew any that are bent.

5 Examine the bearing surface of the tappets which lie on the camshaft. Any indentation in this surface or any cracks indicate serious wear and the tappets should be renewed. Thoroughly clean them out, removing all traces of sludge. It is most unlikely that the sides of the tappets will prove worn, but, if they are a very loose fit in their bores, and can readily be rocked, they should be exchanged for new units. It is very unusual to find any wear, except at very high mileages.

32 Oil pump – examination and renovation

1 Unbolt the pump cover, remove the gasket and slide out the internal rotors.

2 Remove the regulator valve threaded plug and extract the valve and spring (photo).

3 Clean all components and carry out the following checks for wear using a feeler gauge:

(a) *Check the clearance between the outer rotor and the oil pump body. This should be between 0.0059 and 0.0083 in (0.15 and 0.21 mm) with a wear limit of 0.020 in (0.5 mm) (photo)*

(b) *Check the clearance between the high points of the inner and outer rotors. This should be less than 0.005 in (0.12 mm) with a maximum of 0.008 in (0.20 mm) (photo)*

(c) *Using a straight-edge check the clearance between the pump face and rotor; this should be 0.002 in (0.05 mm) with a maximum wear limit of 0.0079 in (0.20 mm)*

(d) *If the clearance at (c) is correct, the rotor side clearance with minimum rotor wear will be a maximum of 0.0047 in (0.12 mm) with the pump cover fitted*

4 Where any of the clearances are outside the specified tolerances, renew the oil pump complete.

32.2 Oil pressure relief valve

32.3a Checking the oil pump rotor tip clearance

32.3b Checking the oil pump rotor to casing clearance

33 Flywheel – servicing

1   Examine the clutch driven plate contact area on the flywheel for scoring or cracks. If these are severe or extensive the flywheel should be renewed. Surface grinding is not recommended as the balance of the crankshaft/flywheel assembly will be upset.
2   If the teeth on the flywheel starter ring are badly worn, or if some are missing then it will be necessary to remove the ring and fit a new one, or exchange the flywheel for a reconditioned unit.
3   Either split the ring with a cold chisel after making a cut with a hacksaw blade between the teeth, or using a soft headed hammer (not steel) to knock the ring off, striking it evenly and alternately at equally spaced points. Take great care not to damage the flywheel during this process.
4   Heat the new ring in either an electric oven to about 392°F (200°C) or immerse in a pan of heated oil.
5   Hold the ring at this temperature for five minutes and then quickly fit it to the flywheel so the chamfered portion of the teeth faces the engine side of the flywheel.
6   The ring should be tapped gently down onto its register and left to cool naturally when the contraction of the metal on cooling will ensure that it is a secure and permanent fit. Great care must be taken not to overheat the ring, indicated by it turning light metallic blue, as if this happens, the temper of the ring will be lost.

34 Driveplate – servicing

1   This component fitted instead of the flywheel in conjunction with automatic transmission, should be checked for distortion and elongation of the bolt holes which secure it to the torque converter.
2   Examine the starter ring gear teeth for wear or chipping.
3   Where any of these faults are evident, renew the driveplate complete.

35 Oil seals – renewal

1   At the time of major overhaul, renew the timing cover oil seal and the crankshaft rear oil seal as a matter of routine.
2   Make sure that the lips of the seals face the correct way as shown (photo).
3   Removal and fitting of the timing cover oil seal should be carried out using a piece of tubing as a drift.

36 Engine reassembly – general

1   Before commencing reassembly, gather together the necessary tools, gaskets and other small items.
2   Observe absolute cleanliness during reassembly and lubricate each component before refitting with clean engine oil. In particular, blow through all oil ways and lubricate them to ensure that they are clear of dirt and metal swarf.
3   Do not use unnecessary force to fit a part, but re-check clearances

and tolerances where difficulties are encountered.
4   Where applicable, always use new lockwashers, gaskets and seals, and tighten all fittings to the specified torques.

37 Engine – reassembly

1   If removed, refit the engine mounting brackets.
2   Reinsert the gauze filter into its recess in the crankcase and refit the baffle plate locating with screws and washers (photos).
3   Lubricate and insert the respective tappets into the crankcase (photo).
4   Lubricate the camshaft bearings and lobes and carefully insert the camshaft into position in the crankcase (photo). Do not force it if it gets stuck during insertion but carefully manoeuvre it through the respective bearings until it is fully home.
5   Locate the camshaft retaining plate with its 'lower' marking facing outwards (photo). Refit and tighten the plate bolts and washers and tighten to the specified torque.
6   Check that the main bearings, caps and shells are perfectly clean, then position the shell halves in the block saddles and bearing caps. Note that the centre bearing shell is the flanged one which takes up the endfloat (photo). Check that the oil holes are in alignment when fitted to those of the cylinder block.
7   Lubricate the bearings and crankshaft journals and oilways using clean engine oil (photo). Carefully lower the crankshaft into position (photo).
8   Before fitting the bearing caps, apply some suitable sealant to the rear main bearing contact corners of the block as indicated in Fig. 1.7.
9   Apply some clean engine oil to the lip of the oilseal and carefully locate it on the rear end of the crankshaft (photo). Use a suitable tube drift to locate it on the shaft.
10   Locate the respective bearing caps and bolts (photo). Tighten the bolts in the sequence shown in Fig. 1.8 progressively to the specified torque. On completion check the crankshaft endfloat and also that it rotates freely (photo). Note that the arrow marks on the cap faces must point to the front of the engine. Check the crankshaft endfloat using a suitable feeler gauge as shown in the photo.
11   The piston and connecting rod assemblies are now to be fitted and it is important that they are clean and well lubricated prior to assembly (photo).
12   Locate the connecting rod bearing shells into the rods and caps and lubricate with clean engine oil.
13   Clean and lubricate with clean engine oil both the piston assemblies and the cylinder bores, then insert each piston and rod assembly into its respective bore. Note that the piston number and small notch on its top outer edge must face to the front (photo). As a further check the oil jet hole in the connecting rod must face to the crankcase right-hand side.
14   Compress the piston rings with a suitable ring compressor and carefully tap the piston crown with the end of a hammer handle to press the piston home into its bore (photo).
15   Engage the connecting rod with the crankshaft when the crankpin is at its lowest point of rotational travel. Lubricate the exposed part of the crankpin.
16   Fit the big-end cap complete with shell bearing, making sure that

35.2 Timing cover oil seal

37.2a Crankcase gauze filter

37.2b Crankcase baffle plate

37.3 Fit the tappets

37.4 Insert the camshaft carefully

37.5 Camshaft retaining plate fitted

37.6 Centre main bearing with thrust flanges

37.7a Lubricate the bearing shells ...

37.7b ... and fit the crankshaft

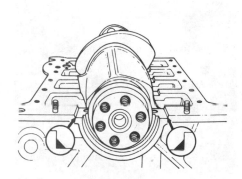
Fig. 1.7 Apply sealant to the areas shown (Sec 37)

37.9 Fit the crankshaft oil seal

37.10a Locate the bearing caps and secure them

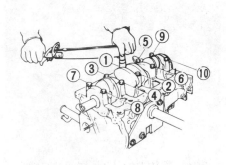
Fig. 1.8 Main bearing cap bolt tightening sequence (Sec 37)

37.10b Check crankshaft endfloat

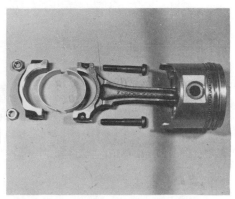
37.11 Check connecting rod ready for fitting

37.13 Notch on outer edge of piston crown to front of engine

37.14 Fitting a piston, using a ring compressor

37.16 Fitting a connecting rod bearing cap

37.17 Tightening a connecting rod bearing cap

37.18 Crankshaft sprocket shim and Woodruff keys in position

37.20a Timing marks aligned

37.20b Fitting the camshaft sprocket bolt and washers

37.21a Ensure that the oil feed hole to the chain tensioner is clear ...

37.21b ... and fit the tensioner

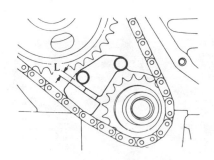
Fig. 1.9 Measuring the tensioner spindle projection L (Sec 37)

37.22 Fit the oil thrower disc with concave side outwards

37.24 Fit the timing cover

the numbers are adjacent and in their correct sequence (photo).

17 Tighten the nuts to the specified torque then repeat the procedure for the remaining pistons/connecting rods and bearings (photo).

18 The crankshaft and camshaft sprocket must now be checked for alignment. Relocate any shim washers originally fitted over the respective shafts and refit the Woodruff keys and sprockets (photo). Now check using a depth gauge that the sprocket alignment heights are within 0·020 in (0·5 mm). Any further adjustment can be made by the use of the special shim washers which are available and are 0·006 in (0·15 mm) thick.

19 When the sprocket alignments are correct, withdraw the sprockets from their shafts and locate them in the timing chain, so that the timing dot on each sprocket is in direct alignment. Position no. 1 piston at top dead centre (TDC).

20 Fit the sprockets and chain onto the crankshaft and camshaft, keeping the timing dots in alignment (photo). Refit the camshaft sprocket retaining bolt with spring and flat washer (photo). Tighten to the specified torque.

21 Check that the timing chain tensioner oil feed hole is clear (photo) and relocate the chain tensioner, securing with the two bolts and spring washers (photo). Now check that the gap between the tensioner body and guide is within 0·6 in (15 mm). If over this tolerance renew the timing chain.

22 Relocate the dished washer over the crankshaft with the concave side facing outwards (photo).

23 Smear a liberal amount of sealant solution over the faces of the timing case and front mating cylinder block faces. Locate the gaskets over the dowels.

24 Check that the oilseal is fully located in the timing case and lubricate its seating lip. Carefully refit the timing case into position (photo) and secure with the retaining bolts tightened to the specified torque.

25 Refit the oil feed suction pipe and gasket, retaining with the two bolts and spring washers.

26 Apply some sealant to the front and rear sump groove seal corners and carefully locate the rubber seals into position with the thick seals at the front and thin to the rear. Fit the sump flange gasket halves into

position over the studs and check that the securing bolt holes are in line (photo).

27 Refit the sump and secure with bolts and nuts (photo).

28 Locate the backplate over the two dowels (photo).

29 Refit the flywheel and secure with the six bolts. Note that the bolt holes are not equidistant and therefore the flywheel will only fit in one position. Tighten the bolts to the specified torque (photo).

30 Refit the crankshaft pulley and secure with bolt and washer (photo).

38 Cylinder head and rocker shaft – reassembly and refitting

1   Fit the valve spring seat over the valve guide.

2   Fit the valve lip seal (photo) over the guide using special drift number KV10104800 if available (Fig. 1.10).

3   Lubricate the stem and fit the valve into the guide (photo).

4   Refit the spring with the white painted coil section to the cylinder head and fit the retainer and collets with the aid of a valve spring compressor. The collets can be retained in the valve stem groove with a dab of grease (photo).

5   Reassemble the rocker shaft assembly in the reverse sequence to dismantling. Lubricate the respective components as they are assembled.

6   Position the cylinder head gasket onto the top of the block locating it over the dowels. Use a non-setting sealant on the joint faces of the head and block if desired.

7   Carefully place the cylinder head into position locating onto the dowels (photo).

8   Insert the respective cylinder head bolts (photo). Note that the longer bolt fits in the centre on the opposite side to the valves. Progressively tighten the bolts to the torque specified in the sequence shown (Fig. 1.11).

9   Lubricate and insert the pushrods into their respective locations (photo).

10 The rocker assembly can now be fitted into position and the ball-pins located in the pushrod cups (photo). Tighten the bolts to the

37.26 Fit the sump and bearing gaskets

37.27 Fit the sump

37.28 Position the engine backplate ...

37.29 ... and fit the flywheel

37.30 Fit the crankshaft pulley

38.2 Valve guide seals

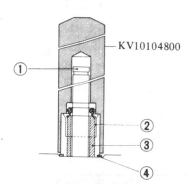

Fig. 1.10 Special tool for fitting valve stem seals (Sec 38)

1   Valve   3   Valve guide
2   Lip seal   4   Valve spring seat

38.3 Inserting the valves

38.4a Fit the valve spring (painted end downwards) and the spring retainer

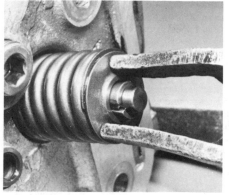

38.4b Inserting the split collets

38.7 Installing the cylinder head

38.8 Inserting the cylinder head bolts

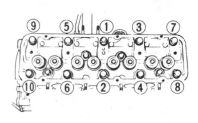

Fig. 1.11 Cylinder head bolt tightening sequence (Sec 38)

38.9 Inserting the pushrods

38.10 Fitting the rocker assembly

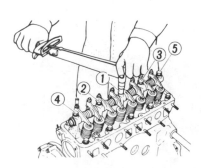

Fig. 1.12 Rocker pedestal bolt tightening sequence (Sec 38)

39.6 Adjusting the valve clearances

40.2 Fitting the oil pump

specified torque (Fig. 1.12).
11 Adjust the valve clearances, as described in Section 39.

39 Valve clearances – adjustment

1 To check the valve clearances, the engine must be turned over and this is best achieved by applying a ring spanner or socket onto the crankshaft pulley bolt and rotating the crankshaft to the positions required. If the engine is in the vehicle it will be easier to turn it over if the spark plugs are removed (to reduce the compression).
2 The valve clearances should preferably be checked when the engine is hot, but if it has been standing and cooled off or is being reassembled, they can be adjusted to the cold clearance specifications initially and checked again later when the engine has been run to warm it up. The clearances are as given in the Specifications.
3 The correct valve clearances are essential for the efficient running of the engine. If the clearances are set too open, the efficiency of the engine is reduced as the valves open late and close earlier than was intended. If, on the other hand the clearances are set too close there is a danger that the stems will expand upon heating and not allow the valves to close properly which will cause burning of the valve head and seat and possible warping.
4 If the engine is in the car to get at the rockers it is merely necessary to remove the rocker cover, and then to lift the rocker cover and gasket away.
5 It is important that the clearance is set when the tappet of the valve being adjusted is on the heel of the cam, (ie opposite the peak). This can be done by carrying out the adjustments in the following order, which also avoids turning the crankshaft more than necessary.

Valve fully open	Check & adjust
Valve No. 8	*Valve No. 1*
Valve No. 6	*Valve No. 3*
Valve No. 4	*Valve No. 5*
Valve No. 7	*Valve No. 2*
Valve No. 1	*Valve No. 8*
Valve No. 3	*Valve No. 6*
Valve No. 5	*Valve No. 4*
Valve No. 2	*Valve No. 7*

6 The correct valve clearance is obtained by slackening the hexagon locknut with a spanner while holding the ballpin against rotation with the screwdriver (photo). Then, still pressing down with the screwdriver, insert a feeler gauge in the gap between the valve stem head and the rocker arm and adjust the ballpin until the feeler gauge will just move in and out without nipping, and, still holding the ballpin in the correct position, tighten the locknut.
7 On completion of all the valve clearance adjustments, refit the rocker cover using a new gasket (when necessary).

40 Engine – refitting external components

1 Refit the fuel pump using new gaskets, and secure with nut, spring and flat washers.
2 Refit the oil pump unit using a new gasket (photo). The two short bolts are fitted at the rear of the pump. The single long bolt is fitted at the front but do not tighten this bolt at this stage if the engine is out of the vehicle. If the engine is fitted then the earth strap can be fitted under the long bolt head and it can be tightened. (Note that the top rear bolt also retains a wire clip).
3 Refit the water pump unit. Clean off any old gasket from the mating surfaces and fit a new one. Secure the pump with three nuts and two bolts.
4 Refit the thermostat with the 'pip' at the top (see Chapter 2) and secure the housing. Note that the bolt on the top right-hand side retains the fuel line clip.
5 Locate the new inlet/exhaust manifold gasket, making sure that the mating surfaces are clean. Refit the manifolds (photo) and secure with nuts and washers. Remember that the air cleaner support bracket fits over the second stud from the rear, and the engine lifting bracket fits over the front stud of the exhaust manifold. The front stud of the inlet manifold retains the fuel line clip.
6 Refit the alternator, but do not fully tighten the bracket and stay nuts at this stage.
7 Refit the distributor. Refer to Chapter 4 for the correct procedure.
8 Locate the fuel line retaining clip on the alternator side of the cylinder head (photo) using the special bolt. Reconnect the feed tube from the fuel pump.
9 Refit the carburettor using new gaskets and check that the mating surfaces are perfectly clean. Reconnect the fuel line.
10 Refer to Chapter 5 and refit the clutch assembly.
11 Refer to Chapter 6 and refit and secure the gearbox (if removed).
12 Relocate and secure the starter motor unit.
13 The engine is now ready for fitting but first check that all external components are secure and correctly attached.

41 Engine and transmission – refitting

1 Install the clutch (where applicable) by following the procedure given in Chapter 5.
2 Reconnect the engine to the manual or automatic transmission by reversing the procedure given in Section 6 or 7.
3 Using the hoist and slings, refit the engine/transmission in the vehicle by reversing the removal procedure given in Section 5.
4 When fitting is complete, check and adjust the fan belt tension as described in Chapter 2.
5 Refill the engine with the correct grade and quantity of oil (where applicable).

40.5 Use new gaskets when fitting the manifolds

40.8 Engine ready for installation
1, 2 and 3 Fuel line clips
4 Engine lifting bracket
5 Air filter bracket

6   Refill the cooling system (Chapter 2).
7   Check the level in the manual or automatic transmission, and top-up if necessary.

42 Initial start-up after major repair

1   With the engine refitted in the vehicle, make a final visual check to see that everything has been reconnected and that no loose rags or tools have been left within the engine compartment.
2   Turn the idling speed adjusting screw in about $\frac{1}{2}$ turn to ensure that the engine will have a faster than usual idling speed during initial start-up and operation.
3   Start the engine. This may take a little longer than usual as the fuel

pump and carburettor bowls will be empty and will require priming.
4   As soon as the engine starts, allow it to run at a fast-idle. Examine all hose and pipe connections for leaks.
5   After the engine has been run for several minutes check the tightness of the cylinder head bolts.
6   Operate the vehicle on the road until normal engine temperature is reached, then remove the rocker cover and adjust the valve clearances hot, as described in Section 39.
7   Where the majority of engine internal bearings or components (pistons, rings etc) have been renewed then the operating speed should be restricted for the first 500 miles (800 km), and the engine oil changed at the end of this period.
8   Check and adjust if necessary the ignition timing (Chapter 4).
9   Check and adjust the carburettor and all exhaust emission control equipment as far as is practicable (Chapter 3).

43 Fault diagnosis – engine

Symptom	Reason/s
Engine will not turn over when starter switch is operated	Flat battery Bad battery connections Bad connections at solenoid switch and/or starter motor Starter motor jammed Defective solenoid Starter motor defective
Engine turns over normally but fails to start	No spark at plugs No fuel reaching engine Too much fuel reaching the engine (flooding)
Engine starts but runs unevenly and misfires	Ignition and/or fuel system faults Incorrect valve clearances Burnt out valves Worn piston rings
Lack of power	Ignition and/or fuel system faults Incorrect valve clearances Burnt out valves Worn out piston rings
Excessive oil consumption	Oil leaks from crankshaft rear oil seal, timing cover gasket and oil seal, rocker cover gasket, oil filter gasket, sump gasket, sump plug washer Worn piston rings or cylinder bores resulting in oil being burnt by engine Worn valve guides and/or defective valve stem seals
Excessive mechanical noise from engine	Wrong valve to rocker clearances Worn crankshaft bearings Worn cylinders/pistons (piston slap) Slack or worn timing chain and sprockets

Chapter 2 Cooling system

For modifications, and information applicable to later models, see Supplement at end of manual

Contents

Specifications

System type .... Thermo syphon with pump and fan assistance

System capacity
Refer to Capacities, dimensions and weights at the beginning of this manual.

Thermostat

	Temperate type	Frigid type	Tropical type
Valve opening temperature	180°F (82°C)	190°F (88°C)	170°F (76·5°C)
Maximum valve lift	0·31 in (8 mm)	0·31 in (8 mm)	0·31 in (8 mm)
Fully open temperature	203°F (95°C)	212°F (100°C)	194°F (90°C)

Radiator cap relief pressure .... 13 lbf/in² (0·9 kgf/cm²)

Fan belt tension
Deflection at mid span .... 0·31 to 0·47 in (8 to 12 mm)

Torque wrench setting

	lbf ft	kgf m
Water pump bolts	6·5 to 10·1	0·9 to 1·4

1 General description

The cooling system comprises the radiator, top and bottom water hoses, water pump, cylinder head and block water jackets, radiator cap with pressure relief valve and flow and return heater hoses. The thermostat is located in a recess at the front of the cylinder head. The principle of the system is that cold water in the bottom of the radiator circulates upwards through the lower radiator hose to the water pump, where the pump impeller pushes the water round the cylinder block and head through the various cast-in passages, to cool the cylinder bores, combustion surfaces and valve seats. When sufficient heat has been absorbed by the cooling water and the engine has reached an efficient working temperature, the water moves from the cylinder head past the now open thermostat, into the top radiator hose and into the radiator header tank.

The water then travels down the radiator tubes and is rapidly cooled by the in-rush of air, when the vehicle is in forward motion. A four bladed fan, mounted on the water pump pulley, assists this cooling action. The water, now cooled, reaches the bottom of the radiator and the cycle is repeated.

When the engine is cold, the thermostat remains closed until the coolant reaches a pre-determined temperature (see Specifications). This assists rapid warming-up.

Water temperature is measured by an electro-sensitive capsule located immediately below the thermostat housing. Connection between the transmitter capsule and the facia gauge is made by a single cable and a spade connector. The cooling system also provides the heat for the heater. The heater matrix is fed directly with water from the hottest part of the engine, returning through a connection on the bottom radiator hose.

2 Cooling system – draining

1   Should the system have to be left empty, both the cylinder block and radiator must be drained, otherwise, with a partly drained system, corrosion of the water pump impeller seal face may occur with subsequent early failure of the pump seal and bearing.
2   Place the car on a level surface and have ready a container having a capacity of two gallons which will slide beneath the radiator and sump.
3   Move the heater control on the facia to 'HOT' and unscrew and remove the radiator cap. If hot, unscrew the cap very slowly, first covering it with a cloth to remove the danger of scalding when the pressure in the system is released.
4   Remove the drain plug from the bottom of the radiator and the drain plug on the left side of the cylinder block to allow the coolant to drain out. If the coolant contains antifreeze and it is reasonably clean, retain it for re-use.

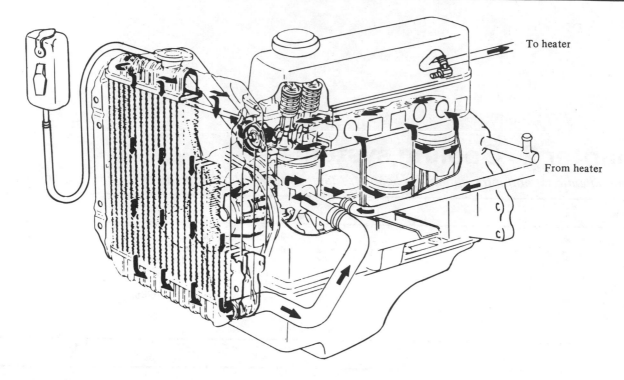

Fig. 2.1 Cooling system schematic view (Sec 1)

3 Cooling system – flushing

1   The radiator and waterways in the engine after some time may become restricted or even blocked with scale or sediment which reduce the efficiency of the cooling system. When this condition occurs or the coolant appears rusty or dark in colour the system should be flushed. In severe cases reverse flushing may be required as described later.
2   Place the heater controls to the HOT position and unscrew fully the radiator and cylinder block drain plugs.
3   Remove the radiator filler cap and place a hose in the filler neck. Allow water to run through the system until it emerges from both drain holes quite clear in colour. Do not flush a hot engine with cold water.
4   In severe cases of contamination of the coolant, or of the system, reverse flush, by first removing the radiator cap and disconnecting the lower radiator hose at the radiator outlet pipe.
5   Remove the top hose at the radiator connection end and remove the radiator as described in Section 6.
6   Invert the radiator and place a hose in the bottom outlet pipe. Continue flushing until clear water comes from the radiator top tank.
7   To flush the engine water jackets, remove the thermostat as described later in this Chapter and place a hose in the thermostat location until clear water runs from the water pump inlet. Cleaning by the use of chemical compounds is not recommended.

4 Cooling system – filling

1   The cooling system is designed to have a mixture of equal volumes of water and ethylene glycol antifreeze all the year round.
2   Refer to the Specification to find the capacity of the cooling system and mix the required volume of antifreeze and water mixture. If possible, use soft water, or clean rainwater.
3   Place the heater control to the HOT position, ensure that the cylinder block drain plug is screwed in and that the radiator drain valve is closed.
4   Pour the coolant mixture into the radiator slowly, so that the air in the system will be expelled and not become trapped and continue pouring until the radiator is full to the cap.
5   Fit the radiator cap and pour coolant into the coolant reservoir up to the MAX mark.

6   Run the engine and check for leaks from the hoses and the drain points.
7   Recheck the level of coolant in the reservoir and top it up if necessary.

5 Antifreeze mixture

1   On leaving the factory the cooling system is filled with an antifreeze/water mixture in equal volumes which ensures protection down to -31°F (-35°C). This concentration should be maintained at all times.
2   The antifreeze solution also serves as a rust inhibitor and additional anti-corrosion products should not be mixed with it.
3   Only ethylene glycol type of antifreeze should be used and the coolant should be drained and renewed by fresh coolant every two or three years as recommended by the antifreeze manufacturers.
4   Antifreeze will mark the paintwork of the car and if coolant is spilt on the bodywork, it should be wiped off immediately.

6 Radiator – removal and refitting

1   Drain the coolant into a clean container.
2   Release the clamps on the upper and lower radiator hoses and disconnect the hoses from the radiator (photo). On models fitted with automatic transmission, disconnect the oil cooler inlet and outlet pipes from the radiator.
3   Remove the fan shroud retaining bolts and remove the fan shroud.
4   Remove the radiator retaining bolts and remove the radiator by lifting it upwards.
5   Refitting the radiator is the reverse of removal, but first inspect the hoses and if they show signs of cracking, or are becoming hard, fit new hoses.
6   Ensure that when the hoses are fitted, the direction arrows on them are visible from above and push all hoses on as far as they will go. To make it easier to fit hoses, smear the inside of their bore at the ends with soap, or rubber grease.
7   Check that there is a clearance of at least 30 mm (1.18 in) between the radiator hoses and any adjacent parts. On models fitted with air conditioning there should be a minimum clearance of 18 mm (0.71 in) between the compressor and the coolant hose.

6.2 Radiator top hose connection

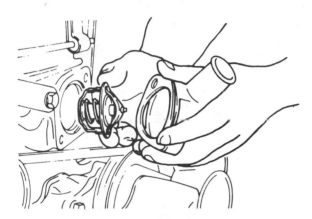

Fig. 2.2 Removing the thermostat (Sec 7)

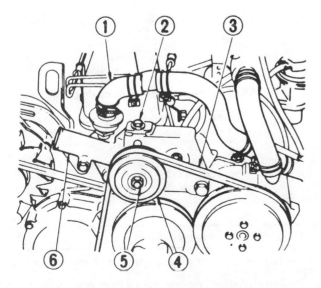

Fig. 2.3 Thermostat installation, air injection models (Sec 7)

1 Air hose	4 Idler pulley
2 Adjusting bolt	5 Pulley nut
3 Drivebelt	6 Water outlet

8   Before tightening the fan shroud bolts, ensure that the fan is clear of the shroud at all points.
9   Tighten the hose clips until they are secure, but do not over tighten them and damage the hoses.
10 Refill the cooling system and examine all joints for leaks.

7   Thermostat – removal and refitting

1   Drain into a clean container enough coolant to reduce the level below the thermostat.
2   Disconnect the upper radiator hose from its connection to the engine.
3   On models with air injection (except non-California models with 5-speed transmission) disconnect the ignition system air hose from the check valve. Also slacken the air injection system drivebelt by loosening the nut and bolt of the idler pulley.
4   Loosen the bolts and remove the idler pulley bracket (except non-California models with 5-speed transmission), or disconnect the air induction pipe (non-California models with 5-speed transmission only).
5   Remove the bolts from the thermostat cover and remove the cover, gasket and thermostat from the thermostat housing.
6   Before refitting the thermostat, check it as described in the following Section.
7   Clean all dirt and pieces of gasket from the mating faces of the thermostat cover and housing.
8   Refit the thermostat and bolt the cover on again, using a new gasket.
9   Replenish the coolant in the system and check for leaks.

8   Thermostat – testing

1   Examine the thermostat to see which type is fitted and then refer to the Specifications for its operating characteristics.
2   Have ready a gauge 8 mm (0.31 in) wide.
3   Submerge the thermostat in hot water at 5°C (9°F) above the temperature for maximum valve lift. Allow sufficient time for the thermostat to open fully and then insert the gauge to check that the full specified lift is obtained.
4   Cool the water to a temperature of 5°C (9°F) below the specified opening temperature and check that the valve closes fully.
5   A thermostat cannot be repaired and if it does not operate within the specification it must be discarded and a new one fitted. Never refit a defective unit. If a new thermostat is not immediately available, the engine can be operated without a thermostat.

9   Water pump – removal and refitting

1   Drain the cooling system, collecting the coolant in a clean container.
2   Remove the bolts securing the radiator shroud and remove the shroud.
3   On vehicles without air conditioning, slacken the fan belt, then remove the bolts from the fan and take off the fan blades, fan spacer and pulley from the hub (photo).
4   On vehicles with air conditioning, slacken the fan belt, then remove the bolts from the fan and take off the fan blades, torque coupling and pulley from the hub.
5   Remove the bolts securing the water pump to the front cover and tap the pump to release it. Remove the pump assembly and gasket (Fig. 2.4). The pump cannot be dismantled and if it is defective must be replaced by an exchange unit.
6   Before refitting the pump by reversing the removal operations, clean all traces of dirt and gasket material from the mating surfaces of the pump and the front cover.
7   Use a new gasket and tighten the bolts to the specified torque.
8   Fill the cooling system, check that there is uniform clearance between the fan and its shroud and tension the fan belt to the specified figure. Run the engine at fast idle speed.
9   Check for leaks and top-up the cooling system if necessary.

9.3 Fan blades, spacer and pulley

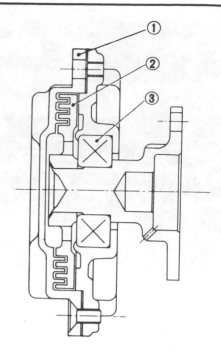

Fig. 2.5 Torque coupling sectional view (Sec 10)

1 Casing   3 Bearing
2 Rotor

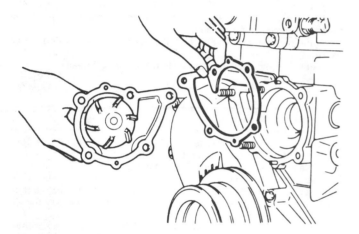

Fig. 2.4 Removing the water pump (Sec 9)

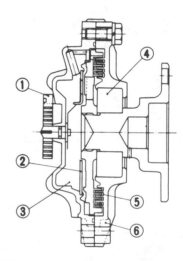

Fig. 2.6 Temperature controlled coupling (Sec 10)

1 Bi-metal thermostat   4 Bearing
2 Slide valve   5 Rotor
3 Reservoir chamber   6 Casing

10 Fluid coupling – general description

1   Models fitted with air conditioning have a fluid coupling fitted between the water pump and the fan blades and two different types of coupling are used.

Torque coupling
2   The torque coupling allows variable slip to occur between the water pump flange and the fan and is designed to keep the fan speed below 2900 rpm.
3   This limitation of fan speed conserves engine power at high engine speeds and also helps to reduce fan noise.
4   The coupling is filled with a special silicone oil and if the coupling leaks, the fluid cannot be replenished.

Temperature controlled coupling
5   The temperature controlled fluid coupling is similar in principle to the torque coupling, but has one important difference.
6   The ordinary torque coupling has its slip controlled only by engine speed, regardless of engine temperature. The temperature controlled coupling has a coiled bi-metallic spring at its front and the movement of this spring operates a valve to control the flow of fluid between the two parts of the coupling.
7   When the air passing through the radiator is relatively cool, the flow of oil in the coupling is restricted and the fan slips at about 2050 rpm.
8   When the temperature of the air through the radiator increases above a certain point, indicating that a higher rate of cooling is

required, the bi-metallic spring operates the valve to allow more oil to enter and slip speed is raised to 2900 rpm.
9   If the coupling leaks and silicone oil is lost, it cannot be replenished.

11 Fluid coupling – removal and refitting

1   Remove the bolts securing the radiator shroud and remove the shroud.
2   Slacken the fan belt, then remove the bolts securing the fan to the fluid coupling and remove the fan.
3   Remove the nuts securing the torque coupling to the water pump hub and pull off the torque coupling.
4   Refit the coupling by reversing the removal operations, but when fitting the fan shroud, ensure that there is a uniform clearance between

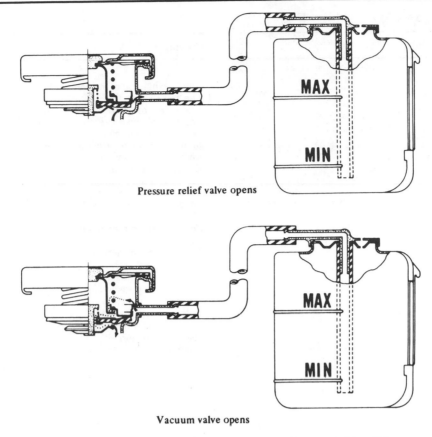

Pressure relief valve opens

Vacuum valve opens

Fig. 2.7 Operation of radiator pressure cap and reservoir (Sec 12)

it and the fan.

5   On completion tension the fan belt.

12 Radiator pressure cap – operation and testing

1   The radiator cap incorporates two valves. A pressure valve maintains a pre-set pressure of 13 lbf/in^2 (0.9 kg/cm^2) above atmospheric pressure, but vents if this pressure is exceeded. This pressurisation of the coolant allows it to operate at a much higher temperature without boiling compared with the temperature at which it would boil under normal atmospheric pressure.

2   When the system cools, the pressure in the system falls to below atmospheric pressure and at a predetermined level of vacuum, the vacuum valve lifts and draws in coolant from the coolant reservoir.

3   Periodically remove the radiator cap and check the rubber seal on it for tears or deterioration.

4   If there is no obvious defect in the cap, but it is suspect because the engine overheats, or the radiator does not replenish itself from the coolant reservoir, the cap can be tested on a special tester which many of the larger garages have.

See overleaf for 'Fault diagnosis – cooling system'

13 Fault diagnosis – cooling system

Symptom	Reason/s
Engine overheating	Insufficient coolant in system
	Fan belt slipping
	Radiator core blocked, or restricted
	Water hose kinked, restricting flow
	Thermostat defective
	Ignition timing incorrect (retarded)
	Carburettor setting incorrect (mixture too lean)
	Oil level in sump too low
	Blown cylinder head gasket, causing loss of coolant
	Defective, or incorrect pressure cap
	Fluid coupling defective
Engine too cool	Thermostat jammed open
	No thermostat
	Outside temperature excessively low
Loss of coolant	Loose clips on hoses
	Water hoses perished and leaking
	Radiator core leaking
	Defective pressure cap
	Blown cylinder head gasket
	Leaking core plug
	Cracked cylinder block, or head

Chapter 3 Fuel, exhaust and emission control systems

For modifications, and information applicable to later models, see Supplement at end of manual

Contents

Specifications

Fuel pump
Type .... Mechanically operated diaphragm
Capacity .... 450 cc (27.46 cu in) per min at 1000 rpm
Pressure .... 3.0 to 3.8 lbf/in² (0.21 to 0.27 kgf/cm²)

Air cleaner
Type .... Renewable paper element
Temperature control:
    Valve partially open .... 100 to 129°F (38 to 54°C)
    Valve fully open .... Above 131°F (55°C)

Carburettor make .... Hitachi

Carburettor application
Europe
    A12 engine .... DCG 306 – 5C
    A14 engine .... DCG 306 – 80
California
    A14 engine, manual transmission .... DCH 306 – 61
    A14 engine, automatic transmission .... DCH 306 – 63
    A15 engine, automatic transmission .... DCH 306 – 69
US (except California)
    A14 engine, manual transmission .... DCH 306 – 60E
    A14 engine, automatic transmission .... DCH 306 – 68
    A14 engine, 5-speed manual transmission .... DCH 306 – 67
    A15 engine, automatic transmission .... DCH 306 – 68
Canada
    A14 engine, manual transmission .... DCH 306 – 60
    A14 engine, automatic transmission .... DCH 306 – 12

Carburettor data

Fuel level adjustment
    Fuel level from top of carburettor body (H') ....   0.75 in (19 mm)
Gap between valve stem and float seat
    H (float up) ....   0.59 in (15 mm)
    h (float down) ....   0.51 to 0.67 in (1.3 to 1.7 mm)
Bi-metal setting ....   Centre of index mark
Bi-metal resistance ....   3.7 to 8.9 ohms at 70°F (21°C)
Fast idle adjustment
    Fast idle cam 2nd step – gap between throttle valve and
    carburettor body
        A12 engine, manual transmission ....   0.046 to 0.054 in (1.17 to 1.38 mm)
        A14 engine, manual transmission ....   0.0287 to 0.0331 in (0.73 to 0.84 mm)
        A14, A15 engine, automatic transmission ....   0.0394 to 0.0449 in (1.00 to 1.14 mm)
    Fast idle speed at 2nd cam step
        Manual transmission ....   1900 to 2700 rpm
        Automatic transmission ....   2400 to 3200 rpm
Vacuum break adjustment
    Gap between choke valve and carburettor body
        All models except Non-California, 5-speed transmission
        models ....   0.0709 to 0.0780 in (1.80 to 1.98 mm)
        Non-California, 5-speed transmission models ....   0.0780 to 0.0850 in (1.98 to 2.16 mm)
Choke unloader adjustment
    Gap between choke valve and carburettor body
        All models except non-California, 5-speed transmission
        models ....   0.0929 in (2.36 mm)
        Non-California, 5-speed transmission models ....   0.0854 in (2.17 mm)
Interlock opening of primary and secondary throttle valves ....   0.2295 in (5.83 mm)
Dash pot adjustment (without loading)
    California ....   1900 to 2100 rpm
    US – except California
        A14 engine, manual transmission ....   2300 to 2500 rpm
        A14, A15 engines, automatic transmission ....   1900 to 2100 rpm
        A14 engine, Non-California, 5-speed transmission ....   1900 to 2100 rpm
    Canada
        A14 engine, manual transmission ....   2300 to 2500 rpm
        A14 engine, automatic transmission ....   1900 to 2100 rpm
Throttle opener operating pressure at sea level and 29.9 in
(760 mm) Hg atmospheric pressure
    California ....   -22.05 ± 0.79 in (-560 ± 20 mm) of mercury
    Canada and US except California ....   -20.47 ± 0.79 in (-520 ± 20 mm) of mercury
Bore diameter
    Primary ....   1.02 in (26 mm)
    Secondary ....   1.18 in (30 mm)
Venturi diameter
    Primary
        A12 engine ....   0.787 in (20 mm)
        A14, A15 engines except non-California 5-speed models ....   0.91 in (23 mm)
        A14 engine, non-California, 5-speed models ....   0.087 in (22 mm)
    Secondary
        A12 engine ....   1.024 in (26 mm)
        A14, A15 engines ....   1.06 in (27 mm)
Main jet (primary)
    Europe   97
    California   107
    US except California
        Manual transmission except 5-speed   106
        5-speed transmission   107
        Automatic transmission   105
    Canada
        Manual transmission   104
        Automatic transmission   104
Main jet (secondary)
    Europe   150
    California   145
    US except California   145
    Canada   145
Main air bleed (primary)
    Europe   80
    California   95
    Canada and US except California
        Manual transmission except 5-speed   110
        5-speed transmission   65
        Automatic transmission   95

Main air bleed (secondary)
    Europe 80
    California 80
    Canada and US except California
        Manual transmission except 5-speed 80
        5-speed transmission 60
        Automatic transmission 80
Slow air bleed (Europe)
    Primary
        A12 engine 220
        A14 engine 170
    Secondary
        A12 engine 100
        A14 engine 100
Slow jet (Canada and US)
    Primary
        All models except non-California, 5-speed models 45
        Non-California, 5-speed models 46
    Secondary
        All models 50
Power jet
    Europe 60
    California 43
    US except California
        Manual transmission except 5-speed 40
        5-speed transmission 48
        Automatic transmission 38
    Canada
        Manual transmission 48
        Automatic transmission 40
Idle compensator
    Partially open
        Bi-metal No 1 . . . . 140 to 158°F (60 to 70°C)
        Bi-metal No 2 . . . . 158 to 176°F (70 to 80°C)
    Fully open
        Bi-metal No 1 . . . . Above 158°F (70°C)
        Bi-metal No 2 . . . . Above 176°F (80°C)
Idling speed
    New Sunny model
        Manual transmission . . . . 600 rpm
        Automatic transmission . . . . 700 rpm in N position
    210 model
        Manual transmission . . . . 700 rpm
        Automatic transmission . . . . 650 rpm in D position

Torque wrench settings

	lbf ft	kgf m
Fuel tank bolts	5.8 to 8.7	0.8 to 1.2
Fuel tank drain plug	12 to 17	1.6 to 2.4
Anti-dieseling solenoid	13 to 16	1.8 to 2.2
Fuel pump	6.5 to 10.0	0.9 to 1.4

1 General description

The fuel system comprises a rear mounted tank from which fuel is drawn through a filter by means of a mechanically operated pump mounted on the right-hand side of the crankcase. The fuel pump is operated by an eccentric on the camshaft and delivers fuel, under pressure, to a twin choke carburettor. The carburettor type varies according to the vehicle model and date of manufacture and reference should be made to the Specifications for full details.

The carburettor fitted to all New Sunny models has a manually-operated choke while the 210 models have a similar carburettor incorporating an electrically-heated automatic choke.

All vehicles are fitted with a crankcase ventilation system and 210 models are additionally equipped with exhaust emission control, fuel evaporative control systems and a temperature controlled air cleaner.

2 Air cleaner – servicing

1 The standard air cleaner comprises a body in which is housed a paper element type filter, a lid and the necessary connecting hoses and brackets.
2 Every 24 000 miles (38 000 km) the element should be renewed.

Other than renewal, no servicing is required.
3 Unscrew and remove the wing nut which secures the air cleaner lid in position, remove the lid and extract the paper element (photo).
4 Wipe the interior of the air cleaner body free from oil and dirt and fit the new element.
5 Set the valve lever to 'SUMMER' or 'WINTER' position as required by climatic conditions (photo).

3 Air cleaner – automatic temperature control type

1 This type of air cleaner is designed to keep air being drawn into the engine for combustion purposes at a consistent temperature of about 43° C (110°F). The system is installed to assist in reducing pollution emitted from the exhaust and consists, essentially, of a temperature sensor and air control valves.
2 The temperature sensor will actuate the air control valve so that the correct mixture of hot air from the exhaust manifold and cold air entering the air cleaner inlet tube will be supplied to the carburettor at the specified temperature irrespective of the operating temperature of the engine itself.
3 Repair maintenance of this type of air cleaner is not required beyond renewal of the element as described for the standard air cleaner in the preceding Section. However, in the event of a fault developing and evidence of increased exhaust fumes being emitted,

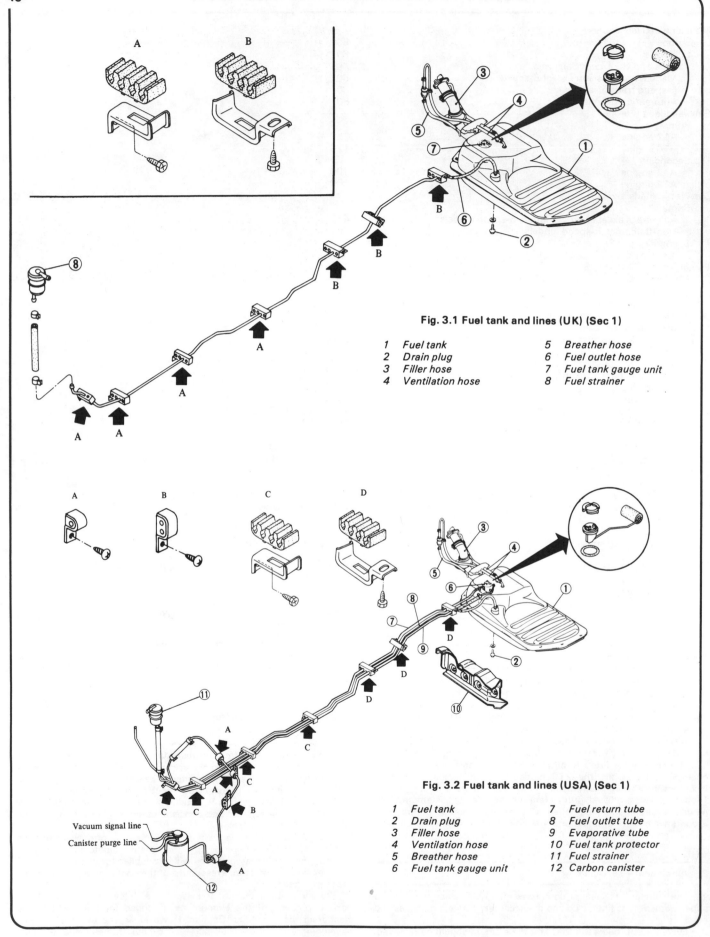

Fig. 3.1 Fuel tank and lines (UK) (Sec 1)

1	Fuel tank	5	Breather hose
2	Drain plug	6	Fuel outlet hose
3	Filler hose	7	Fuel tank gauge unit
4	Ventilation hose	8	Fuel strainer

Fig. 3.2 Fuel tank and lines (USA) (Sec 1)

1	Fuel tank	7	Fuel return tube
2	Drain plug	8	Fuel outlet tube
3	Filler hose	9	Evaporative tube
4	Ventilation hose	10	Fuel tank protector
5	Breather hose	11	Fuel strainer
6	Fuel tank gauge unit	12	Carbon canister

Vacuum signal line

Canister purge line

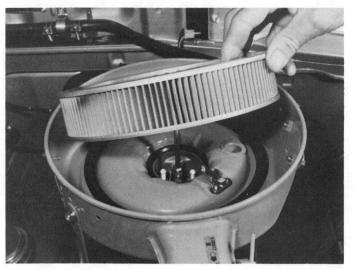

2.3 Air cleaner element

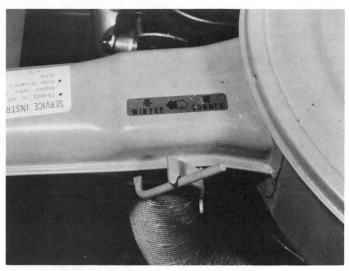

2.5 Air intake control lever

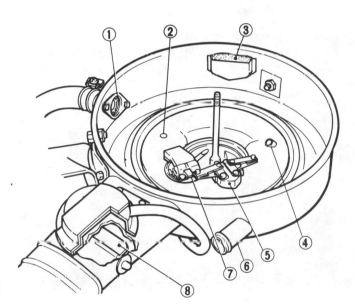

Fig. 3.3 Automatic temperature control air cleaner – US models except non-California, 5-speed models (Sec 3)

1	Air relief valve (Non-California models)	5	Idle compensator
2	Air hole for TCS	6	Outlet for CAC valve (California models)
3	PCV filter	7	Temperature sensor
4	Air hole for AB valve	8	Heat control valve

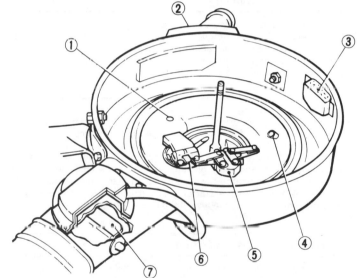

Fig. 3.4 Automatic temperature control air cleaner – Canada and non-California, 5-speed models (Sec 3)

1	Air hole for TCS	4	Air hole for AB valve
2	Air induction valve and filter	5	Idle compensator
3	PCV filter	6	Temperature sensor
		7	Heat control valve

carry out the following operations.

4   Check the security, condition and correct location of all vacuum air supply hoses.

5   With the engine at normal operating temperature, switch off the ignition and holding a mirror to reflect the interior of the air cleaner intake pipe, check the position of the valve. The valve should be closed to exhaust manifold heated air. If this is not the case, check the valve linkage.

6   Disconnect the vacuum hose which connects the vacuum capsule to the inlet manifold. Suck the tube to actuate the vacuum capsule and check that the valve closes to cold air intake. If this is not the case then the air cleaner must be renewed as an assembly.

7   With the engine cold, check that the ambient temperature of the sensor is below 30°C (86°F).

8   Using a mirror as previously described, check that the valve is in the 'open to cold air' position.

9   Start the engine and run it at idling speed, the valve should close immediately to cold air and permit exhaust manifold heated air to be drawn into the cleaner.

10   As the engine warms up observe that the valve gradually opens to permit the entry of cold air into the air cleaner intake tube.

11   If the valve does not operate correctly at within the temperature range 38 to 55°C (100° to 131°F) (checked by using a thermometer adjacent to its location)) remove and renew the sensor unit by bending back the tabs of its retaining clips.

4   Idle compensator – checking and renewal

1   The idle compensator is a thermostatic valve located in the air cleaner to compensate for over-rich mixture when the under bonnet temperature is very high. The valve opens under temperature conditions of between 60° and 75°C (140° and 167°F).
2   A faulty idle compensator may be checked in-situ by making sure that the valve is shut (under bonnet temperature cool) and then disconnecting the hose and alternately blowing and sucking with the mouth. If any air leakage is evident around the valve, renew it.
3   Operation of the valve can be checked by removing it (two screws after detaching air cleaner cover), and immersing it in water which is being heated to the valve operating temperature.

5   Fuel filter – servicing

1   The fuel filter is located in the tank to pump hose and is of the sealed paper element type (photo).
2   Every 24 000 miles (38 000 km) renew the filter. It is preferable to carry out this operation when the fuel tank level is low otherwise when the fuel hoses are disconnected from the filter, the tank line will have to be plugged to prevent loss of fuel.
3   Check that the new filter is fitted in the correct attitude.

6   Fuel pump – description

The fuel pump is actuated by the movement of its rocker arm on a camshaft eccentric. This movement is transferred to a flexible diaphragm which draws the fuel from the tank and pumps it under pressure to the carburettor float chamber. Inlet and outlet valves are incorporated to control the flow of fuel irrespective of engine speed.

7   Fuel pump – testing

Presuming that the fuel lines and unions are in good condition and that there are no leaks anywhere, check the performance of the fuel pump in the following manner: Disconnect the fuel pipe at the carburettor inlet union, and the high tension lead to the coil, and with a suitable container or a large rag in position to catch the ejected fuel, turn the engine over on the starter motor solenoid. A good spurt of petrol should emerge from the end of the pipe every second revolution.

8   Fuel pump – removal and refitting

1   Disconnect the fuel pipes by unscrewing their two hose clips on the fuel pump which is located on the right-hand side of the engine. Where the fuel tank contains more than a small amount of fuel it will probably be necessary to plug the inlet fuel line from the tank.
2   Remove the two nuts which secure the fuel pump to the crankcase. Lift away the pump noting carefully the number of gaskets used between the pump and crankcase mating faces.
3   Refitting is a reversal of removal but note the routing of the fuel pipe to the carburettor.

9   Fuel pump – dismantling, inspection, reassembly

1   Scratch an alignment mark across the edges of the upper and lower body flanges to ensure correct assembly.
2   Unscrew and remove the body securing screws.
3   Remove the cover screws and lift off the cover and gasket.
4   Remove the fuel pipe stubs.
5   Remove the retainer (two screws) and extract the two valves.
6   Press the diaphragm downwards and then grip the top of the pull rod and move the bottom end of the rod so that a sideways movement will disengage it from the rocker arm link. The diaphragm, diaphragm spring, lower body and washer may then be withdrawn.
7   The rocker arm pin is an interference fit and if it is essential to remove it, then it should be pressed or drifted out.
8   Check all components for wear and renew as necessary. Hold the diaphragm up to the light and inspect for splits or pin holes. Check the

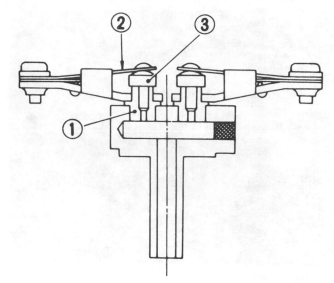

Fig. 3.5 Idle compensator (Sec 4)

1   Orifice   3   Rubber valve
2   Bi-metal

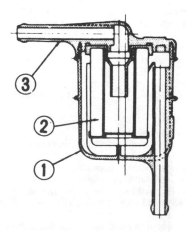

5.1 Fuel filter and fuel pump (arrowed)

Fig. 3.6 Fuel filter (Sec 5)

1   Body   3   Cover
2   Paper element

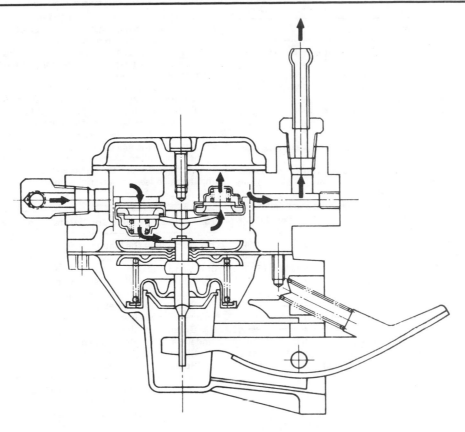

Fig. 3.7 Fuel pump – schematic (Sec 6)

upper and lower body halves for cracks.

9   Reassembly is a reversal of dismantling. Apply grease to the rocker arm mechanism and fit a new cover gasket.

10 When the pump has been reassembled, test its efficiency by either placing a finger over the inlet pipe and actuating the rocker arm when a good suction noise should be heard or by connecting it to the tank fuel line and after actuating the rocker arm a few times, each successive stroke should be accompanied by a well defined spurt of fuel from the outlet pipe.

11 Refit the pump as described in the preceding Section.

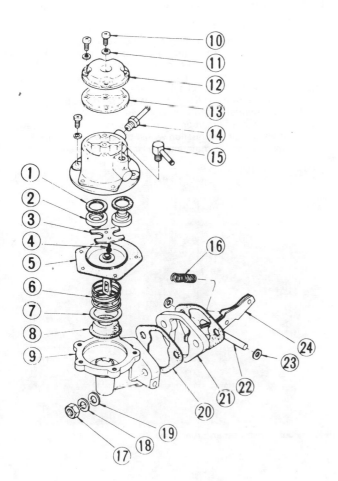

Fig. 3.8 Fuel pump – exploded view (Sec 9)

1   Packing
2   Valve assembly
3   Retainer
4   Screw
5   Diaphragm assembly
6   Diaphragm spring
7   Retainer
8   Oil seal
9   Body lower complete
10   Screw
11   Spring washer
12   Fuel pump cap
13   Cap gasket
14   Inlet connector
15   Outlet connector
16   Rocker arm spring
17   Nut
18   Spring washer
19   Plain washer
20   Gasket
21   Spacer
22   Rocker pin
23   Spacer
24   Rocker arm

10 Fuel tank – description and maintenance

1   The same fuel tank is used on all models and it is mounted at the rear, beneath the luggage compartment

2   The cap of the fuel filler pipe forms a seal over the pipe and as fuel is drawn from the tank, air enters the tank through a check valve which is mounted beneath the trim covering the fuel pipe.

3   The fuel tank is fitted with a fuel level transmitter and a drain plug and vehicles equipped with emission control have additional fuel tank connections for the control of fuel vapour emission.

4   Occasionally check the condition of the fuel hoses and the tightness of the fuel hose clips.

5   Because of condensation inside the fuel tank, water can accumulate at the bottom of the tank which causes the tank to corrode and may eventually result in water entering the carburettor. The accumulation of water in the tank can be minimised by keeping the level of fuel in the tank high. Periodically, when the level of fuel in the tank is very low, remove the tank filler cap and the drain plug, drain the tank completely and strain the fuel through a water separating filter. Do not have the car over a pit when draining out the fuel. Carry out the draining in a well ventilated place and make sure that there are no naked flames, or other possible sources of ignition.

11 Fuel level transmitter – removal, testing and refitting

1   Disconnect the lead from the battery negative terminal.

2   *On the Saloon model,* remove the panel to the right of the spare wheel in the luggage boot to expose the fuel tank and transmitter unit (photos).

3   *On Coupe and Estate car models,* remove the small inspection cover from the floor of the luggage compartment.

4   Disconnect the leads from the tank transmitter unit and using a 'C' wrench or carefully applying a hammer and drift to the tags of the locking ring, unscrew the unit and carefully remove it.

5   If a malfunction occurs in the fuel gauge, first check all leads and connections between the gauge and transmitter unit.

6   If the fuel gauge and the water temperature gauge become faulty at the same time, the instrument voltage stabiliser may be at fault.

7   Refitting is a reversal of removal but take care not to damage the float or arm of the transmitter unit when inserting it into the tank and always use a new rubber sealing ring. Ensure that the projection on the tank gauge unit aligns with the notch in the fuel tank.

12 Fuel tank (Saloon) – removal and refitting

1   Disconnect the lead from the battery negative terminal

2   With the car in a well ventilated place, which is free from any risk of igniting fuel vapour, remove the drain plug from the tank and drain the fuel into a correctly labelled container, suitable for petrol. Seal the container and store it in a safe place.

3   Slacken the hose clip and disconnect the fuel hose from the tank.

4   Remove the filler hose protector and the inspection cover from the luggage compartment.

5   Disconnect the fuel filler hose, vent hoses (emission control models) and the electrical connector on the fuel gauge transmitter.

6   Remove the fuel tank protector (if fitted).

7   Remove the bolts from the fuel tank flange and remove the tank.

8   Refitting is the reverse of removal, but it is necessary to ensure that the fuel tank has been secured in place before the fuel filler hose is connected. Failure to do this may result in fuel leakage from the hose connections. Ensure that all hoses are fitted free from kinks, or strain and that all hose clips are tightened.

13 Fuel tank (Coupe and Estate) – removal and refitting

1   Disconnect the lead from the battery negative terminal.

2   With the car in a well ventilated place, which is free from any risk of igniting fuel vapour, remove the drain plug from the tank and drain the fuel into a correctly labelled container, suitable for petrol. Seal the container and store it in a safe place. Disconnect the fuel inlet hose.

3   Remove the carpet and the floor from the luggage compartment, then remove the inspection cover and side trim.

4   Disconnect the fuel filler hose, vent hoses (emission control models) and the electrical connector to the fuel gauge transmitter.

5   Remove the fuel tank protector (if fitted).

6   Remove the bolts from the fuel tank flange and remove the tank.

7   Refitting is the reverse of removal, but it is necessary to ensure that the fuel tank has been secured in place before the fuel filler hose is connected. Failure to do this may result in fuel leakage from the hose connections. Ensure that all hoses are fitted free from kinks, or strain and that the hose clips are tightened.

14 Fuel evaporative emission control – description and maintenance

1   This system is designed to prevent vapour from the tank escaping to the atmosphere and is fitted to vehicles operating in areas where stringent anti-pollution regulations are enforced.

2   The system comprises a tight sealing filler cap, a vapour-liquid separator, a vent line and a check valve.

3   The principle of operation is that with the engine switched off, the vent line, the separator and fuel tank are filled with fuel vapour. When the engine is started, the vapour which has accumulated is drawn into the inlet manifold for combustion within the engine cylinders.

4   Periodic preventive maintenance of the system should be carried

11.2a Fuel transmitter cover panel

11.2b Fuel transmitter and fuel pipes

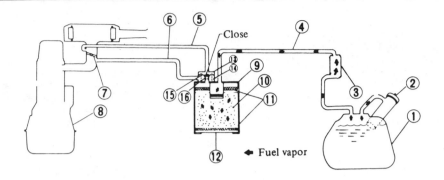

Fig. 3.9 Evaporative emission control system – schematic (Sec 14)

1 Fuel tank	5 Vacuum signal line	9 Carbon canister	13 Purge control valve
2 Fuel filler cap with vacuum relief valve	6 Canister purge line	10 Activated carbon	14 Diaphragm spring
3 Fuel check valve	7 Throttle valve	11 Screen	15 Diaphragm
4 Vapor vent line	8 Engine	12 Filter	16 Fixed orifice

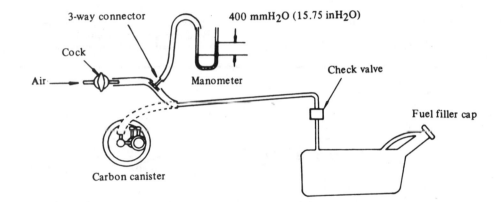

Fig. 3.10 Evaporative emission control system testing (Sec 14)

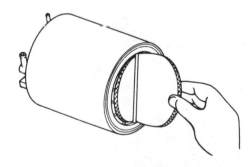

Fig. 3.11 Renewing the carbon canister filter (Sec 14)

out. Inspect all hoses and the fuel filler cap for damage or deterioration. Leakage at the fuel cap can only be determined by fitting a three-way connector, cock and manometer (U-shaped glass tube will do) into the vent line as shown in Fig. 3.10.

5 Blow through the cock until the level in the U-tube is approximately at the higher level illustrated. Close the cock and after a period of $2\frac{1}{2}$ minutes check that the level in the U-tube has not dropped more than indicated in the illustration. If the levels in the U-tube quickly become equalised, the filler cap is not sealing correctly.

6 Assuming the previous test has proved satisfactory, again blow into the U-tube and shut the cock. Remove the filler cap quickly when the height of the liquid in the U-tube should immediately drop to zero, failure to do this will indicate a clogged or obstructed vent line.

7 The fuel filler cap incorporates a vacuum release valve and this may be checked by gently sucking with the mouth. A slight resistance

Fig. 3.12 Carbon canister purge control valve (Sec 14)

1 Cover	3 Retainer
2 Diaphragm	4 Diaphragm spring

accompanied by a click shows the valve is in good condition. Further suction will cause the resistance to cease as soon as the valve clicks.

8 To check the operation of the check valve, blow into it from the fuel tank. Resistance should be felt but a little air should engage from the engine end of the valve. Blow into the check valve from the engine end and check that the resistance is minimal and that the flow of air is smooth. Renew the valve if it is proved faulty (Figs. 3.13 and 3.14).

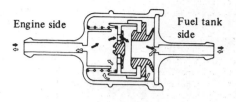

Fresh air flow

⇦ Evaporative fuel flow
← Fresh air flow

Fig. 3.13 Fuel check valve (Sec 14)

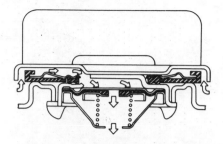

Fig. 3.14 Fuel filler cap (Sec 14)

15 Accelerator linkage – adjustment

1   After a considerable mileage, the accelerator cable may stretch and the following adjustment may be carried out to remove the slack.
2   Check the security of the inner cable to the accelerator pedal and the threaded portion of the outer cable which is held by a nut to the engine bulkhead. Refer to Fig. 3.16. Loosen clamp '1' and pull the outer cable in the direction 'P', until any further movement would cause the throttle arm on the carburettor to move. Now ease the outer cable in the opposite direction 'Q' no more than 0·04 in (1 mm). Tighten the clamp.
3   The accelerator pedal should be adjusted by means of its stop bolt

so that the pedal travel is as indicated and the carburettor butterfly valve is fully open when the pedal is fully depressed.
4   On vehicles having automatic transmission, adjust the 'kick-down' switch to operate when the accelerator pedal is fully depressed.

16 Carburettors – general description

All models are equipped with a Hitachi twin barrel carburettor of the down draught type. An automatic, electrically heated choke is fitted to the carburettors on 210 vehicles while the New Sunny models have carburettors equipped with a manually operated choke.

The carburettors vary in calibration details and those fitted on 210

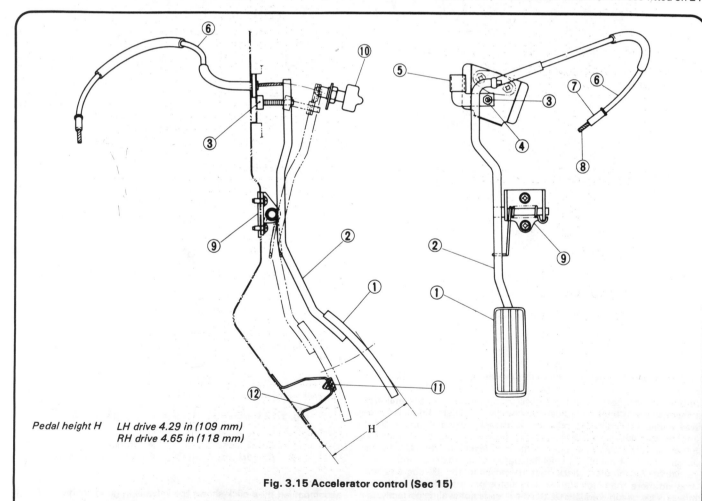

Pedal height H   LH drive 4.29 in (109 mm)
                  RH drive 4.65 in (118 mm)

Fig. 3.15 Accelerator control (Sec 15)

1 Accelerator pedal	5 Kickdown switch striker (Automatic transmission models only)	7 Accelerator wire socket	10 Kickdown switch
2 Accelerator pedal arm		8 Accelerator inner wire	11 Accelerator pedal stopper rubber
3 Stopper bolt	6 Accelerator wire outer case	9 Accelerator pedal bracket and return spring	12 Accelerator pedal stopper bracket
4 Stopper locknut			

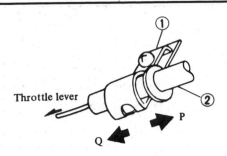

Fig. 3.16 Accelerator cable adjustment (Sec 15)

1 *Clamp*   2 *Outer case*

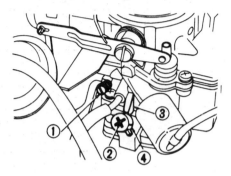

Fig. 3.17 Carburettor adjustment screws (Sec 17)

1 *Throttle speed screw*   3 *Mixture screw stop*
2 *Mixture control screw*   4 *Limiter cap*

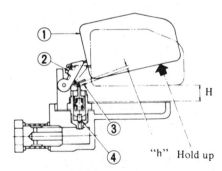

Fig. 3.18 Float level adjustment (Sec 18)

See Specification for dimensions H and h

1 *Float*   3 *Float tang*
2 *Float stop*   4 *Needle valve*

models having manual transmission incorporate a throttle opener device. When these carburettors are fitted in conjunction with automatic transmission a dashpot is incorporated in the carburettor to prevent any tendency to stall the engine during deceleration. Refer to the Specifications Section for details and applications.

The carburettor is conventional in operation and incorporates a primary and main jet system and a mechanically operated accelerator pump.

Manually operated choke: This comprises a butterfly valve which closes one of the venturi choke tubes and is so synchronized with the throttle valve plate that the latter opens sufficiently to provide a rich mixture and an increased slow running speed for easy starting.

Automatic choke: This is essentially an electrically heated bi-metal strip. When the engine is switched on, the bi-metal strip which is linked to the now fully closed choke valve (cold engine) is heated electrically and over a pre-set period causes the choke valve to open until its fully open position coincides with the engine reaching normal operating temperature.

For idling and slow running, the fuel passes through the slow running jet, the primary slow air bleed and the secondary slow air bleed. The fuel is finally ejected from the by-pass and idle holes.

The accelerator pump is synchronized with the throttle valve. During periods of heavy acceleration, the pump which is of simple piston and valve construction, provides an additional metered quantity of fuel to enrich the normal mixture. The quantity of fuel metered can be varied according to operating climatic conditions by adjusting the stroke of the pump linkage.

The secondary system provides a mixture for normal motoring conditions by means of a main jet and air bleed. The float chamber is fed with fuel pumped by the mechanically operated pump on the crankcase. The level in the chamber is critical and must at all times be maintained as specified.

17 Slow running – adjustment

1 Run the engine to normal operating temperature and then set the throttle adjusting screw (1) (Fig. 3.17) to provide the correct idling speed as given in the Specifications, according to the particular model. If the vehicle is fitted with a tachometer then the setting of engine speed will be no problem. Where an instrument is not available then a useful guide may be obtained from the state of the ignition warning lamp. This should just be going out at the correct idling speed.
2 Setting of the mixture screw (2) may be carried out using 'Colortune' or a vacuum gauge attached to the inlet manifold. In either case follow the equipment manufacturer's instructions.
3 In certain territories, the use of a CO meter is essential and if this is used then the throttle adjusting screw and the mixture screw must be turned to provide a reading on the meter of 1·5% ± 0·5% at the specified engine idling speed.
4 As a temporary measure, the adjustment screws may be rotated progressively, first one and then the other until the engine idles at the correct speed without any 'hunting' or stalling. Turning the mixture screw clockwise weakens the mixture and anti-clockwise enriches it. Never screw the mixture screw in too far or the idle limiter cap will break. Should this happen, a new cap must be fitted in accordance with the installation diagram, first making sure that the mixture screw has been correctly set to give the specified CO exhaust gas analysis.

18 Float level – adjustment

1 Where the appropriate adjustments have been carried out and there is evidence of fuel starvation or conversely, flooding or excessively rich mixture, the float level should be checked.
2 Remove the carburettor as described in Section 25.
3 Disconnect choke connecting rod, accelerator pump lever and return spring.
4 Unscrew and remove the five securing screws which secure the upper choke chamber to the main body.
5 Turn the float chamber upside down and check the dimension 'H' with the float hanging down under its own weight, (Fig. 3.18).
6 Gently push the float upwards to the full extent of its travel and check the clearance 'h' between the end face of the inlet needle valve and the float tongue. Adjustment to correct either of these dimensions is carried out by bending the float tang (3).

19 Fast idle adjustment

Type DCG 306 – manual choke

1 Ensure that the choke control is fully out and that the air cleaner having been removed, the choke butterfly valve can be seen to be in the fully closed position.
2 Check the position of the primary throttle valve plate. This should be open sufficiently to give a gap of 0·046 to 0·054 in (1·17 to 1·38 mm) between the edge of the plate and the venturi wall.
3 If adjustment is required, bend the choke connecting rod.

Type DCH 306 – automatic choke

4 Remove the automatic choke bi-metal cover.
5 Within the bi-metal housing, set the fast idle arm on the second

step of the fast idle cam.

6   Turn the fast idle adjusting screw so that the clearance between the edge of the primary throttle valve plate and the carburettor is within the following tolerances:

Manual transmission 0·0287 to 0·0331 in (0·73 to 0·84 mm)
Automatic transmission 0·0394 to 0·0449 in (1·00 to 1·14 mm)

These settings will give a fast idle speed for a cold engine of (manual transmission) 1900 to 2700 rpm and (automatic transmission) 2400 to 3200 rpm.

20 Vacuum break (DCH 306 carburettor) – adjustment

1   Close the choke valve plate fully and retain it in this position by using a rubber band.

2   Grip the vacuum break stem with a pair of long-nosed pliers and extend it fully from the vacuum capsule. Measure dimension 'B' (Fig. 3.20) which should be 0·0709 to 0·0780 in (1·80 to 1·98 mm) for all models except non-California, 5-speed models, 0·0780 to 0·0850 in (1·98 to 2·16 mm) on non-California, 5-speed models.

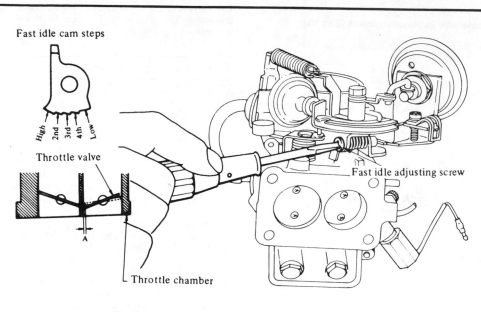

Fig. 3.19 Fast idle adjustment – DCH 306 (Sec 19)

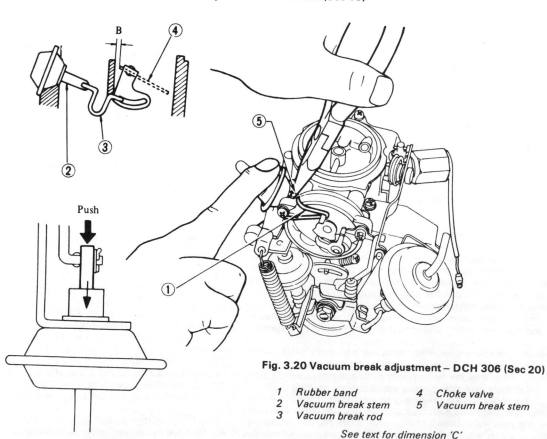

Fig. 3.20 Vacuum break adjustment – DCH 306 (Sec 20)

1	*Rubber band*	4	*Choke valve*
2	*Vacuum break stem*	5	*Vacuum break stem*
3	*Vacuum break rod*		

See text for dimension 'C'

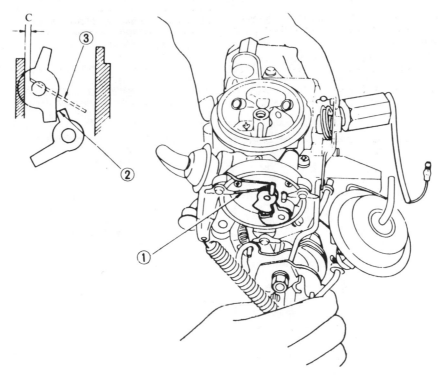

Fig. 3.21 Choke valve release adjustment – DCH 306 (Sec 21)

1   Rubber band   3   Choke valve
2   Unloader tongue   See text for dimension 'C'

3   Where necessary, bend the vacuum break rod to achieve the specified clearance.

21 Choke valve release (DCH 306 carburettor) – adjustment

1   Close the choke valve plate fully and retain it in this position with a rubber band.
2   Open the throttle lever fully and then check the dimension 'C' (Fig. 3.21) between the edge of the choke valve and the carburettor body. This should be 0·0929 in (2·36 mm) for all models except non-California, 5-speed models and 0·0854 in (2·17 mm) on non-California, 5-speed models.
3   If necessary bend the unloader tongue to achieve the correct dimension.

22 Automatic choke bi-metal (DCH 306 carburettor) – adjustment and testing

1   Depress the accelerator pedal fully and ensure that the choke valve closes fully. Push the choke valve with a finger to ensure that it moves freely, without binding.
2   Check that the index mark on the bi-metal cover is set at the centre of the choke housing index mark (Fig. 3.22). The bi-metal cover must not be in any position except on the centre mark.
3   Where there is evidence that the bi-metal resistance is unserviceable, this should be tested by connecting a sensitive ohmmeter between the choke heater wire terminal and the carburettor body. With the ignition off the resistance should be between 3·7 and 8·9 ohms measured at an ambient temperature of approximately 21°C (70°F).

23 Dashpot – adjustment (DCH 306 carburettor)

1   Run the engine to the normal operating temperature.
2   Actuate the throttle linkage by hand until the dashpot just impinges upon the return spring lever. At this position the engine

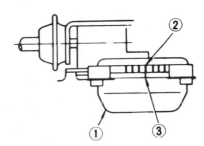

Fig. 3.22 Choke bi-metal setting (Sec 22)

1   Thermostat cover   2   Thermostat housing   3   Groove in cover

tachometer should register 2000 rpm. If this is not the case, adjust the dashpot stop nut.
3   Finally when the engine is running at 3000 rpm release the throttle linkage and ensure that the engine speed falls smoothly from this level to 1000 rpm in about three seconds. If the speed does not fall smoothly and progressively then the dashpot is probably worn and must be renewed.

24 Primary and secondary throttle butterfly valves – adjustment of interlock mechanism

1   Actuate the primary throttle valve until the secondary throttle valve is just about open. Measure the distance (G1 – Fig. 3.23) between the edge of the primary valve plate and the wall of the bore, this should be 0·23 in (5·8 mm).
2   If the clearance requires adjustment, bend the rod which connects the two throttle plates.

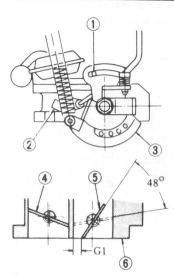

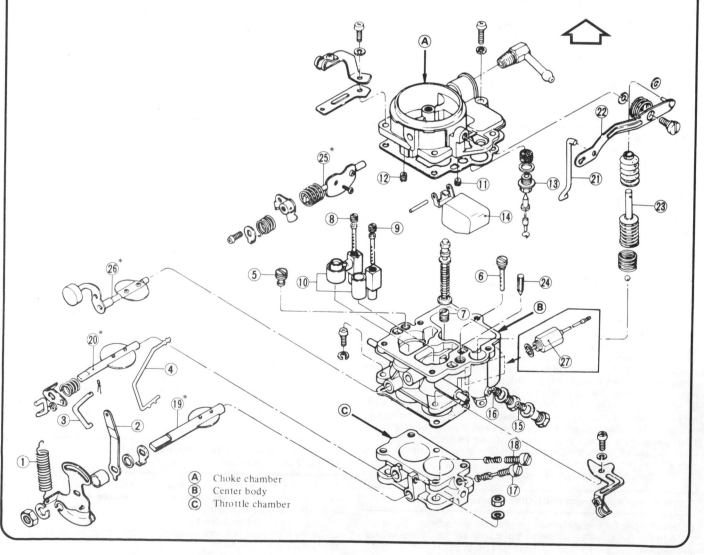

Fig. 3.24 Manual choke carburettor (DCG 306) – exploded view (Sec 27)

1   Throttle return spring
2   Starting lever
3   Connecting rod
4   Choke connecting rod
5   Secondary slow jet
6   Primary slow jet
7   Power jet
8   Secondary main air bleed
9   Primary main air bleed
10 Primary and Secondary small venturi
11 Primary slow air bleed
12 Secondary slow air bleed
13 Needle valve
14 Float
15 Primary main jet
16 Secondary main jet
17 Idle adjust screw
18 Throttle adjust screw
19*Primary throttle valve
20*Secondary throttle valve
21 Accelerating pump rod
22 Accelerating pump lever
23 Accelerating pump
24 Injector weight
25*Choke valve
26*Auxiliary valve
27 Anti-dieseling solenoid valve (A12 Engine only)

Note: Do not remove the parts marked with an asterisk

Fig. 3.23 Primary and secondary throttle adjustment (Sec 24)

1   Connecting rod
2   Secondary connecting lever
3   Throttle lever
4   Secondary throttle valve
5   Primary throttle valve
6   Throttle chamber

See text for dimention 'G1'

A   Choke chamber
B   Center body
C   Throttle chamber

25 Carburettor – removal and refitting

1   Remove the air cleaner.
2   Disconnect the fuel inlet pipe.
3   Disconnect the vacuum pipe from the distributor.
4   Disconnect the lead to the automatic choke, or the choke control cable according to type of carburettor.
5   Disconnect the lead from the anti-dieseling (anti-run on) solenoid on 210 vehicles, see Section 33.
6   Disconnect the throttle cable from the carburettor.
7   Remove the four nuts and washers which secure the carburettor to the inlet manifold and lift it away.
8   Refitting is a reversal of removal, but always use a new flange gasket between the carburettor and the manifold.

26 Carburettors – servicing general

1   In time, the components of a carburettor will wear and fuel consumption will inevitably increase. The diameters of drillings and jets may increase due to the passage of air and fuel and leaks may develop round spindles and other moving parts. When a carburettor is well worn it is better to obtain a new or rebuilt unit rather than attempt to recondition the old one when so many parts need renewal.
2   Where it is decided to dismantle the carburettor for cleaning, or to renew a jet, or other small component, proceed by first obtaining the appropriate repair kit, which will contain all the necessary gaskets and other components.
3   Never probe jets with wire to clear them but blow them out with air from a tyre pump.
4   Before starting to dismantle, clean the outside of the carburettor, using a brush and some fuel.

27 Carburettor (DCG 306 – manual choke) – dismantling and reassembly

1   The main jets and needle valves are accessible from the exterior of the carburettor.
2   These should be unscrewed, removed and cleaned by blowing them through with air from a tyre pump; never probe a jet or needle valve seat with wire.
3   Detach the choke chamber by removing the connecting rod, accelerator pump lever, return spring and the five securing screws.
4   The primary and secondary emulsion tubes are accessible after removing the main air bleeds.
5   Remove the accelerator pump cover, retaining the spring, piston and ball valve carefully.
6   Separate the float chamber from the throttle housing by unscrewing and removing three securing screws. Slide out the float pivot pin and remove the float.
7   Unless imperative, do not dismantle the throttle butterfly valves from their spindles.
8   Take great care when disconnecting the interlock rods that they are not bent or twisted or the settings and adjustments will be upset.
9   With the carburettor dismantled, clean all components in clean fuel and blow through the internal body passages with air from a tyre pump.
10   Inspect all components for wear and the body and chamber castings for cracks.
11   Clean the small gauze filter and if corroded or clogged, renew it.
12   If wear is evident in the throttle spindle, the carburettor should be renewed on an exchange basis.
13   Check all jet and air bleed sizes with those specified in Specifications in case a previous owner has changed them for ones of incorrect size.
14   Check the ejection of fuel when the accelerator pump is actuated.
15   Reassembly is a reversal of dismantling using all the items supplied in the repair kit.
16   Carry out the adjustments described in Sections 18, 19 and 24, of this Chapter.

28 Carburettor (DCH 306 – automatic choke)– dismantling and reassembly

1   Remove the main jets and needle valves from the primary and secondary sides. They are accessible from outside the carburettor.
2   Detach the throttle return spring.
3   Unscrew the accelerator pump lever shaft, remove the pump operative lever and connecting rod.
4   Remove the rubber pipe from the choke piston.
5   Remove the servo-diaphragm (manual transmission models).
6   Remove the choke assembly bolts and withdraw the assembly, at the same time disconnecting the interconnecting rods.
7   Remove the air bleeds and extract the primary and secondary emulsion tubes.
8   Slide out the float pivot pin and remove the float.
9   Unscrew and remove the fuel inlet needle valve.
10   Invert the carburettor and eject the components of the accelerator pump. Take care not to lose the ball and weight.
11   Separate the throttle chamber from the main body by removing the three securing screws.
12   Do not dismantle the throttle valves unless absolutely essential.
13   Take great care when disconnecting the interlock rods that they are not bent or twisted or the settings and adjustments will be upset.
14   With the carburettor dismantled, clean all components in clean fuel and blow through the body passages with air from a tyre pump.
15   Inspect all components for wear and the body and chamber castings for cracks.
16   Clean the small gauze filter and if corroded or clogged, renew it.
17   If wear is evident in the throttle spindle, the carburettor should be renewed on an exchange basis.

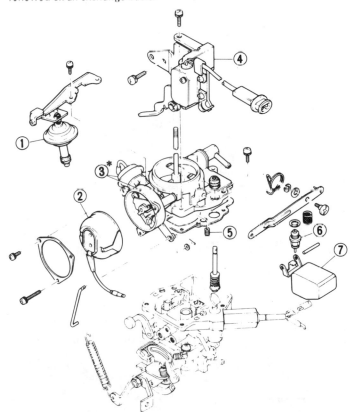

Fig. 3.25 Choke chamber parts non-California, 5-speed models (Sec 28)

1	Dashpot	4	Throttle valve switch
2	Automatic choke cover		assembly
3*	Automatic choke body and	5	Primary slow air bleed
	diaphragm chamber	6	Needle valve
		7	Float

Note: Do not remove the parts marked with an asterisk

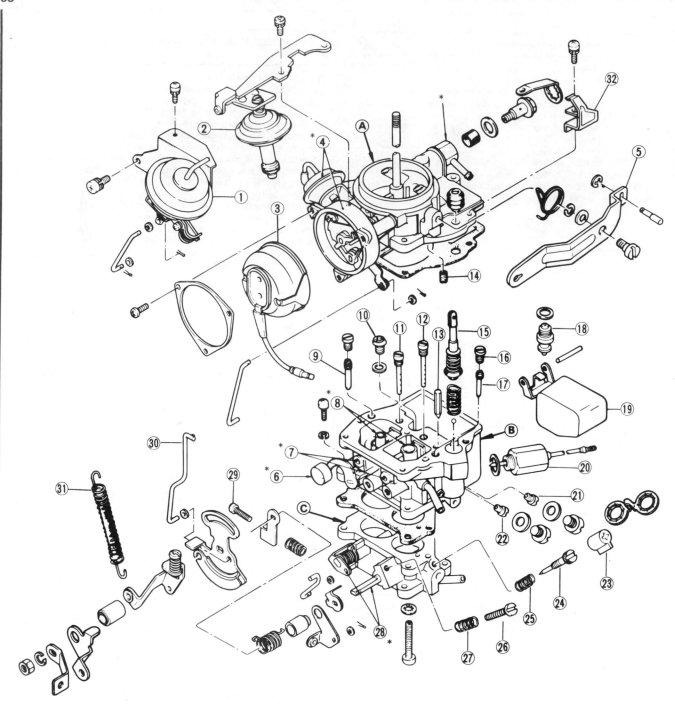

Fig. 3.26 Exploded view of DCH 306 automatic choke carburettor – non-California 5-speed models (Sec 28)

1 Servo diaphragm of throttle opener	8* Primary and secondary small venturi
2 Dashpot	9 Secondary slow jet
3 Automatic choke cover	10 Power valve
4* Automatic choke body and diaphragm chamber	11 Secondary main air bleed
5 Accelerating pump lever	12 Primary main air bleed
6* Auxiliary valve	13 Injector weight
7* Venturi stopper screw	14 Primary slow air bleed
	15 Accelerator pump

16 Plug	25 Spring
17 Primary slow jet	26 Throttle adjust screw
18 Needle valve	27 Spring
19 Float	28* Primary and secondary throttle valves
20 Anti-dieseling solenoid valve	29 Fast idle adjust screw
21 Primary main jet	30 Accelerating pump rod
22 Secondary main jet	31 Throttle return spring
23 Idle limiter cap	32 Stroke limiter
24 Idle adjust screw	

Ⓐ Choke chamber
Ⓑ Centre body
Ⓒ Throttle chamber

Note: Do not remove the parts marked with an asterisk

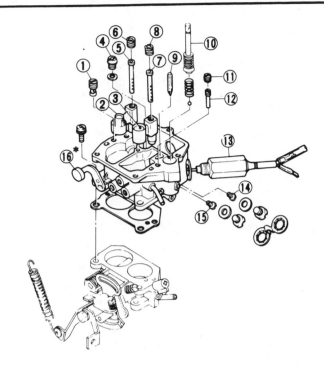

Fig. 3.27 Centre body parts – non-California, 5-speed models (Sec 28)

1	Secondary slow jet	5	Secondary main air bleed	9	Injector weight	13	Anti-dieseling solenoid
2	Secondary small venturi	6	Plug	10	Accelerator pump		valve
3	Primary small venturi	7	Primary main air bleed	11	Plug	14	Secondary main jet
4	Power valve	8	Plug	12	Primary slow jet	15	Primary main jet
						16*	Auxiliary valve

*Note: Do not remove the parts
marked with an asterisk*

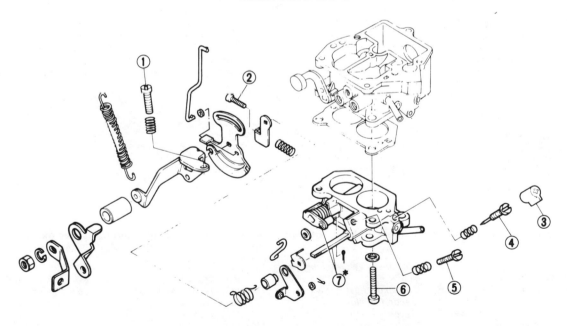

Fig. 3.28 Throttle chamber parts – non-California, 5-speed models (Sec 28)

1	Throttle valve switch adjust screw	2	Fast idle adjust screw	4	Idle adjust screw	6	Vacuum screw
		3	Limiter cap	5	Throttle adjust screw	7*	Primary and secondary throttle valves

*Note: Do not remove the parts
marked with an asterisk*

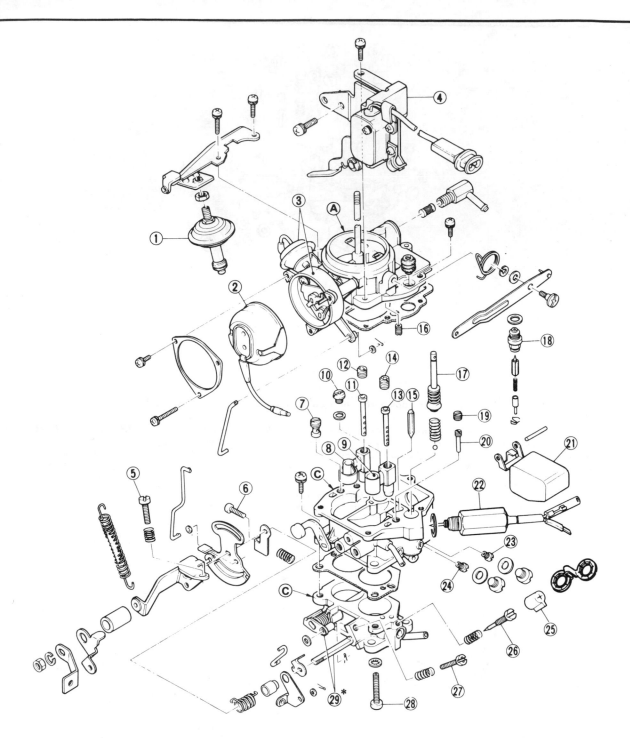

Fig. 3.29 Exploded view of DCH 306 automatic choke carburettor – all models except non-California 5-speed models (Sec 28)

A	Choke chamber	5	Throttle valve switch adjust screw
B	Centre body		
C	Throttle chamber	6	Fast idle adjust screw
		7	Secondary slow jet
1	Dashpot	8	Secondary small venturi
2	Automatic choke cover	9	Primary small venturi
3*	Automatic choke body and diaphragm chamber	10	Power valve
		11	Secondary main air bleed
4	Throttle valve switch assembly	12	Plug
		13	Primary main air bleed

14	Plug
15	Injector weight
16	Primary slow air bleed
17	Accelerator pump
18	Needle valve
19	Plug
20	Primary slow jet
21	Float
22	Anti-dieseling solenoid valve

23	Secondary main jet
24	Primary main jet
25	Idle limiter cap
26	Idle adjust screw
27	Throttle adjust screw
28	Vacuum screw
29*	Primary and secondary throttle valves

Note: Do not remove the parts marked with an asterisk

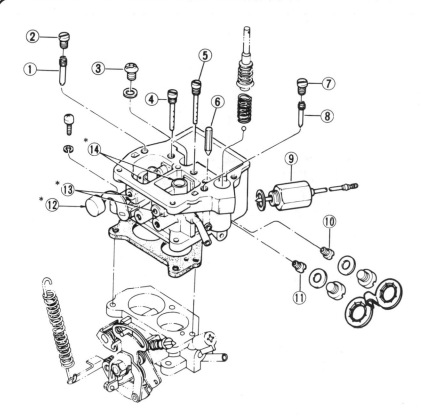

Fig. 3.30 Centre body parts – all models except non-California, 5-speed models (Sec 28)

1 Secondary slow jet
2 Plug
3 Power valve
4 Secondary main air bleed
5 Primary main air bleed
6 Injector weight
7 Plug
8 Primary slow jet
9 Anti-dieseling solenoid valve
10 Primary main jet
11 Secondary main jet
12* Auxiliary valve
13* Venturi stopper screw
14* Primary and secondary small venturis
Note: Do not remove the parts marked with an asterisk

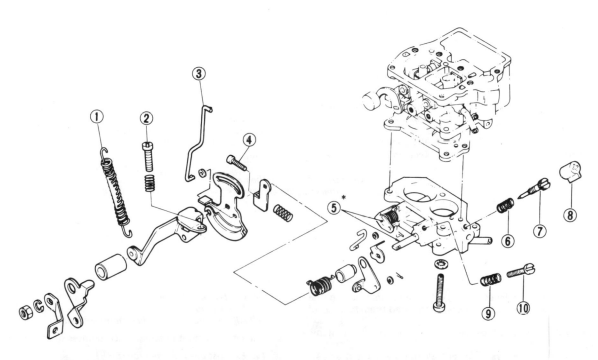

Fig. 3.31 Throttle chamber parts – all models except non-California, 5-speed models (Sec 28)

1 Throttle return spring
2 Throttle opener adjust screw
3 Accelerating pump rod
4 Fast idle adjust screw

5* Primary and secondary throttle valve
6 Spring
7 Idle adjust screw

8 Idle limiter cap
9 Spring
10 Throttle adjust screw

Note: Do not remove the parts marked with an asterisk

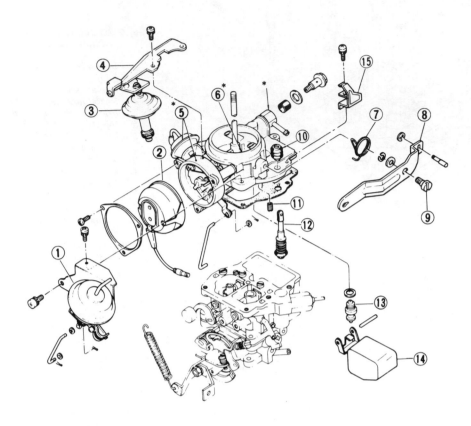

Fig. 3.32 Choke chamber parts – all models except non-California, 5-speed models (Sec 28)

1 Servo diaphragm of throttle opener	5 *Automatic choke body and diaphragm chamber	9 Accelerating pump lever shaft	12 Primary slow air bleed
2 Automatic choke cover	6 *Choke valve	10 Accelerating pump dust cover	13 Needle valve
3 Dashpot	7 Pump lever return spring	11 Accelerating pump	14 Float
4 Spring hanger	8 Accelerating pump lever		15 Stroke limiter

*Note: Do not remove the parts
marked with an asterisk*

18 Check all jet and air bleed sizes with those specified in the Specifications in case a previous owner has changed them for ones of incorrect size.

19 Reassembly is a reversal of dismantling, using all the items supplied in the repair kit.

20 During reassembly, always carry out all the checks and adjustments described in Sections 18 to 24, of this Chapter.

29 Exhaust emission control system – description

1 The maintenance of a 'clean exhaust' without loss of power or economy is dependent not only upon the correct adjustment of the specific components described in this Section but also upon the correct tune of other components of the engine.

2 Regularly check the adjustment of the following:

 (a) Valve clearances
 (b) Ignition timing

 (c) Contact breaker points
 (d) Spark plugs
 (e) All the carburettor adjustments described in this Chapter

3 The emission control system incorporates the following:

 (a) Exhaust gas recirculation (EGR)
 (b) Throttle opener control (manual transmission)
 (c) Transmission controlled vacuum advance (manual transmission)
 (d) Anti-dieseling (anti-run on) solenoid valve
 (e) Crankcase emission control valve
 (f) Fuel evaporative control (refer to Section 14, of this Chapter)
 (g) Temperature controlled air cleaner (refer to Section 3, of this Chapter)
 (h) Air injection system and Catalytic converter (California)

4 Maintenance and servicing of these components is described in the following Sections.

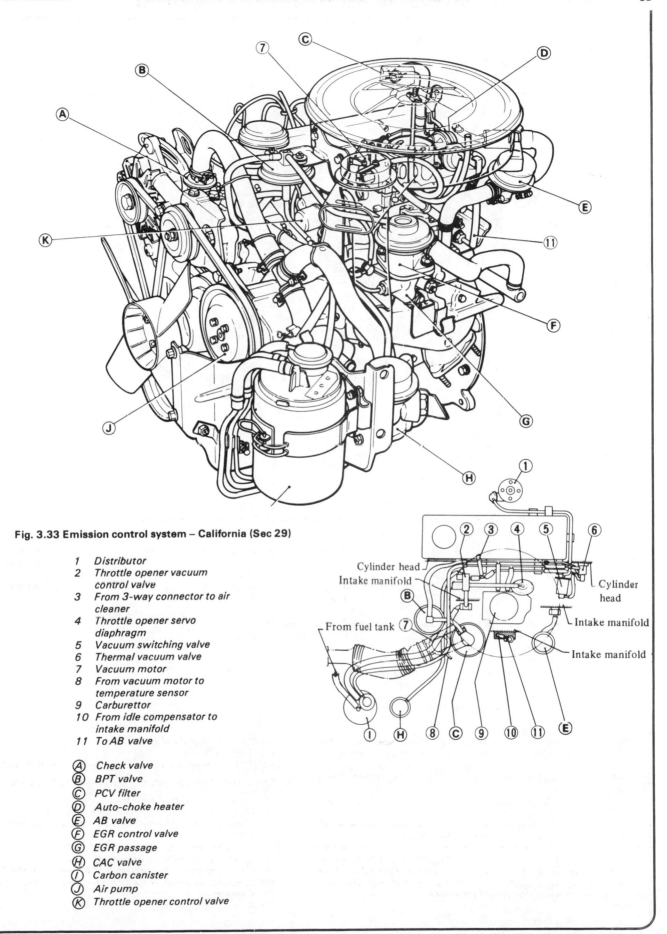

Fig. 3.33 Emission control system – California (Sec 29)

1 Distributor
2 Throttle opener vacuum control valve
3 From 3-way connector to air cleaner
4 Throttle opener servo diaphragm
5 Vacuum switching valve
6 Thermal vacuum valve
7 Vacuum motor
8 From vacuum motor to temperature sensor
9 Carburettor
10 From idle compensator to intake manifold
11 To AB valve

A Check valve
B BPT valve
C PCV filter
D Auto-choke heater
E AB valve
F EGR control valve
G EGR passage
H CAC valve
I Carbon canister
J Air pump
K Throttle opener control valve

Cylinder head
Intake manifold
From fuel tank
Cylinder head
Intake manifold
Intake manifold

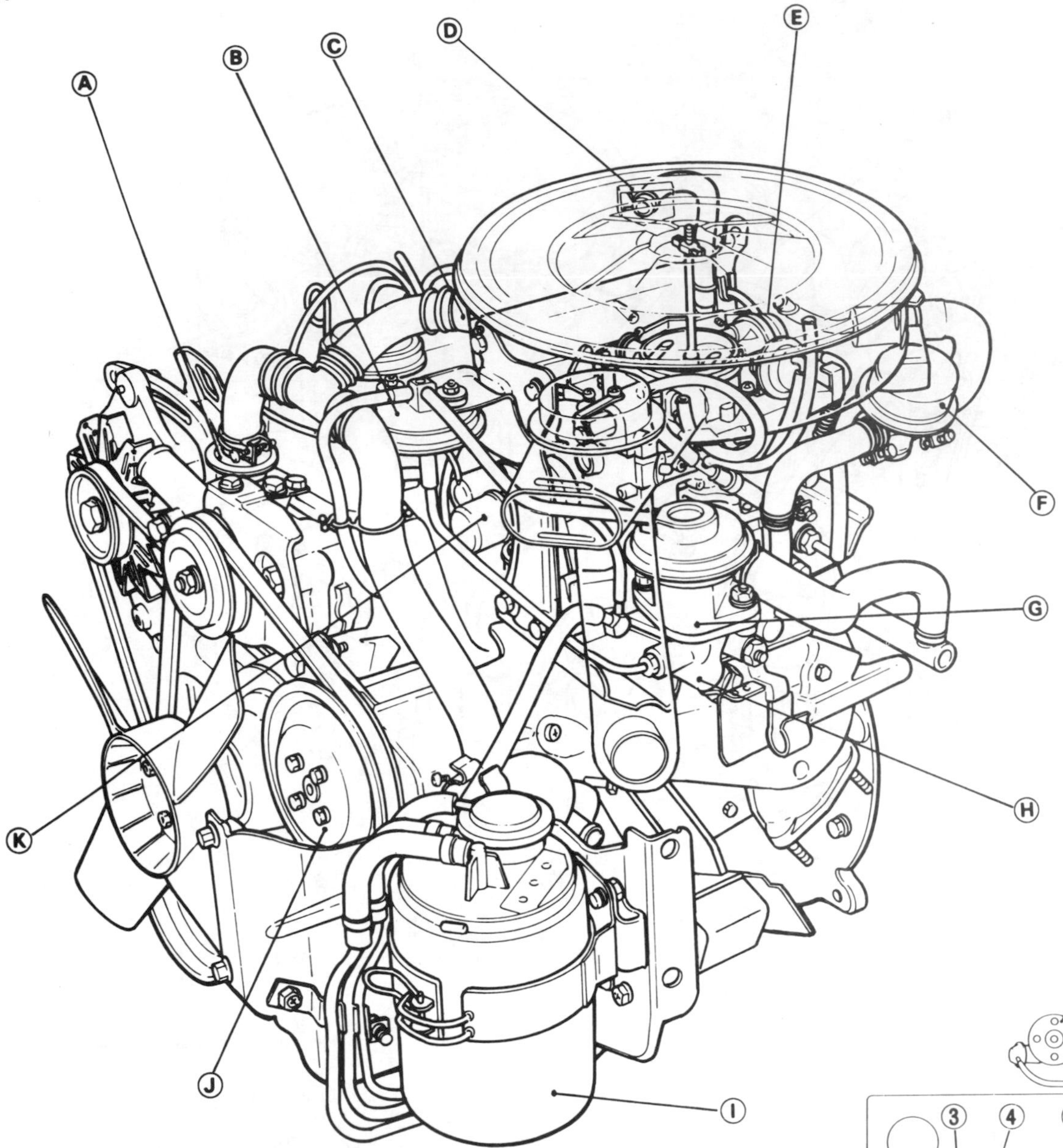

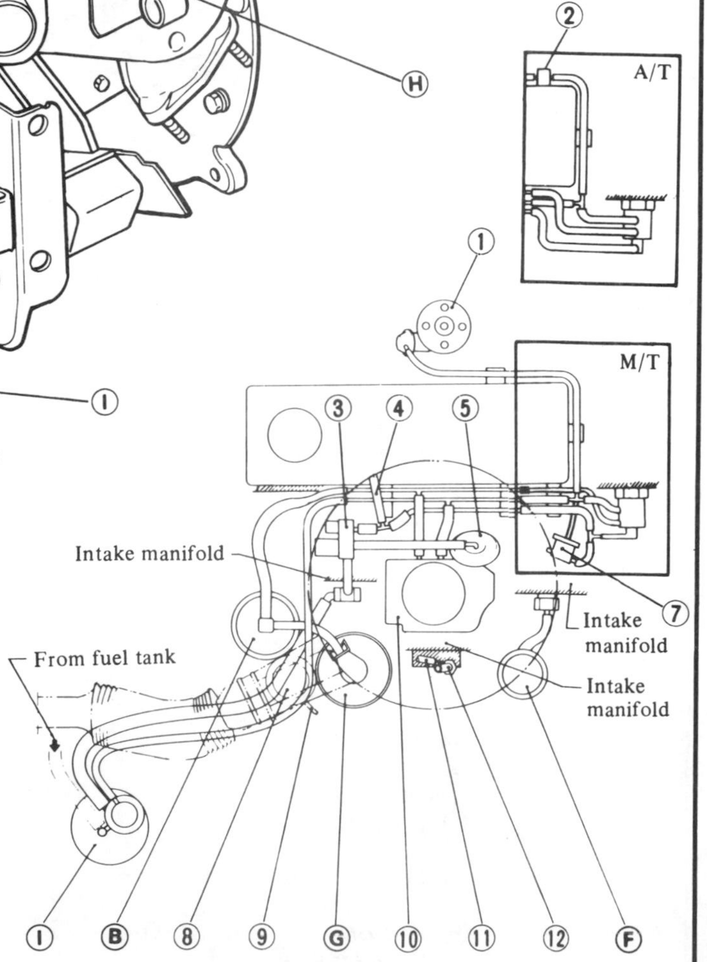

Fig. 3.34 Emission control system – US except California (Sec 29)

1　Distributor
2　Spark delay valve (A/T)
3　Throttle opener vacuum control valve
4　From 3-way connector to air cleaner
5　Throttle opener servo diaphragm
6　Thermal vacuum valve (3-port type)
7　Vacuum switching valve (M/T)
8　Vacuum motor
9　From vacuum motor to temperature sensor
10　Carburettor
11　From idle compensator to intake manifold
12　To AB valve

A　Check valve
B　BPT valve
C　Air pump relief valve
D　PCV filter
E　Auto-choke heater
F　AB valve
G　EGR control valve
H　EGR passage
I　Carbon canister
J　Air pump
K　Throttle opener control valve

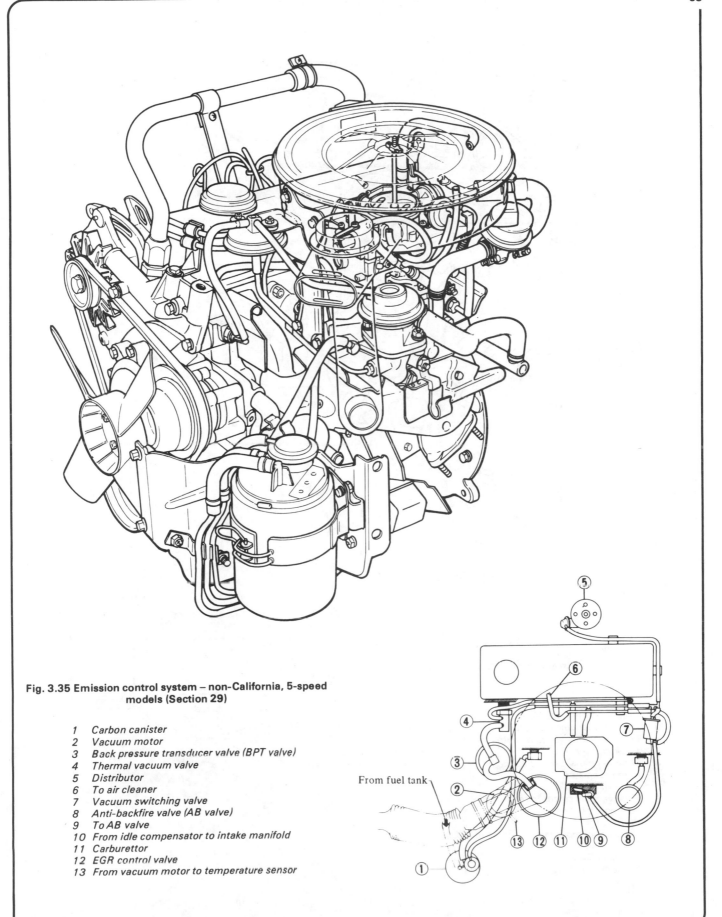

Fig. 3.35 Emission control system – non-California, 5-speed models (Section 29)

1   Carbon canister
2   Vacuum motor
3   Back pressure transducer valve (BPT valve)
4   Thermal vacuum valve
5   Distributor
6   To air cleaner
7   Vacuum switching valve
8   Anti-backfire valve (AB valve)
9   To AB valve
10 From idle compensator to intake manifold
11 Carburettor
12 EGR control valve
13 From vacuum motor to temperature sensor

From fuel tank

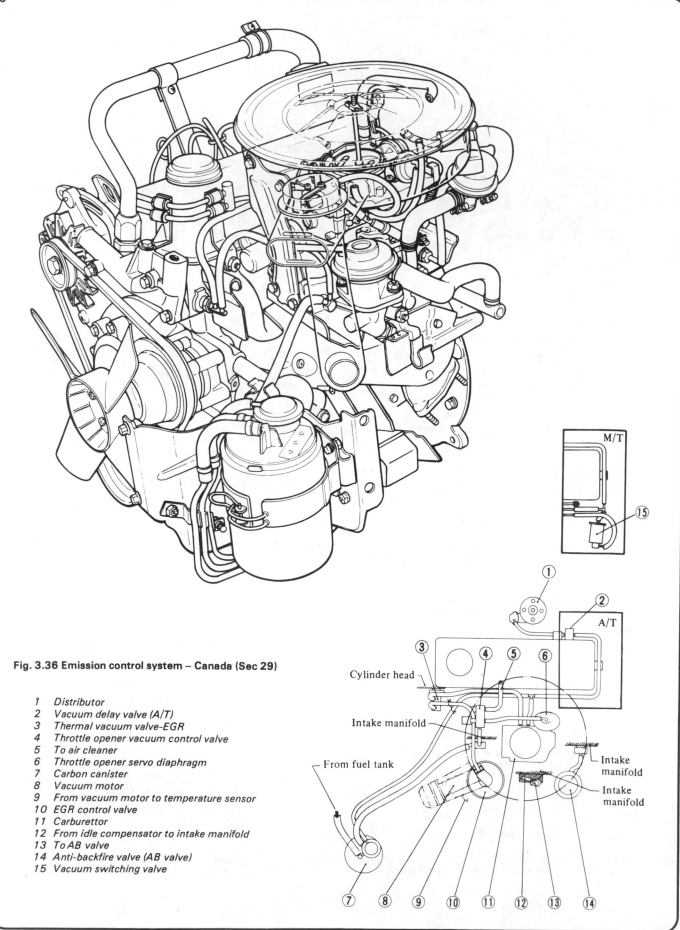

Fig. 3.36 Emission control system – Canada (Sec 29)

1 Distributor
2 Vacuum delay valve (A/T)
3 Thermal vacuum valve-EGR
4 Throttle opener vacuum control valve
5 To air cleaner
6 Throttle opener servo diaphragm
7 Carbon canister
8 Vacuum motor
9 From vacuum motor to temperature sensor
10 EGR control valve
11 Carburettor
12 From idle compensator to intake manifold
13 To AB valve
14 Anti-backfire valve (AB valve)
15 Vacuum switching valve

30 Exhaust gas recirculation (EGR) system

1   The system is designed to recirculate exhaust gases into the inlet manifold where they will re-enter the combustion chambers of the engine and so help to reduce the combustion temperatures and reduce the emission of noxious gases.

2   The system incorporates a control valve, a vacuum valve controlled by coolant temperature and a back pressure transducer (BPT) valve which monitors exhaust pressure (Figs. 3.39 – 3.42).

3   When the EGR valve opens, exhaust gases from the exhaust manifold are directed through the valve into the inlet manifold. Metering of the gases is controlled by the valve which itself is operated by vacuum pressure according to the throttle opening.

4   The thermal vacuum valve is temperature controlled and during starting or cold running conditions, it seals the vacuum passage to prevent gas recirculation.

5   At intervals specified in the Routine Maintenance Section, check the condition and security of all hoses.

6   Visually check that with the engine running, the control valve is open at part throttle and shut at full throttle.

7   Remove the control valve and clean deposits from its seat with a wire brush.

8   Check the thermal vacuum valve by removing it from the engine and attaching a length of plastic tube to each of its ports. Immerse the valve in water, taking care not to let water enter any of the tubes and heat the water. Suck with the mouth on the pipe attached to the top valve port and check that the valve opens and admits air only below 50 to 63°C (122 to 145°F) for the 3-port valve. On the 2-port valve, air should only be admitted if the temperature exceeds 40 to 63°C (104 to 145°F).

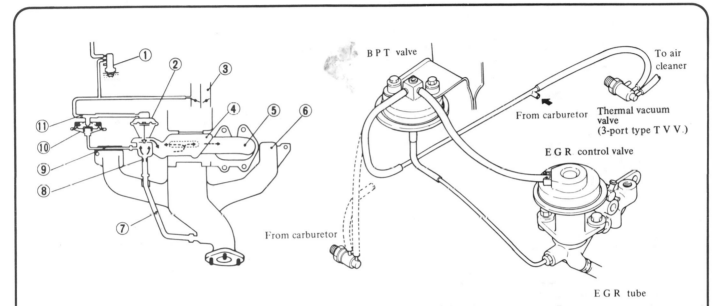

Fig. 3.37 Exhaust gas recirculation (EGR) system – US models (Sec 30)

Thermal vacuum valve (2-port type TVV for non-California, 5-speed)

1 EGR thermal vacuum valve	4 EGR passage	7 EGR tube	9 BPT tube
2 EGR control valve	5 Intake manifold	8 Orifice	10 BPT valve
3 Carburettor	6 Exhaust manifold		

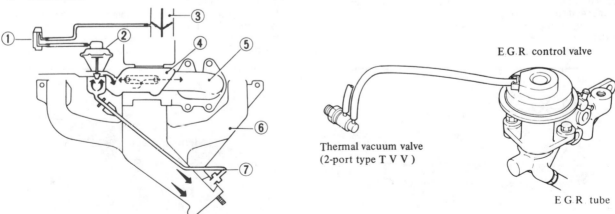

Fig. 3.38 Exhaust gas recirculation (EGR) system – Canada models (Sec 30)

1 Thermal vacuum valve	3 Carburettor	5 Intake manifold	7 EGR tube
2 EGR control valve	4 EGR passage	6 Exhaust manifold	

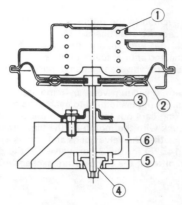

Fig. 3.39 EGR control valve (Sec 30)

1	Diaphragm spring	4	Valve
2	Diaphragm	5	Valve seat
3	Valve shaft	6	Valve chamber

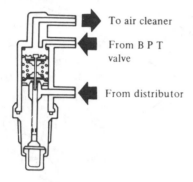

Fig. 3.40 Thermal vacuum valve – 2-port type (Sec 30)

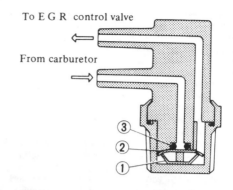

Fig. 3.41 Thermal vacuum valve – 3-port type (Sec 30)

1	Spring	3	O-ring
2	Bi-metal		

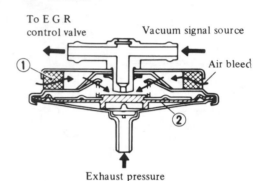

Fig. 3.42 BPT valve (Sec 30)

1	Air filter	2	Diaphragm

31 Throttle opener control system

1   A throttle opening device is fitted which is designed to open the throttle slightly during engine deceleration and to reduce the concentration of unburned hydrocarbons in the exhaust system by admitting a mixture sufficient to maintain complete combustion within the cylinders. The device comprises a servo diaphragm attached to the carburettor and a control valve bolted to the inlet manifold. The system is actuated by vacuum within the inlet manifold. A solenoid actuated by the speedometer needle, prevents the throttle opener device operating at speeds below 10 mph (16 km/h).

2   Run the engine until normal operating temperature is reached (check valve plate fully open).

3   Disconnect the vacuum hose which runs between the inlet manifold and the automatic temperature controlled air cleaner.

4   Disconnect the leads from the throttle opener solenoid.

5   Check and adjust the engine idling.

6   Connect the servo diaphragm (using a temporary hose) directly to the inlet manifold bypassing the vacuum control valve.

7   The engine speed under these conditions should be between 1650 and 1850 rpm (except California) and 1900 to 2100 rpm for California. If necessary, adjust the engine speed until it is within the specified range, turning the adjusting screw clockwise to increase the speed and anticlockwise to lower it.

8   Reconnect the throttle opener solenoid and reconnect the vacuum hoses to their original positions

9   In the event of failure to respond to adjustment with either component, renew as assemblies as they are not capable of repair.

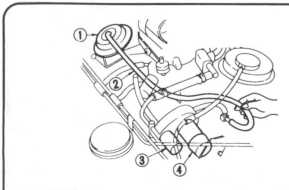

Fig. 3.43 Throttle opener control system components (Sec 31)

1	Servo diaphragm	3	TOCS solenoid valve
2	Rubber hose	4	TOCS control valve

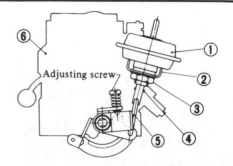

Fig. 3.44 Throttle positioner adjustment (Sec 31)

1	Servo diaphragm	4	Stopper
2	Bracket	5	Link
3	Locknut	6	Carburettor

32 Transmission controlled vacuum advance

1   This system installed on manual transmission vehicles provides operation of the distributor vacuum advance only when top gear is selected. The retarded ignition timing in other gear positions helps to maintain complete combustion.

2   A switch screwed into the gearbox housing actuates a solenoid valve which in turn allows air to enter the distributor vacuum capsule in all gear positions except top gear with the result that there is little vacuum advance in the low gear positions.

3   To check the operation of the system, have the engine running and depress the clutch and select each forward gear in turn. Arrange for an assistant to pull the vacuum hose from the distributor and feel for vacuum at the open end of the hose. This should be apparent when top gear is selected but not in the other gears.

4   Where this check does not prove satisfactory, inspect the electrical leads and hose connections and for a faulty solenoid or gearbox switch.

33 Anti-dieseling (anti-run on) valve

1   This is installed directly into the carburettor and operates by means of a solenoid which closes immediately the ignition is switched off to cut off fuel to the engine and prevent run on. This can be caused by overheating or a heavy carbon build up within the combustion chambers causing ignition of the fuel mixture even though the ignition is switched off.

2   In the event of failure of the valve, check the electrical connection first. If renewal is required, carefully unscrew the solenoid valve and then screw in the new one after coating all threads with a thread locking compound.

3   Do not use the carburettor for 12 hours to give the locking compound time to set.

34 Crankcase ventilation system

1   The crankcase ventilation system comprises a hose connected between the crankcase and the inlet manifold, and a further hose connected between the dust side of the air cleaner and the rocker cover. A vacuum operated PCV valve regulates the quantity of blow-by gas admitted to the inlet manifold.

2   Under closed throttle and partial throttle operation, the crankcase blow-by gases are drawn through the PCV valve, into the inlet manifold, and then into the engine for further combustion. Ventilating air is also drawn from the air cleaner into the rocker cover.

3   Under full throttle operation, the inlet manifold vacuum is insufficient to open the PCV valve, and the blow-by gases are then forced through the rocker cover and hose to the air cleaner where they are drawn through the inlet manifold into the engine.

4   Periodically examine the hoses for condition and security and every 12 000 miles (38 000 km) disconnect them and clean away any accumulated sludge. The PCV valve and air cleaner filter should be renewed at the specified intervals.

35 Manifolds and exhaust system

1   The inlet manifold is of aluminium construction while the exhaust manifold is cast iron. The latter incorporates a deflector valve with bi-metal coil spring to give quick warm up of the inlet manifold during initial starting of the engine when running during cold weather.

2   The exhaust system is of two section design and incorporates an expansion box and silencer. The system is supported on rubber rings and a flexible strap (photos).

3   Examination of the exhaust pipe and silencers at regular intervals is worthwhile as small defects may be reparable when, if left they will almost certainly require renewal of one of the sections of the system. Also, any leaks, apart from the noise factor, may cause poisonous

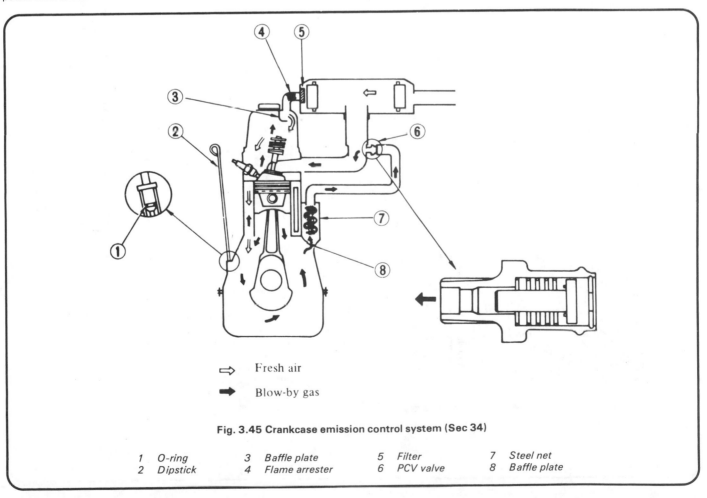

⇨   Fresh air

➡   Blow-by gas

Fig. 3.45 Crankcase emission control system (Sec 34)

1 O-ring	3 Baffle plate	5 Filter	7 Steel net
2 Dipstick	4 Flame arrester	6 PCV valve	8 Baffle plate

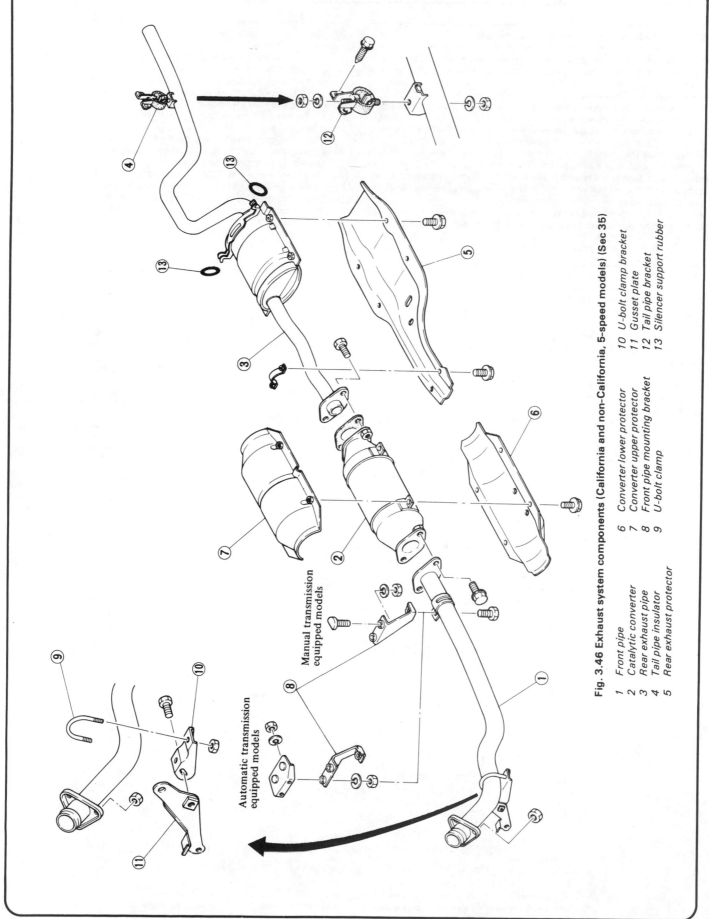

Fig. 3.46 Exhaust system components (California and non-California, 5-speed models) (Sec 35)

1 Front pipe
2 Catalytic converter
3 Rear exhaust pipe
4 Tail pipe insulator
5 Rear exhaust protector
6 Converter lower protector
7 Converter upper protector
8 Front pipe mounting bracket
9 U-bolt clamp
10 U-bolt clamp bracket
11 Gusset plate
12 Tail pipe bracket
13 Silencer support rubber

Manual transmission equipped models

Automatic transmission equipped models

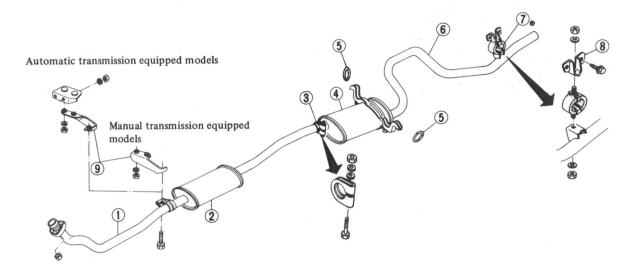

Fig. 3.47 Exhaust system components (except California) (Sec 35)

1 Front pipe assembly	4 Main silencer	7 Tail pipe insulator
2 Front silencer	5 Silencer clamp rubber	8 Tail pipe mounting bracket
3 Exhaust pipe clip	6 Rear pipe	9 Front pipe support bracket

35.2a Rear silencer

35.2b Tail pipe support

exhaust gases to get inside the car which can be unpleasant, to say the least, even in mild concentrations. Prolonged inhalation could cause sickness and giddiness.

4   As the sleeve connections and clamps are usually very difficult to separate it is quicker and easier in the long run to remove the complete system from the car when renewing a section. It can be expensive if another section is damaged when trying to separate a bad section from it.

5   To remove the system first remove the bolts holding the tail pipe bracket to the body. Support the rear silencer on something to prevent cracking or kinking the pipes elsewhere.

6   Unhook the rubber rings supporting the silencer.

7   Disconnect the manifold to downpipe connecting flange and then withdraw the complete exhaust system from below and out to the rear of the vehicle. If necessary, jack-up the rear of the vehicle to provide more clearance.

8   When separating the damaged section to be renewed cut away the damaged part from the adjoining good section rather than risk damaging the latter.

9   If small repairs are being carried out it is best, if possible, not to try and pull the sections apart.

10   Refitting should be carried out after connecting the two sections together. De-burr and grease the connecting socket and make sure that the clamp is in good condition and slipped over the front pipe but do not tighten it at this stage.

11   Connect the system to the manifold and connect the rear support strap. Now adjust the attitude of the silencer so that the tension on the two rubber support rings will be equalized when fitted.

12   Tighten the pipe clamp, the manifold flange nuts and the rear suspension strap bolts. Check that the exhaust system will not knock against any part of the vehicle when deflected slightly in a sideways or upward direction.

36 Fault diagnosis – carburation and fuel system

Symptom	Reason/s
Excessive fuel consumption	Air filter choked
	Leakage from pump, carburettor or fuel lines or fuel tank
	Float chamber flooding
	Distributor capacitor faulty
	Distributor weights or vacuum capsule faulty
	Mixture too rich
	Contact breaker gap too wide
	Incorrect valve clearances
	Incorrect spark plug gaps
	Tyres under inflated
	Dragging brakes
Insufficient fuel delivery or weak mixture	Fuel tank air vent or pipe blocked or flattened
	Clogged fuel filter
	Float chamber needle valve clogged
	Faulty fuel pump valves
	Fuel pump diaphragm split
	Fuel pipe unions loose
	Fuel pump lid not seating correctly
	Inlet manifold gasket or carburettor flange gasket leaking
	Incorrect adjustment of carburettor

37 Fault diagnosis – emission control system

Symptom	Reason/s
High engine idling speed	Sticking dash-pot (auto. trans.)
	Faulty throttle opener system (manual trans.)
	Faulty automatic choke
Rough or uneven idling	Faulty auto. temperature controlled air cleaner
	Faulty EGR control valve
	Faulty idle compensator in air cleaner
Back fire	Faulty auto. temperature controlled air cleaner
	Faulty EGR control valve
Dieseling (running on)	Faulty anti-dieseling (anti-run on) solenoid

Chapter 4 Ignition system

For modifications, and information applicable to later models, see Supplement at end of manual

Contents

Specifications

Firing order 1-3-4-2

Ignition timing

A12 engine, manual transmission	7° BTDC at 600 rpm
A14 engine, manual transmission (Europe)	7° BTDC at 650 rpm
A14 and A15 manual transmission	
California and non-California 5-speed models	5° BTDC at 700 rpm
Non-California and Canada	10° BTDC at 700 rpm
A14 and A15 automatic transmission	
California	5° BTDC at 650 rpm in D position
Non-California	8° BTDC at 650 rpm in D position
Canada	10° BTDC at 650 rpm in D position

Ignition coil

Type	
210	CIT-30 or STC-30
New Sunny	
A12	C6R-205 or HP5-13E11
A14	C6R-206 or HP5-13E10
Voltage	12V
External resistance	1.6 ohms

Distributor

Type	
210	D4K8
New Sunny	D411
Rotation	Anti-clockwise
Contact breaker gap (D411)	0.018 to 0.022 in (0.45 to 0.55 mm)
Dwell angle (D411)	49 to 55°
Condenser capacity (D411)	0.20 to 0.24 mfd
Reluctor gap (D4K8)	0.012 to 0.020 in (0.3 to 0.5 mm)

Spark plugs

	USA	Non-California, 5-speed model	Canada
Type			
210			
Standard	NGK BP5ES-11	NGK BP5EQ-13	NGK BPR5ES
	Hitachi L46PW-11	Hitachi L45PM-13	
Hot	NGK BP4ES-11	NGK BP4EQ-13	NGK BPR4ES
	Hitachi L47PW-11	Hitachi L47PM-13	
Cold	NGK BP6ES-11	NGK BP6EQ-13	NGK BPR6ES
	NGK BP7ES-11	NGK BP7EQ-13	NGK BPR7ES
	Hitachi L44PW-11	Hitachi L45PM-13	
	Hitachi L45PW-11	Hitachi L44PM-13	
Plug gap	0.039 to 0.043 in	0.043 to 0.051 in	0.031 to 0.035 in
	(1.0 to 1.1 mm)	(1.1 to 1.3 mm)	(0.8 to 0.9 mm)
	UK		
New Sunny	NGK BP5ES		
	NGK BPR5ES		
	Hitachi L46PW		
Plug gap	0.031 to 0.035 in		
	(0.8 to 0.9 mm)		

Torque wrench settings

	lbf ft	kgf m
Spark plugs	11 to 18	1.5 to 2.5

Torque wrench settings

	lbf ft	kgf m
Spark plugs	11 to 18	1.5 to 2.5

1 General description

For an engine to run at maximum efficiency, the spark must ignite the fuel/air charge in the combustion chamber at exactly the right moment for the particular engine speed and load conditions.

The ignition system comprises the ignition coil which is two windings which are coupled electromagnetically; and the distributor which is a rotating switch, controlling the current in the ignition coil primary winding and applying the high voltage of the ignition coil secondary winding to the appropriate spark plug. In the conventional distributor, which is fitted to European models, the ignition coil primary current is controlled by a mechanical switch whose contacts are opened by the distributor cam. On North American models, the distributor shaft carries a magnetic reluctor instead of a cam and the position of the reluctor is sensed by a pick-up coil. The electrical signal which the reluctor generates in the pick-up coil is conducted to an electronic switch controlling the ignition coil primary current.

A vacuum diaphragm, which is controlled by the suction of the inlet manifold, causes the instant of switching of the low tension winding of the coil to be varied according to the inlet manifold suction and therefore engine load, while a centrifugally operated cam produces a variation in switching which is dependent upon engine speed. The vacuum and centrifugal mechanisms are similar on both types of distributor.

2 Contact breaker – adjustment

1   Pull off the two clips securing the distributor cap to the body (photo) and lift the cap off. Clean the inside and outside of the cap with a clean, dry cloth and examine the inside of the cap for signs of cracking of the plastic, or evidence that the insulation has broken down. If the insulation is defective, there will be signs of charring of the plastic. Check that the four metal segments inside the cap have not burned excessively and make sure that the carbon brush in the middle of the distributor cap moves freely out again after being pressed in. Fit a new distributor cap if any defect is found.
2   Pull off the rotor arm, clean it and inspect it for cracks, or excessive burning of the metal contact.
3   Using a screwdriver which is free from oil and dirt, prise the contacts apart to see whether they are burned, or pitted. If they are not satisfactory, remove the contact breaker assembly as described in the following Section.
4   If the contacts are in good condition, or a new contact breaker assembly has been fitted, turn the engine until the heel of the contact breaker arm is at the highest point of the cam and the contacts are at their maximum distance apart.
5   Measure the gap between the contacts, using an oil free feeler gauge and check the measurement with that given in the Specification (photo).
6   If it is necessary to adjust the gap, slacken the two screws which secure the contact breaker baseplate and turn the adjuster screw until the correct gap is obtained.
7   Tighten the two clamp screws and recheck the gap.
8   Smear the surface of the cam lightly with grease. Refit the rotor arm and the distributor cap.

3 Contact breaker assembly – removal and refitting

1   Pull off the rotor arm.
2   Slacken the screw which secures the primary lead to the contact breaker assembly and pull the primary lead off.
3   Remove the two clamp screws from the contact breaker baseplate

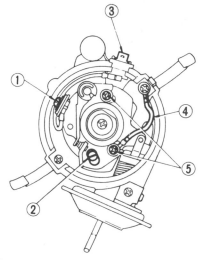

Fig. 4.1 Contact breaker adjustment (Sec 2)

1 Primary lead clamp screw
2 Gap adjusting screw
3 Primary lead terminal
4 Earth lead
5 Clamping screws

2.1 Distributor cap and clips

2.5 Adjusting the contact breaker gap

and lift off the contact breaker assembly.

4 If the contact faces are dirty, or slightly pitted they may be cleaned with very fine sand paper, but if the wear is more than slight, discard the assembly and fit a new one.

5 Refitting is the reverse of removal, but take care to fit the primary lead to the clamp screw on the side of the contact breaker and the earth lead to the baseplate clamp screw.

6 Smear a light coating of grease on to the cam, adjust the contact breaker gap and refit the rotor arm.

4 Gap adjustment – electronic ignition

1 Pull off the two clips securing the distributor cap to the body and lift the cap off. Clean the inside and outside of the cap with a clean, dry cloth and examine the inside of the cap for signs of cracking of the plastic, or evidence that the insulation has broken down. If the insulation is defective, there will be signs of charring of the plastic. Check that the four metal segments inside the cap have not burned excessively and make sure that the carbon brush in the middle of the distributor cap moves freely out again after being pressed in. Fit a new distributor cap if any defect is found.

2 Pull off the rotor arm, clean it and inspect it for cracks, or excessive burning of the metal contact.

3 Turn the engine until the teeth on the reluctor and the stator are opposite each other and then check the gap between each of the four pairs of teeth with a feeler gauge. The gap should be the same in all cases and within the limits given in the Specification.

4 To centre the stator to give a uniform gap, slacken the three screws which clamp the stator plate and move the stator plate to achieve the same gap between all four pairs of teeth.

5 Tighten the clamp screws and recheck the gap.
6 Refit the rotor arm and the distributor cap.

5 Distributor – removal and refitting

1 The method is similar for the contact breaker and the electronic types.

2 Pull off the two clips securing the distributor cap and lift off the cap.

3 To simplify refitting the distributor, turn the engine until the engine is on TDC for number 1 cylinder. This position is when the distributor rotor arm is opposite the number 1 cylinder mark on the distributor cap (Fig. 4.3) and the notch in the rim of the crankshaft pulley is opposite the O-mark on the scale on the timing chain cover (photo).

4 Disconnect the connector from the primary lead of the contact breaker distributor, or the plug from the ignition unit on the electronic distributor.

5 Pull the vacuum pipe off the vacuum unit.

6 To ensure that the distributor is fitted without altering the ignition timing, note which graduation on the scale marked on the clamp plate is opposite the line marked on the distributor mounting face of the cylinder block (photo).

7 Remove the screw from the distributor clamp plate and lift the distributor out.

8 When fitting the distributor, set the rotor so that it is about 30° to the left of the number 1 cylinder position before inserting it. As the distributor is inserted, its gear will mesh with the drive gear on the camshaft and the rotor will turn. When the distributor is fully home, check that the rotor is in the number 1 cylinder position and also check that the crankshaft pulley switch is still opposite the O-mark.

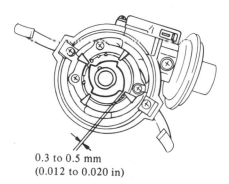

0.3 to 0.5 mm
(0.012 to 0.020 in)

Fig. 4.2 Air gap adjustment – electronic ignition (Sec 4)

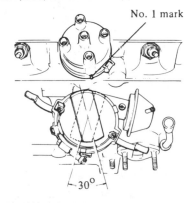

No. 1 mark

30°

Fig. 4.3 Distributor rotor position for No 1 cylinder (Sec 5)

5.3 Crankshaft pulley notch and timing marks in alignment. Note method of timing crankshaft

5.6 Distributor clamp plate graduations

9   Align the graduation on the clamp plate with the line on the distributor mounting face as it was before removal. Insert the clamp screw and tighten it.
10 Connect the primary lead, or the ignition unit plug and refit the distributor cap. Fit the vacuum pipe.

6   Condenser – removal and refitting

1   A condenser (capacitor) is connected in parallel with the contact breaker points to reduce sparking of the points and to increase their life.
2   A defective condenser may result in the engine failing to start, or if the engine starts it may misfire and run erratically.
3   To test a condenser satisfactorily requires a high voltage insulation tester and if a condenser is suspect, it is easier to substitute a new one. As the cost is fairly small, it is worth renewing the condenser whenever new contact breaker points are fitted.
4   To remove the condenser, slacken the screw of the primary lead terminal assembly and disconnect the condenser lead. Remove the screw clamping the condenser to the distributor body and remove the condenser.
5   Refitting is the reverse of the operations required for removal, but it is necessary to make sure that the electrical connections are clean and free from grease.

7   Distributor – dismantling and reassembly

Contact breaker type

1   Pull off the two clips securing the distributor cap to the body and lift the cap off.
2   Pull the rotor arm off the cam assembly.
3   Remove the screws securing the vacuum unit to the distributor body. Unhook the eye of the vacuum unit spindle from the contact breaker baseplate (photo) and remove the vacuum unit.
4   Slacken the screw of the primary lead terminal assembly and disconnect the condenser lead. Remove the screw clamping the condenser to the distributor body and remove the condenser.
5   Slacken the screw which secures the primary lead to the contact breaker assembly and pull the primary lead off. Remove the two screws from the baseplate and remove the contact breaker assembly.
6   Remove the two screws securing the contact breaker baseplate to the distributor body and remove the baseplate.
7   Mark the position of the distributor gear on its spindle and then drive out the spring pin and remove the gear. Withdraw the rotor shaft and drive assembly from the distributor body.
8   Mark the rotor and the drive shafts so that they will be refitted in their same relative positions. If this is not done the two parts may be reassembled 180° apart and the ignition timing will be similarly incorrect.

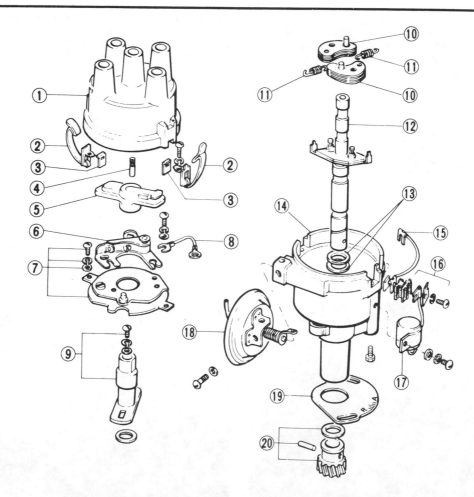

Fig. 4.4 Distributor – exploded view – contact breaker type (Sec 7)

1 Cap assembly	6 Contact set	11 Governor spring	16 Terminal assembly
2 Cap clip	7 Breaker plate	12 Shaft assembly	17 Condenser assembly
3 Dust seal	8 Earth wire	13 Thrust washer	18 Vacuum control assembly
4 Carbon brush assembly	9 Cam assembly	14 Housing	19 Fixing plate
5 Rotor head	10 Governor weight	15 Lead wire	20 Drive gear

7.3 Vacuum unit connection to baseplate

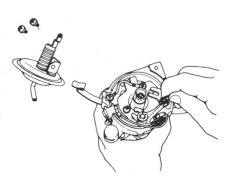

Fig. 4.5 Removing the vacuum unit and contact breaker assembly (Sec 7)

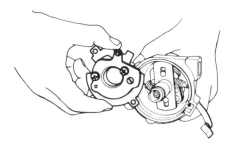

Fig. 4.6 Removing the breaker plate (Sec 7)

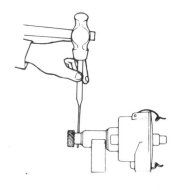

Fig. 4.7 Removing the drive gear roll pin (Sec 7)

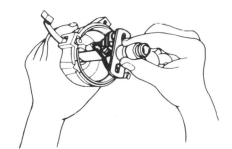

Fig. 4.8 Removing the rotating parts (Sec 7)

Fig. 4.9 Unscrewing the cam screw (Sec 7)

9   Remove the felt packing from the top of the rotor shaft. Unscrew and remove the rotor shaft setscrew from the top of the rotor spindle.

10   Mark one of the governor springs and its bracket. Also mark one of the governor weights and its pivot pin to ensure that all these parts are in their original positions. When removing the governor springs, take care not to stretch, or damage them.

11   Clean all the parts and examine them for wear. It is difficult to get small replacement parts and if any parts are unserviceable, an exchange distributor should be fitted.

12   Check the vacuum unit by sucking the vacuum connection to make sure that the operating rod moves and that the diaphragm does not leak. New vacuum units are available as replacements.

13   Smear grease on to the governor weight pivots and on to the sliding surfaces of the weights.

14   Reassemble the distributor in reverse order to dismantling, taking care to ensure that all parts are fitted exactly as they were before dismantling. When refitting the drive gear, use a new roll pin.

Electronic type

15   Remove the distributor cap and rotor as described in paragraphs 1 and 2.

16   Remove the two screws which secure the ignition unit to the distributor body and detach the unit to give access to the connections.

17   Use a pair of sharp nosed pliers to disconnect the pick-up coil terminal from the ignition unit.

18   Remove the three screws securing the stator and magnet assembly and carefully lift out the assembly.

19   Remove the screw securing the vacuum unit to the distributor body. Unhook the eye of the vacuum unit spindle from the breaker plate assembly and remove the vacuum unit.

20   Using two screwdrivers, or levers, carefully prise the reluctor from the shaft. Do not prise against the teeth of the reluctor, because this may damage them. After removing the reluctor, recover the roll pin.

21   Remove the breaker plate setscrews and take out the breaker plate after removing the pick-up coil assembly (Fig. 4.14).

22   Remove the gear and dismantle the rotor shaft and drive assembly as described in paragraphs 7 to 13.

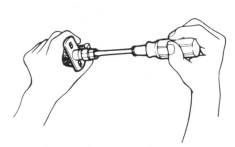

Fig. 4.10 Removing the electronic type ignition unit (Sec 7)

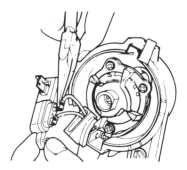

Fig. 4.11 Disconnecting the pick-up coil terminal (Sec 7)

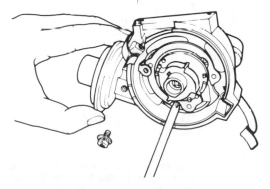

Fig. 4.12 Removing the vacuum unit (electronic distributor) (Sec 7)

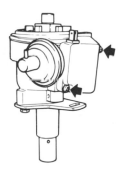

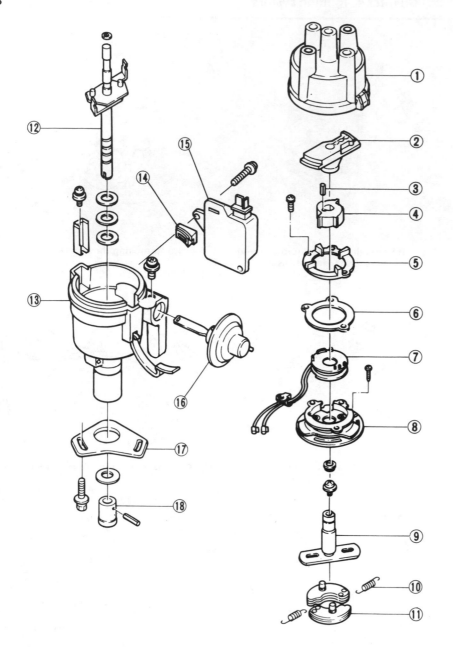

Fig. 4.13 Distributor (electronic type) – exploded view (Sec 7)

1 Cap assembly
2 Rotor head assembly
3 Roll pin
4 Reluctor
5 Stator
6 Magnet assembly
7 Pick-up coil assembly
8 Breaker plate assembly
9 Rotor shaft assembly
10 Governor spring
11 Governor weight
12 Shaft assembly
13 Housing
14 Grommet
15 Ignition unit
16 Vacuum unit
17 Fixing plate
18 Collar

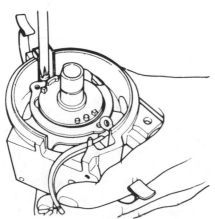

Fig. 4.14 Removing the breaker plate screws (electronic distributor) (Sec 7)

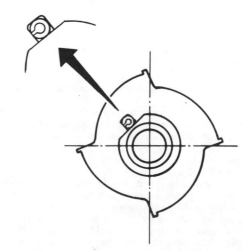

Fig. 4.15 Reluctor roll pin position

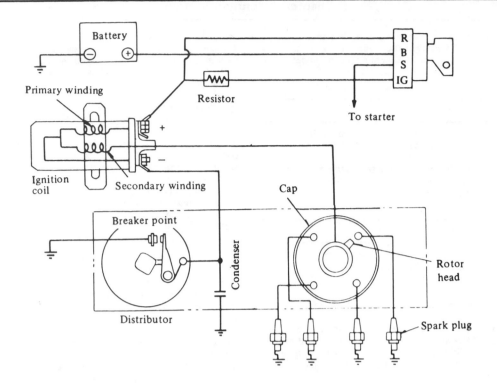

Fig. 4.16 Ignition circuit diagram (contact breaker distributor) (Sec 8)

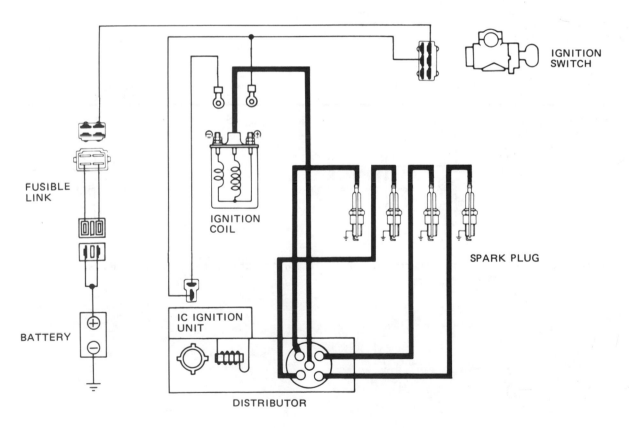

Fig. 4.17 Ignition circuit diagram (electronic type) (Sec 9)

23 Assemble the distributor in the reverse order to dismantling, taking care that all parts are installed exactly as they were before dismantling. Use new roll pins when refitting the drive gear and the reluctor and position the reluctor drive pin as shown in Fig. 4.15.

8 Ignition coil – polarity

1 If the ignition coil is not connected properly there will be a severe reduction in spark efficiency which may result in difficult starting and rough idling.
2 Ensure that the (+) positive terminal of the ignition coil is connected to the ignition starter switch and that the (-) negative terminal of the coil is connected to the distributor.

9 Electronic ignition – testing

1 If the electronic ignition system is suspected of malfunctioning, carry out the following checks in the order given.

Power supply
2 Ensure that the ignition switch is turned OFF and then disconnect the plug from the ignition unit.
3 Connect a DC voltmeter with a range of at least 12 V or a test lamp, as shown in Fig. 4.18 and turn the ignition switch ON. If battery voltage is not indicated by the meter, or lamp, turn the ignition switch OFF and check the power supply wiring, fusible link, ignition switch and connectors.

Primary circuit
4 Ensure that the ignition switch is turned OFF and then disconnect the plug from the ignition unit.
5 Connect a DC voltmeter with a range of at least 12V, or a test lamp to the terminal of the ignition unit shown in Fig. 4.19 and turn the ignition switch ON. If battery voltage is not indicated by the meter, or lamp, turn the ignition switch OFF and check the primary circuit wiring and connectors. If the result of these tests is satisfactory, check the ignition coil.

Ignition coil
6 Ensure that the ignition switch is turned OFF and then remove the connector from the (-) negative terminal of the ignition coil.
7 Connect an ohm meter between the (-) negative and (+) positive terminals of the ignition coil. If the resistance is within the range given in the Specification, the coil is satisfactory. It if is outside this range, fit a new ignition coil.

Ignition unit and pick-up coil
8 Ensure that the ignition switch is turned OFF and then remove the distributor cap and rotor.
9 Connect an ohm meter between the two terminals of the pick up coil. If a resistance of about 400 ohms is indicated the pick-up coil is satisfactory and the ignition unit is defective.
10 Remove the defective ignition unit as described in paragraphs 16 and 17 of Section 7.
11 Fit a new ignition unit, ensuring that the contact faces of the ignition unit and the distributor body are clean, so that there is good electrical contact.

10 Ignition – timing

1 The setting of the ignition timing to give optimum engine performance, requires the use of a stroboscopic timing light.
2 Ensure that the spark plugs are clean and that their gaps are set at the dimension given in the Specification. Also ensure that on the contact breaker type of distributor, the contact opening setting is correct.
3 Warm the engine up to its normal operating temperature and on models with manual transmission adjust the idling speed to 700 rpm. On automatic transmission models, apply the handbrake, block the front and rear wheels with chocks, move the transmission selector lever to D and adjust the idling speed to 650 rpm.
4 Switch the engine OFF. Connect the timing light in accordance with its manufacturer's instructions and mark with chalk, or white paint the notch on the crankshaft pulley and the pointer on the front cover timing scale which corresponds to the ignition setting point given in the Specification.
5 With the engine running at its correct idling speed and with the vacuum hose disconnected from the distributor and the end of the hose plugged (except on non-California, 5-speed models which should have the hose left open) shine the timing light on to the timing scale.
6 If the mark on the crankshaft pulley is not aligned with the correct

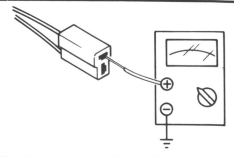

Fig. 4.18 Checking the power supply circuit (electronic ignition) (Sec 9)

Fig. 4.19 Checking the primary circuit (electronic ignition) (Sec 9)

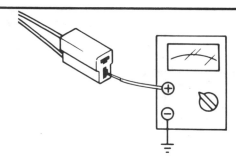

Resistance: × 1 range

Fig. 4.20 Checking the ignition coil primary winding (Sec 9)

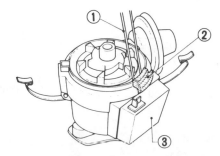

Fig. 4.21 Measuring pick-up coil resistance (electronic ignition) (Sec 9)

1 *Test meter probes*   3 *Ignition unit*
2 *Grommet*

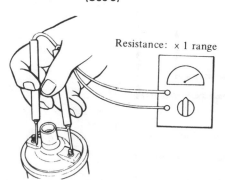

Measuring plug gap. A feeler gauge of the correct size (see ignition system specifications) should have a slight 'drag' when slid between the electrodes. Adjust gap if necessary

Adjusting plug gap. The plug gap is adjusted by bending the earth electrode inwards, or outwards, as necessary until the correct clearance is obtained. Note the use of the correct tool

Normal. Grey-brown deposits, lightly coated core nose. Gap increasing by around 0.001 in (0.025 mm) per 1000 miles (1600 km). Plugs ideally suited to engine, and engine in good condition

Carbon fouling. Dry, black, sooty deposits. Will cause weak spark and eventually misfire. Fault: over-rich fuel mixture. Check: carburettor mixture settings, float level and jet sizes; choke operation and cleanliness of air filter. Plugs can be re-used after cleaning

Oil fouling. Wet, oily deposits. Will cause weak spark and eventually misfire. Fault: worn bores/piston rings or valve guides; sometimes occurs (temporarily) during running-in period. Plugs can be re-used after thorough cleaning

Overheating. Electrodes have glazed appearance, core nose very white – few deposits. Fault: plug overheating. Check: plug value, ignition timing, fuel octane rating (too low) and fuel mixture (too weak). Discard plugs and cure fault immediately

Electrode damage. Electrodes burned away; core nose has burned, glazed appearance. Fault: pre-ignition. Check: as for 'Overheating' but may be more severe. Discard plugs and remedy fault before piston or valve damage occurs

Split core nose (may appear initially as a crack). Damage is self-evident, but cracks will only show after cleaning. Fault: pre-ignition or wrong gap-setting technique. Check: ignition timing, cooling system, fuel octane rating (too low) and fuel mixture (too weak). Discard plugs, rectify fault immediately

pointer, slacken the distributor clamp screw and turn the distributor body until the timing marks are aligned.

7   Clamp the distributor and recheck the timing.

8   Switch the engine OFF, disconnect the timing light, remove the plug from the vacuum hose (except on non-California, 5-speed models) and reconnect the vacuum pipe to the vacuum unit.

9   Check the slow running speed and readjust if necessary.

11 Spark plugs and HT leads

1   For good fuel economy and optimum engine performance the spark plugs need to be in good condition, of the correct type and set to the specified gap.

2   Every 12 000 miles or 12 months fit a new set of spark plugs and remove the plugs for cleaning and readjusting every six months.

3   Poor starting during damp weather is usually the result of dirt on the HT leads and plug insulators. The HT leads should be wiped with a dry cloth at monthly intervals and the external porcelain surface of the spark plugs should be cleaned at the same frequency.

4   When fitting spark plugs, initially screw them in with the fingers to avoid cross threading. Tighten them to the specified torque, do not overtighten them.

5   Ensure that all four plugs are of the same brand and the same heat range.

12 Ignition system – fault diagnosis

There are two main symptoms indicating ignition faults. Either the engine will not start or fire, or the engine is difficult to start and misfires. If it is a regular misfire, ie the engine is only running on two or three cylinders, the fault is almost sure to be in the high tension circuit. If the misfiring is intermittent, the fault could be in either the high or low tension circuits. If the car stops suddenly, or will not start at all, it is likely that the fault is in the low tension circuit. Loss of power and overheating, apart from faulty carburation settings, are normally due to faults in the distributor or incorrect ignition timing.

Engine fails to start

1   If the engine fails to start and the car was running normally when it was last used, first check there is fuel in the petrol tank. If the engine turns over normally on the starter motor and the battery is evidently well charged, then the fault may be in either the high or low tension circuits. First check the HT circuit. If the battery is known to be fully charged, the ignition light comes on, and the starter motor fails to turn the engine, check the tightness of the leads on the battery terminals and the security of the earth lead to its connection to the body. It is quite common for the leads to have worked loose, even if they look and feel secure. If one of the battery terminal posts gets very hot when trying to work the starter motor, this is a sure indication of a faulty connection to that terminal.

2   One of the most common reasons for bad starting is wet or damp spark plug leads and distributor. Remove the distributor cap. If condensation is visible internally dry the cap with a rag and wipe over the leads. Refit the cap.

3   If the engine still fails to start, check that current is reaching the plugs, by disconnecting each plug lead in turn at the spark plug end, and holding the end of the cable about $\frac{3}{16}$ inch (5 mm) away from the cylinder block. Spin the engine on the starter motor.

4   Sparking between the end of the cable and the block should be fairly strong with a regular blue spark. (Hold the lead with rubber to avoid electric shocks). If current is reaching the plugs, then remove them and clean and regap them. The engine should now start.

5   If there is no spark at the plug leads, take off the HT lead from the centre of the distributor cap and hold it to the block as before. Spin the engine on the starter once more. A rapid succession of blue sparks between the end of the lead and the block indicate that the coil is in order and that the distributor cap is cracked, the rotor arm faulty or the carbon brush in the top of the distributor cap is not making good contact with the rocker arm.

6   If there are no sparks from the end of the lead from the coil, check the connections at the coil end of the lead. If it is in order carry out the checks contained in the electronic ignition test procedure (Section 9).

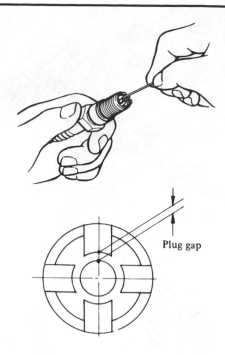

Fig. 4.22 Checking the spark plug gap on a multi-electrode spark plug (Sec 11)

Engine misfires

7   If the engine misfires regularly, run it at a fast idling speed. Pull off each of the plug caps in turn and listen to the note of the engine. Hold the plug cap in a dry cloth or with a rubber glove as additional protection against a shock from the HT supply.

8   No difference in engine running will be noticed when the lead from the defective circuit is removed. Removing the lead from one of the good cylinders will accentuate the misfire.

9   Remove the plug lead from the end of the defective plug and hold it about $\frac{3}{16}$ inch (5 mm) away from the block. Restart the engine. If the sparking is fairly strong and regular, the fault must lie in the spark plug.

10   The plug may be loose, the insulation may be cracked, or the points may have burnt away, giving too wide a gap for the spark to jump. Worse still, one of the points may have broken off. Either renew the plug, or clean it, reset the gap and then test it.

11   If there is no spark at the end of the plug lead, or if it is weak and intermittent, check the ignition lead from the distributor to the plug. If the insulation is cracked or perished, renew the lead. Check the connections at the distributor cap.

12   If there is still no spark, examine the distributor cap carefully for tracking. This can be recognised by a very thin black line running between two or more electrodes, or between an electrode and some other part of the distributor. These lines are paths which now conduct electricity across the cap, thus letting it run to earth. The only answer in this case is a new distributor cap.

13   Apart from the ignition timing being incorrect, other causes of misfiring have already been dealt with under the section dealing with the failure of the engine to start. To recap, these are that:

(a)   The coil may be faulty giving an intermittent misfire
(b)   There may be a damaged wire or loose connection in the low tension circuit.
(c)   There may be a fault in the electronic ignition system
(d)   There may be a mechanical fault in the distributor (broken driving spindle or contact breaker spring)

14   If the ignition timing is too far retarded it should be noted that the engine will tend to overheat, and there will be a quite noticeable drop in power. If the engine is overheating and the power is down, and the ignition timing is correct, then the carburettor should be checked, as it is likely that this is where the fault lies.

Chapter 5 Clutch

For modifications, and information applicable to later models, see Supplement at end of manual

Contents

Specifications

Type .... Single dry plate, with diaphragm spring

Clutch control .... Cable (rhd models), hydraulic (lhd models)

Clutch disc type .... 180 CBL

Facing dimensions
Outside diameter .... 7.09 in (180 mm)
Inside diameter .... 4.92 in (125 mm)
Thickness .... 0.138 in (3.5 mm)

Facing wear limit
Depth of rivet head below facing surface .... 0.012 in (0.3 mm)

Run out limit .... 0.020 in (0.5 mm) measured at a radius of 3.35 in (85.0 mm)

Clutch master cylinder
Diameter .... $\frac{5}{8}$ in (15.87 mm)
Bore to piston clearance .... Less than 0.006 in (0.15 mm)

Clutch slave cylinder
Diameter .... $\frac{11}{16}$ in (17.46 mm)
Bore to piston clearance .... Less than 0.006 in (0.15 mm)

Clutch pedal adjustments

	Hydraulic control	Cable control
Pedal height	5.63 to 5.87 in (143 to 149 mm)	6.42 to 6.65 in (163 to 169 mm)
Pedal free play	0.04 to 0.20 in (1 to 5 mm)	
Withdrawal lever free play	0.039 to 0.079 in	0.118 to 0.157 in
	(1.0 to 2.0 mm)	(3.0 to 4.0 mm)
Pedal free travel	0.63 to 1.30 in (16 to 33 mm)	0.51 to 0.67 in (13 to 17 mm)

Torque wrench settings

	lbf ft	kgf m
Pedal stop locknut	5.8 to 8.7	0.8 to 1.2
Master cylinder push rod locknut	5.8 to 8.7	0.8 to 1.2
Slave cylinder push rod locknut	5.8 to 8.7	0.8 to 1.2
Slave cylinder bleed screw	5.1 to 6.5	0.7 to 0.9
Master cylinder to dash securing nut	5.8 to 8.7	0.8 to 1.2
Clutch tube flare nut	11 to 13	1.5 to 1.8
Slave cylinder to clutch housing securing bolt	22 to 30	3.1 to 4.1
Clutch hose to slave cylinder	12 to 14	1.7 to 2.0
Clutch cover bolt	12 to 15	1.7 to 2.1

1 General description

The function of the clutch is to allow the engine to run without it being coupled to the transmission. It enables the engine torque to be applied to the gearbox progressively, so that the car can move off from rest smoothly and it permits the gears to be changed easily and smoothly as the car speed increases or decreases.

The principal parts of the clutch assembly are the driven, or friction plate, the driving plate and cover assembly and the release bearing assembly. When the clutch is engaged, the driven plate, which is splined to the gearbox input shaft, is sandwiched between the flywheel and the driving plate by the pressure of the diaphragm spring and so engine torque is transmitted from the flywheel and driven plate to the input shaft of the gearbox.

When the clutch pedal is depressed, the clutch release arm and

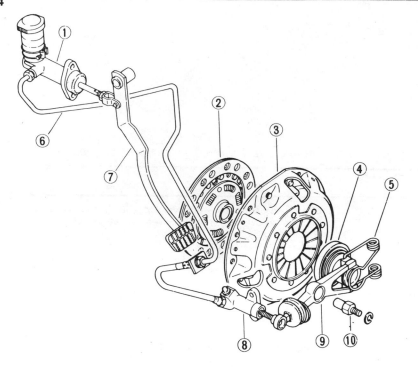

Fig. 5.1 Clutch system components – hydraulic type (Sec 1)

1 Clutch master cylinder
2 Clutch disc assembly
3 Clutch cover assembly
4 Release bearing and sleeve assembly
5 Return spring
6 Clutch hydraulic pipe
7 Clutch pedal
8 Slave cylinder
9 Withdrawal lever
10 Withdrawal lever ball pin

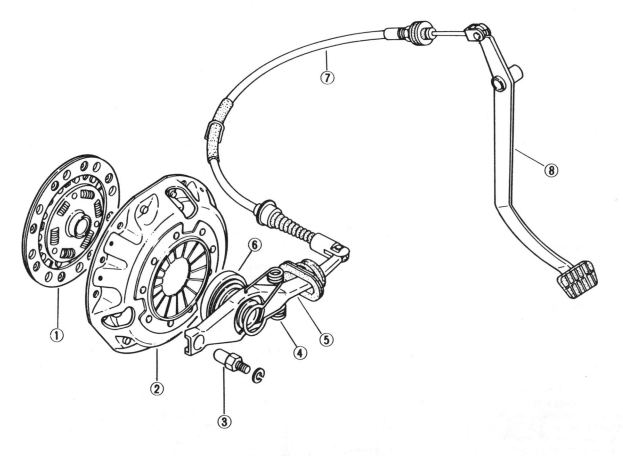

Fig. 5.2 Clutch system components – cable type (Sec 1)

1 Clutch plate assembly
2 Clutch cover assembly
3 Withdrawal lever ball pin
4 Return spring
5 Withdrawal lever
6 Release bearing and sleeve assembly
7 Clutch control cable
8 Clutch pedal

bearing are pushed against the centre of the diaphragm spring, releasing the pressure on the driven plate and so disconnecting the drive between the engine and the gearbox.

When the clutch is released, the diaphragm spring forces the pressure plate against the friction plate, which moves forward until it is against the flywheel. When the friction plate is again clamped between the flywheel and the driving plate, the drive is reconnected.

The control of the clutch from the pedal to the clutch withdrawal lever may be by a cable, or by a hydraulic system. When the clutch is operated hydraulically, the clutch pedal is connected to a short pushrod to a master cylinder with an integral fluid reservoir.

Depressing the clutch pedal moves the piston of the master cylinder forward and forces fluid through the hydraulic pipe to the slave cylinder. The piston in the slave cylinder is moved forward by the fluid and the pushrod which connects the slave cylinder piston to the clutch withdrawal lever transmits this movement to the lever, causing the clutch to operate.

As the friction linings on the clutch disc wear, the pressure plate moves automatically towards the friction plate to compensate for wear.

When a cable clutch operating mechanism is fitted, movement of the clutch pedal is transmitted directly to the clutch release lever. On a cable operated clutch it is important that the length of cable is set correctly and kept in adjustment. If this is not done, it may be difficult to change gear and there may be excessive and unnecessary wear on the clutch friction plate and release bearing.

2 Clutch – adjustment (hydraulic control)

1 The adjustments are carried out when the vehicle is built and will not normally require to be changed unless new components have been fitted.

2 The highest point of the pedal rubber must be at the specified height from the car floor. This is adjusted by releasing the locknut from the pedal stop screw and moving the adjusting nut to give the correct adjustment. After making the adjustment, tighten the locknut and then press and release the clutch pedal over its entire range to check that it operates smoothly and without noise.

3 There must be a small amount of free play between the master cylinder piston and its pushrod, so that the clutch pedal can be moved the specified amount before the master cylinder piston moves. To adjust the clutch pedal free travel, loosen the locknut on the master cylinder pushrod and turn the pushrod until the pedal pad can be moved the specified amount without there being any resistance from the master cylinder piston. When the free movement is correct, tighten the locknut.

4 To avoid unnecessary wear to the clutch release bearing and the fingers of the diaphragm spring, there must be a clearance between the release bearing and the diaphragm spring. To make the adjustment, loosen the locknut on the rod of the clutch slave cylinder and turn the adjusting nut on the rod until the release bearing touches the diaphragm spring and there is no free movement of the clutch operating lever. Fron this position, unscrew the adjusting nut to give the correct clearance, which will be about $1\frac{1}{4}$ turns of the nut. While taking care not to disturb the adjustment, tighten the locknut.

5 Depress the clutch pedal several times, then recheck the operating lever free play and readjust if necessary.

3 Clutch – adjustment (cable control)

1 Because of wear in the linkages and stretching of the cable, it is necessary to check the clutch adjustment as a maintenance item and to adjust it whenever the clutch does not disengage properly, or if new clutch components are fitted.

2 The highest point of the pedal rubber must be at the specified height from the car floor. This is adjusted by releasing the locknut from the pedal stop screw and moving the adjusting nut to give the correct adjustment (Fig. 5.5). After making the adjustment, tighten the locknut and then press and release the clutch pedal over its entire range to check that it operates smoothly and without noise.

3 There must be the specified amount of free play at the end of the clutch operating lever, so that when the clutch pedal is released the thrust bearing is not being pressed against the fingers of the diaphragm spring.

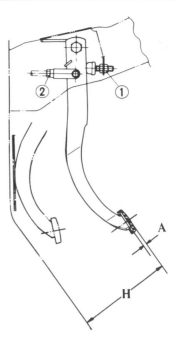

Fig. 5.3 Clutch pedal adjustments – hydraulic type (Sec 2)

1   Pedal stop locknut
2   Master cylinder pushrod locknut
Dimension A – pedal free play (see Specification)
Dimension H – pedal height (see Specification)

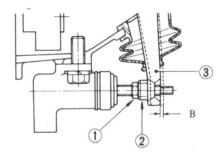

Fig. 5.4 Clutch slave cylinder adjustment – hydraulic type (Sec 2)

1   Locknut   Dimension B – withdrawal lever
2   Adjuster nut   free play (see Specification)
3   Withdrawal lever

4 Remove the E-ring from the slot in the end of the clutch outer cable (photo). If the free play is too much, fit a new E-ring into a slot nearer to the bulkhead, so that the effective length of the outer cable is increased. If free play is insufficient, the E-ring must be moved towards the front of the car, to decrease the effective length of the outer cable. After moving the E-ring, measure the free play of the clutch operating lever and readjust if necessary to achieve the correct dimension.

5 Depress and release the clutch pedal several times and again check the free play dimension. As a final check, measure the free play at the centre of the pedal pad and ensure that this is as specified.

4 Clutch pedal – removal and refitting (hydraulic control)

1 Extract the spring clip from the clevis pin and push the clevis pin out.

2 Separate the clutch pedal from the clevis and then fit the pin and clip back into the clevis to prevent their being lost.

3 Remove the E-ring from the slot in the end of the pivot pin, withdraw the pin, the clutch pedal and spring.

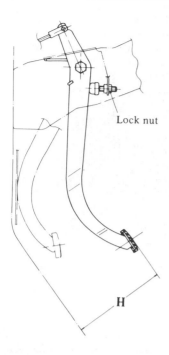

Fig. 5.5 Clutch pedal adjustment – cable type (Sec 3)

Dimension H – pedal height (see Specification)

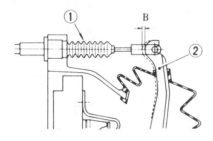

Fig. 5.6 Clutch lever adjustment – cable type (Sec 3)

Dimension B – withdrawal lever free play (see Specification)

1   Clutch control cable   2   Withdrawal lever

3.4 Clutch cable adjustment. Use a new E-ring

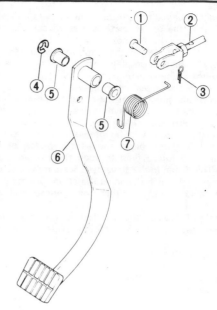

Fig. 5.7 Clutch pedal assembly – hydraulic type (Sec 4)

1   Clevis pin   5   Bush
2   Master cylinder pushrod   6   Clutch pedal
3   Snap pin   7   Return spring
4   E-ring

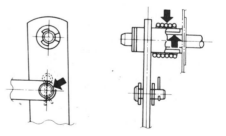

Fig. 5.8 Clutch pedal lubrication – hydraulic type (Sec 4)
Apply grease to arrowed parts

4   Refitting is the reverse of removal, but fit new bushes if the old ones are worn and grease the spring and all moving surfaces. Fit the clevis pin from left to right.
5   Check the operation of the clutch and check the adjustment as described in Section 2.

---

5   Clutch pedal and cable – removal and refitting

1   Remove the E-ring from the clutch outer cable and fit it into the slot which is furthest from the cable end. This will give sufficient slack in the cable to allow the cable end to be unhooked from the clutch pedal.
2   Remove the E-ring from the slot in the end of the pivot pin, withdraw the pin, the clutch pedal and spring.
3   Unhook the cable from the end of the clutch operating lever (photo) and pull out the clutch cable assembly.
4   Refitting is the reverse of removal, but fit new pivot bushes to the clutch pedal if the old ones are worn and grease the spring and all moving surfaces. Renew the E-ring.
5   Check the operation of the clutch and check its adjustment as described in Section 3.
6   Ensure that the clutch cable is not kinked, or strained and that it is well clear of all moving parts and is well clear of the fuel hose. The

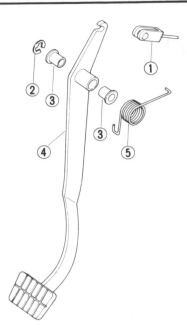

Fig. 5.9 Clutch pedal assembly – cable type (Sec 5)

1 Clutch control cable
2 E-ring
3 Bush

4 Clutch pedal
5 Return spring

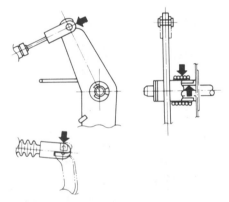

Fig. 5.10 Clutch pedal lubrication – cable type (Sec 5)
Apply grease to arrowed parts

hose clips of the fuel hose should be fitted so that the clamping screws are on the opposite side of the hose to the clutch cable.

6 Hydraulic system – bleeding

1   Liquids cannot be compressed to any significant extent and if a system is full of liquid, any force applied to the master cylinder will immediately be transferred in full to the slave cylinder.
2   If the hydraulic system contains any air, the air will compress as pressure is applied, much of the movement of the master cylinder piston will be ineffective and the clutch pedal operation will be incorrect.
3   Air can enter the system when any joint, or seal leaks, when the system is dismantled to fit new parts, or if hydraulic fluid containing air bubbles is put into the system. Removal of air, known as bleeding is carried out as follows.
4   Unless using a proprietary device which enables the system to be bled without assistance, the help of a second person is necessary.
5   Have ready a tin of fresh brake/clutch fluid of approved specification, a short length of flexible tubing which is a snug fit over the bleed nipple and a small transparent jar.

5.3 Attachment of clutch cable to operating lever

6   If there is a cap over the bleed nipple on the clutch slave cylinder, remove the cap. Clean the nipple and fit one end of the flexible tube over the nipple. Pour hydraulic fluid into the jar to a depth of about half an inch and place the jar so that the free end of the flexible tube is below the surface of the fluid.
7   Remove the cover from the clutch system reservoir and fill the reservoir with fluid.
8   With an assistant sitting in the car ready to operate the clutch pedal, open the slave cylinder bleed screw about one turn. With the bleed screw in this position, the clutch pedal should be depressed to its fullest extent and held in this position until the bleed screw has been tightened. With the bleed screw tightened, release the clutch pedal.
9   Repeat the sequence of opening the bleed valve, depressing the pedal, closing the bleed valve and releasing the pedal about four times and then top-up the level of fluid in the reservoir.
10 Continue the sequence until when fluid is expelled from the system into the jar by the operation of the clutch pedal, no air bubbles emerge with the fluid.
11 Top-up the reservoir and fit the reservoir cap.
12 The fluid which is ejected from the system during bleeding should be discarded.
13 Remove the flexible tube from the slave cylinder bleed nipple and fit a plastic cap to the nipple.
14 Check that the operation of the clutch is satisfactory. If all the air has been removed from the system and the movement of the clutch operating lever is unsatisfactory, it is likely that the master, or slave cylinder needs overhauling.

7 Clutch master cylinder – removal, overhaul, reassembly and refitting

1   Remove the spring pin and clevis pin from the yoke attaching the clutch pedal to the master cylinder pushrod.
2   Remove the reservoir cap, place a piece of plastic film over the top of the reservoir and screw the cap on again. This will minimise the amount of fluid running out when the hydraulic pipe is disconnected from the master cylinder.
3   Using a properly fitting spanner, so that the flare nut is not damaged, disconnect the hydraulic pipe from the master cylinder. Have ready a piece of rag to prevent any fluid from falling on to the car's paintwork and after disconnecting the pipe, cover its end and plug the hole in the master cylinder.
4   Unscrew and remove the two bolts securing the master cylinder to the bulkhead and take the master cylinder off.
5   Remove the master cylinder cap, pour out and discard the fluid.
6   Pull the dust cover off the end of the cylinder.
7   Remove the stopper ring from the end of the cylinder and take out the pushrod assembly.

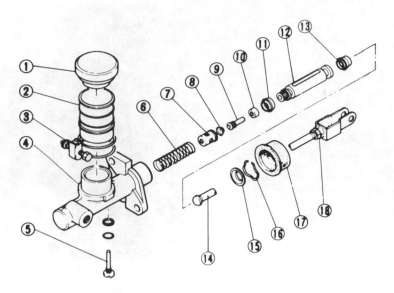

Fig. 5.11 Clutch master cylinder components (Sec 7)

1 Reservoir cap	6 Return spring	11 Primary cup	16 Stopper ring
2 Reservoir	7 Spring seat	12 Piston	17 Dust cover
3 Reservoir band	8 Valve spring	13 Secondary cup	18 Lock nut
4 Body	9 Supply valve rod	14 Pushrod	
5 Support valve stopper	10 Supply valve	15 Stopper	

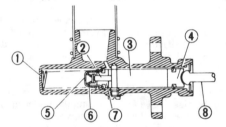

Fig. 5.12 Master cylinder piston assembly (Sec 7)

1 Return spring		5 Spring seat	
2 Supply valve rod		6 Valve spring	
3 Piston		7 Primary cup	
4 Secondary cup		8 Pushrod	

8   Unscrew and remove the supply valve stopper from the bottom of the cylinder and shake the piston assembly, spring seat and return spring out of the cylinder.

9   Look carefully at the piston assembly and note which way round the piston cups are fitted. Remove the piston cups and the dust cover and discard them.

10 Do not detach the reservoir from the cylinder body. If the reservoir does become detached, it must be discarded and a new one fitted.

11 Clean all components of the master cylinder in clean brake fluid. The parts must be cleaned with mineral oil derivatives such as petrol or paraffin. Ensure that the parts are scrupulously clean and either dry them by leaving them on clean kitchen paper, or use a clean, lint-free cloth.

12 Check the cylinder bore and the piston for rust and for scoring. If either of them is evident, discard the component and fit a new one.

13 Measure the clearance between the piston and its bore with feeler gauges. If the clearance exceeds the specified value, fit a new piston and/or master cylinder assembly.

14 Check that all recesses, openings and passages are clean and free from obstruction and then reassemble by reversing the dismantling operations.

15 Dip the piston cups in hydraulic fluid before fitting them to the piston and make sure that they are fitted the same way round as the old ones. Dip the piston assembly in hydraulic fluid and pour a small quantity of hydraulic fluid into the bore before fitting the piston and when inserting it. Take care that the lips of the piston cups are not turned back, or damaged.

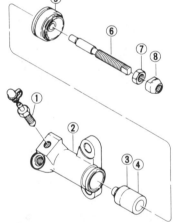

Fig. 5.13 Clutch slave cylinder assembly (Sec 8)

1 Bleeder screw		5 Dust cover	
2 Cylinder body		6 Pushrod	
3 Piston cup		7 Locknut	
4 Piston		8 Pushnut	

16 Refitting is the reverse of the removal procedure.

17 After refitting the master cylinder, bleed the hydraulic system (Section 6) and check the clutch adjustment (Section 2).

---

8   Clutch slave cylinder – removal, overhaul, reassembly and refitting

1   Remove the two bolts securing the clutch slave cylinder to the bellhousing. Take the cylinder off and pull out the pushrod.

2   Fit a spanner to the hexagon on the flexible hose connection to the slave cylinder, hold the hexagon stationary and screw the slave cylinder off the hose. Do not twist the flexible hose.

3   Remove and discard the dust cover.

4   Shake the piston assembly out of the bore. Note which way round the piston cup is fitted, then remove the piston cup and discard it.

5   Remove the bleed screw.

6 Clean all the parts of the slave cylinder in clean hydraulic fluid. The parts must not be cleaned with mineral oils such as petrol, or paraffin. Ensure that the parts are scrupulously clean and dry them either by leaving them on clean kitchen paper, or wipe them with a clean, lint-free cloth.

7 Check the cylinder bore and the piston for rust and for scoring. If either is evident, discard the component and fit a new one.

8 Measure the clearance between the piston and its bore with feeler gauges. If the clearance exceeds the specified value, fit a new piston and/or cylinder.

9 Check the bleed valve and its bore to make sure that they are clean and then reassemble, by reversing the dismantling operations.

10 Dip the piston cup in hydraulic fluid before fitting it to the piston and make sure that it is fitted the same way round as the old one. Dip the piston assembly in hydraulic fluid and pour a small quantity of hydraulic fluid into the bore before fitting the piston and when inserting it; take care that the lip of the piston cup is not turned back, or damaged.

11 Refitting is the reverse of the removal procedure.

12 After refitting the slave cylinder, bleed the hydraulic system (Section 6) and check the clutch adjustment (Section 2).

9 Clutch assembly – removal, inspection and refitting

1 Access to the clutch can be obtained either by removing the engine (Chapter 1), or by removing the gearbox (Chapter 6). Unless major work is required on the engine, it is simpler to remove the gearbox.

2 Mark the clutch cover and flywheel, so that the clutch can be refitted in its original position.

3 Progressively slacken the bolts securing the clutch assembly to the flywheel. Turn each bolt about one turn at a time in diagonal sequence to release pressure evenly and so prevent distortion of the casing.

4 Remove the screws, cover assembly and pressure plate. Note which way round the pressure plate is fitted and mark the side which is towards the flywheel.

5 Clean the face of the flywheel, the pressure plate and the friction plate, using a damp cloth. The dust from clutch facings may be harmful to the lungs, so it should not be inhaled and it is inadvisable to remove the dust by brushing, or blowing.

6 Inspect the friction surfaces of the friction plate and if worn, a new plate must be fitted. A new plate should be fitted if the depth of the rivets below the face of the friction material is less than 0.3 mm (0.012 in). The use of a plate which is worn more than this may lead to scoring of the pressure plate and flywheel. Check that the friction linings show no signs of heavy glazing, or oil impregnation. If evident, a new plate must be fitted. If a small quantity of lubricant has found its way on to the friction material, it will tend to be burnt off by the heat generated in the resultant clutch slipping. This is not serious provided that the grain of the facing material can be seen clearly, but if there is any doubt about the serviceability of the plate, fit a new one. If it is evident that the plate has been impregnated with oil, the source of the oil must be found and stopped before a new plate is fitted.

7 Carefully inspect the pressure plate and the flywheel contact faces for signs of overheating, distortion, cracking and scoring. If there is serious scoring, they must be renewed, or refaced by a specialist workshop.

8 Mount the pressure plate on to the input shaft and check for looseness, or wear on the hub splines. Also check the pressure plate cushion springs for damage, or looseness.

9 Inspect the clutch operating lever for wear and fit a new lever assembly if necessary.

10 Inspect the clutch release bearing for wear, indicated by roughness, or sloppiness between the inner and outer tracks. If wear is evident, discard the bearing and fit a new one. Draw the oil bearing off the bearing sleeve and press on the new bearing being careful to apply pressure to the inner track only.

11 Using a light coat of multi-purpose grease, lubricate the inner groove of the release bearing, the contact surfaces of the withdrawal lever, ball pin and bearing sleeve and also the bearing sleeve sliding surface of the transmission case front cover. Make sure that the return spring is correctly located when refitting the release bearing components.

12 Lubricate the splines of the gearbox input shaft and the hub of the clutch pressure plate with molybdenum disulphide grease (Fig. 5.17).

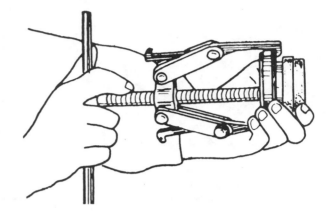

Fig. 5.14 Removing the clutch release bearing (Sec 9)

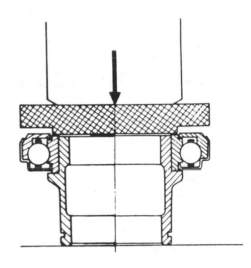

Fig. 5.15 Pressing on the clutch release bearing (Sec 9)

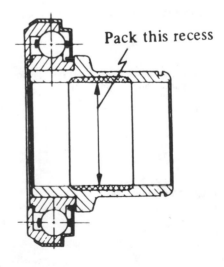

Pack this recess

Fig. 5.16 Lubricating recess of bearing sleeve (Sec 9)

13 Take care not to use excess grease which could later melt and contaminate the clutch facing.

14 Inspect the pilot bearing in the end of the crankshaft. If the bearing is worn, or damaged, screw a threading tap into the bearing to withdraw it, clean the hole in the crankshaft thoroughly and fit a new

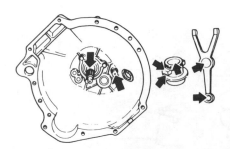

Fig. 5.17 Clutch assembly lubrication (Sec 9)
Apply grease to arrowed parts

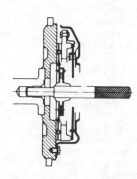

Fig. 5.18 Sectional view of clutch
centraliser (Sec 9)

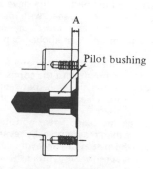

Fig. 5.19 Position of clutch pilot bush
(Sec 9)
Dimension A – 0.110 in (2.8 mm)

bearing. The new bearing should be pressed in until its end is 0.110 in (2.8 mm) below the face of the crankshaft flange.

15 Place the friction plate against the flywheel, with the marked face of the plate against the flywheel. Align the mating marks on the flywheel and clutch cover and fit the cover, securing it in place by screwing in two bolts loosely.

16 The friction plate must now be centralised so that when the engine and gearbox are mated, the gearbox input shaft splines will pass through the splines in the centre of the friction plate hub.

17 If the gearbox has been dismantled, centralisation can be carried out easily by using the gearbox input shaft and inserting it through the friction plate splines and locating its end in the crankshaft pilot bearing.

18 In the absence of an input shaft, or clutch aligning tool, a mock tool can be made with a piece of metal, or wooden rod and adhesive tape. Wind adhesive tape round one end of the rod until it is a snug fit in the end of the crankshaft, then wind tape on that part of the rod which passes through the centre of the friction plate, until a snug fit at this point is achieved.

19 With the clutch plate supported on the centraliser, insert the remaining clutch cover screws and tighten the screws a turn at a time in a diagonal sequence so that the cover plate is pulled down evenly, without distortion to its flange. Before tightening the screws to their final torque, prevent the flywheel from rotating by jamming the starter ring with a spanner or screwdriver located between the teeth of the starter ring gear and a bellhousing bolt.

20 Withdraw the clutch centralising tool, mate the gearbox to the engine and adjust the clutch as described in Section 2 or 3.

10 Fault diagnosis – clutch

Symptom	Reason/s
Judder when taking up drive	Loose engine or gearbox mountings
	Badly worn friction surfaces or contaminated with oil
	Worn splines on gearbox input shaft or driven plate hub
	Worn input shaft spigot bush in flywheel
Clutch spin (failure to disengage) so that gears cannot be meshed	Incorrect release bearing to diaphragm spring finger clearance
	Driven plate sticking on input shaft splines due to rust. May occur after vehicle standing idle for long period
	Damaged or misaligned pressure plate assembly
Clutch slip (increase in engine speed does not result in increase in vehicle road speed – particularly on gradients)	Incorrect release bearing to diaphragm spring finger clearance
	Friction surfaces worn out or oil contaminated
Noise evident on depressing clutch pedal	Dry, worn or damaged release bearing
	Insufficient pedal free travel
	Weak or broken pedal return spring
	Weak or broken clutch release lever return spring
	Excessive play between driven plate hub splines and input shaft splines
Noise evident as clutch pedal released	Distorted driven plate
	Broken or weak driven plate cushion coil springs
	Insufficient pedal free travel
	Weak or broken clutch pedal return spring
	Weak or broken release lever return spring
	Distorted or worn input shaft
	Release bearing loose on retainer hub

Chapter 6 Manual gearbox and automatic transmission

For modifications, and information applicable to later models, see Supplement at end of manual

Contents

Specifications

Manual gearbox

Type .... 4-speed F4W 56A or F4W 60L and 5-speed FS5W 60L with Warner synchromesh on all forward gears

	F4W 56A	F4W 60L	FS5W 60L
Number of forward speeds	4	4	5
Gear ratios			
First	3.757:1	3.513:1	3.513:1
Second	2.169:1	2.170:1	2.170:1
Third	1.404:1	1.378:1	1.378:1
Fourth	1.000:1	1.000:1	1.000:1
Fifth	–	–	0.846:1
Reverse	3.640:1	3.764:1	3.464:1
Final gear ratio	3.889:1	3.889:1 (3.700:1 for North American models)	3.889:1 (3.700:1 for North American models)
Oil capacity			
Pints	$2\frac{1}{8}$	$2\frac{1}{4}$	$2\frac{1}{8}$
US pints	$2\frac{1}{2}$	$2\frac{3}{4}$	$2\frac{1}{2}$
Litres	1.2	1.3	1.2
Gear endplay			
First in (mm)	0.0059 to 0.0098 (0.15 to 0.25)	0.0059 to 0.0098 (0.15 to 0.25)	0.0059 to 0.0098 (0.15 to 0.25)
Second in (mm)	0.0059 to 0.0098 (0.15 to 0.25)	0.0118 to 0.0157 (0.30 to 0.40)	0.0059 to 0.0098 0.15 to 0.25)
Third in (mm)	0.004 to 0.012 (0.1 to 0.3)	0.0059 to 0.0118 (0.15 to 0.30)	0.0118 to 0.0157 (0.30 to 0.40)
Fifth in (mm)	–	–	0.0059 to 0.0118 (0.15 to 0.30)
Countergear in (mm)	0 to 0.008 (0 to 0.2)	0.0039 to 0.0079 (0.10 to 0.20)	0.0039 to 0.0079 (0.10 to 0.20)
Reverse idler gear in (mm)	–	0.0039 to 0.0106 (0.10 to 0.27)	0.0059 to 0.0157 (0.15 to 0.40)
Baulk ring to gear clearance in (mm)	0.0413 to 0.0551 (1.05 to 0.40)	0.0315 to 0.650 (0.80 to 1.65)	0.0315 to 0.0650 (0.80 to 1.65)

	F4W 56A	F4W 60L	FS5W 60L
Gear backlash			
Main drive and counter drive gear in (mm)	0.0020 to 0.0059 (0.05 to 0.15)	0.0020 to 0.0059 (0.05 to 0.15)	0.0020 to 0.0059 (0.05 to 0.15)
First in (mm)	0.0020 to 0.0059 (0.05 to 0.15)	0.0020 to 0.0059 (0.05 to 0.15)	0.0020 to 0.0059 (0.05 to 0.15)
Second in (mm)	0.0020 to 0.0059 (0.05 to 0.15)	0.0020 to 0.0059 (0.05 to 0.15)	0.0020 to 0.0059 (0.05 to 0.15)
Third in (mm)	0.0020 to 0.0059 (0.05 to 0.15)	0.0020 to 0.0059 (0.05 to 0.15)	0.0020 to 0.0059 (0.05 to 0.15)
Fifth in (mm)	—	—	0.0020 to 0.0059 (0.05 to 0.15)
Reverse counter to reverse idler in (mm)	0.0020 to 0.0071 (0.05 to 0.18)	0.0020 to 0.0071 (0.05 to 0.18)	0.0020 to 0.0071 (0.05 to 0.18)
Reverse idler to reverse main in (mm)	0.0020 to 0.0071 (0.05 to 0.18)	0.0020 to 0.0071 (0.05 to 0.18)	0.0020 to 0.0071 (0.05 to 0.18)
Main drive gear rotating torque lbf in (kgf cm)	Less than 1.6 (Less than 1.8)	Less than 1.6 (Less than 1.8)	Less than 1.6 (Less than 1.8)

Torque wrench settings

	lbf ft	kgf m
All models		
Rear extension bolt	12 to 16	1.6 to 2.2
Front cover bolt	7 to 12	1.0 to 1.6
Speedometer sleeve locking plate bolt	2.2 to 3.6	0.3 to 0.5
Top detecting switch	14 to 25	2.0 to 3.5
Reversing light switch	14 to 25	2.0 to 3.5
Return spring plug	3.6 to 7.2	0.5 to 1.0
Filler plug	18 to 29	2.5 to 4.0
Drain plug	18 to 29	2.5 to 4.0
Transmission to engine bolts	12 to 16	1.6 to 2.2
Transmission to engine rear plate bolts	12 to 16	1.6 to 2.2
Transmission to gusset bolt	33 to 44	4.6 to 6.1
Starter motor to transmission bolt	22 to 29	3.0 to 4.0
Rear mounting insulator to transmission bolt	6.5 to 8.7	0.9 to 1.2
Crossmember mounting bolt	23 to 31	3.2 to 4.3
Rear engine mounting bolt	6.5 to 8.7	0.9 to 1.2
Clutch slave cylinder bolt	22 to 30	3.1 to 4.1
Propeller shaft to differential	17 to 24	2.4 to 3.3
Exhaust mounting bracket to front pipe	23 to 31	3.2 to 4.3
Ball pin	14 to 22	2.0 to 3.0
F4W 56A		
Striking lever set screw	4.3 to 7.2	0.6 to 1.0
F4W 60L		
Striking lever locknut	6.5 to 8.7	0.9 to 1.2
Mainshaft bearing retainer screw	5.1 to 7.2	0.7 to 1.0
Stopper pin bolt	3.6 to 5.8	0.5 to 0.8
Control lever pin nut	9 to 12	1.3 to 1.7
FS5W 60L		
Striking lever locknut	6.5 to 8.7	0.9 to 1.2
Shift arm bracket	59 to 72	8.2 to 10
Mainshaft bearing retainer screw	5.8 to 9.4	0.8 to 1.3
Mainshaft locknut	72 to 80	10 to 11
Control lever pin nut	9 to 12	1.3 to 1.7

Automatic transmission

Type . . . . JATCO 3N71B. Three forward speeds and reverse. Three element torque converter with planetary gear train

Gear ratios
First 2.458:1
Second 1.458:1
Third 1.000:1
Reverse 2.182:1

Stall speed
A14 engine . . . . 1900 to 2200 rpm
A15 engine . . . . 1850 to 2150 rpm

Fluid capacity . . . . 4$\frac{7}{8}$ Imp qt; 5$\frac{7}{8}$ US qt; 5.5 litres

Torque converter capacity . . . . 2$\frac{3}{8}$ Imp qt; 2$\frac{7}{8}$ US qt; 2.7 litres

Fluid type . . . . Dexron

Torque wrench settings	lbf ft	kgf m
Drive plate to crankshaft		
A14 engine	58 to 65	8.0 to 9.0
A15 engine	61 to 69	8.5 to 9.5
Drive plate to torque converter	29 to 36	4.0 to 5.0
Converter housing to engine		
Hexagon bolts with washer	14 to 18	2.0 to 2.5
Hexagon flange head bolts	12 to 16	1.6 to 2.2
Transmission case to converter housing	33 to 40	4.5 to 5.5
Oil pan to transmission case	3.6 to 5.1	0.5 to 0.7
Inhibitor switch to transmission case	3.6 to 5.1	0.5 to 0.7
Manual shaft locknut	22 to 29	3.0 to 4.0
Oil cooler pipe to transmission case	22 to 36	3.0 to 5.0
Test plug (oil pressure gauge connection)	10 to 15	1.4 to 2.1

Part A MANUAL GEARBOX

1 General description

There are three different models of gearbox fitted to the cars within the range covered. Two of these are four-speed and although it is basically the same gearbox, there are different gear ratios for the A12 and A14 engine.

The five-speed gearbox, which is an option on most models with the A14 engine, is similar in general construction to the four-speed box.

Synchromesh is provided on all forward gears and gearshift control is by means of a centrally mounted lever on the car floor.

The gear trains are mounted on an adaptor plate, to which the main transmission casing and rear extension are secured by tie bolts. Removal of the main casing and rear extension gives complete access to the gears and shafts.

2 Gearbox – removal and refitting

1 Disconnect the lead from the battery negative terminal.
2 From inside the vehicle remove the console from the transmission tunnel.
3 Unscrew and remove the rubber boot and retainer from the base of the gear lever (photo). Make certain that the lever is in neutral and then remove the circlip and pivot pin from the remote control rod guide (photos). Withdraw the gear lever.
4 If possible carry out the removal of the gearbox over a pit or with the car on ramps. Failing this, jack the vehicle up sufficiently to give enough clearance to remove the clutch bellhousing. Support the vehicle securely with its wheels chocked and with the body supported on stands, or baulks of timber.
5 Disconnect the exhaust front pipe from the manifold and remove

2.3a Gearshift lever rubber boot removal

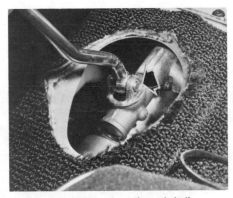
2.3b Gearshift lever pivot pin and circlip (arrowed)

2.3c Remove the gearshift lever bolt from underneath (F4W 60L)

Fig. 6.1 Removing the gear lever – nut arrowed (Sec 2)

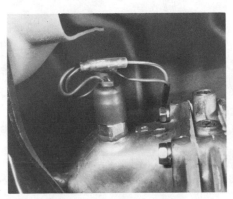
2.6 Reversing light switch connections

2.7 Disconnecting the speedometer cable

the bolt securing the mounting bracket to the front pipe.

6   Disconnect the leads from the reversing lamp switch (photo).

7   Disconnect the speedometer cable from the rear extension (photo). If the gearbox is to be dismantled, drain the oil and then screw the drain plug back into place. Disconnect the top gear detecting switch wires on North American models (when fitted).

8   Remove the propeller shaft, as described in Chapter 7. Cover the opening in the rear extension with a plastic bag held in place by a strong rubber band to prevent any oil coming from the gearbox.

9   Unbolt the clutch slave cylinder from the bellhousing and tie it up out of the way, or disconnect the operating cable from the release lever depending upon whether the clutch is hydraulic, or cable controlled. Refer to Chapter 5 if necessary.

10   Place a jack under the sump using a piece of wood between the jack and the sump and taking care not to foul the drain plug, take the weight of the engine on the jack.

11   Unscrew the gearbox rear mounting bolts, place a supporting jack under the gearbox and remove the securing bolts from the gearbox support member.

12   Remove the starter motor cable connection and the two bolts securing the motor. Remove the starter motor.

13   Unscrew and remove the bellhousing to engine securing bolts and also the gusset plate bolts.

14   Lower the two jacks progressively, until the gearbox can be withdrawn rearwards from beneath the vehicle. Do not allow the weight of the gearbox to hang even momentarily upon the gearbox input shaft while the shaft is being withdrawn from the clutch assembly, because the shaft, or clutch may be damaged. Do not lower the jacks more than is necessary for the gearbox to clear the underside of the body floor to avoid unnecessary strain on the engine mountings.

15   Before refitting the gearbox, lightly grease the splines of the clutch disc and the gearbox input shaft. Also grease the moving surfaces of the gear lever and striking rod and ensure that the mating faces of the engine rear plate and the gearbox casing are clean.

16   Carefully align the engine rear plate and the gearbox casing before attempting to enter the input shaft into the clutch and do not use any force to engage the shaft. If necessary turn the gearbox slightly to align the splines.

17   After fitting the gearbox, remove the filler plug and pour in the specified quantity of recommended gear oil, so that the level of oil is up to the filler plug hole. Coat the threads of the filler plug with jointing compound, screw in the plug and tighten it.

3 Gearbox (F4W56A) – dismantling into major assemblies

1   Before dismantling, clean the external surfaces thoroughly with paraffin or water soluble solvent. Drain the oil into a suitable container.

2   Detach the flexible dust cover from the release lever aperture in the clutch bellhousing and then remove the release lever and release bearing (see Chapter 5).

3   Remove the reversing lamp switch (photo) and the neutral and top gear switches (where fitted); see Section 9.

4   Unscrew and remove the two bolts which secure the speedometer pinion assembly to the extension housing and withdraw the pinion assembly (photo).

5   Remove the circlip and the remote control rod guide stop pin.

6   Remove the threaded plug which is located above and slightly to the rear of the speedometer pinion aperture and then withdraw the plunger, return spring and bush (photo).

7   From within the clutch bellhousing, unbolt and remove the front cover, O-ring and shim.

8   Unscrew and remove the rear extension housing to gearbox casing tie-bolts.

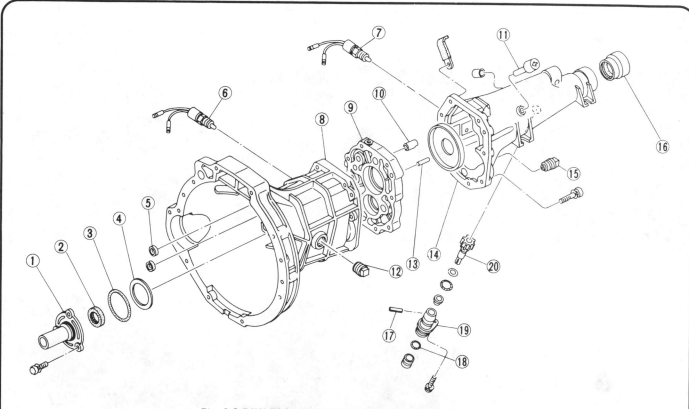

Fig. 6.2 F4W 56A transmission case components (Sec 3)

1 Front cover	6 Top gear detecting switch	11 Breather	16 Rear extension dust cover
2 Front cover oil seal	7 Reversing light switch	12 Filler plug	with oil seal
3 Front cover O-ring	8 Transmission case assembly	13 Rear extension dowel pin	17 Retaining pin
4 Front cover adjusting shim	9 Adapter plate	14 Rear extension assembly	18 Speedometer pinion O-ring
5 Welch plug	10 Striking rod bushing	15 Drain plug	19 Speedometer sleeve
			20 Speedometer pinion

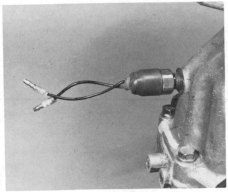

3.3 Removing the reversing light switch

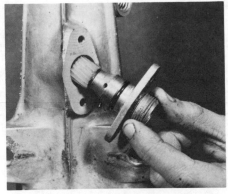

3.4 Removing the speedometer drive pinion assembly

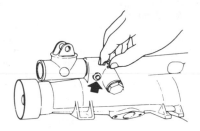

Fig. 6.3 Remote control rod guide stop pin and circlip (arrowed) (Sec 3)

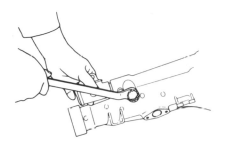

Fig. 6.4 Removing plunger threaded plug (Sec 3)

3.6 Removing the return spring plug

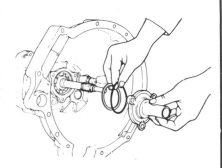

Fig. 6.5 Removing front cover, O-ring and input shaft bearing shim (Sec 3)

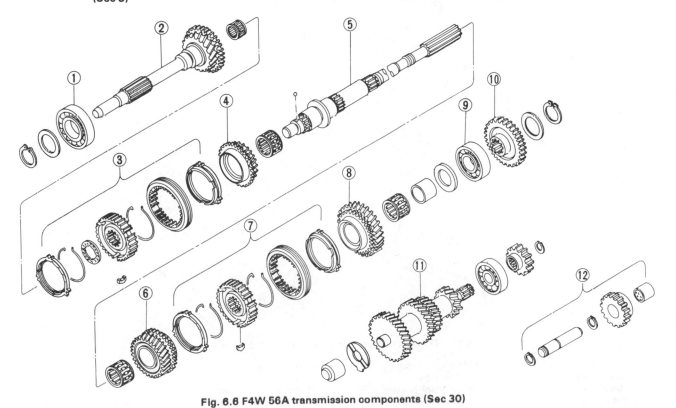

Fig. 6.6 F4W 56A transmission components (Sec 30)

1 Main drive bearing	4 3rd gear, mainshaft	7 1st and 2nd synchronizer	10 Reverse gear, mainshaft
2 Main drive gear	5 Mainshaft	8 1st gear, mainshaft	11 Counter gear assembly
3 3rd and 4th synchronizer	6 2nd gear, mainshaft	9 Mainshaft bearing	12 Idler gear assembly

9   Rotate the remote control rod guide as far as it will go in a clockwise direction and then drive off the rear extension housing using a soft-faced mallet.

10 Tap off the single piece clutch bellhousing/casing in a similar manner to that applied to the rear extension.

11 Make up a suitable support plate and secure it in the jaws of a vice and then bolt the adaptor plate to it so that the countergear assembly

is at the top.

12 Remove the countergear thrust washer.

13 Drive out the pins which secure the three shift forks to the selector rods. There is no need to remove the dogs from the ends of the selector rods unless they are to be renewed.

14 Remove the reverse shift fork and reverse idle gear.

15 Invert the adaptor plate in the vice so that the shift forks and

Fig. 6.7 Removing the rear extension housing (Sec 3)

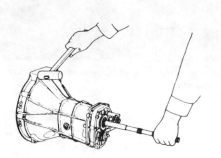

Fig. 6.8 Removing the gearbox casing from the adapter plate (Sec 3)

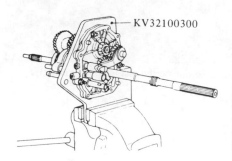

Fig. 6.9 Adaptor plate bolted to support plate (Sec 3)

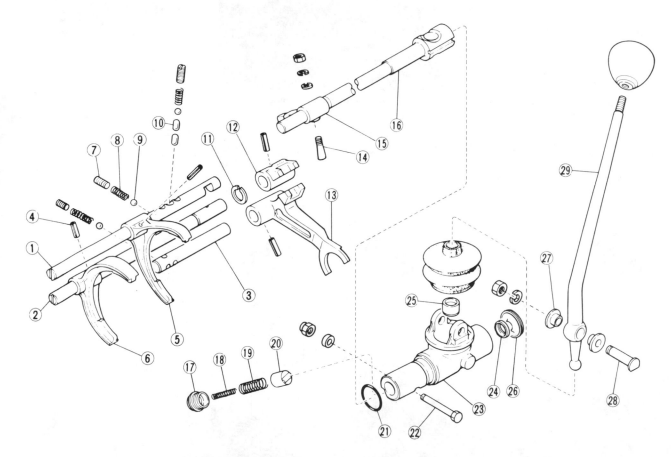

Fig. 6.10 F4W 56A transmission gearshift components (Sec 3)

1	1st and 2nd fork rod	8	Check ball spring	15	Striking lever	22	Stopper pin bolt
2	3rd and 4th fork rod	9	Check ball	16	Striking rod	23	Striking guide assembly
3	Reverse fork rod	10	Interlock plunger	17	Return spring plug	24	Striking guide oil seal
4	Retaining pin	11	Stopper ring	18	Reverse check spring	25	Control lever bushing
5	1st and 2nd shift fork	12	Shift rod A bracket	19	Return spring	26	Expansion plug
6	3rd and 4th shift fork	13	Reverse shift fork	20	Plunger	27	Control pin bushing
7	Checking ball plug	14	Lock pin	21	O-ring	28	Control arm pin
						29	Control lever

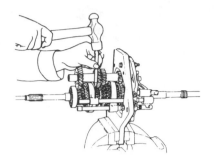

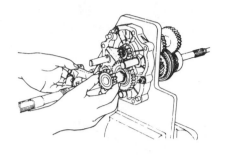

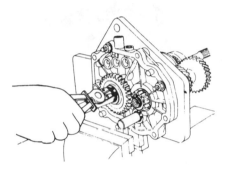

Fig. 6.11 Driving out a shift fork retaining pin (Sec 3)

A   Reverse gear shift rod
B   3rd/4th gear shift rod
C   1st/2nd gear shift rod

Fig. 6.12 Removing reverse gear shift fork and reverse idler gear (Sec 3)

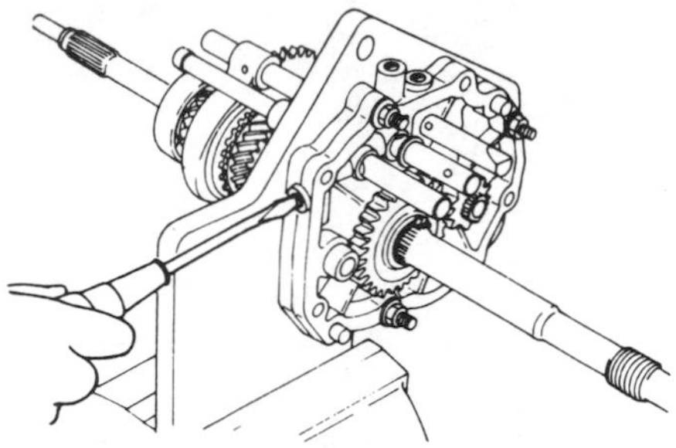

Fig. 6.13 Removing a detent ball plug (Sec 3)

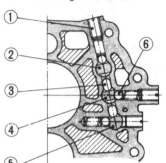

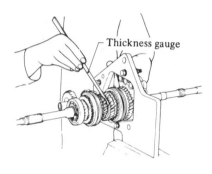

Fig. 6.14 Detent ball and interlock plunger positions (Sec 3)

1   Plug
2   1st/2nd gear selector rod
3   Interlock plunger
4   3rd/4th gear selector rod
5   Reverse gear selector rod
6   Detent ball

Fig. 6.15 Measuring gear endplay (Sec 3)

Fig. 6.16 Extracting reverse gear circlip (Sec 3)

selector rods are uppermost.

16   Unscrew and remove the three detent ball plugs.

17   Tap out the selector rods from the adaptor plate (towards the rear) and take off the shift forks. Retain the detent balls, springs and interlock plungers as the selector rods are withdrawn. The selector rods need only be driven far enough to permit removal of the shift forks. The selector rods remaining attached to the adaptor plate will not impede removal of the shafts or gears later on.

18   At this stage, check for backlash in the gears, this should be within the tolerances given in the Specifications Section. Also check the mainshaft gears for endfloat which again should be as specified for the particular gears. Where the tolerances are exceeded, the drive and driven gears must be renewed as matched sets.

19   Inspect the teeth of the gearwheels for wear or chipping which if evident will necessitate renewal of the gears concerned.

20   From the rear of the mainshaft, extract the reverse gear circlip, the thrust washer and reverse gear.

21   Using a soft-faced mallet, tap the rear end of the mainshaft and eject both the mainshaft and countershaft assemblies from the adaptor plate. Hold the two gear trains in mesh during the removal operation and then detach the countergear also the input shaft from the front end of the mainshaft.

22   Unless the necessary press facilities are available, it is recommended that dismantling of the mainshaft, countergear and input shaft be left to your Datsun dealer. Where suitable equipment is available, proceed as described in the following Sections.

4   Mainshaft (F4W56A) – dismantling, examination and reassembly

1   From the front end of the mainshaft, remove the pilot needle roller

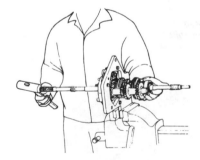

Fig. 6.17 Removing gear assemblies from adaptor plate (Sec 3)

bearing, the thrust washer and its steel locking ball, 3rd/4th synchro assembly, baulk rings, 3rd gear and needle roller bearing (photo).

2   Supporting the mainshaft bearing, press the mainshaft from it.

3   From the rear end of the mainshaft withdraw the thrust washer, 1st gear, needle roller bearing, bush, 1st/2nd synchro assembly, baulk rings, 2nd gear and another needle roller bearing.

4   With the mainshaft dismantled, check it for twist or spline wear and renew it if necessary.

5   Check the needle roller bearings and the main bearing for wear and renew if necessary.

6   Examine the synchronizer units for wear or damage. If there has been a history of noisy or slow gear selection, renew the synchronizer unit complete. If there is slight wear on any component (sleeve, hub, thrust washer etc), this should be renewed individually.

7   Examine each of the baulk rings for wear and damage. Place each baulk ring on its appropriate gear cone and measure the gap between them. This should be between 0.041 and 0.060 in (1.05 and 1.40

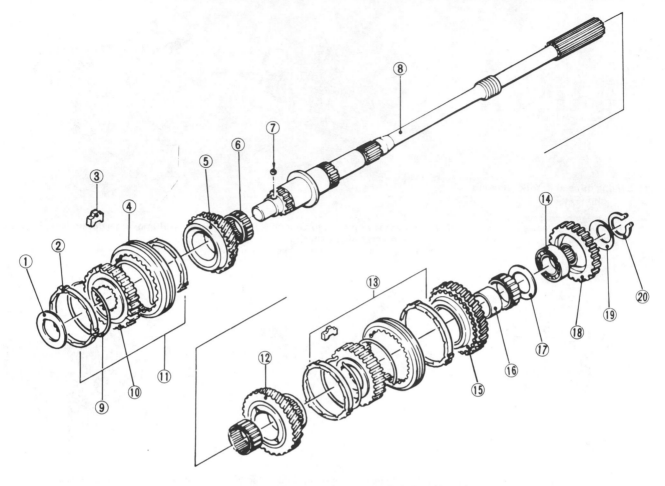

Fig. 6.18 Mainshaft assembly – exploded view (Sec 4)

1	Thrust washer	6	Needle bearing	11	3rd/4th synchro assembly	16	Bush
2	Baulk ring	7	Ball	12	2nd gear	17	Thrust washer
3	Synchro shift key	8	Mainshaft	13	1st/2nd synchro assembly	18	Reverse gear
4	Synchro sleeve	9	Synchro spring	14	Mainshaft bearing	19	Thrust washer
5	3rd gear	10	Synchro hub	15	1st gear	20	Circlip

4.1 Front end of mainshaft showing needle roller bearing, thrust washer and 3rd/4th gear synchro

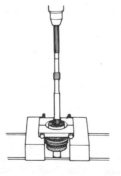

Fig. 6.19 Removing the mainshaft bearing (Sec 4)

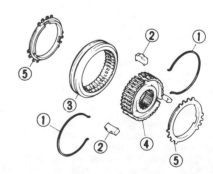

Fig. 6.20 Synchronizer components (Sec 4)

1	Spring	4	Hub
2	Shift key	5	Baulk ring
3	Sleeve		

mm). Where the clearance is found to be smaller, renew the baulk ring.

8   To assemble a synchronizer, insert the hub into the sleeve and locate the three shift keys in grooves at equidistant points.

9   Install the springs which retain the shift keys but make quite sure that the ends of opposite springs are not engaged in the same key.

10   To the rear end of the mainshaft, assemble the 2nd gear needle

bearing, 2nd gear, the baulk ring, 1st and 2nd speed synchro unit, 1st gear baulk ring, 1st gear bush and needle bearing, 1st gear and the thrust washer, in that sequence.

11   Now press on the mainshaft bearing making sure that pressure is applied only to the inner track.

12   To the front end of the mainshaft, fit the 3rd gear needle bearing,

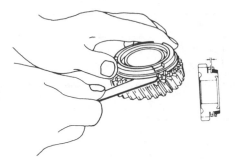

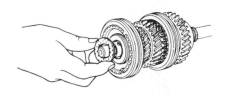

Fig. 6.21 Checking baulk ring to cone clearance (Sec 4)

Fig. 6.22 Fitting a synchronizer spring (Sec 4)

Fig. 6.23 Fitting the thrust washer to front of mainshaft (Sec 4)

3rd gear, the baulk ring, 3rd/4th synchro unit, the thrust washer with its locking ball. Apply grease to the thrust washer before fitting and make sure that the oil grooves are against the synchro hub.

---

5 Countergear (F4W56A) – dismantling, examination and reassembly

1 Extract the circlip from the rear end of the countergear.

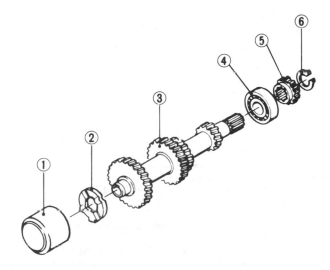

Fig. 6.24 Countershaft gear assembly – exploded view (Sec 5)

1	Needle bearing holder	4	Bearing
2	Thrust washer	5	Countershaft reverse gear
3	Counter gear	6	Circlip

2 Support the reverse gear and press the countergear assembly from it.
3 Remove the rear bearing in a similar manner.
4 Inspect the gearteeth for wear or chipping and renew if necessary the complete countergear assembly.
5 Examine the rear bearing for wear, roughness or noise when spinning it with the fingers and renew where necessary.
6 Press the rear bearing onto the countergear, applying pressure only to the bearing inner track.
7 Temporarily fit a countershaft thrust washer into the recess at the front end of the gearbox casing. A height gauge (service tool ST 23050000) must now be borrowed from your Datsun dealer. With the tool held against the adaptor plate mating face of the gearbox casing and using feeler blades, measure the countershaft endplay which should be between 0.000 and 0.008 in (0 and 0.02 mm). In order to correct the endplay, extract the thrust washer and substitute one of the appropriate thickness from those available in the following range of sizes:

> 0.0906 to 0.0925 in (2.30 to 2.35 mm)
> 0.0925 to 0.0945 in (2.35 to 2.40 mm)
> 0.0945 to 0.0965 in (2.40 to 2.45 mm)
> 0.0965 to 0.0984 in (2.45 to 2.50 mm)
> 0.0984 to 1.004 in (2.50 to 2.55 mm)
> 0.1004 to 0.1024 in (2.55 to 2.60 mm)

8 Remove the countergear assembly from the gearbox casing and press the reverse gear onto the countergear.
9 Fit the circlip to the rear end of the countergear.

---

6 Input shaft (F4W56A) – examination, dismantling and reassembly

1 Inspect the gear teeth and splines of the input shaft for wear or damage. If apparent, renew the shaft complete.
2 Check the bearing for wear or rough or noisy operation when it is turned with the fingers.
3 To remove the bearing, first extract the circlip and thrust washer

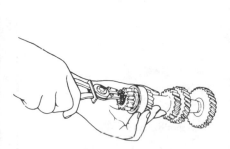
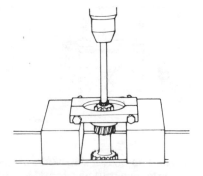
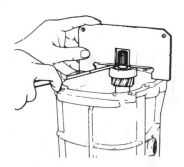

Fig. 6.25 Removing circlip from end of counter gear (Sec 5)

Fig. 6.26 Removing reverse gear from countershaft (Sec 5)

Fig. 6.27 Using a height gauge to measure counter gear endplay (Sec 5)

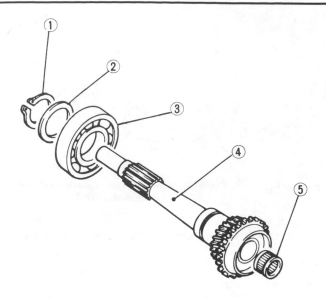

Fig. 6.28 Input shaft – exploded view (Sec 6)

1	Circlip	4	Input shaft
2	Thrust washer	5	Pilot bearing
3	Bearing		

and then using a suitable puller or press, draw the bearing from the shaft.

4   Press the new bearing onto the input shaft, applying pressure to the inner track only and making sure that the circlip groove on the shaft is fully exposed.

5   Locate the thrust washer on the bearing so that the chamfered face of the washer faces the front of the input shaft.

6   Fit a new circlip to the input shaft.

7   Finally, check the condition of the pilot needle bearing and renew it if it is worn.

7   Gearbox oil seals and casing (F4W56A)

1   At time of major overhaul, always check the gearbox casing and rear extension housing for cracks.

2   Renew the front cover oil seal.

3   Renew the oil seal in the rear extension housing. If the bush in the rear extension is worn then the rear extension housing will have to be renewed complete.

4   If the countershaft needle bearing requires renewal, press it into the gearbox interior from the outside. Install the new one from the inside so that it will project by 0.079 in (2.0 mm) beyond the front face of the gearbox casing.

5   Finally, check the condition of the gearbox rear mounting and renew it if the rubber component has deteriorated.

8   Gearbox (F4W56A) – reassembly

1   Fit the baulk ring to the input shaft and then joint the input shaft to the front of the mainshaft (photo).

2   Mesh the mainshaft and countergear assemblies and then fit them simultaneously into the adaptor plate by striking them alternately with a soft-faced mallet (photo).

3   Fit the reverse gear and thrust washer to the rear end of the mainshaft and secure with circlip. Make sure that the chamfered face of the thrust washer is towards the front of the gearbox. Some washers are dished type, fit with the concave side to the reverse gear (photos).

4   Insert the spring and detent ball into the reverse hole in the adaptor plate. A useful tool can be made from a piece of rod having a sloping surface at one end to depress the detent ball and compress the spring pending installation of the reverse selector rod (photo).

5   Fit the reverse selector rod so that it displaces the tool without releasing the detent ball or spring.

6   Apply thread locking compound to the plug and screw it into the adaptor plate until it is flush with the surface of the plate (photo).

7   Insert the interlock plunger which lies between the reverse and 3rd/4th selector rods. Using the special tool maintain pressure on the plunger until by moving the reverse selector rod, the plunger can be felt to engage in the notch in the reverse selector rod.

8   Engage the 3rd/4th shift fork with the groove in the 3rd/4th synchro sleeve (longer arm of fork *furthest* from countergear) and then slide the 3rd/4th selector rod through the adaptor plate and shift fork. The 3rd/4th shift fork is identical with the 1st/2nd shift fork (photo).

9   Fit the detent ball, spring and plug into the 3rd/4th hole in the adaptor plate. Apply thread locking compound to the plug and screw it in until flush with the surface of the adaptor plate. Make sure that the detent notch in the selector rod is in the correct attitude to engage with the detent ball.

10 Engage the 1st/2nd shift fork wth the groove in the 1st/2nd synchro sleeve (longer arm of fork *nearest* countergear), (photo).

11 Insert the interlock plunger which lies between the 1st/2nd and 3rd/4th selector rod holes in the adaptor plate. Make sure that the 3rd/4th selector rod notch is aligned to receive the plunger.

12 Slide the 1st/2nd selector rod through the adaptor plate and the shift fork.

13 Insert the detent ball, spring and plug into the 1st/2nd hole in the adaptor plate. Apply thread locking compound to the plug and screw it in until flush with the surface of the adaptor plate. Make sure that the detent notch in the selector rod is in the correct attitude to engage with the detent ball (photos).

14 Fit the reverse idler gear and shift fork (photo).

15 Secure the three shift forks to their selector rods using new retaining pins (photo).

16 Check the operation of the selector mechanism by moving the 3rd/4th selector rod to engage 3rd and then 4th gear. With either of these gears selected, movement of either of the other two selector rods should not cause any other gears to mesh. If they do, then the interlock plungers are not operating correctly which may be due to the selector rods having been fitted with their notches 180° out of alignment.

17 Apply gear oil to all internal components and select each gear in

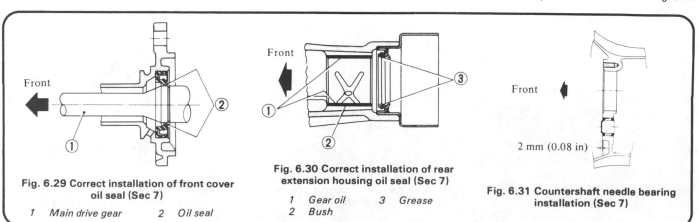

Fig. 6.29 Correct installation of front cover oil seal (Sec 7)

1 Main drive gear	2 Oil seal

Fig. 6.30 Correct installation of rear extension housing oil seal (Sec 7)

1	Gear oil	3	Grease
2	Bush		

2 mm (0.08 in)

Fig. 6.31 Countershaft needle bearing installation (Sec 7)

8.1 Input shaft ready for coupling to mainshaft

8.2 Fitting the mainshaft and counter gear assemblies to adaptor plate

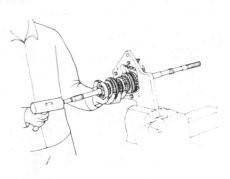

Fig. 6.32 Fitting the gear assemblies to adaptor plate (Sec 8)

8.3a Reverse gear fitted on mainshaft rear end

8.3b Thrust washer fitted on mainshaft rear end

8.3c Securing reverse gear and thrust washer to mainshaft with circlip

8.4 Detent ball and spring inserted into adaptor plate

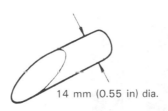

14 mm (0.55 in) dia.

Fig. 6.33 Detent ball and interlock plunger installation tool (Sec 8)

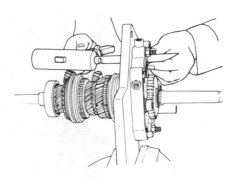

Fig. 6.34 Fitting the reverse gear selector rod (Sec 8)

8.6 Inserting detent plug

8.8 Fitting 3rd/4th selector rod and shift fork

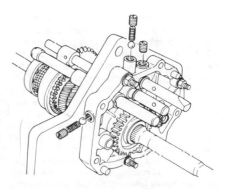

Fig. 6.35 Fitting the detent balls and springs (Sec 8)

8.10 Fitting 1st/2nd selector rod and shift fork
  1   1st/2nd   3   Reverse
  2   3rd/4th

8.13a Inserting 1st/2nd detent ball and spring into adaptor plate

8.13b Inserting 1st/2nd detent plug

8.14 Reverse idler gear and shift fork

8.15 Shift fork to selector rod and roll pin

8.19 Counter gear thrust washer at front of gearcase interior

8.20 Fitting adaptor plate in gearbox casing

Wooden block

Fig. 6.36 Fitting the transmission casing (Sec 8)

turn to check for positive and smooth operation.
18 Clean the mating surfaces of the adaptor plate and the gearbox casing and apply jointing compound to both surfaces.
19 Stick the countergear thrust washer previously selected (see Section 5) into the recess at the front of the gearbox, holding it in position with a dab of thick grease and making sure that the oil grooves on the washer are not visible when it is fitted (photo).
20 Connect the gearbox casing to the adaptor plate making sure that the locating dowel engages correctly and then tap the adaptor plate fully home with a soft-faced mallet. Take great care that the input shaft bearing enters the front face of the gearbox squarely and the nose of the countershaft enters the needle bearing in correct alignment during the later stages of the mating operation (photo).
21 Clean the mating surfaces of the adaptor plate and the rear extension and apply jointing compound to them.
22 Set the selector rods in neutral and then gradually slide the rear extension onto the adaptor plate ensuring that the selector cross lever engages correctly with the dogs on the ends of the selector rods.

During this operation, make sure that the remote control rod passes down the right-hand side of the mainshaft when viewed from the bottom of the gearbox (photo).
23 Fit the tie-bolts and washers and tighten them to the specified torque.
24 Apply jointing compound to the remote control rod guide stop in the hole in the rear extension, insert the pin and secure with the circlip (photos).
25 Grease the plunger, and springs and insert them into the hole in the rear extension housing (photo).
26 Apply jointing compound to the threaded plug and fit it. Fit the speedometer pinion assembly (two bolts) (photo).
27 Using a vernier type depth gauge or feeler blades and a straight-edge, measure the distance by which the input shaft bearing outer race is recessed from the front cover mating face of the transmission casing. Select a shim from the range of thicknesses available – 0·020 in (0·5 mm) 0·008 in (0·2 mm) 0·004 in (0·1 mm) 0.012 (0.03 mm) – which will reduce the dimension 'A' (Fig. 6.39) to between 0·1969

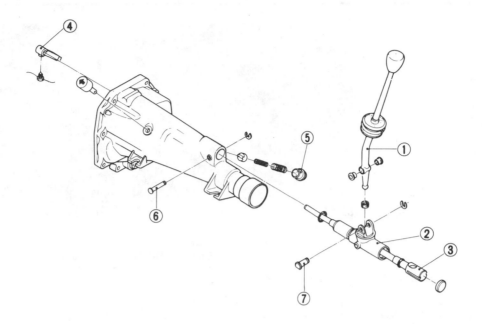

Fig. 6.37 Rear extension housing – exploded view (Sec 8)

1 Gearshift lever
2 Remote control rod guide
3 Remote control rod
4 Selector cross lever
5 Return spring plug
6 Guide stop pin
7 Gearshift lever pivot

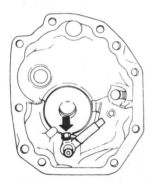

Fig. 6.38 Selector cross lever and securing bolt (arrowed) (Sec 8)

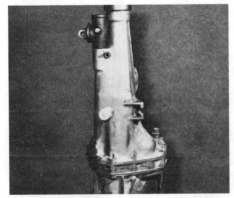

8.22 Fitting gearbox extension to adaptor plate

8.24a Gearshift remote control rod guide stop pin

8.24b Fitting circlip to remote control rod guide stop pin

8.25 Fitting plunger assembly to rear extension housing

8.26 Fitting speedometer drive pinion assembly

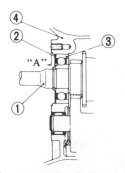

Fig. 6.39 Input shaft bearing shim selection
diagram (Sec 8)

1   Input shaft   3   Bearing
2   Shim   4   Casing

8.27 Input shaft bearing shim and recess

8.28 Front cover showing input shaft oil seal
and O-ring

and 0·2029 in (5·00 and 5·15 mm). Stick the selected shim in position using a dab of thick grease (photo).

28 Clean the mating surfaces of the front cover and the gearbox casing, fit the front cover using a new O-ring seal and tightening the securing bolts to the specified torque (photo).

29 Refit the reversing lamp switch, top gear and neutral indicator switches, apply jointing compound to their threads before screwing them in. Check that the breather on the rear extension housing has its directional arrow pointing to the front of the gearbox.

30 Fit the release bearing and lever, coating the sliding and pivot surfaces with a little high melting point grease.

31 Temporarily connect the gear shift lever and check for smooth and positive gear selection.

9 Gearbox (F4W 60L) – dismantling into major assemblies

1 Before commencing work on the gearbox, clean off it's external surfaces using a water soluble solvent or paraffin.

2 If not already done on removal, drain the transmission lubricant.

3 Refer to Chapter 5 and remove the clutch release mechanism.

4 If still attached, remove the crossmember mounting support bracket from the extension housing.

5 Unscrew and withdraw the reverse light switch.

6 Unscrew and remove the retaining bolt from the speedometer drivegear retaining housing flange and withdraw the unit.

7 Unscrew and remove the nut and stopper pin-bolt from the rear

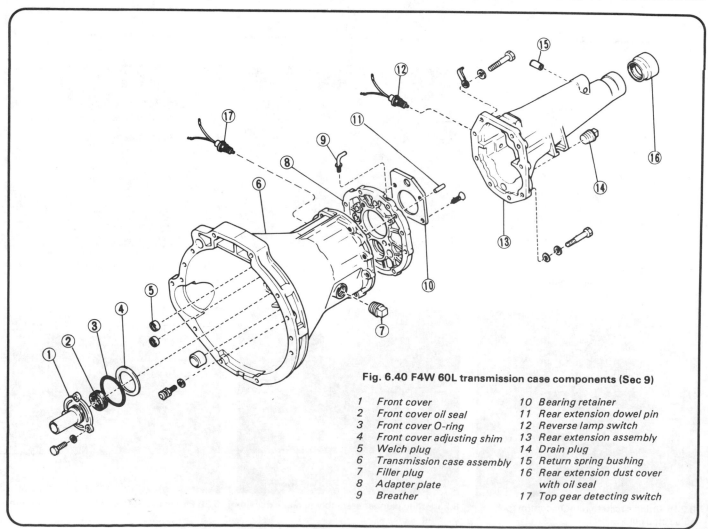

Fig. 6.40 F4W 60L transmission case components (Sec 9)

1 Front cover	10 Bearing retainer
2 Front cover oil seal	11 Rear extension dowel pin
3 Front cover O-ring	12 Reverse lamp switch
4 Front cover adjusting shim	13 Rear extension assembly
5 Welch plug	14 Drain plug
6 Transmission case assembly	15 Return spring bushing
7 Filler plug	16 Rear extension dust cover
8 Adapter plate	with oil seal
9 Breather	17 Top gear detecting switch

extension (Fig. 6.41).

8 The return spring plug, spring, reverse check spring and plunger can now be carefully removed from the rear extension unit.

9 Unscrew the retaining bolts from the front cover and withdraw it together with the O-ring and adjustment shim over the input shaft. Keep the shim with the O-ring and cover.

10 Using a suitable pair of circlip pliers, extract the front main drive bearing retaining circlip from the bearing orifice.

11 Unscrew and remove the rear extension unit retaining bolts, and note the position of the cable retainer clip.

12 Check that the gearbox is in neutral and rotate the striker rod (selector rail) in a clockwise direction and simultaneously drive the

extension rearwards from the main housing. Lightly tap around the housing using a soft head mallet. Do not use a screwdriver to prise the two housings apart. If the extension housing is reluctant to part company with the main housing check that the striker rod is fully positioned to release it from the shift rod/fork.

13 Support the mainshaft and tap the gearbox housing with a soft head mallet as shown (Fig. 6.43) to enable the housing and adaptor plate assembly to be disconnected.

14 Now that the gear assembly is removed an initial inspection can be made of the components. If it is decided to dismantle the complete assembly, it is a good system to devise a method of supporting the adaptor plate assembly. An adaptor plate retainer can easily be

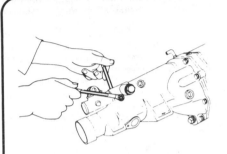

Fig. 6.41 Removing the stopper pin bolt (Sec 9)

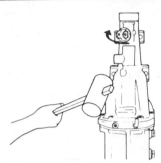

Fig. 6.42 Removing the rear extension – turn striker rod in direction of arrow (Sec 9)

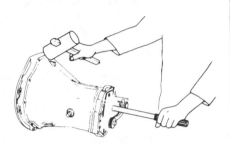

Fig. 6.43 Withdrawing the adaptor plate assembly (Sec 9)

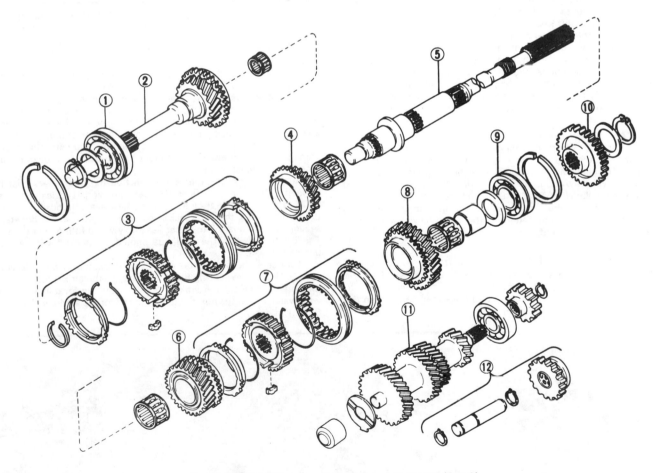

Fig. 6.44 F4W 60L transmission gear components (Sec 9)

1	Main drive bearing	4	3rd gear, mainshaft	7	1st and 2nd synchronizer	10	Reverse gear, mainshaft
2	Main drive gear	5	Mainshaft	8	1st gear, mainshaft	11	Counter gear assembly
3	3rd and 4th synchronizer	6	2nd gear, mainshaft	9	Mainshaft bearing	12	Idler gear assembly

fabricated and bolted to the adaptor plate so that it can be securely held in a vice for convenience when working. Figure 6.45 shows the special adaptor setting plate tool manufactured by Datsun (Tool No. KV32100300).

15 Remove the thrust washer from the counter gear (laygear) taking note which way round it is fitted (slot to front).

Shift forks and rods – dismantling

16 Using a suitable pin punch, drive out the respective roll pins retaining the shift forks to the rods.

17 Withdraw the reverse idler gear and shift fork.

18 Unscrew and remove the three check ball plugs and extract the springs and balls.

19 Lightly tap the selector rods on the front end and extract them together with their shift forks. Note which way round the shift forks are fitted and refit them to their respective shafts on removal to avoid confusion during assembly.

Gear assemblies – dismantling

20 Using a suitable pair of circlip pliers, remove the circlip at the rear of the mainshaft. Then withdraw the thrust washer and reverse gear from the mainshaft, but note which way round the gear is facing.

21 The bearing retainer plate can now be removed by unscrewing the four cross-head screws. We found them to be extremely tight and had to use a large cross-head screwdriver and grip the screwdriver shaft with a pair of molegrips to provide the additional effort required to loosen the screws.

22 Using circlip pliers, extract the circlip locating the mainshaft rear bearing.

23 The mainshaft gear assembly can now be driven from the adaptor together with the counter gear unit. Support both gear assemblies and tap them free with a soft head mallet hitting their rear end faces (Fig. 6.47). Take care not to drop or damage the gears during removal.

24 The gearbox major components are now removed and can be inspected and if necessary dismantled further for repair or renewal, but note that further operations should not be undertaken unless the facilities of a press and/or a bearing puller are available. With this in mind, read the further dismantling procedures through and decide whether or not you have suitable facilities to undertake further work.

Mainshaft – dismantling

25 Extract the circlip from the mainshaft at the front using suitable pliers. Withdraw the 3rd and 4th synchronizer unit complete with baulk rings, 3rd gear and the needle roller bearing. Using a suitable bearing puller withdraw the mainshaft bearing. If available use special Datsun bearing puller No. ST30031000, and press the bearing free as in Fig. 6.19. Withdraw the thrust washer, 1st gear together with its bush and needle roller bearing. Remove the 1st/2nd synchronizer unit together with baulk rings and needle roller bearing.

Main drivegear (input shaft) – dismantling

26 Using suitable circlip pliers, remove the circlip and withdraw the spacer. A bearing puller, or if available Datsun special tool No ST22730000 and a press are needed to remove the bearing from the shaft. Do not drop the shaft and gear.

Counter gear (laygear) – dismantling

27 Remove the circlip from the counter shaft and using a suitable puller or Datsun special puller No ST22730000, withdraw the countershaft reverse gear. Use the same puller and remove the counter gear rear bearing.

10 Synchromesh hubs (F4W60L) – dismantling and inspection

1 The synchro hubs are only too easy to dismantle – just push the centre out and the whole assembly flies apart. The point is to prevent this happening, before you are ready. Do not dismantle the hubs without reason and do not mix up the parts of the two hubs.

2 It is most important to check backlash in the splines between the outer sleeve and inner hub. If any is noticeable the whole assembly must be renewed.

3 Mark the hubs and sleeve so that you may reassemble them on the same splines. With the hub and sleeve separated, the teeth at the end of the splines which engage with corresponding teeth of the gear wheels, must be checked for damage and wear.

4 Note the keystone shape at the ends of the teeth. This shape matches the gear teeth shape and it is a design characteristic to minimise jump-out tendencies.

5 If the synchronizing cones are being renewed it is sensible also to renew the sliding keys and springs which hold them in position.

11 Rear extension (F4W60L) – dismantling, inspection and assembly

1 To remove the striking lever from the striking rod, unscrew the lockpin nut and remove with washers. Extract the pin and withdraw the lever.

2 Withdraw the striker rod and guide from the rear extension housing.

3 The oil seal can be prised out of its housing, and should normally be renewed during an overhaul of the gearbox.

4 Do not remove the bush from the rear extension.

5 Clean and check the housing for signs of cracks, or damage. In particular, look for any damage or distortion to the mating face of the adaptor plate. Clean off any small protrusions, or sealant, taking care not to damage or score the surface. Should the rear extension bush be damaged, or show any signs of wear, the housing and bush must be renewed, as an assembly.

6 To reassemble the rear extension housing, first check that it is perfectly clean, in particular the seal housing. Lubricate the seal housing with clean gear oil and press a new seal into position, using a tube drift. Check that the seal is correctly located and lubricate the sealing lip with gear oil to assist assembly when fitting over the shaft. The cavity between the seal lips should be packed with a multi-purpose grease.

7 Lubricate the striker rod guide in the extension and the O-ring groove. With a new O-ring fitted, carefully fit the striker rod and when fully home, relocate the striking lever. Insert the lockpin and secure with washers and the nut, tightening to the torque settings given in the Specifications.

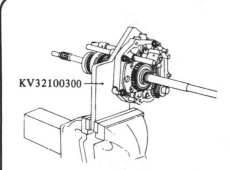

Fig. 6.45 Securing the adaptor plate with special tool KV 32100300 (Sec 9)

KV32100300

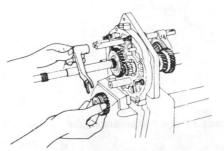

Fig. 6.46 Removing reverse shift fork and idler gear (Sec 9)

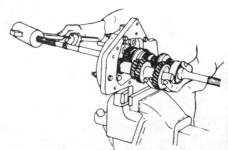

Fig. 6.47 Removing the gear assemblies from the adaptor plate (Sec 9)

8   If a new welch plug is to be fitted, smear its aperture with sealant prior to fitting.

12 Gearbox (F4W60L) – inspection

1   It is assumed that the gearbox has been dismantled for reasons of excessive noise, lack of synchromesh action on certain gears, or for failure to stay in gear. If anything more drastic than this, (total failure, seizure or main casing cracked) it would be better to leave it alone and look for a replacement, either secondhand or an exchange.

2   With the exception of oil seals, clean all components using a suitable solvent, ready for inspection.

3   All oil seals and O-rings should be renewed as a matter of course.

4   Examine all gears for excessively worn, chipped or damaged teeth, and renew any defective gears.

5   Use feeler gauges and check the baulk ring to cone clearance. Apply hand pressure to the baulk ring and insert the feeler gauge. The clearance must be at least 0·020 in (0·5 mm), if not, renew the baulk ring.

6   Check the gear endplay using feeler gauges. The gear endplay is given in the Specifications.

7   All ball race bearings should be checked for chatter and roughness after they have been flushed out. It is advisable to renew these anyway, even though they may not appear too badly worn. Circlips which are all important in locating bearings, gears and hubs, should be checked to ensure that they are undistorted and undamaged. In any case a selection of new circlips of varying thicknesses should be obtained, to compensate for variations in new components fitted, and wear in old ones. The specifications given in the respective reassembly sequences (Section 12) indicate what shims are available.

8   The thrust washers at the ends of the counter gear cluster should be renewed, as they will almost certainly have worn if the gearbox is of any age.

9   Needle roller bearings are usually found in good order, but if in any doubt renew the needle rollers as necessary.

10   Further details regarding the inspection of the synchro hub assemblies is given in Section 10.

11   If renewing the counter shaft needle roller bearing in the gearbox case, refer to Fig. 6.31 and ensure that it projects 0·08 in (2 mm) from the front face of the gearbox case. Never refit a bearing once removed, always renew it.

12   Any wear or damage found in the counter gear assembly will necessitate renewal of the complete assembly. The needle roller bearings and thrust washers can be renewed separately. When renewing a counter shaft, it is normal to renew the corresponding mainshaft gears as matched sets.

13   Examine reverse gears for wear or damage and renew as appropriate.

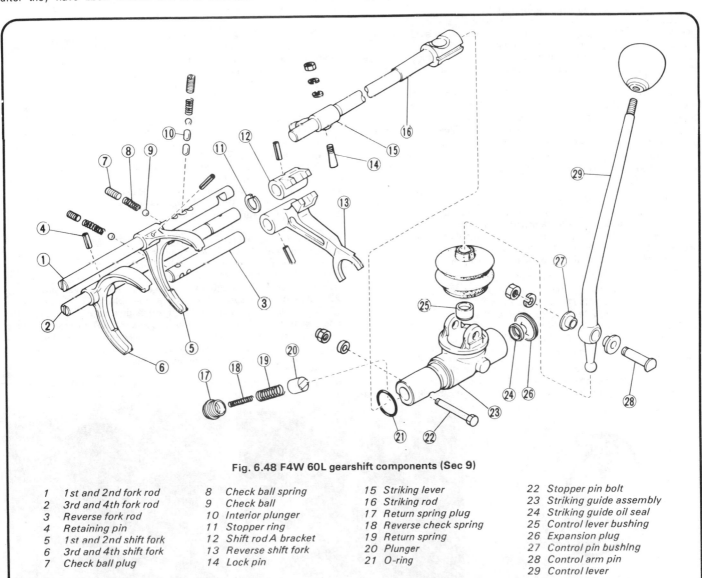

Fig. 6.48 F4W 60L gearshift components (Sec 9)

1	1st and 2nd fork rod	8	Check ball spring
2	3rd and 4th fork rod	9	Check ball
3	Reverse fork rod	10	Interior plunger
4	Retaining pin	11	Stopper ring
5	1st and 2nd shift fork	12	Shift rod A bracket
6	3rd and 4th shift fork	13	Reverse shift fork
7	Check ball plug	14	Lock pin

15	Striking lever	22	Stopper pin bolt
16	Striking rod	23	Striking guide assembly
17	Return spring plug	24	Striking guide oil seal
18	Reverse check spring	25	Control lever bushing
19	Return spring	26	Expansion plug
20	Plunger	27	Control pin bushing
21	O-ring	28	Control arm pin
		29	Control lever

13 Gearbox (F4W60L) – reassembly

1 Clean and lubricate with gear oil all components prior to assembly. Commence by reassembling the synchromesh hubs.

Synchromesh hubs – reassembly

2 Insert a synchro hub into its respective coupling sleeve and then locate the three shift inserts into their grooves.

3 Refit the spread spring with its protrusion located in the groove to retain the insert on the inside of the coupling sleeve. Fit the second spread spring to the opposing side of the hub. When fitting the synchromesh springs they must be located so that their respective opposing positions are offset to each other (Fig. 6.49).

4 Operate the hub and sleeve by hand to ensure that they function correctly.

Mainshaft – reassembly

5 Grease and locate the 2nd gear needle roller bearing onto the mainshaft, then fit the 2nd gear (photo).

6 Locate the baulk ring on to the 2nd gear and fit the 1st/2nd gear synchromesh unit (photo).

7 Slide the 1st gear needle bearing onto the shaft (photo) and then locate the bearing (photo).

8 Fit the baulk ring and 1st gear (photo).

9 Locate the thrust washer against the 1st gear and then fit the ball bearing with the circlip groove in its outer track offset away from the 1st gear as shown (photo) and press into position.

10 Grease the 3rd gear needle roller bearing and locate it on the front end of the mainshaft against the distance piece, then fit the 3rd gear and its baulk ring (photo).

11 Fit the 3rd/4th synchromesh unit (photo), then select a suitable circlip to locate the synchro hub unit (photo). Circlips are available in different thicknesses and a thickness should be selected to ensure minimum clearance between the synchro and the circlip. Circlips are available in the following thicknesses:-

  0·0610 to 0·0630 in (1·55 to 1·60 mm)
  0·0630 to 0·0650 in (1·60 to 1·65 mm)
  0·0650 to 0·0669 in (1·65 to 1·70 mm)

Main drive gear – assembly

12 Press the main drive gear ball bearing in to position on the shaft, with the groove in the outer track towards the front.

13 Locate the spacer against the bearing and then select and fit a circlip of suitable thickness to take up any clearance.

  Circlips are available in the following thicknesses:-

  0·0528 to 0·0551 in (1·34 to 1·40 mm)
  0.0551 to 0.0575 in (1.40 to 1.46 mm)
  0·0575 to 0·0598 in (1·46 to 1·52 mm)
  0·0598 to 0·0622 in (1·52 to 1·58 mm)
  0·0622 to 0·0646 in (1·58 to 1·64 mm)
  0·0646 to 0·0669 in (1·64 to 1·70 mm)
  0·0669 to 0·0693 in (1·70 to 1·76 mm)

When fitted, the circlip must be fully located in its groove,

14 Lubricate the caged roller bearing with a medium grease and locate it in the main drive gear (photo). Locate the baulk ring in the main drive gear then mate the main drive gear to the mainshaft and check for correct engagement.

Counter gear (layshaft) – reassembly

15 Press the ball bearing onto the countershaft.

16 Fit the countershaft thrust washer and gear and locate in the gearbox casing. Now using a clock gauge or special Datsun height gauge, tool No. KV 32100100 as shown in Fig. 6.27, check the end-float of the counter gear. Thrust washers are available in varying thicknesses to provide the necessary endplay which should ⌐ 0·0039 to 0·0079 in (0·10 to 0·20 mm). The available thrust washer thicknesses are:

  0·0866 to 0·0886 in (2·20 to 2·25 mm)
  0·0866 to 0·0906 in (2·25 to 2·30 mm)
  0·0906 to 0·0925 in (2·30 to 2·35 mm)
  0·0925 to 0·0945 in (2·35 to 2·40 mm)
  0·0945 to 0·0965 in (2·40 to 2·45 mm)
  0·0965 to 0·0984 in (2·45 to 2·50 mm)
  0·0984 to 0·1004 in (2·50 to 2·55 mm)
  0·1004 to 0·1024 in (2·55 to 2·60 mm)

17 Having decided on the correct washer thickness required, withdraw the counter gear from the gearbox case.

18 The reverse gear can now be pressed onto the countershaft and when fully positioned fit the circlip into the shaft groove against the gear (photo).

Main components – assembly

19 Align the corresponding gears of the mainshaft, countershaft and input shaft assemblies as shown (photo).

20 Locate them as a unit into the adaptor plate (photo). To do this the adaptor plate will have to be firmly supported whilst the mainshaft and countershaft are pressed and/or tapped carefully into position.

21 Fit the circlip to the mainshaft rear bearing groove as shown (photo) and ensure that the circlip is fully located.

22 Refit the bearing retainer plate and secure with setscrews (photo). Tighten them to the specified torque (see Specifications). Punch mark the screw edges to lock them.

23 Now fit the reverse gear to the mainshaft, followed by the thrust washer and circlip (photo). Ensure that the circlip is fully located in its groove, and the washer, which is dished must have its concave face to the front (Fig. 6.50). When fitting, locate the washer and circlip and tap home using a tube drift as shown.

Selector rods and forks

24 Engage neutral when reassembling the selector rod and forks. Insert the reverse shift rod through the adaptor plate and locate the reverse shift fork and idler gear as shown (photo). Align the roll pin hole in the rod and fork and drive home a new roll pin to secure.

25 Lubricate and insert an interlock plunger (photos).

26 Insert the 3rd and 4th gear shift rod (aligning the notches with the interlock ball holes) and locate the shift fork (photo). Refit the shift rod 'A' bracket on the rear end of the rod if it has been removed and secure both bracket and fork using roll pins.

27 Lubricate and insert an interlock plunger.

28 Insert 1st gear shift rod and fork (photo). Secure the two, using a roll pin (photo), but ensure that the rod interlock plunger detent is aligned correctly.

Fig. 6.49 Synchromesh hub spring positions – ends of opposite springs staggered 120° (Sec 13)

13.5 Locate 2nd gear over the needle roller bearing

13.6 Fit the baulk ring and 1st/2nd synchro hub

13.7a Slide 1st gear bearing bush into position ...

13.7b ... followed by the bearing

13.8 Fit 1st gear and baulk ring

13.9 Locate thrust washer and fit bearing

13.10 Fit roller bearing, 3rd gear and baulk ring

13.11a Fit the synchro unit ...

13.11b ... check the circlip thickness required ...

13.11c ... and fit the circlip

13.14 Insert the needle bearing into the main drive gear

13.18 Reverse gear and circlip in position

13.19 The mainshaft, countershaft and main drive gear assemblies realigned

13.20 Locate the gear assemblies in the adaptor plate

13.21 Fit the mainshaft rear bearing circlip

13.22 The bearing retainer plate in position

13.23 Reverse gear, thrust washer and circlip

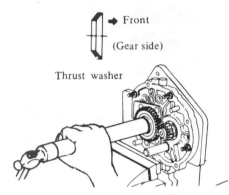
Fig. 6.50 Fitting reverse gear and thrust washer (Sec 13)

13.24 Reverse gear shift rod and idler gear (note rod position)

13.25a Using a magnet to insert an interlock plunger

13.25b Interlock plunger in position

13.26 Insert 3rd/4th selector rod and fork

13.28a Fitting 1st gear selector rod and fork

13.28b Driving home the roll pin

13.32 Correct installation of thrust washer

13.33 Lowering the adaptor plate on to the transmission. Note alignment dowels

29 Refit the respective check balls, springs and plugs. Apply a locking solution to each plug to prevent it from working loose, but make sure the threads are clean when applying. Screw the plugs down so that their heads are flush with the adaptor plate outside edge. Note that the check ball plug for the 1st/2nd fork rod is longer than the others.

30 On completing the assembly of the shift rods and forks check that the shift rods and gears operate in the correct manner. The gears must engage smoothly.

Adaptor plate assembly to gearbox

31 Before fitting the adaptor plate and gears to the gearbox, check that the mating surfaces of both are perfectly clean and then apply an even amount of sealant to them.

32 Position the previously selected thrust washer, as shown in the photo, with the oil groove face towards the roller bearing. Smear the faces of the thrust washer with grease before fitting.

33 The adaptor plate assembly and gearbox housing can now be carefully reassembled (photo). Check that the dowel pin and location hole are in line before lightly tapping home.

34 If they have been removed and not yet refitted, refit the main drive ball bearing and the counter gear needle roller bearing into their respective housings. Press, or drive them in, using a suitable tube drift, but ensure that they are exactly in line before pressing or driving home.

35 Refit the circlip to the mainshaft groove. Check that the mainshaft assembly rotates freely.

36 Insert the circlip to the main bearing housing (photo).

Rear extension – refitting

37 If it has been removed, refit the striking rod through the extension housing and relocate the striking lever. Secure with the lockpin, washers and nut (photo).

38 Check that the mating surfaces of both the rear extension and adaptor plate are clean and smear them with some sealant.

39 Ensure that the fork rods are in neutral and rotate the strike rod in the extension In a clockwise direction. Carefully refit the extension to the gearbox and check that the striker rod lever fully engages with the selector fork brackets. Locate the retaining bolts and washers (don't

forget the wire location clip fitted to the top right-hand bolt), but do not fully tighten just yet.

40 The stopper pin-bolt must now be fitted and the guide unit may have to be manoeuvered to allow the bolt to pass through fully (photo). Smear the bolt with sealant before refitting.

41 Before tightening the bolts retaining the extension, use a long handled screwdriver and pass it through the guide unit, engage with the striking rod and check the gear selection action (photo). If satisfactory, tighten the bolts to the specified torque.

42 Carefully tap, or press the rear extension oil seal into position (photo).

43 Smear the plunger assembly with grease and refit it into the extension housing (photo) with springs and plug. Apply some locking sealant to the threads of the plug, prior to fitting.

44 Refit the speedometer pinion unit and tighten the retaining bolt to the specified torque.

45 Refit the reversing light switch. Apply locking sealant to the switch threads prior to refitting

Front cover – refitting

46 Before refitting the front cover, the adjustment shim thickness must be checked using a vernier/depth gauge as shown in Fig. 6.51. The depth is measured between the front face of the transmission case and the main drive bearing outer race, 'A' in Fig. 6.39 with the shim in place. According to the depth calculation the shim should be selected as given on the table below:

If 'A' equals:	Use shim thickness
0·2382 to 0·2398 in (6·05 to 6·09 mm)	0·0197 in (0·50 mm)
0·2402 to 0·2417 in (6·10 to 6·14 mm)	0·0217 in (0·55 mm)
0·2421 to 0·2437 in (6·15 to 6·19 mm)	0·0236 in (0·60 mm)
0·2441 to 0·2457 in (6·20 to 6·24 mm)	0·0256 in (0·65 mm)
0·2461 to 0·2476 in (6·25 to 6·29 mm)	0·0276 in (0·70 mm)
0·2480 to 0·2496 in (6·30 to 6·34 mm)	0·0295 in (0·75 mm)
0·2500 to 0·2516 in (6·35 to 6·39 mm)	0·0315 in (0·80 mm)

47 Having selected a suitable shim, the front cover can now be

13.36 Fit the circlips on the main bearing

13.37 The striking lever, showing nut and washers

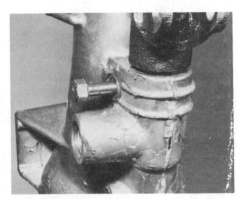

13.40 Fit the stopper pin bolt

13.41 Checking gear engagement

13.42 Fitting a new oil seal in the rear extension

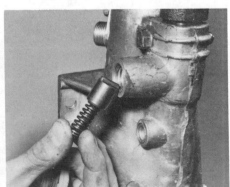

13.43 Fitting the plunger and spring

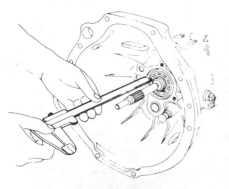

Fig. 6.51 Measuring the dimension for the front cover shim (Sec 13)

13.47 Fit the front cover

13.48 Fit the clutch release mechanism

refitted, together with the new O-ring (photo). Tighten the cover bolts to the specified torque.

48 Refit the clutch release lever and bearing assembly (Chapter 5) to complete the gearbox assembly (photo).

14 Gearbox (FS5W 60L) – dismantling into major assemblies

1 Refer to Section 9 and carry out the steps detailed in paragraphs 1 to 11 inclusive.

2 Turn the striking rod anti-clockwise and then using a standard puller, draw the rear extension off. Do not attempt to remove the rear extension by prising it off the adaptor plate.

3 Hold the mainshaft and then separate the transmission case from the adaptor plate by tapping round the case evenly with a soft headed hammer. Do not attempt to prise the transmission case off the adaptor plate.

4 With the gear assembly removed, make an initial inspection of the components. If it is decided to dismantle the entire assembly, it is desirable to devise a method of supporting the adaptor plate assembly. An adaptor plate mounting can easily be fabricated and bolted to the adaptor plate so that it can be supported in a vice securely for convenience when working. Figure 6.45 shows the special adaptor plate setting tool manufactured by Datsun (Tool No. KV 32100300), which is suitable for the F4W60L or the FS5W60L transmissions.

5 Note which way round the counter gear thrust washer is fitted and

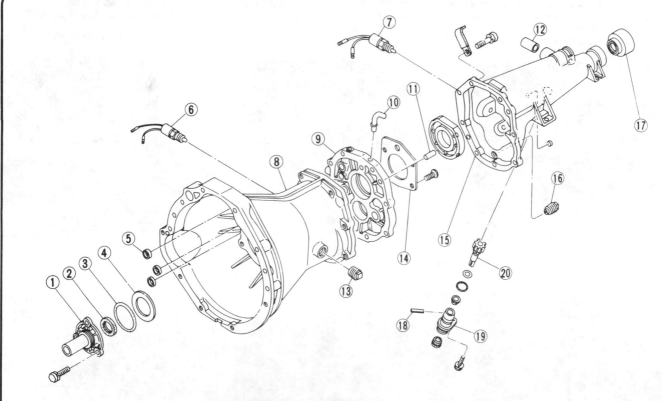

Fig. 6.52 FS5W 60L transmission case components (Sec 14)

1 Front cover	6 Top gear detecting switch	11 Rear extension dowel pin	16 Drain plug
2 Front cover oil seal	7 Reverse lamp switch	12 Return spring bushing	17 Rear extension dust cover
3 Front cover O-ring	8 Transmission case assembly	13 Filler plug	with oil seal
4 Front cover adjusting shim	9 Adapter plater	14 Bearing retainer	18 Retaining pin
5 Welch plug	10 Breather	15 Rear extension assembly	19 Speedometer sleeve
			20 Speedometer pinion

Fig. 6.53 Removing the rear extension (FS5W 60L) (Sec 14)

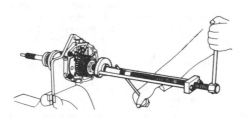

Fig. 6.54 Pulling the mainshaft bearing off (Sec 14)

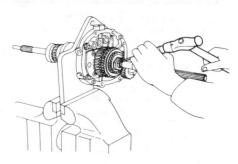

Fig. 6.55 Releasing the staking of the mainshaft nut (Sec 14)

then remove it.

Shift forks and rods – dismantling

6   Use a suitable pin punch to drive the selector fork retaining pins from the respective fork rods.

7   Unscrew and remove the check ball plugs and extract the detent balls and springs. Drive the selector rods out of the adaptor plate by tapping them lightly on the front end. When the rods are removed, take care to recover the two interlock plungers. Having removed the shift rods, remove the shift forks and place them with their respective rods.

Mainshaft and countershaft – removal and dismantling

8   Using suitable circlip pliers, remove the circlip from the rear end of the mainshaft. The bearing must now be pulled off and this can be achieved with a suitable puller.

9   Remove the second circlip from its position on the shaft behind the bearing.

10   Position the 1st and 2nd gears so that they are both in engagement and the transmission is locked, then relieve the staking of the mainshaft nut, unscrew the nut and remove it.

11   Remove the components from the mainshaft and as they are removed, note which way round they are fitted and their sequence of

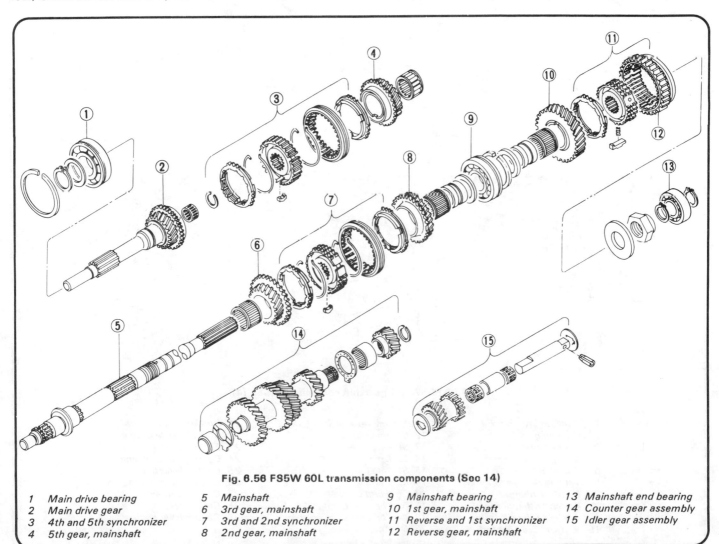

Fig. 6.56 FS5W 60L transmission components (Sec 14)

1 Main drive bearing	5 Mainshaft	9 Mainshaft bearing	13 Mainshaft end bearing
2 Main drive gear	6 3rd gear, mainshaft	10 1st gear, mainshaft	14 Counter gear assembly
3 4th and 5th synchronizer	7 3rd and 2nd synchronizer	11 Reverse and 1st synchronizer	15 Idler gear assembly
4 5th gear, mainshaft	8 2nd gear, mainshaft	12 Reverse gear, mainshaft	

removal so that they can be refitted correctly.

12 Remove the washer from the shaft and then the synchro hub with reverse gear.

13 With one hand remove the 1st gear and its needle bearing and at the same time use the other hand to remove reverse idler gear and its needle bearing.

14 Remove the thrust washer.

15 Use an impact screwdriver to remove the four screws from the bearing retainer and then remove the bearing retainer.

16 Remove the retaining ring from the end of the countergear shaft and then use a puller to draw the gear off the shaft, taking care not to

damage the gear teeth.

17 With a pair of suitable circlip pliers, remove the circlip from the mainshaft rear bearing.

18 Support the mainshaft and the counter gear assembly and gently tap the rear end of the mainshaft with a soft headed hammer to drive out the mainshaft gear assembly.

19 Remove the counter gear assembly, the main drive gear and then the mainshaft assembly in that order, taking care not to drop any of the gears.

20 The gearbox major components have now been removed and can be inspected. If further dismantling is necessary the use of a press is

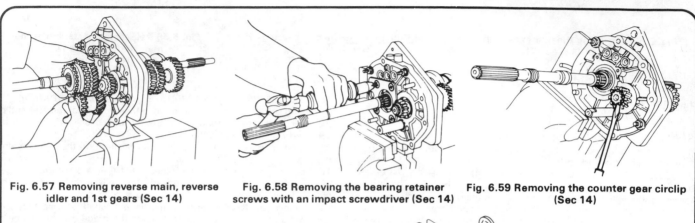

Fig. 6.57 Removing reverse main, reverse idler and 1st gears (Sec 14)

Fig. 6.58 Removing the bearing retainer screws with an impact screwdriver (Sec 14)

Fig. 6.59 Removing the counter gear circlip (Sec 14)

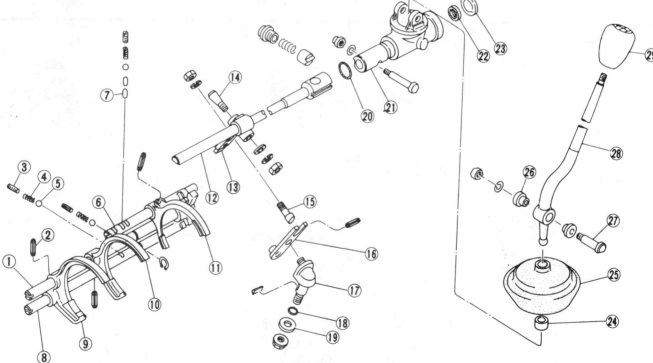

Fig. 6.60 FS5W 60L gearshift components (Sec 14)

1 2nd and 3rd fork rod	11 1st and reverse shift fork	21 Striking guide
2 Retaining pin	12 Striking rod	22 Striking guide oil seal
3 Check ball plug	13 Striking lever	23 Expansion plug
4 Check ball spring	14 Lock pin	24 Control lever bushing
5 Check ball	15 Striking pin	25 Control lever boot
6 1st and reverse fork rod	16 Shift arm	26 Control pin bushing
7 Interlock plunger	17 Shift arm bracket	27 Control arm pin
8 4th and 5th fork rod	18 Arm bracket O-ring	28 Control lever
9 4th and 5th shift fork	19 Arm bracket plain washer	29 Control lever knob
10 2nd and 3rd shift fork	20 O-ring	

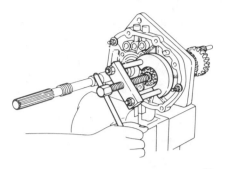

Fig. 6.61 Removing 1st gear counter gear (Sec 14)

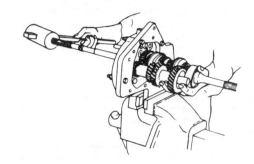

Fig. 6.62 Removing the gear assemblies from the adaptor plate (Sec 14)

required and a precision measuring instrument such as a micrometer is also necessary.

Mainshaft – dismantling

21 Remove the circlip from the front end of the mainshaft.
22 Remove the 4th and 5th gear synchronizer assembly and its baulk rings.

23 Pull the 5th gear and its needle bearing off the front of the shaft.
24 Press the mainshaft bearing off the shaft (Fig. 6.19), holding the shaft to prevent it from falling when the bearing is released.
25 Remove the thrust washer, 2nd gear, its needle bearing and sleeve.
26 Remove the 2nd and 3rd gear synchronizer and baulk rings.
27 Remove the 3rd gear and its needle bearing.

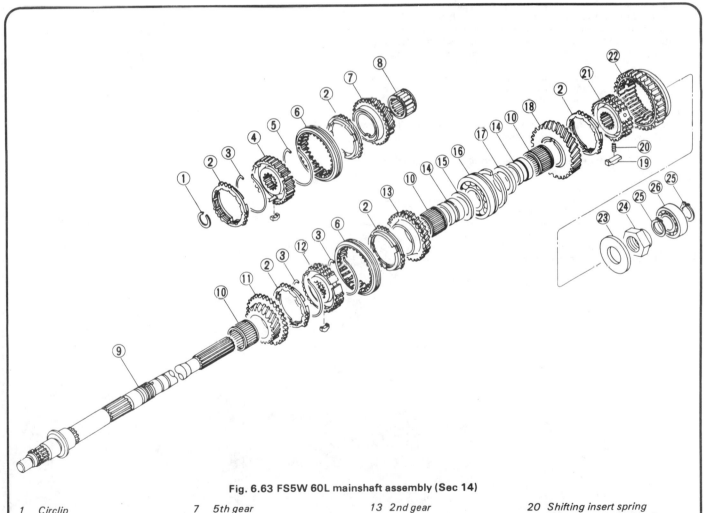

Fig. 6.63 FS5W 60L mainshaft assembly (Sec 14)

1	Circlip	7	5th gear	13	2nd gear
2	Baulk ring	8	5th gear bearing	14	1st gear bushing
3	Spread ring	9	Mainshaft	15	Thrust washer
4	Synchronizer 4th and 5th hub	10	Needle bearing	16	Mainshaft bearing
5	Shifting insert	11	3rd gear	17	Washer
6	Coupling sleeve	12	Synchronizer 2nd and 3rd hub	18	1st gear
				19	Shifting insert

20	Shifting insert spring
21	Reverse mainshaft hub
22	Reverse gear
23	Shifting insert retainer
24	Mainshaft nut
25	Mainshaft end bearing circlip
26	Mainshaft end bearing

Main drive gear (input shaft) – dismantling
28 Using suitable circlip pliers, remove the circlip and withdraw the spacer. A bearing puller, or if available Datsun special tool No. ST 22730000 and a press are needed to remove the bearing from the shaft. Take care not to drop the shaft and gear.

15 Synchromesh hubs (FS5W60L) – dismantling and inspection

1   Refer to Section 10 for 2nd/3rd and 4th/5th synchro hubs.
2   When dismantling the 1st/reverse synchro hub, note the position of the shift inserts; the hooked end must face 1st gear. Mark the reverse gear/sleeve in relation to the hub, and after dismantling, prise the insert retainer from the sleeve.

16 Rear extension (FS5W60L) – dismantling, inspection and assembly

1   Remove the lock pin nut and the lock pin from the striking lever (Fig. 6.65) and then remove the striking lever.
2   Remove the oil seal and dust cover from the rear end of the rear extension, then remove the striking rod and striking guide. Do not remove the rear extension bushing from the rear extension. Check all components for wear and renew them as necessary.
3   To reassemble the rear extension, use a drift tube and drive, or press the new oil seal into position in the rear cover. The outer rim of the seal and the seal lip must be smeared with gear oil before fitting. Fill the cavity between the seal lips with a medium grade grease as shown in Fig. 6.30.
4   Smear the O-ring and plunger grooves in the striker rod with medium grade grease and fit the O-ring.
5   Fit the striking rod and striking rod guide through the hole in the rear extension.
6   Fit the striking lever on the front end of the striking rod. Fit the lock pin, plain washer, spring washer and nut. Tighten the nut to the specified torque.
7   Before fitting the dust cover in the end of the striking rod guide, coat the edges of the cover with sealant.

17 Gearbox components (FS5W60L) – inspection

1   In general the gearbox inspection procedures should follow those details given in Section 12, paragraphs 1 to 5.
2   If the adaptor plate bearing is to be removed, unscrew the retainer

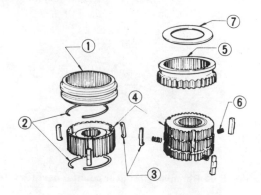

Fig. 6.64 Synchronizer components (FS5W 60L) (Sec 15)

1	Coupling sleeve	5	Reverse gear
2	Spread spring	6	Spread spring
3	Shifting insert	7	Shifting insert retainer
4	Synchro hub		

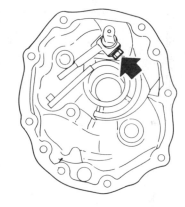

Fig. 6.65 Removing the lock pin nut (Sec 16)

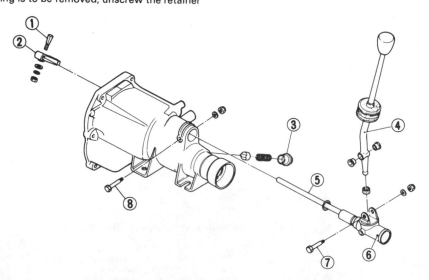

Fig. 6.66 Gear shift mechanism (FS5W 60L) (Sec 16)

1	Lock pin	3	Return spring plug	5	Striking rod	7	Control lever pin
2	Striking lever	4	Control lever	6	Striking rod guide	8	Stopper pin bolt

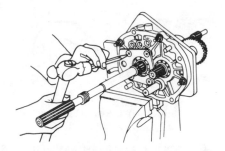

Fig. 6.67 Staking the bearing retainer screws (Sec 17)

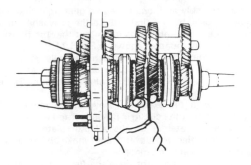

Fig. 6.68 Measuring gear endplay (Sec 17)

plate screws. These will probably be tight and will require the use of a good size cross-head screwdriver and possibly a mole grip wrench around its shaft to give assistance. The bearing can be driven or pressed out. Reassemble in the reverse order but torque tighten the retaining screws to 5.8 to 9.4 lbf ft (0.8 to 1.3 kgf m). Stake each screw edge as shown using a punch (Fig. 6.67) to prevent them working loose.

3   Measure the endplay of the gears as shown in Fig. 6.68 using feeler gauges. The normal gear endplay is as given in the Specifications.

4   Check all bearings for wear or signs of damage after they have been cleaned. Renew any suspect or defective parts.

5   Check the condition of the circlips but don't get them mixed up as they are of selected thicknesses. The circlips should generally be renewed as a matter of practice and if other corresponding components are being renewed then it will be advisable to get an assortment of thicknesses to compensate for any variation in fitting tolerances (sizes are given in the assembly instructions).

6   Thrust washers are almost certainly fairly worn if the gearbox is of any age, and should therefore be renewed as a matter of course.

7   Any wear or damage of the counter gear assembly will necessitate the renewal of the complete assembly. When renewing the countershaft assembly it is advisable to also renew the corresponding mainshaft gears so that they wear in equally.

8   Examine the reverse gears and renew if badly worn or damaged.

18 Gearbox (FS5W60L) – reassembly

1   Refer to Section 13 paragraphs 1 to 4 inclusive for 2nd/3rd and 4th/5th synchro hubs. For the 1st/reverse synchro hub, locate the three coil springs and shift inserts into the hub, then slide the reverse gear/sleeve onto the hub and over the inserts. Press the retainer into the sleeve. Make sure that the inserts are located with their hooked ends towards the 1st gear end of the hub.

Mainshaft assembly

2   Lubricate 3rd gear needle roller bearing and fit it on the mainshaft, then fit the 3rd gear and its baulk ring.

3   Fit the 2nd and 3rd gear synchroniser assembly, taking care that it is the correct way round (Fig. 6.69) and then fit the 2nd gear baulk ring.

4   Lubricate the 2nd gear bushing and second gear needle roller bearing. Slide the bushing on to the shaft and fit the needle roller bearing on the bushing.

5   Fit the 2nd gear on its bearing and then fit the thrust washer.

6   Using a tube drive the mainshaft bearing on to the mainshaft.

7   Lubricate the 5th gear needle roller bearing and fit it on the front end of the mainshaft. Fit the 5th gear and its baulk ring.

8   Fit the 4th and 5th gear synchroniser assembly and then fit a new circlip so that there will be minimum clearance between the end face of the hub and the ring. Available circlip thicknesses are:-

0.0610 to 0.0630 in (1.55 to 1.60 mm)
0.0630 to 0.0650 in (1.60 to 1.65 mm)
0.0650 to 0.0669 in (1.65 to 1.70 mm)

9   Fit the circlip, making sure that it seats correctly in the groove.

Main drive gear – assembly

10   Refer to Section 13, paragraphs 12 to 14 inclusive.

Counter gear (layshaft) – reassembly

11   Fit a counter gear thrust washer in the transmission case and then with the transmission case resting on the bellhousing end, insert the counter gear.

12   Place a straight edge across the top face of the transmission case and use feeler gauges to measure the gap between the straight edge and the face of the gear (Fig. 6.70). Move the straight edge to at least one other position across the gear and again measure the clearance.

13   Select a thrust washer to ensure that the endplay of the counter gear will be the specified amount. Available thicknesses are:-

0.0866 to 0.0886 in (2.20 to 2.25 mm)
0.0886 to 0.0906 in (2.25 to 2.30 mm)
0.0906 to 0.0925 in (2.30 to 2.35 mm)
0.0925 to 0.0945 in (2.35 to 2.40 mm)
0.0945 to 0.0965 in (2.40 to 2.45 mm)
0.0965 to 0.0984 in (2.45 to 2.50 mm)
0.0984 to 0.1004 in (2.50 to 2.55 mm)
0.1004 to 0.1024 in (2.55 to 2.60 mm)

14   Remove the counter gear and the thrust washer from the transmission case and place the counter gear, the removed thrust washer and the selected thrust washer together for later reassembly.

Gear assemblies to adaptor plate

15   With the adaptor plate mounted and supported firmly, fit the mainshaft assembly as follows. First check that the main drive gear is located correctly with the mainshaft.

16   Mesh the gears of the mainshaft assembly with those of the

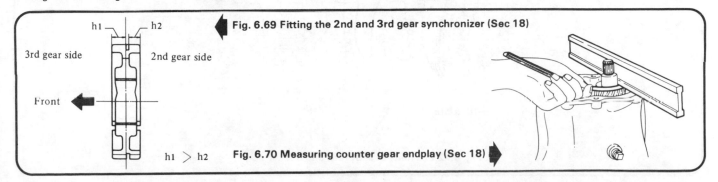

Fig. 6.69 Fitting the 2nd and 3rd gear synchronizer (Sec 18)

h1   h2
3rd gear side   2nd gear side
Front
h1 > h2

Fig. 6.70 Measuring counter gear endplay (Sec 18)

counter gear assembly and insert the two gear trains into the adaptor plate simultaneously, having first fitted a thrust washer on to the end of the counter gear assembly. It is important that the thrust washer is fitted the correct way round as shown in Fig. 6.71.

17 While still holding the gears in mesh, carefully tap the shaft ends with a soft headed hammer until the countershaft assembly is fully home and the circlip groove of the mainshaft bearing is clear of the rear face of the adaptor plate.

18 Fit the circlip in the external groove of the main bearing outer track, making sure that the circlip is properly fitted to the groove.

19 Fit the bearing retainer on the adaptor plate, tighten the four screws to the specified torque and then stake the screws by centre punching their heads at two points.

20 Use a drift tube to press or drive the first counter gear on to the splines of the counter gear shaft and retain the gear in place by fitting a circlip into the groove. The circlip should be selected to give minimum clearance between the face of the counter gear and the circlip. Available thicknesses of circlip are:-

0.0492 to 0.0531 in (1.25 to 1.35 mm)
0.0531 to 0.0571 in (1.35 to 1.45 mm)

21 Fit the thrust washer on the mainshaft rear end. Fit the thrust washer to the idler shaft rear.

22 Lubricate the needle roller bearings of the idler gear and of 1st gear. Fit to their respective shafts simultaneously, the synchro hub with reverse gear, 1st gear with its needle roller bearing and bushing, the idler gear and its needle roller bearing.

23 Screw the mainshaft nut on to the shaft finger tight.

24 Engage 1st and 2nd gears simultaneously to lock the transmission and then tighten the mainshaft nut to the specified torque. Stake the nut by punching the collar of the nut in to the groove in the mainshaft.

25 Fit a 0.039 in (1.0 mm) thick circlip to the groove in the mainshaft and then, using a tubular drift, drive on the mainshaft bearing.

26 Fit a thick circlip to the groove in the mainshaft to secure the bearing with a minimum of endplay. Available circlip thicknesses are:

0.039 in (1.0 mm)
0.047 in (1.2 mm)

Selector forks and rods – reassembly

27 Fit the 1st and reverse shift fork into the groove in its synchroniser unit and then thread its rod through the fork and through the adaptor plate. Position the rod in its neutral position, insert an interlock plunger into the adaptor plate and align the groove in the shift rod with the end of the interlock plunger.

28 Thread the 2nd and 3rd shift rod through the adaptor plate and fit the 2nd and 3rd and the 4th and 5th gear shift forks into the grooves in their respective synchroniser units.

29 With the 2nd and 3rd gear shift rod set to its neutral position insert an interlock plunger into the adaptor plate.

30 Thread the 4th and 5th gear shift rod through the adaptor plate and its shift fork.

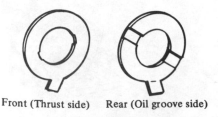

Front (Thrust side)   Rear (Oil groove side)

Fig. 6.71 Counter gear thrust washer (Sec 18)

31 With the holes of the selector forks and shift rods in exact alignment, locate and drive new roll pins into position, so that the ends of the pins are flush with the outside surface of the forks.

32 Fit the check balls and the check ball springs, ensuring that the ball is aligned with the centre notch in each of the fork rods.

33 Apply locking compound to the threads of the ball plugs and screw the plugs in flush. Note that the plug for the 1st and reverse fork rod is longer than the plugs for the other two rods.

34 To ensure that the interlock plungers have been fitted correctly, slide the 2nd and 3rd fork rod to engage either 2nd, or 3rd gear. With the gear engaged, slide the other two shift rods to ensure that no other gear can be engaged at the same time.

35 Lubricate all sliding surfaces with gear oil and then check that all three shift rods move smoothly and that the gears engage easily and correctly.

19 Gearbox (FS5W60L) – major components assembly

1   Remove the adaptor plate from the mounting fixture which was used to support it during assembly.

2   Clean the mating surfaces of the adaptor plate and the transmission case and apply sealant to them.

3   Stand the bellhousing end of the transmission case on blocks of wood at least 0.79 in (20 mm) thick so that the case is level.

4   Apply grease to the two faces of the counter gear thrust washer which was selected (Section 17, paragraph 13) and fit the washer, taking care to fit it the correct way round (Fig. 6.73).

5   Lower the adaptor plate assembly on to the transmission case. Align the dowels and the dowel holes and then tap the adaptor plate lightly, but evenly with a soft-headed hammer until the plate is bearing against its mating face on the transmission case and the main drive bearing and the front needle bearing are positioned correctly.

6   Make certain that the mainshaft rotates freely and then fit the circlip in the groove in the outer track of the main drive bearing, ensuring that the circlip is fitted into the groove properly.

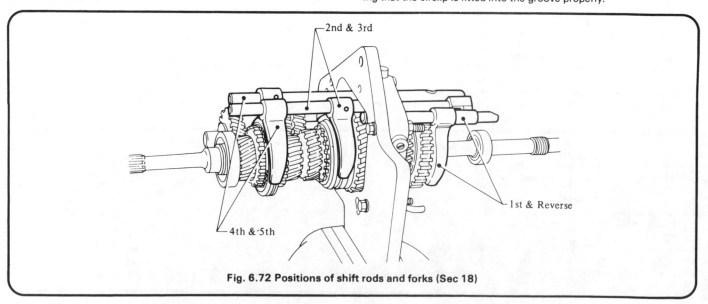

Fig. 6.72 Positions of shift rods and forks (Sec 18)

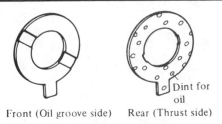

Front (Oil groove side)   Rear (Thrust side)

Fig. 6.73 Counter gear thrust washer (Sec 19)

Rear extension – refitting

7   Clean the mating surfaces of the adaptor plate and the rear extension and apply sealant to them.

8   Select 5th gear, set the striking rod to neutral and turn it clockwise. Set the striking lever and shift arm as shown in Fig. 6.74.

9   With the components in these positions, align the shift arm pin with the groove in the fork rod and lower the rear extension on to the adaptor plate. While doing this, take care that the shift arm does not come out of the striking lever.

10 Fit the through bolts and washers and tighten the bolts evenly until the recommended torque is achieved.

11 Smear grease on to the rear extension plunger and insert it in its hole, then insert its spring.

12 Apply locking compound to the threads of the return spring plug and screw the plug in to the recommended torque.

13 Fit the speedometer pinion assembly. Screw in its securing bolt on

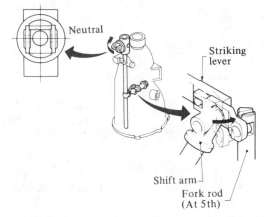

Fig. 6.74 Fitting the rear extension assembly (Sec 19)

the locking plate, tightening it to the specified torque.

14 Apply locking compound to the threads of the reversing light switch and the top gear selecting switch, if the gearbox has one. Screw the switches in until they are firmly fitted.

Front cover

15 The installation of the front cover is identical with that on the F4W60L gearbox, described in Section 13, paragraphs 46 to 48.

20 Fault diagnosis – manual gearbox

Symptom	Reason/s
Weak or inefficient synchromesh	Synchro cones worn or damaged Baulk rings worn Defective synchro unit
Jumps out of gear	Worn interlock plunger Worn detent ball Weak or broken detent spring Worn shift fork or synchro sleeve groove Worn gear
Excessive noise	Incorrect oil grade Oil level too low Worn gear teeth Worn mainshaft bearings Worn thrust washers Worn input or mainshaft splines
Difficult gear changing or selection	Incorrect clutch free movement

Part B AUTOMATIC TRANSMISSION

21 General description

The automatic transmission unit used is the JATCO 3N71B.

The unit provides three forward ratios and one reverse. Changing of the forward gear ratios is completely automatic in relation to the vehicle speed and engine torque input and is dependent upon the vacuum pressure in the manifold and the vehicle road speed to actuate the gear change mechanism at the precise time.

The transmission has six selector positions:

P – parking position which locks the output shaft to the interior wall of the transmission housing. This is a safety device for use when the vehicle is parked on an incline. The engine may be started with 'P' selected and this position should always be selected when adjusting the engine while it is running. Never attempt to select 'P' when the vehicle is in motion.

R – reverse gear.

N – neutral. Select this position to start the engine or when idling in traffic for long periods.

D – drive, for all motoring conditions.

2 – locks the transmission in second gear for wet road conditions or steep hill climbing or descents. The engine can be over revved in this position. The maximum speed in this gear should not exceed 66 mph (105 kph) or for USA models 70 mph (110 kph). Never change down into this gear at speeds above those given.

1 – The selection of this ratio above road speeds of approximately 37 mph (60 kph) or 40 mph (66 kph) for USA models will engage 2nd gear but as the speed drops below these speeds the transmission will engage first gear. This position gives maximum retardation on steep gradients.

Due to the complexity of the automatic transmission unit, any internal adjustment or servicing should be left to a Datsun agent or

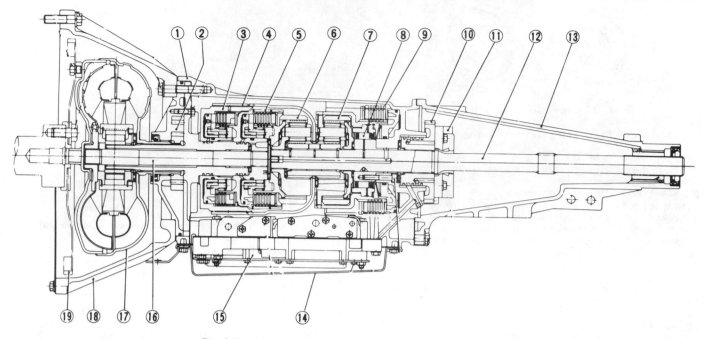

Fig. 6.75 Automatic transmission – sectional view (Sec 21)

1	Transmission case	6	Front planetary gear	11 Governor	16 Input shaft

1   Transmission case
2   Oil pump
3   Front clutch
4   Band brake
5   Rear clutch

6   Front planetary gear
7   Rear planetary gear
8   One-way clutch
9   Low and reserve brake
10 Oil distributor

11 Governor
12 Output shaft
13 Rear extension
14 Oil sump
15 Control valve

16 Input shaft
17 Torque converter
18 Converter housing
19 Drive plate

automatic transmission specialist. The information given in this Chapter is therefore confined to those operations which are considered within the scope of the home mechanic. An automatic transmission should give many tens of thousands of miles service provided normal maintenance and adjustment is carried out. When the unit finally requires major overhaul, consideration should be given to exchanging the old transmission for a factory reconditioned one, the removal and refitting being well within the capabilities of the home mechanic as described later in this Chapter. The hydraulic fluid does not require periodic draining or refilling, but the fluid level must be regularly checked (see next Section).

Periodically clean the outside of the transmission housing as the accumulation of dirt and oil is liable to cause overheating of the unit under extreme conditions.

Adjust the engine idling speed as specified, (see Chapter 3 for further details).

22 Fluid level – checking

1   Run the vehicle on the road until the normal operating temperature is attained.
2   With the engine idling, select each gear position in turn and then place the speed selector lever in 'P'.
3   Allow the engine to continue to idle and after a period of two minutes, withdraw the dipstick, wipe it on a piece of clean lint-free cloth; re-insert it, quickly withdrawing it and reading off the oil level.
4   Top-up as necessary but do not overfill.
5   Switch off the engine.
6   The need for frequent topping-up indicates a leak either in the transmission unit itself, or from the fluid cooler or connecting pipes.

23 Automatic transmission – removal and refitting

1   Removal of the engine and automatic transmission as a combined unit is described in Chapter 1 of this manual. Where it is decided to remove the transmission leaving the engine in position in the vehicle, proceed as follows.

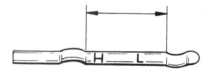

Fig. 6.76 Transmission fluid level. Maintain within the range indicated (Sec 22)

2   Disconnect the battery earth lead.
3   Jack the vehicle to an adequate working height and support on stands or blocks. Alternatively position the vehicle over a pit.
4   Disconnect the exhaust downpipe from the manifold.
5   Disconnect the leads from the starter inhibitor switch.
6   Disconnect the wire from the downshift solenoid.
7   Disconnect the vacuum pipe from the vacuum capsule which is located just forward of the downshift solenoid.
8   Separate the selector lever from the selector linkage.
9   Disconnect the speedometer drive cable from the rear extension housing.
10 Disconnect the fluid filler tubes. Plug the opening.
11 Disconnect the fluid cooler tubes from the transmission casing and plug the openings.
12 Remove the propeller shaft; for further information see Chapter 7.
13 Support the engine sump with a jack; use a block of wood to prevent damage to the surface of the sump.
14 Remove the rubber plug from the lower part of the engine rear plate. Mark the torque converter housing and driveplate in relation to each other for exact alignment.
15 Unscrew and remove the four bolts which secure the torque converter to the driveplate. Access to each of these bolts, in turn is obtained by rotating the engine slowly, using a wrench on the crankshaft pulley bolt.
16 Unbolt and withdraw the starter motor.
17 Support the transmission with a jack (preferably a trolley type).
18 Detach the rear transmission mounting from the transmission housing and the vehicle body.
19 Unscrew and remove the transmission to engine securing bolts.
20 Lower the two jacks sufficiently to allow the transmission unit to

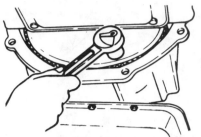

Fig. 6.77 Removing the drive plate to converter bolts (Sec 23)

Fig. 6.78 Torque converter alignment notch (Sec 23)

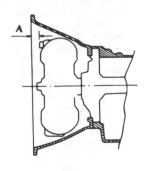

Fig. 6.79 Torque converter fitted dimension measured at 'A' (Sec 23)

be withdrawn from below and to the rear of the vehicle. The help of an assistant will probably be required due to the weight of the unit. Do not forget that the transmission is still filled with fluid. If necessary, this can be drained by removing the sump or standing the unit on end to allow the fluid to drain from the extension housing.

21 Refitting is basically the reverse of the removal procedure but should the torque converter have been separated from the main assembly, ensure that the notch on the converter is correctly aligned with the corresponding one on the oil pump. To check that the torque converter has been correctly fitted, the dimension 'A' should exceed 0.846 in (21.5 mm). See Fig. 6.79.

22 Tighten all bolts to the specified torque settings. Refill the unit with the correct grade and quantity of fluid lf any was spilled or drained.

23 Check the operation of the inhibitor switch and the selector linkage and adjust, if necessary, as described later in this Chapter.

24 Selector linkage – removal and refitting

1 Remove the two small screws which secure the knob to the speed selector lever. Remove the knob.

2 Remove the console from the transmission tunnel.

3 Unbolt the selector lever bracket and the lever on the side of the transmission, and withdraw the complete selector linkage.

4 Refitting is the reverse of the removal procedure but adjust the linkage as described in the following Section before fitting the control knob.

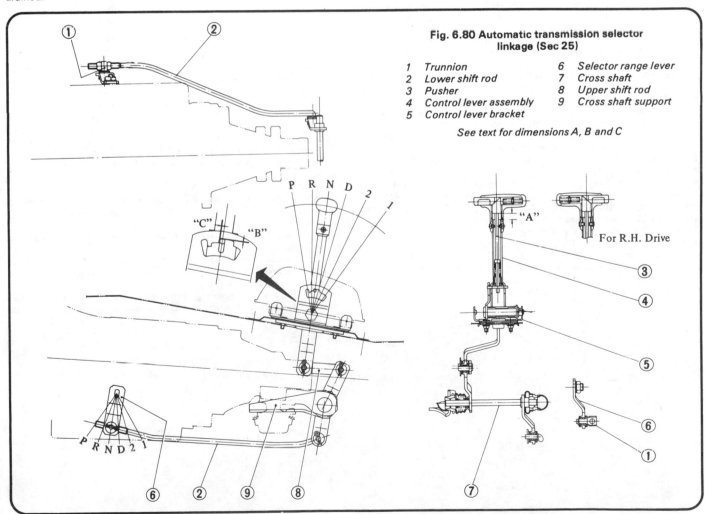

Fig. 6.80 Automatic transmission selector linkage (Sec 25)

1	Trunnion	6	Selector range lever
2	Lower shift rod	7	Cross shaft
3	Pusher	8	Upper shift rod
4	Control lever assembly	9	Cross shaft support
5	Control lever bracket		

See text for dimensions A, B and C

For R.H. Drive

25 Selector linkage – adjustment

1   Set dimension 'A' (Fig. 6.80) with the control knob removed, then fit the control knob again. Dimension 'A' = 0.43 to 0.47 in (11 to 12 mm).

2   Check dimension 'B' and adjust, if necessary, by rotating the pusher. Dimension 'B' = 0.004 to 0.020 in (0.1 to 0.5 mm).

3   Loosen the trunnion nuts. Set the control lever selector lever at 'N' and obtain clearance 'C' by adjustment of the nuts as necessary. Dimension 'C' = 0.04 in (1 mm).

4   Ensure that the linkage operates satisfactorily throughout the selection range.

26 Kick-down switch and downshift solenoid – checking

1   If the kick-down facility fails to operate or operates at an incorrect change point, first check the security of the switch on the accelerator pedal arm and the wiring between the switch and the solenoid.

2   Turn the ignition key so that the ignition and oil pressure lamps illuminate but without operating the starter motor. Depress the accelerator pedal fully and as the switch actuates, a distinct click should be heard from the solenoid. Where this is absent a new switch or solenoid must be installed. **Note:** *when the solenoid is removed fluid will drain out. This can be re-used if collected in a clean container. Do not forget to refill with fluid on completion.*

27 Starter inhibitor switch – testing and adjustment

1   Check that the starter motor operates only in 'N' and 'P' and the reversing lamps illuminate only with the selector lever in 'R'.

2   Any deviation from this arrangement should be rectified by adjustment, first having checked the correct setting of the selector linkage (Fig. 6.80).

3   Refer to Fig. 6.82 and detach the range selector lever (9) from the selector rod which connects it to the hand control. Move the range selector lever to the 'N' position, (slot in shaft vertical).

4   Connect an ohmmeter (or a test lamp) to the black and yellow wires of the inhibitor switch. With the ignition switch ON, the meter should indicate continuity of circuit when the range selector lever is within 3 degrees either side of the 'N' and 'P' positions.

5   Repeat the test with the meter connected to the red and black wires and the range lever in 'R'.

6   Where the switch requires adjusting to provide the correct range of switching in the three selector positions, move the range level to 'N' and then remove the retaining nut (6), the two inhibitor switch securing bolts and the screw located below the switch.

7   Align the hole, from which the screw was removed, with the pinhole in the manual shaft (2). A thin rod or piece of wire may be used to do this. Holding this alignment, fit the inhibitor switch securing bolts and tighten them. Remove the alignment rod and fit the screw.

8   Refit the remaining switch components and test for correct operation as previously described. If the test procedure does not prove satisfactory, renew the switch.

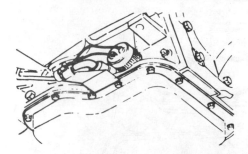

Fig. 6.81 Downshift solenoid location (Sec 26)

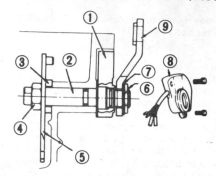

Fig. 6.82 Starter inhibitor switch (Sec 27)

1	*Inhibitor switch*	*6*	*Nut*
2	*Manual shaft*	*7*	*Washer*
3	*Washer*	*8*	*Inhibitor switch*
4	*Nut*	*9*	*Range select lever*
5	*Manual plate*		

28 Rear extension oil seal – renewal

1   After a considerable mileage, leakage may occur from the seal which surrounds the shaft at the rear end of the automatic transmission extension housing. This leakage will be evident from the state of the underbody and from the reduction in the level of the hydraulic fluid.

2   Remove the propeller shaft as described in Chapter 7.

3   Taking care not to damage the splined output shaft and the alloy housing, pry the old oil seal from its location. Drive in the new one using a tubular drift.

4   Should the seal be very tight in its recess, support the transmission on a jack and remove the rear mounting. Unbolt the rear extension housing from the transmission casing.

5   Pull the extension housing straight off over the output shaft and governor assembly.

6   Using a suitable drift applied from the interior of the rear extension housing, remove the old oil seal. At the same time check the bush and renew it if it is scored, or worn.

7   Refitting is the reverse of the removal procedure, but always use a new gasket between the rear extension and main housing.

29 Fault diagnosis – automatic transmission

In addition to the information given in this Chapter, reference should be made to Chapter 3 for the servicing and maintenance of the emission control equipment (where applicable) used on models equipped with automatic transmission

Symptom	Reason/s
Engine will not start in 'N' or 'P'	Faulty starter or ignition circuit Incorrect linkage adjustment Incorrectly installed inhibitor switch
Engine starts in selector positions other than 'N' or 'P'	Incorrect linkage adjustment Incorrectly installed inhibitor switch
Severe bump when selecting 'D' or 'R' and excessive creep when idling	Idling speed too high Vacuum circuit leaking
Poor acceleration and low maximum speed	Incorrect oil level Incorrect linkage adjustment

The most likely causes of faulty operation are incorrect oil level and linkage adjustment. Any other faults or mal-operation of the automatic transmission unit must be due to internal faults and should be rectified by your Datsun dealer. An indication of a major internal fault may be gained from the colour of the oil which under normal conditions should be transparent red. If it becomes discoloured, or black, then burned clutch or brake bands must be suspected

Chapter 7 Propeller shaft

For modifications, and information applicable to later models, see Supplement at end of manual

Contents

Specifications

Type . . . . Single piece, tubular steel with two universal joints and splined sliding coupling

Length
Manual transmission . . . . 46.34 in (1177 mm)
Automatic transmission . . . . 41.14 in (1045 mm)

Outside diameter . . . . 2.713 in (68.9 mm)

Torque wrench setting

	lbf ft	kgf m
Shaft flange bolts	17 to 24	2.4 to 3.3

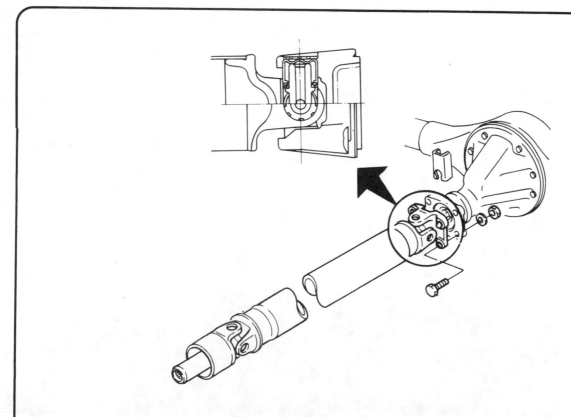

Fig. 7.1 Propeller shaft assembly (Sec 1)

1 General description

The propeller shaft is of one piece, tubular steel construction having a universal joint at each end to allow for axial misalignment between the gearbox output shaft and the rear axle.

At the front end of the shaft is a sliding sleeve which mates with the splined output shaft of the transmission and accommodates the changes in shaft length required by the vertical movement of the rear axle.

There is a difference in the length and the design of the sliding sleeve on the shafts used with the manual gearbox and the automatic transmission and the assemblies are not interchangeable.

The needle bearing cups of the universal joints are staked in position and the shaft cannot be dismantled. If there is play in the bearings, or if the shaft becomes damaged, a new shaft must be fitted.

2 Universal joints – testing for wear

1   Wear in the needle roller bearings is characterised by a clonking noise when taking up the drive. There may also be vibration of the transmission and metallic squeaking and grating.
2   The condition of the needle roller bearings can be checked without removing the shaft. For the front joint, grip the front half coupling to stop it from rotating and grip the shaft with the other hand and see if it can be moved. If one part can be moved perceptibly relative to the other, considerable bearing wear is indicated.
3   To check the rear bearing, grip the rear axle flange and hold it stationary while gripping the propeller shaft and testing it for movement.
4   If wear is evident, a complete propeller shaft must be fitted as a replacement.

3 Propeller shaft – removal and refitting

1   Either position the car over a pit and apply the brakes, or chock the front wheels, jack-up the rear of the vehicle and support it securely.
2   Mark the two edges of the rear coupling parts so that they can be refitted in the same relative position. Failure to do this may result in propeller shaft vibration.
3   Unscrew and remove the four bolts which secure the flanges together and push the propeller shaft forward slightly to separate the flanges.
4   Place a drip tray beneath the rear end of the transmission to catch any oil which runs out and then carefully pull the propeller shaft sleeve yoke out from the end of the transmission, ensuring that the oil seal is

3.4 Propeller shaft sleeve yoke

not damaged (photo).
5   Remove the shaft assembly and then plug the end of the transmission to prevent further loss of oil.
6   Refitting is the reverse of removal, but the flanges of the axle joint must be positioned so that the mating marks on their edges are aligned and the bolts must be fitted with the heads of the bolts toward the front of the car.

4 Propeller shaft – vibration

1   If propeller shaft vibration is experienced, first clean the shaft to remove any dirt or undersealing material which may be adhering to it.
2   Road test the vehicle to check whether vibration is still present.
3   If vibration is noted during the road test, put mating marks on the two parts of the differential flange joint and remove the four bolts which secure the two flange parts.
4   Rotate one part of the flange joint 180°, refit the bolts and tighten them.
5   Again road test the car to check for vibration and if it is still evident, fit a replacement propeller shaft assembly.

5 Fault diagnosis – propeller shaft

Symptom	Reason(s)
Vibration	Wear in sliding sleeve splines Worn universal joint bearings Propeller shaft unbalanced Propeller shaft bent
Knock or clonk when taking up drive	Worn universal joint bearings Loose bolts in flange couplings Differential fault

Chapter 8 Rear axle and rear suspension

For modifications, and information applicable to later models, see Supplement at end of manual

Contents

Specifications

Rear axle

Type .... Rigid, semi-floating with hypoid gears

Construction .... Pressed steel casing, cast iron differential carrier

Ratio .... 3.889:1 or 3.700:1 for North American manual gearbox models

Oil capacity .... $1\frac{5}{8}$ Imp pints; $1\frac{7}{8}$ US pints; 0.9 litres

Rear suspension

Type .... Coil spring and link with double acting shock absorbers

Coil springs
Wire diameter:
    Coupe .... 0.402 in (10.2 mm)
    Saloon and Estate .... 0.413 in (10.5 mm)
Coil diameter .... 3.54 in (90 mm)
Free length:
    Saloon .... 14.13 in (359 mm)
    Coupe .... 14.53 in (369 mm)
    Estate .... 14.41 in (366 mm)
Effective turns 8.75
Spring rate:
    Saloon and Coupe .... 95.8 lbf/in (17.1 kgf/cm)
    Estate .... 107.0 lbf/in (19.1 kgf/cm)
Identification colour:
    Saloon .... Green and yellow
    Coupe .... Cream and khaki
    Estate .... Khaki and white

Shock absorbers
Maximum length .... 21.26 in (540 mm)
Stroke .... 7.40 in (187.8 mm)

Torque wrench settings

	lbf ft	kgf m
Brake pipe nuts	11 to 13	1.5 to 1.8
Brake backplate nuts	16 to 20	2.2 to 2.7
Propeller shaft flange bolts	17 to 24	2.4 to 3.3
Wheel nuts	58 to 72	8.0 to 10.0
Drain and filler plugs	43 to 72	6.0 to 10.0
Differential carrier to axle case bolts	12 to 17	1.6 to 2.4
Shock absorber upper end nut	11 to 14	1.5 to 2.0

	lbf ft	kgf m
Shock absorber lower end nut	51 to 58	7.0 to 8.0
Upper link fixing bolt	51 to 58	7.0 to 8.0
Upper link fixing nut	51 to 58	7.0 to 8.0
Lower link fixing nut	51 to 58	7.0 to 8.0

1 General description

The rear axle is of the pressed steel banjo type which carries a malleable cast iron differential assembly of the hypoid gear type. The differential can be removed from the axle casing as a unit and if worn, or defective, should be replaced as a unit.

The rear axle has a suspension of coil springs and double-acting telescopic dampers. The axle is braced by four trailing links.

2 Routine Maintenance

1   If there is no loss of oil from the rear axle resulting from failure of the oil seals and other sources of leakage, topping-up of the oil level should not be required.

2   At the specified intervals drain the oil from the rear axle and refill it with the specified quantity and grade of oil.

3   Inspect the rear axle casing regularly for signs of damage and oil leaks and wipe away the accumulated oil and dirt from the breather outlet on the top of the axle casing.

3 Rear axle – removal and refitting

1   Block the front wheels with chocks, loosen the nuts of the rear wheels and raise the rear of the car high enough to permit working underneath. Place securely based stands under the body member at each side of the vehicle, or support the body member on substantial baulks of timber.

2   Support the centre of the differential carrier with a jack, but place a block of wood between the head of the jack and the carrier, to spread the load.

3   Remove the rear road wheels.

4   Mark a line across the edge of the two flanges of the differential to propeller shaft joint. Remove the four bolts from the joint flange, separate the two flanges and lower the free end of the propeller shaft to the ground.

5   Disconnect the brake hose from its connection to the brake pipe

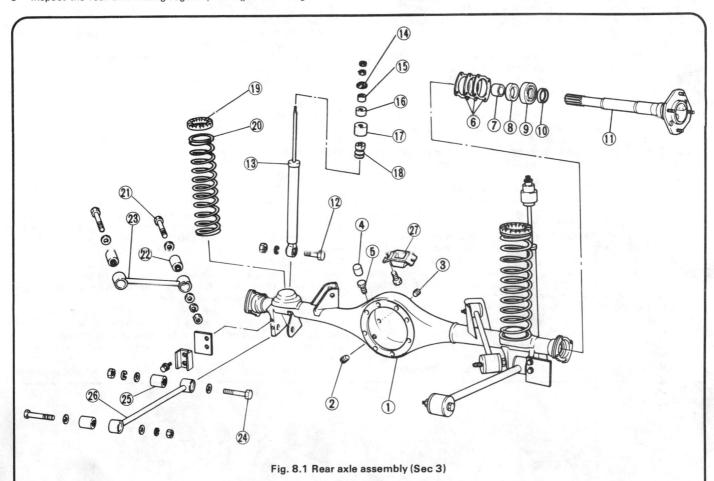

Fig. 8.1 Rear axle assembly (Sec 3)

1 Rear axle case	9 Rear axle bearing (wheel bearing)	15 Shock absorber mounting bush	20 Coil spring
2 Drain plug			21 Upper link bush bolt
3 Filler plug	10 Bearing spacer	16 Shock absorber mounting bush	22 Upper link bush
4 Breather cap	11 Rear axle shaft		23 Upper link
5 Breather	12 Shock absorber lower end bolt	17 Bump stop cover	24 Lower link bush bolt
6 Rear axle case end shim		18 Bump stop rubber	25 Lower link bush
7 Bearing collar	13 Shock absorber assembly	19 Shock absorber mounting insulator	26 Lower link
8 Oil seal	14 Special washer		27 Torque arrester

on the car body and plug the open ends of the pipe and the hose to prevent loss of fluid and the entry of dirt.

6 Slacken the locknut of the brake cable adjuster and disconnect the cable from the adjuster.

7 Remove the bolt from the lower end of each of the rear shock absorbers and pull the shock absorber vertically, to disengage it from the bracket.

8 Lower the jack beneath the axle slowly, until the coil springs are fully extended. Mark the springs to show which side of the vehicle they are fitted and also which is the top and the bottom of the spring, then remove the springs.

9 Raise the jack to its original position and remove the four bolts which secure the links to the axle.

10 Steady the axle to ensure that it does not fall off the jack. Lower the jack slowly until the axle is on the ground and remove the axle.

11 Refitting is the reverse of removal, but smear grease over the link attachment and shock absorber bolts before inserting them. After inserting the link bolts, raise the axle until the links are almost horizontal before tightening the nuts.

12 After connecting the brake pipe and cable, bleed the braking system and adjust the handbrake, as described in Chapter 9.

4 Axle half-shaft – removal and refitting

1 Block the front wheels with chocks and loosen the nuts of the rear wheel on the side from which the half-shaft is to be removed.

2 Raise the rear of the car and support the rear axle case on secure stands, or baulks of timber.

3 Remove the road wheel.

4 Pull off the spring from the brake backplate and disconnect the brake cable from the lever by removing the clevis pin.

5 Disconnect the brake pipe from the brake cylinder and plug the open end of the pipe and the brake cylinder to prevent loss of fluid and the entry of dirt.

6 Remove the brake drum. On models with self-adjusting rear brakes it may be necessary to back off the automatic adjuster before the drum can be removed (Chapter 9).

7 Using a socket inserted through one of the holes in the axle shaft flange, unscrew and remove the four nuts which secure the backplate to the axle casing.

8 To extract the half-shaft, fit an extractor with a slide hammer attachment to the wheel studs. It is not possible to pull the shaft out without using a slide hammer and any attempt to do so may be dangerous and result in pulling the car off its stands.

9 Before fitting the half-shaft, which is the reverse of removal, it is recommended that a new oil seal is fitted as described in the following Section. When passing the half-shaft through the oil seal, keep the shaft aligned with the axle casing exactly, so that the lip of the seal is not damaged. If any shims were fitted to the end of the axle casing flange, it is important that they are fitted again.

10 To check whether shims are required, first ensure that the half-shaft has entered fully, by entering the splines on the end of the shaft into those in the differential unit and then carefully tapping the shaft home. Place a straight edge across the end of the axle tube to check whether the front face of the bearing is proud of the end of the axle tube. If the bearing is proud, a shim must be fitted to the end of the

tube, the shim thickness being at least equal and not more than 0.004 in (0.1 mm) greater than the amount by which the bearing projects.

11 Tighten the backplate bolts to the specified torque, connect the handbrake linkage and brake pipe then bleed the brakes (Chapter 9).

12 Fit the roadwheel and lower the vehicle to the ground.

13 Check the oil level in the rear axle.

5 Axle shaft oil seal – renewal

1 Oil seepage into the rear brake drums is an indication of failure of the axle housing oil seals. Where oil contamination is observed, always check that this is not hydraulic brake fluid leaking from a faulty wheel operating cylinder.

2 Remove the axle half shaft as described in the preceding Section.

3 Using a screwdriver as a lever, prise the oil seal from the recess in the end of the axle casing.

4 Tap the new oil seal squarely into position using a piece of tube as a drift. Fill the space between the lips of the seal with grease.

5 Refit the axle half shaft, as described in Section 4.

6 Axle shaft bearing – removal and refitting

1 The removal and fitting of half shaft bearings and spacer/collars is best left to a service station having suitable extracting and pressing equipment. Where the home mechanic has such facilities available, proceed as follows.

2 With the half shaft removed as described in Section 4, secure it in a vice fitted with jaw protectors.

3 Using a sharp cold chisel and a hammer, split open the bearing collar and remove it from the axle shaft. Take great care not to damage or distort the axle shaft during this operation.

4 Using a suitable extractor, remove the bearing from the axle shaft and finally the bearing spacer.

5 Press wheel bearing grease into the bearing and then locate the spacer, new bearing and new collar in position on the shaft. Press the components into position on the axle shaft using a suitable press to bear on the end of the collar.

6 Refit the reassembled half shaft to the rear axle casing, as described in Section 4.

7 Differential carrier – removal and refitting

1 The overhaul of the rear axle differential unit is not within the scope of the home mechanic due to the specialized gauges and tools which are required. Where the unit requires servicing or repair due to wear or excessive noise it is most economical to exchange it for a factory reconditioned assembly and this Section is limited to a description of the removal and refitting procedure.

2 Drain the oil from the rear axle.

3 Jack-up the axle and support it on axle axle-stands and withdraw the axle half-shafts as described in Section 4 of this Chapter.

4 Disconnect and remove the propeller shaft as previously described.

5 Unscrew, evenly and in opposite sequence, the bolts from the

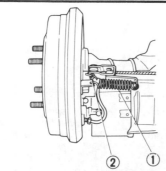

Fig. 8.2 Disconnecting the brakes (Sec 4)

1   *Spring*   2   *Clevis pin*

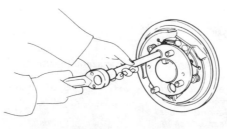

Fig. 8.3 Removing the brake backplate nuts (Sec 4)

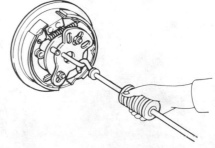

Fig. 8.4 Removing the half-shaft with a slide hammer (Sec 4)

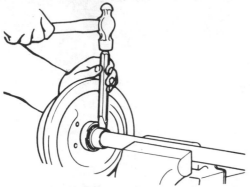

Fig. 8.5 Splitting the bearing collar (Sec 6)

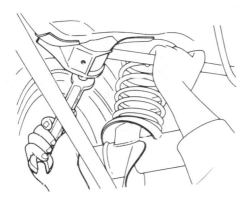

Fig. 8.6 Removing the upper link (Sec 8)

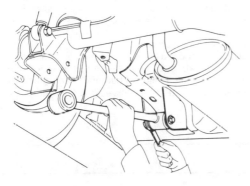

Fig. 8.7 Removing the lower link (Sec 8)

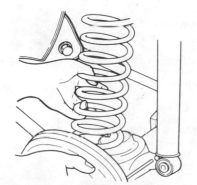

Fig. 8.8 Removing a coil spring (Sec 10)

differential unit. Pull the differential unit from the main axle casing.

6   Scrape all traces of old gasket from the mating surface of the axle casing. Locate a new gasket in position, having first lightly coated it with jointing compound.

7   Clean the mating surface of the differential carrier and remove any burrs. Install the carrier so that the pinion is at the lowest point.

8   Coat the threads of the securing bolts with a suitable sealant then tighten them to the specified torque.

9   Refit the half shafts and the propeller shaft.

10   Refit the roadwheels and lower the jack.

11   Fill the differential unit to the correct level with the specified grade of oil.

8   Link assembly – removal and refitting

1   It is possible to remove one link assembly on its own, but if two or more assemblies are to be taken off, first remove the rear axle assembly as described in Section 3.

2   Remove the links by removing the bolts from each end, but take care to note the link from which each bolt was taken, because the bolts in the lower link are a different length from those in the upper link. If the bolts are inserted into the wrong position they cannot be tightened securely.

3   When fitting the links, insert the bolts and screw the nuts on without tightening them. With the vehicle unloaded, jack-up the centre of the differential carrier until the upper and lower links are almost horizontal and then tighten the link bush bolts and nuts to the specified torque.

9   Link bushes – renewal

1   If the rubber of the link bushes shows pronounced cracking, or distortion, new bushes should be fitted.

2   Because the bushes need to be pressed in, using the correct size of die and mandrel, it is more satisfactory if the bushes are renewed by a Datsun agent.

3   It is important not to try and fit bushes by tapping the end face of the bush directly because this may result in the deformation of the bush and incorrect fitting of the bolt.

10 Coil springs – removal and refitting

1   Block the front wheels with chocks, loosen the nuts of the rear wheels and raise the rear of the car high enough to permit working underneath. Place securely based stands under the body member at each side of the vehicle, or support the body member on substantial baulks of timber.

2   Support the centre of the differential carrier with a jack, but place a block of wood between the head of the jack and the carrier, to spread the load.

3   Remove the rear roadwheels.

4   Remove the bolt from the lower end of each of the rear shock absorbers and pull the shock absorber vertically, to disengage it from the bracket.

5   Lower the jack beneath the axle slowly, until the coil springs are fully extended. Mark the springs to show to which side of the vehicle they are fitted and also which is the top and the bottom of the spring, then remove the springs.

6   Check the springs for deformation and cracks and test them for comparison with the specification.

7   When fitting the springs, which is the reverse of the removal operations, make sure that the springs have seated properly and squarely before raising the axle jack and applying load to the suspension.

8   If either of the springs is unsatisfactory, fit a new pair of springs. While the suspension is dismantled, inspect all rubber components and renew any which are defective.

11 Shock absorbers – removal, testing and refitting

1   On saloon models open the boot lid to gain access to the top fixing of the shock absorber and on Coupe and Estate versions, prise off the

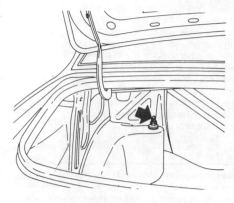

Fig. 8.9 Shock absorber top fixing (Saloon) (Sec 11)

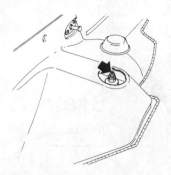

Fig. 8.10 Shock absorber top fixing (Coupe and Estate) (Sec 11)

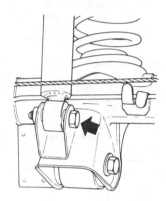

Fig. 8.11 Shock absorber lower fixing (Sec 11)

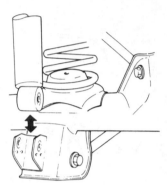

Fig. 8.12 Disconnecting the shock absorber (Sec 11)

cover plug.
2   While preventing the piston rod from rotating, unscrew and remove the piston rod nut.
3   Remove the bolt from the shock absorber attachment to the axle, and pull the shock absorber vertically to disengage it from the bracket.
4   Shock absorbers may be tested without removing them by pushing one corner of the car down as far as possible and then releasing. If the oscillation ceases after one and a half strokes, the shock absorber is likely to be satisfactory, but a better check is to have the vehicle tested at a service centre which has special equipment for measuring shock absorber performance.

5   When off the car, inspect the shock absorbers for leaks and for obvious signs of damage such as bent or damaged piston rods.
6   Check all rubber parts of the suspension for signs of wear, damage and deterioration. Renew any parts which are defective.
7   Operate the shock absorbers several times over their entire length of travel to check that the movement is smooth and uniform.
8   Fit the shock absorbers by first tightening the upper mounting nut on the piston rod to its specified torque and then tighten the locknut securely. Smear grease on the shock absorber lower end fixing bolt before fitting it.

12 Fault diagnosis – rear axle and rear suspension

Symptom	Reason(s)
Noise on drive, or overrun	Low oil level
	Loose crownwheel bolts
	Loose bearing cap bolts
	Wear in bearings or, gear teeth
Noise when turning	Stiff, broken or damaged pinion, pinion bearing or thrust washer
Knock when taking up drive	Excessive crownwheel to pinion backlash
	Worn gears
	Worn half-shaft splines
	Drive pinion nut loose
	Loose crownwheel bolts, or bearing cap bolts
	Worn side gear splines
Body lower on one side	Weak, or broken spring

Chapter 9 Braking system

For modifications, and information applicable to later models, see Supplement at end of manual

Contents

Specifications

System type	Disc brakes at front and self-adjusting drum brakes at rear, hydraulically operated with vacuum servo assistance. Mechanical handbrake on rear wheels only

Front brakes
Type	AN20
Pad size (width x thickness x length)	1.622 x 0.394 x 2.417 in (41.2 x 10.0 x 61.4 mm)
Disc diameter	9.65 in (245.0 mm)
Disc run-out	0.0047 in (0.12 mm) maximum
Wear limit	
Pad thickness	0.063 in (1.6 mm) minimum
Disc thickness	0.331 in (8.4 mm) minimum
Caliper bore diameter	2.012 in (51.1 mm)

Rear brakes
Type	LT20 automatic adjustment
Lining size (width x thickness x length)	1.378 x 0.189 x 7.68 in (35.0 x 4.8 x 195.0 mm)
Drum diameter	8.0 in (203.2 mm)
Wear limit	
Lining thickness	0.059 in (1.5 mm) minimum
Drum diameter	8.05 in (204.5 mm) maximum
Cylinder diameter	0.812 in (20.64 mm)

Master cylinder
Type	Tandem with independent reservoirs
Diameter	0.812 in (20.64 mm)
Piston to cylinder clearance	0.0059 in (0.15 mm) maximum

Brake booster
Type	M60
Diaphragm diameter	6 in (152.4 mm)
Pushrod length	0.384 to 0.394 in (9.75 to 10.00 mm)
Operating rod length	5.31 in (135 mm)

Brake pedal
Free height	
Left-hand drive	5.63 to 5.87 in (143 to 149 mm)
Right-hand drive	6.42 to 6.65 in (163 to 169 mm)
Pedal free play at pad	0.04 to 0.20 in (1 to 5 mm)
Pedal stroke at pad with brake booster	5.51 in (140 mm)
Depressed height	More than 2.76 in (70 mm)

Handbrake

Operating pull . . . . 44 lbf (20 kgf)
Stroke . . . . 3.66 to 4.17 in (93 to 106 mm)

Torque wrench settings

	lbf ft	kgf m
Master cylinder to brake booster	5.8 to 8.0	0.8 to 1.1
Brake booster to body	5.8 to 8.0	0.8 to 1.1
Brake tube flare nut	11 to 13	1.5 to 1.8
Brake hose connector	12 to 14	1.7 to 2.0
Air bleed screw	5.1 to 6.5	0.7 to 0.9
3-way connector mounting	5.8 to 8.0	0.8 to 1.1
Brake warning lamp switch	9 to 11	1.2 to 1.5
Caliper fixing bolts	53 to 72	7.3 to 9.9
Disc fixing bolts	28 to 38	3.9 to 5.3
Rear wheel cylinder mounting bolts	4.3 to 5.8	0.6 to 0.8
Front brake baffle plate bolts	2.5 to 3.2	0.34 to 0.44
Rear brake back plate mounting bolts	16 to 20	2.2 to 2.7
Brake booster operating rod nut	12 to 16	1.6 to 2.2
Pushrod adjusting nut	12 to 16	1.6 to 2.2

1   General description

The brake system fitted to models covered by this manual have disc brakes at the front and drum brakes at the rear, and these are operated hydraulically with power assistance by a Master-Vac servo unit.

The hydraulic system is of the dual line type whereby the front brakes and rear brakes are operated by individual circuits, so that if a line should fail, braking action will still be available on two wheels.

The rear drum brakes are of the internal expanding type, the shoes and linings moving outwards and into frictional contact with the rotating brake drum. The brake shoes are actuated by a single wheel cylinder on each wheel.

The front disc brakes are of the rotating disc and semi-rigid mounted caliper design. The disc is secured to the flange of the hub and the caliper mounted on the steering swivel.

Each caliper contains two piston operated friction pads, which on application of the footbrake pinch the disc between them.

Application of the footbrake creates hydraulic pressure in the master cylinder and fluid from the cylinder travels via steel and flexible pipes to the cylinder in each caliper, pushing the pistons, to which are attached the friction pads, into contact with either side of the disc.

Two seals are fitted to the operating cylinder; the outer seal prevents moisture and dirt entering the cylinder, while the inner seal, which is retained in a groove inside the cylinder, prevents fluid leakage.

As the friction pads wear, so the pistons move further out of the cylinder due to the elasticity of the seals and the level of the fluid in the hydraulic reservoir drops. Disc pad wear is therefore taken up automatically and eliminates the need for periodic adjustment by the owner.

A Nissan Proportioning (NP) valve is incorporated into the hydraulic circuit and this regulates the fluid flow to prevent the rear brakes locking before the front brakes.

The twin master cylinder reservoirs have level indicators fitted to the caps and should the level fall below the specified level, a warning light is actuated to inform the driver.

The handbrake is a centrally mounted lever, which operates cables to the rear brakes only. When the handbrake is applied, a switch is actuated and when the ignition is switched ON, a warning light on the dashboard is illuminated when the handbrake is applied.

2   Brakes – adjustment

1   The front disc brakes do not require adjustment because pad wear is compensated for automatically by the brake pistons.
2   The rear drum brakes have ratchet type adjusters which adjust the drum to shoe clearance automatically when the handbrake is operated. Separate adjustment of the rear brake shoes is not necessary, but the handbrake must be kept in adjustment.

3   Handbrake – adjustment

1   Slacken the locknut on the brake adjusting turnbuckle and rotate the turnbuckle so that the brake control lever stroke is seven or eight notches of its ratchet.
2   Return the handbrake to its OFF position and check that all the brake toggle levers return to their original positions and that the rear cables are not excessively slack.
3   Hold the turnbuckle stationary and tighten the locknut against it.

4   Handbrake warning light switch adjustment

1   Bend the warning lamp switch bracket as necessary so that when the lever is pulled on by one notch, the light comes on and when the lever is fully released, the light goes out.

5   Bleeding the hydraulic system

1   Removal of all air from the hydraulic system is essential for the correct working of the braking system. Before undertaking this, examine the fluid reservoir caps to ensure that the vent holes are clear. Check the level of fluid in the reservoir(s) and top-up if required.
2   Check all brake line unions and connections for seepage, and at the same time check the condition of the rubber hoses, which may be perished.
3   If the condition of the wheel cylinder is in doubt, check for signs of fluid leakage.
4   If there is any possibility that incorrect fluid has been used in the system, drain the fluid out and flush through with methylated spirit. Renew all piston seals and cups because they may have been affected and could fail under pressure.
5   Gather together a clean glass jar, a 12 inch (300 mm) length of tubing which fits tightly over the bleed valve and a tin of the correct brake fluid.
6   To bleed the system, clean the area around the bleed valves and start at the master cylinder by removing the rubber or plastic cover from one bleed valve.
7   Place the end of the tube in the clean jar which should contain sufficient fluid to keep the end of the tube underneath during the operation.
8   Open the bleed valve $\frac{1}{4}$ turn with a wrench, depress the brake pedal and close the bleed valve again just before full travel of the brake pedal is reached. This will expel brake fluid and air from the end of the tube.
9   Repeat this operation until no more air is expelled from that particular bleed valve, then tighten the valve to the specified torque. During the bleeding operation ensure that the master cylinder reservoir is topped-up as necessary, or more air will be introduced into the system.
10   Repeat this operation on the second master cylinder bleed valve then the rear brakes, starting with the left-hand brake followed by the front brakes (photo).
11   When completed, check the level of fluid in the reservoir and then check the feel of the brake pedal, which should be firm and free from any 'spongy' action, which is normally associated with air in the system.
12   It will be noticed that during the bleeding operation, the effort

5.10 Front brake assembly with bleed valve (arrowed)

required to depress the pedal the full stroke will increase, because of loss of the vacuum assistance, as it is destroyed by repeated operation of the servo unit. Although the servo unit will be inoperative as far as assistance is concerned, it does not affect the brake bleeding operation.

6 Brake hoses – inspection, removal and refitting

1   Inspect the condition of the flexible hydraulic hoses. If they are swollen, damaged or chafed they must be renewed.

2   Wipe the top of the brake master cylinder reservoir and unscrew the cap. Place a piece of polythene sheet over the top of the reservoir and refit the cap. This is to stop hydraulic fluid syphoning out during subsequent operations. Note that tandem master cylinders have two reservoirs, but it is not necessary to cover both cylinders unless both front and rear hoses are being removed.

Front brake hose

3   First jack-up the vehicle and remove the wheel. To remove the hose, wipe the unions and bracket free of dust, and undo the union nut from the metal pipe end.

4   Withdraw the metal clip securing the hose to the bracket and detach the hose from the bracket. Unscrew the hose from the caliper.

5   Refitting is the reverse of the removal procedure but ensure that the hose is connected at the caliper end first, with the wheels in the 'straight-ahead' position. On completion, the front brakes must be bled of air, as described in the previous Section.

Rear brake hose

6   To remove a rear flexible hose, wipe the unions, bracket and three way adaptor free of dust, and undo the union nut from the metal pipe end.

7   Withdraw the metal clip securing the hose to the bracket and detach the hose from the bracket. Unscrew the hose from the three-way adaptor.

8   Refitting is a direct reversal of the removal procedure. Ensure that the hose is connected at the three-way adaptor end first. The brake lines must be secured in position against the axle housing by fastening the retaining clips.

9   On completion bleed the rear brakes, as described previously.

7 Front disc brake pads – removal, inspection and refitting

1   Loosen the wheel nuts and then jack-up the front of the car and support it securely on stands, or wood blocks.

2   Remove the roadwheel.

3   Remove the clips and pull out the pins, extracting the coil springs and the pad springs by hand (photo).

4   Using thin nosed pliers, extract the pads from the caliper assembly. Do not depress the brake pedal while the pads are not in place, because the pistons will be ejected.

5   Check that the pads are not contaminated with oil or grease and are not distorted. Damaged and contaminated pads must be renewed.

6   Check that the thickness of friction material is greater than the minimum specified.

7   Clean the exposed parts of the pistons with hydraulic fluid. The

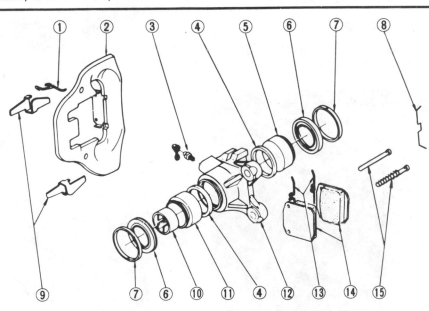

Fig. 9.1 Front brake caliper components (Sec 7)

1 Bias spring	5 Piston B	9 Yoke spring	13 Pad spring
2 Yoke	6 Boot	10 Bias ring	14 Pad
3 Bleed valve	7 Retaining ring	11 Piston A	15 Pin
4 Piston seal	8 Clip	12 Cylinder body	

7.3 Front brake caliper showing pads, clips, pins and springs

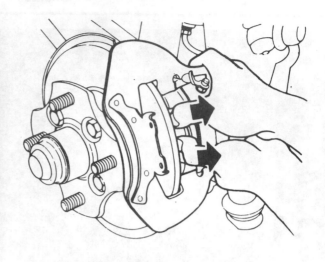

Fig. 9.2 Pushing in piston B (Sec 7)

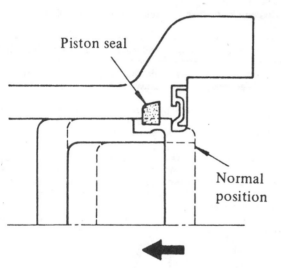

Piston seal

Normal position

Fig. 9.3 Pushing in the piston – do not push in further than position shown by dotted piston (Sec 7)

7.10 Piston B pushed in

7.11 Fitting the inner brake pad

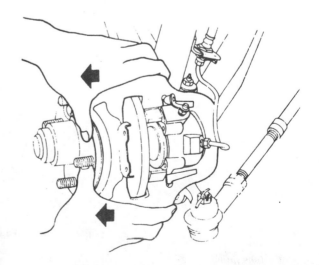

Fig. 9.4 Pulling in piston A (Sec 7)

piston sliding surface is plated and must not be polished with emery cloth even if rust or dirt is adhering to its surface.

8   Check the condition of the brake disc (Section 10).

9   Clean the yoke guide groove on the cylinder body, the sliding surfaces of the yoke and the end face of the piston. Coat these surfaces with PBC grease. Do not use common brake grease and take care not to get grease on the brake disc and pads.

10   Loosen the air bleed screw and very carefully push the outer piston (piston B, Fig. 9.2) until the end surface of the piston is in line with the end of the retaining ring on the boot (photo). The piston can be pushed in by hand, but the operation requires great care because it is easy to push the piston in so that the piston groove goes past the piston seal (Fig. 9.3). If this happens the brake caliper must be removed, dismantled and reassembled (Section 9).

11   When the outer piston has been pushed in, the inner pad can be fitted (photo).

12   Push the inner piston (piston A) into its cylinder by pulling the yoke assembly outwards towards the hub (Fig. 9.4) and then fit the outer pad.

13   Close the bleed screw and fit the pad pins and springs.

14   Depress the brake pedal several times to settle the pads in position.

15   Refit the roadwheels and lower the vehicle to the ground.

16   If worn brake pads are replaced by new ones and the bleed screw is not opened while the pistons are pushed in, there is a danger that the brake fluid reservoir may overflow. When renewing brake pads, always fit a new set of four pads, four pad pins and springs and two clips.

8   Front disc brake caliper – removal and refitting

1   Remove the brake pads as described in the previous Section.

2   Disconnect the brake hose from the caliper assembly and plug both the end of the hose and the hole in the caliper to prevent loss of fluid and the entry of dirt.

3   Remove the two bolts securing the caliper assembly to the steering knuckle and detach the caliper.

4   Installation is the reverse of removal. Tighten the caliper securing bolts to the torque wrench setting given in the Specification, refit the brake pads and bleed the hydraulic system as described in Section 5.

9   Disc brake caliper – dismantling and assembling

1   Drain the brake fluid from the caliper through the flexible hose connection.

2   Unscrew and remove the bleed nipple.

3   Depress each piston in turn as described in Section 7.

4   Secure the longer edge of the caliper yoke in a vice and tap the top of the yoke lightly with a hammer. This action will disconnect the caliper body from the yoke.

5   Remove the bias ring from the inner piston.

6   Remove the retaining rings and boots from the ends of both pistons.

7   Eject both pistons. This may be achieved by blocking the fluid inlet hole and applying air pressure at the bleed nipple hole.

8   Carefully extract the piston seals from their grooves in the cylinders.

9   Detach the spring from the yoke.

10   Clean all components in methylated spirit or clean hydraulic fluid. Inspect the cylinder walls for scoring, bright spots or corrosion. Minor damage to the cylinder bore may be eliminated by polishing the surface with fine emery cloth. If the damage is major, a new cylinder must be used. The surface of the piston is plated and emery cloth must not be used on it and a corroded piston must be renewed.

11   Obtain a repair kit which will contain all the necessary seals and new parts. Check that the rubber seals have not deteriorated or become deformed in storage.

12   Dip the new seals in hydraulic fluid and locate them in their grooves in the cylinder bores. Use only the fingers to manipulate them into position. Note the correct fitting of the seal chamfer.

13   Insert the bias ring into the inner piston so that the radiused end of the ring is to the bottom. Make sure that the inner and outer pistons are correctly identified. Piston A has a recess at the bottom of its bore (Fig. 9.9)

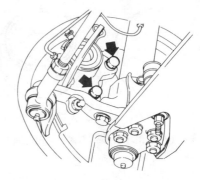

Fig. 9.5 Brake caliper retaining bolts (arrowed) (Sec 8)

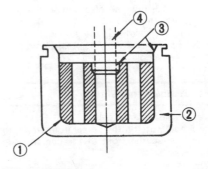

Fig. 9.6 Disconnecting the yoke and caliper (Sec 9)

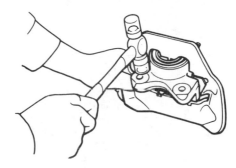

Fig. 9.7 Cylinder body and piston (Sec 9)

1   Bias ring   3   Retaining ring
2   Boot

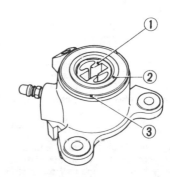

Fig. 9.8 Assembling bias ring to piston A (Sec 9)

1   Rounded end   3   Chamfer
2   Piston 'A'   4   Yoke

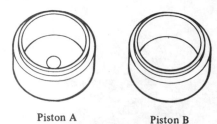

Piston A   Piston B

Fig. 9.9 Identification of piston A and piston B (Sec 9)

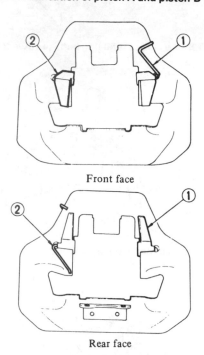

Front face

Rear face

Fig. 9.10 Yoke and yoke spring (Sec 9)

1   Bias spring   2   Yoke spring

14   Dip each of the pistons in clean hydraulic fluid and insert them into their respective cylinders. Do not push the pistons too far into their cylinders or the seal will be damaged by the piston groove. Position the inner piston so that the yoke groove of the bias ring coincides with the yoke groove of the cylinder.
15   Fit the boots and retaining rings.
16   Fit the yoke springs.
17   Fit the bias spring to the yoke.
18   Apply a smear of PBC grease to the yoke sliding surface of the cylinder body then reposition the bias ring so that the groove of the bias ring coincides with the yoke.
19   With the yoke spring located in the groove in the cylinder, connect the cylinder body and yoke, by applying pressure with the thumbs.
20   Screw in the bleed nipple.

10   Brake disc – removal and refitting

1   Chock the rear wheels of the car.
2   Loosen the wheel nuts on the wheel from which the brake disc is to be removed, Jack-up the front of the car and support the body securely on stands, or blocks.
3   Remove the roadwheel.
4   Remove the brake pads, as described in Section 7.
5   Remove the two bolts securing the brake caliper to the steering knuckle. Remove the caliper without disconnecting the brake hose and tie the caliper assembly to the body so that the caliper is out of the way, but the brake hose is not strained.
6   Use two screwdrivers to prise off the hub cap, but take care not to damage the O-ring.

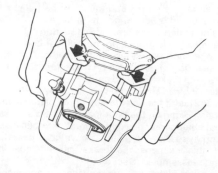

Fig. 9.11 Assembling the yoke and cylinder (Sec 9)

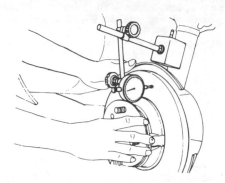

Fig. 9.12 Measuring disc run-out with a dial gauge (Sec 10)

7   Pinch together the splayed ends of the cotter pin and withdraw the pin. Lift the adjusting cap off the nut and screw off the wheel bearing nut. If necessary refer to Chapter 11, Section 9. Lever off the thrust washer.
8   Pull the hub assembly forward and extract the outer roller bearing, then pull the hub and disc assembly off the stub axle.
9   Mark the position of the brake disc on the hub assembly, so that it can be refitted in the same position.
10   Remove the four bolts securing the brake disc and separate the disc from the hub.
11   Clean the disc thoroughly and inspect it for signs of corrosion, scoring, or burning. A scored disc may be reground within the limit given in the Specification.
12   Fitting the disc to the hub is the reverse of removal, but first make sure that the mating faces are clean and the mating marks made before dismantling are lined up.
13   Fit the hub assembly on the stub axle and adjust the wheel bearing as described in Chapter 11, Section 8.
14   Make a bracket which can be attached to the suspension arm and support a piece of metal which just touches the face of the brake disc on its highest spot. Turn the disc to various positions and use a feeler gauge to measure the gap between the disc face and the metal datum. If the maximum deviation (run-out) exceeds that specified remove the disc and check for the presence of dirt on one of the mating faces. If a new disc has been fitted and the run-out is excessive, remove the disc from the hub, rotate it 180° relative to the hub and refit it.
15   When the run-out is satisfactory, pack the wheel bearing with grease and refit the hub cap and roadwheel.

11   Rear drum brakes – removal, inspection and refitting

1   After high mileages it will be necessary to fit new shoes and linings. Fitting new linings to shoes is not normally economic or possible, without the use of special equipment. However, if the services of a local garage or workshop having brake relining equipment are available, there is no reason why the original shoes should not be successfully relined. Ensure that the correct specification linings are fitted to the shoes.
2   Chock the front wheels, jack-up the rear of the car and support on firmly based stands, remove the roadwheel.
3   Engage the handbrake and extract the split pin from the stopper.

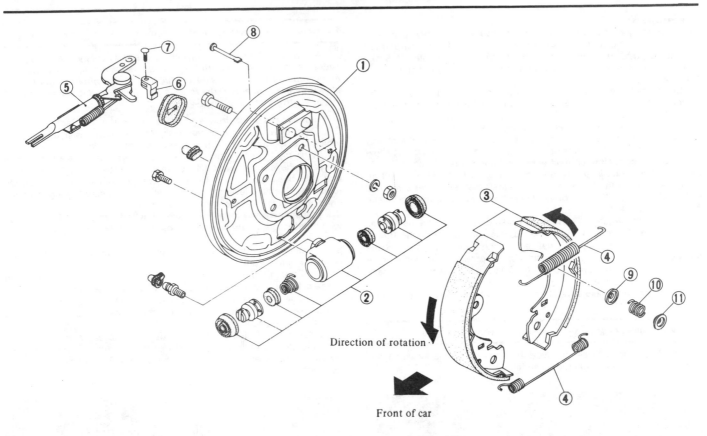

Direction of rotation

Front of car

Fig. 9.13 Rear brake components (Sec 11)

1	Brake back plate	4	Return spring
2	Wheel cylinder assembly	5	Adjuster assembly
3	Brake shoe assembly	6	Stopper

7	Stopper pin	10	Anti-rattle spring
8	Anti-rattle pin	11	Retainer
9	Spring seat		

11.4 Removing a brake drum using jacking screws

11.6 Removing a spring retainer

Remove the stopper from the toggle lever. Release the handbrake lever.

4   The drum can now be removed but mark its relative position to the hub before withdrawal. If it proves reluctant to move, screw in two suitable bolts into the holes in the drum to draw it from the studs (photo). Alternatively try tapping the outside rim of the drum, using a soft faced hammer and rotate the drum to free it.

5   Check the lining thickness (see Specifications), and inspect the drum friction surface for wear or scoring.

6   Use a pair of pliers to rotate the brake shoe antirattle spring retainer through 90° and lift away the retainer cup, spring and spring seat (photo). Remove the handbrake cable retaining clevis pin.

7   Make a note of the locations of the shoe return springs and the way round they are fitted. Carefully ease the shoes from the slots in the wheel cylinder and anchor.

8   Lift the shoes and return springs from the backplate.

9   If the shoes are to be left off for a while, do not depress the brake pedal, otherwise the pistons will be ejected from the cylinders causing

unnecessary work.

10 Thoroughly clean all traces of dust from the shoes, backplate and brake drums using a stiff brush. It is recommended that compressed air is not used, as it blows up dust which should not be inhaled. Brake dust can cause judder or squeal and it is important to clean out as described.

11 Check that the pistons are free to move in the cylinders, that the rubber dust covers are undamaged and in position and that there are no hydraulic fluid leaks.

12 Apply brake grease to the adjuster threads.

13 Prior to reassembly, smear a trace of brake grease to the steady platforms and shoe locations on the cylinder and anchor. Do not allow any grease to come into contact with the linings or rubber parts.

14 Refit the shoes in the reverse sequence to removal. The pull off springs should preferably be renewed every time new shoes are fitted, and must be refitted in their original web holes. Position them between the web and backplate (photos).

15 Back off the adjuster and refit the brake drum. Refit the roadwheel.

16 Note that the right-hand brake adjuster has a right-hand thread whilst the left-hand adjuster has a left-hand thread. Lubricate the adjuster as shown in Fig. 9.14 using brake grease. Also apply brake grease to those items arrowed in Fig. 9.15, being the principal brake pivot and contact areas.

17 Apply the handbrake several times to reset the brake shoes.

12 Rear brake backplate – removal and refitting

The backplate can be removed after removing the axleshaft and axleshaft bearing (see Chapter 8 Section 6)

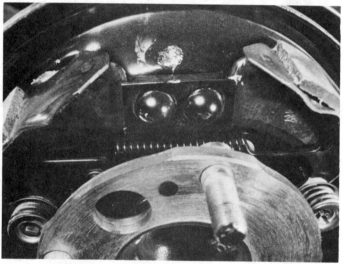

11.14a Position of upper shoe spring

13 Rear brake wheel cylinder – removal, servicing and refitting

If hydraulic fluid is leaking from the brake wheel cylinder, it may be necessary to dismantle it and renew the seals. Should brake fluid be found running down the side of the wheel or a pool of liquid forms alongside one wheel and the level in the master cylinder has dropped, it is indicative that the seals have failed..

1 Remove the brake drum and shoes as described in Section 11.

2 Clean down the rear of the backplate to catch any hydraulic fluid which may issue from the open pipe or wheel cylinder.

3 Wipe the top of the brake master cylinder reservoirs and unscrew the caps. Place a piece of thick polythene over the top of the reservoirs and refit the caps. This is to stop hydraulic fluid syphoning out. On models with a fluid level indicator it will be necessary to plug the open ends of the pipe to prevent loss of hydraulic fluid.

4 Disconnect the brake line to wheel cylinder nut and plug the pipe when detached to prevent any possible leakage or ingress of dirt (photo).

5 Unscrew and remove the wheel cylinder retaining bolts and withdraw the cylinder unit.

6 To dismantle the cylinder unit prise the dust covers from each end of the cylinder body and withdraw the pistons, cups and spring, noting the position of each as they are extracted. Do not use any hard or sharp objects to extract the piston assemblies as the boss must not be scored or damaged in any way.

7 Inspect the inside of the cylinder for score marks caused by impurities in the hydraulic fluid. **Note:** *if the wheel cylinder requires renewal, always ensure that the replacement is identical to the one removed.*

11.14b Position of lower shoe spring

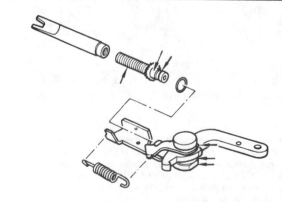

Fig. 9.14 Brake adjuster lubrication points (arrowed) (Sec 11)

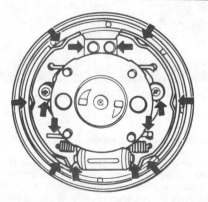

Fig. 9.15 Brake shoe lubrication points (arrowed) (Sec 11)

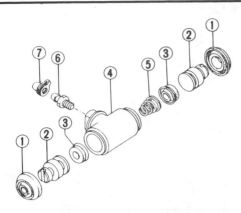

Fig. 9.16 Wheel cylinder components (Sec 13)

1	Dust cover	5	Spring
2	Piston	6	Bleed valve
3	Piston cup	7	Bleed valve cap
4	Wheel cylinder body		

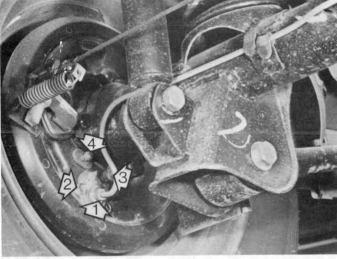

13.4 Wheel cylinder removal

1 Brake pipe connection
2 Retaining bolt
3 Bleed nipple
4 Rubber plug for access to brake adjuster

14.1 Master cylinder

8 If the cylinder is sound, thoroughly clean it out with fresh hydraulic fluid.
9 If a new kit is obtained, ensure that it is suitable for your cylinder as there are two types fitted, Nabco or Tokico, and their respective components are not interchangeable. It is therefore important to quote which type you require when ordering replacements, better still take the cylinder along for comparison.
10 Smear new seals with clean hydraulic fluid to assist assembly to pistons, and make certain they are facing the correct way.
11 Lubricate the cylinder bore with clean hydraulic fluid and reassemble the spring and piston assemblies and fit new rubber dust seals onto each end of the cylinder to complete.
12 Relocate the cylinder unit into the backplate and loosely fit the retaining bolts.
13 Remove the plug from the hydraulic pipe, and carefully screw the pipe retaining nut back into the cylinder.
14 When the hydraulic pipe is located, tighten the wheel cylinder retaining bolts to the specified torque and then tighten the pipe nut – but don't overtighten.
15 Reassembly of the brake shoes, springs and drum is a reversal of the removal procedure as given in Section 11.
16 Bleed the rear brakes on completion (Section 5) and check the cylinder for signs of possible fluid leakage and efficient operation.

14 Master cylinder – removal and refitting

1 Wipe clean the master cylinder and caps to prevent the ingress of dirt to components during the following operations (photo).
2 Unscrew the hydraulic unions from the master cylinder and drain the fluid into a suitable container. Disconnect the fluid level gauge wiring where fitted.
3 Unscrew the master cylinder securing nuts at the flange to the servo unit and carefully withdraw the cylinder unit.
4 Refitting is the reversal of the removal procedure. After topping-up the reservoirs, bleed the hydraulic system as described in Section 5.

15 Master cylinder – dismantling and reassembly

1 Assuming that the cylinder has been removed (see previous Section) and drained out, commence dismantling by extracting the stopper ring from the end of the bore.
2 Extract the stopper using a small screwdriver.
3 Unscrew and remove the stopper screw from underneath the cylinder body.
4 The primary and secondary piston assemblies may now be withdrawn from the cylinder bore. Make a special note of the assembly order as the parts are removed.
5 Carefully remove the seals, making a note of which way round they are fitted.
6 Unscrew the plugs located on the underside of the cylinder body and withdraw the check valve parts. These must be kept in their respective sets.
7 Thoroughly clean the parts in brake fluid, or methylated spirit. After drying the items, inspect the seals for signs of distortion, swelling, splitting or hardening; although it is recommended new rubber parts are always fitted after dismantling as a matter of course.
8 Inspect the bore and piston for signs of deep scoring marks which, if evident, means a new cylinder should be fitted. Make sure that the ports in the bore are clean, by poking gently with a piece of wire.
9 If for any reason the reservoir tanks have to be removed, they must be renewed on assembly. Do not refit the old ones.
10 The fluid level gauge assemblies are not repairable and they should not therefore be interfered with. If they are defective, they must be renewed as a unit.
11 Before assembly, check that you have the correct seal kit or exchange parts/unit, as there are two types of master cylinder fitted. Although basically similar in design, one is manufactured by Tokico and the other by Nabco (Figs. 9.17 and 9.18). As the components of each are not interchangeable, it is most important to specify which type you have when ordering spare parts or replacements. Better still, take the old parts along to the dealer for direct comparison.
12 As the parts are refitted to the cylinder bore, make sure that they are thoroughly wetted with clean hydraulic fluid.
13 Fit new seals to the pistons, making sure they are the correct way

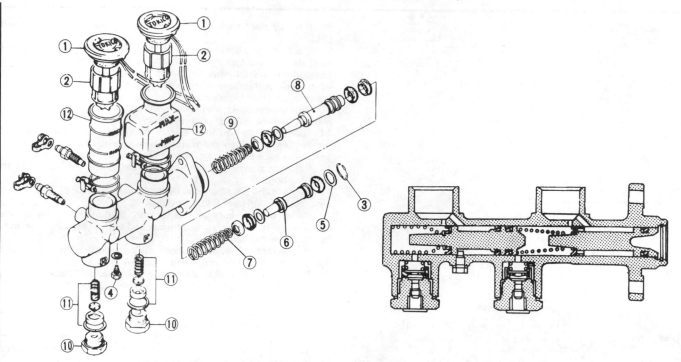

Fig. 9.17 Master cylinder (Tokico) – exploded view (Sec 15)

1 Reservoir cap	4 Stopper screw	7 Primary piston return spring	10 Plug
2 Filter	5 Stopper	8 Secondary piston	11 Check valve
3 Stopper ring	6 Primary piston	9 Secondary piston return spring	12 Reservoir

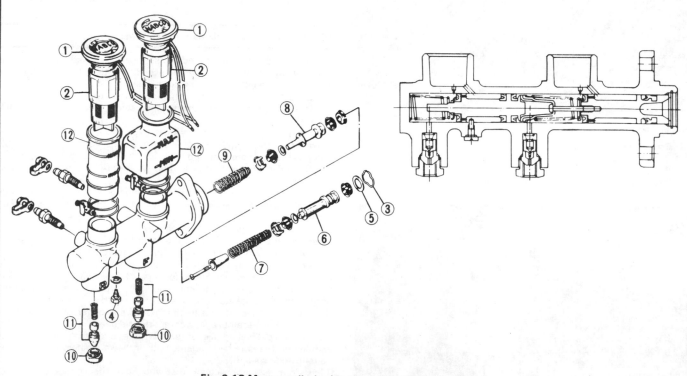

Fig. 9.18 Master cylinder (Nabco) – exploded view (Sec 15)

1 Reservoir cap	4 Stopper screw	7 Primary piston return spring	10 Plug
2 Filter	5 Stopper	8 Secondary piston	11 Check valve
3 Stopper ring	6 Primary piston	9 Secondary piston return spring	12 Reservoir

round, as noted during removal.

14 With the cylinder bore well lubricated, insert the secondary return spring, secondary piston, primary return spring and primary piston into the bore. Take care not to roll the seal lips whilst inserting into the bore.

15 Refit the stopper and stopper ring to secure.

16 Insert the check valve assemblies and secure with plugs.

17 Don't forget to insert the stopper screw and use a new washer.

16 Master-Vac servo unit – description

A Master-Vac vacuum servo unit is fitted and operates in series with the master cylinder to provide assistance to the driver when the brake pedal is depressed. This reduces the effort required by the driver to operate the brake under all braking conditions.

The unit operates by vacuum, obtained from the intake manifold and comprises basically a booster diaphragm and control valve assembly.

The servo unit and hydraulic master cylinder are connected together so that the servo unit piston rod (valve rod) acts as the master cylinder pushrod. The driver's braking effort is transmitted through another pushrod, to the servo unit piston and its built-in control system. The servo unit piston is attached to a rolling diaphragm, which ensures an airtight seal between the two major parts of the servo unit casing. The forward chamber is held under vacuum conditions created in the intake manifold of the engine and during periods when the brake pedal is not in use, the controls open a passage to the rear chamber, so placing it under vacuum conditions as well. When the brake pedal is depressed, the vacuum passage to the rear chamber is cut off and the chamber opened to atmospheric pressure. The consequent pressure difference across the servo piston pushes the piston forward in the vacuum chamber and operates the main pushrod to the master cylinder.

The controls are designed so that assistance is given under all conditions and, when the brakes are not required, vacuum in the rear chamber is established when the brake pedal is released.

Under normal operating conditions, the vacuum servo unit is very reliable and does not require overhaul except at very high mileage.

17 Master-Vac servo unit – removal and refitting

1 Remove the suction hose from the connection on the servo unit.

2 Remove the master cylinder; refer to Section 14 if necessary.

3 Using a pair of pliers, extract the split pin in the end of the brake pedal to pushrod clevis pin. Withdraw the clevis pin. To assist this it may be necessary to release the pedal return spring.

4 Undo and remove the four nuts and spring washers that secure the unit to the bulkhead. Lift the unit away from the engine bulkhead.

5 Refitting of the servo unit is the reverse sequence to removal, but check the adjustments given in Section 18.

18 Master-Vac servo unit – testing and adjustment

1 Failure of the servo may result from a faulty check valve, or from air leakage inside the servo. The servo can be tested with a vacuum gauge without removing the unit from the vehicle and this work should be done by a Datsun dealer.

2 If a servo is found to be faulty, the only part which can be renewed is the check valve. In the event of any other fault, an exchange unit is required.

3 Before fitting the master cylinder to the servo measure the projection of the pushrod beyond the rear face of the servo (Fig. 9.20). If Dimension "A" is outside the limits 0.384 to 0.394 in (9.75 to 10.0 mm), release the locknut, screw the top of the rod clockwise to decrease the length and anti-clockwise to increase it. When the length is correct, tighten the locknut.

4 Measure the projection of the hole centre of the pushrod clevis from the rear face of the servo (Fig. 6.21). If dimension "B" is not 5.31 in (135 mm), slacken the locknut and adjust the length in a similar way to the adjustment of the pushrod.

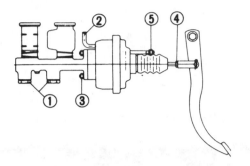

Fig. 9.19 Brake booster removal (Sec 17)

1   Brake pipe connections
2   Vacuum pipe
3   Booster to master cylinder nuts
4   Brake pedal clevis
5   Bulkhead nuts

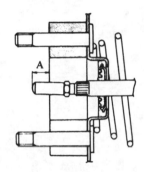

Fig. 9.20 Pushrod adjustment (Sec 18)
See text for Dimension A

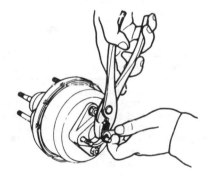

Fig. 9.21 Adjusting the pushrod (Sec 18)

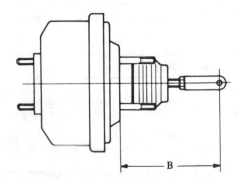

Fig. 9.22 Operating rod adjustment (Sec 18)
See text for dimension B

Fig. 9.23 Vacuum check valve location (Sec 19)

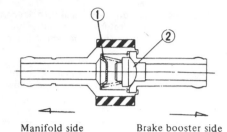

Manifold side   Brake booster side

Fig. 9.24 Vacuum check valve – sectional view (Sec 19)

1   Spring   *2   Valve*

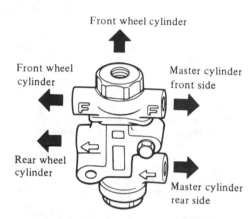

Front wheel cylinder

Front wheel
cylinder

Master cylinder
front side

Rear wheel
cylinder

Master cylinder
rear side

Fig. 9.25 NP valve connections (Sec 19)

19.0 NP valve installation

20.3 Brake fluid level gauge

19 Nissan Proportioning (NP) valve

The NP valve (photo) is fitted between the front and rear brake lines and enables the front brakes to operate normally even when the rear brake line has developed a serious leak. Also should there be a leak in the front brake line the rear brake will still function.

It is recommended that every 24 000 miles (38 000 km) valve operation be checked for correct operation. Remove all luggage and then drive the car on a dry road. With the car travelling at 30 mph (50 km/h) apply the brakes suddenly.

The valve is functioning normally when the rear wheels lock simultaneously with the front wheels or when the front wheels lock before the rear wheels.

Should the rear wheels lock before the front wheels then it is probable that the NP valve has developed an internal fault and it should be renewed.

20 Brake fluid level gauge

1   A brake fluid level gauge is fitted into the reservoir on some models and is designed to light the brake warning light on the instrument panel when the level of fluid falls below a certain level in the reservoir.

2   The float rides on the surface of the hydraulic fluid and when the level drops to the danger point a magnet in the float operates a switch so completing the circuit.

3   To check the operation of the switch, first release the handbrake, then with the ignition switched on, but the engine not running, slowly raise the cap and ascertain that the brake warning light comes on when the float contacts the lower stop (photo).

21 Brake pedal – removal and refitting

1   Extract the split pin from the clevis to pedal pin. Withdraw the pin from the clevis and pedal to separate.

2   Unscrew and remove the fulcrum pin bolt, remove the E-ring, and withdraw the fulcrum pin.

3   The pedal and spring can be removed together but note the way round that the spring is attached. If necessary, drift out the bushes.

4   Refitting is a direct reversal of removal but smear the bushes and return spring with a general purpose grease. Use a new split pin to secure the clevis pin.

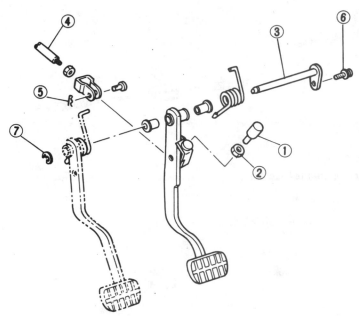

Fig. 9.26 Brake pedal assembly (Sec 21)

1	Brake lamp switch	5	Snap pin
2	Locknut	6	Bolt
3	Fulcrum pin	7	E-ring
4	Brake pushrod or operating rod		

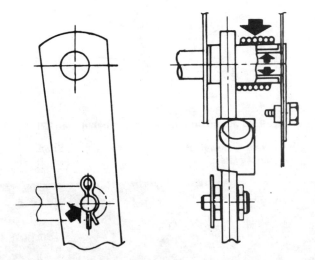

Fig. 9.27 Brake pedal lubrication points (arrowed) (Sec 21)

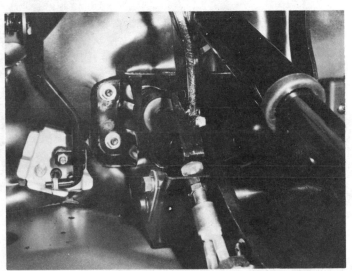

21.5 Brake pedal switch

5 Check the pedal height and fully depressed positions and adjust as necessary at the pushrod yoke or switch (photo) until correct movement is obtained.

22 Handbrake lever and cables – removal and refitting

Control lever and front cable
1 Disconnect the battery earth cable.
2 Remove the central console box where applicable to gain access to the handbrake lever and warning switch.
3 Detach the handbrake warning switch wire at the terminal connector.

4 Unscrew and remove the handbrake lever bolts and detach the grommet rubber.
5 Working underneath the car, remove the locking plate and disconnect the cable adjuster, then carefully withdraw the cable together with the control lever unit through the interior (photo).

6 To detach the cable, remove the split pin and extract the clevis pin.

7 Refitting is a direct reversal of the removal procedure but ensure that a new split pin is used to secure the clevis pin when reassembling the cable. Check that the cable is clear of surrounding components and is able to operate without binding. Readjust the handbrake as described in Section 3. Check that the warning light switch operates correctly before refitting the central console.

144

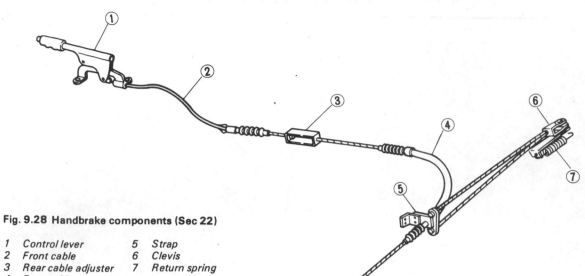

Fig. 9.28 Handbrake components (Sec 22)

1 Control lever   5 Strap
2 Front cable   6 Clevis
3 Rear cable adjuster   7 Return spring
4 Rear cable

22.5 Handbrake cable locking plate and adjuster

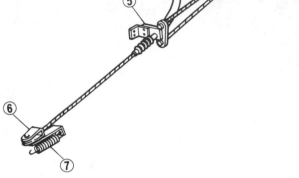

Fig. 9.29 Removing the rear brake cable (Sec 22)

1 Rear cable adjuster   3 Strap
2 Lock plate

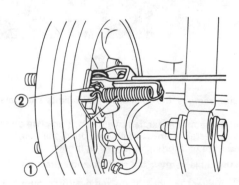

Fig. 9.30 Brake cable to brake attachments (Sec 22)

1 Return spring   2 Clevis pin

22.9 Cable located in lockplate

22.10 Brake strap retainer unit

22.11 Brake lever connection and return spring

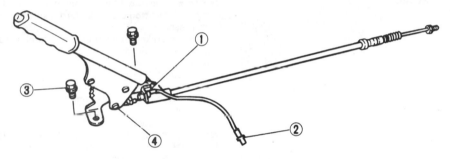

Fig. 9.31 Handbrake lever assembly (Sec 22)

1	Hand brake warning switch	3	Bolt
2	Terminal	4	Pin

Rear cable

8 Working underneath the car, detach the adjuster from the front cable.

9 Prise the lockplate free (photo) at the cable's rear axle location.

10 Unscrew the securing set screws and disconnect the strap retainer unit on the rear axle casing (photo).

11 Disconnect the return spring and detach the cable from the operating lever in the backplate (photo). The cable is retained to the lever by a clevis and pin. Extract the split-pin and withdraw the clevis pin to separate.

12 Refitting is a reversal of the removal procedure but use a new split-pin to retain the clevis pin. Smear the clevis pin/s and adjuster with grease during assembly and to other sliding contact surfaces. Check that the cables are clear of surrounding components and do not bind when operated. Adjust the handbrake as described in Section 3.

See overleaf for 'Fault diagnosis – braking system'

23 Fault diagnosis – braking system

Symptom	Reason/s
Pedal travels almost to floor before brakes operate	Brake fluid level too low Wheel cylinder leaking Master cylinder leaking (bubbles in master cylinder fluid) Brake flexible hose leaking Brake line fractured Brake system unions loose Shoe linings excessively worn
Brake pedal feels 'springy'	New linings not yet bedded-in Brake drums or discs badly worn or cracked Master cylinder securing nuts loose
Brake pedal feels 'spongy' and 'soggy'	Wheel cylinder leaking Master cylinder leaking (bubbles in master cylinder reservoir) Brake pipe line or flexible hose leaking Unions in brake system loose Blocked reservoir cap vent hole
Excessive effort required to brake vehicle	Shoe or pad linings badly worn New linings recently fitted – not yet bedded-in Harder linings fitted than standard resulting in increase in pedal pressure Linings and brake drums or discs contaminated with oil, grease or hydraulic fluid Servo unit inoperative or faulty Scored drums or discs
Brakes uneven and pulling to one side	Linings and drums or discs contaminated with oil, grease or hydraulic fluid Tyre pressure unequal Radial ply tyres fitted at one end of the vehicle only Brake shoes fitted incorrectly Different type of linings fitted at each wheel Anchorages for front or rear suspension loose Brake drums or discs badly worn, cracked or distorted Incorrect front wheel alignment Incorrectly adjusted front wheel bearings
Brakes tend to bind, drag or lock-on	Air in hydraulic system Wheel cylinders seized Handbrake cables too tight Weak shoe return springs Incorrectly set foot pedal or pushrod Master cylinder seized

Chapter 10 Electrical system

For modifications, and information applicable to later models, see Supplement at end of manual

Contents

Specifications

System type	12 volt, negative earth		

Battery

	Europe	USA	Canada
Capacity:			
Volts	12	12	12
Amp hour	40	60	65

Alternator – New Sunny models

Model	**LT 135-35C**		or **LT 150-22B**
Rating	12V, 35A		12V, 50A
Brush length (minimum)		0.295 in (7.5 mm)	
Slip ring diameter (minimum) . . .		1.18 in (30 mm)	

Alternator – 210 models

Model	LR 150-49
Rating	12V, 50A
Brush length (minimum)	0.295 in (7.5 mm)
Slip ring diameter (minimum) . . .	1.18 in (30 mm)

Regulator

	TLIZ-57B	or **RQB 2220 B**
Type		
Regulating voltage	14.3 to 15.3 volts at 68°F (20°C)	14.3 to 15.3 volts at 68°F (20°C)
Voltage coil resistance	10.5 ohms at 68°F (20°C)	23.6 ohms at 68°F (20°C)
Rotor coil inserting resistance . .	10 ohms	10 ohms
Voltage coil series resistance . . .	31 ohms	38 ohms
Core gap	0.024 to 0.039 in (0.6 to 1.0 mm)	0.028 to 0.051 in (0.7 to 1.3 mm)
Point gap	0.012 to 0.016 in (0.3 to 0.4 mm)	0.012 to 0.016 in (0.3 to 0.4 mm)
Charge relay:		
Release voltage	4.2 to 5.2 volts at N terminal	4.2 to 5.2 volts at N terminal
Voltage coil resistance	37.8 ohms at 68°F (20°C)	23.6 ohms at 68°F (20°C)
Core gap	0.031 to 0.039 in (0.8 to 1.0 mm)	0.035 to 0.055 in (0.9 to 1.4 mm)
Point gap	0.016 to 0.024 in (0.4 to 0.6 mm)	0.028 to 0.043 in (0.7 to 1.1 mm)

Starter motor – non-reduction gear type

Type	S114-160, S114-160B, S114-163E or MCA02-0
No load current	Less than 60A

Magnetic switch:

Series coil resistance	0.324 ohms
Shunt coil resistance	0.694 ohms
Gap between pinion and pinion stopper	0.012 to 0.059 in (0.3 to 1.5 mm)

Armature shaft to bearing clearance:

Pinion side	0.0012 to 0.0055 in (0.03 to 0.14 mm)
Rear side	0.012 to 0.055 in (0.03 to 0.14 mm)

Minimum outer diameter of commutator:

S114-160, S114-160B, S114-163E	1.260 in (32 mm)
MCA02-0	1.236 in (31.4 mm)

Brush length (minimum):

S114-160, S114-160B, S114-163E	0.472 in (12 mm)
MCA02-0	0.453 in (11.5 mm)
Clearance between pinion front edge and pinion stopper	0.012 to 0.098 in (0.3 to 2.5 mm)

Starter motor – reduction gear type

Type	S114-253
No load current	Less than 100A
Minimum outer diameter of commutator	1.14 in (29 mm)
Brush length (minimum)	0.43 in (11 mm)
Difference in height of pinion	0.012 to 0.059 in (0.3 to 1.5 mm)

Fuses – UK models

Wiper, washer	10 A
Horn, cigarette lighter	15 A
Stop light, interior light	15 A
Tail lamp – right-hand	10 A
Tail lamp – left-hand	10 A
Heater, radio	15 A
Engine control	10 A
Flasher, meter	10 A
Rear window demister	20 A
Headlamp cleaner	10 A

Fuses – 210 models

Clock, cigarette lighter, interior light	15 A
Stop light, horn, hazard lights	15 A
Tail, parking, interior lights	10 A
Radio, rear window demister	20 A
Wiper, washer, heater	15 A
Engine control	10 A
Flasher, meter, reversing light	10 A
Air conditioner	20 A (separate from fuse box)

Fusible link

	Colour	Size
Power supply	Green	0.0008 in² (0.5 mm²)
Headlight circuit	Brown	0.0005 in² (0.3 mm²)

Bulbs – UK models

Headlights – sealed beam	50/40 W
Headlights – bulb	45/40 W

Front combination light

Turn	21 W
Clearance	5W
Side turn light	5 W

Rear combination light

Turn	21 W
Stop-tail	21/5W
Reversing	21 W

Number plate light

Saloon and Coupe	10 W
Estate	5 W
Interior light	10 W
Luggage compartment light	5W

Bulbs – 210 models

Headlights – sealed beam	60/50W

Front combination light

Turn	23 W
Clearance	8 W

Side marker light

Front	8 W
Rear	8 W

Rear combination light
    Turn . . . . 23 W
    Stop/tail . . . . 23/8 W
    Tail (Saloon only) . . . . 8 W
    Reversing . . . . 23 W
Number plate light . . . . 7.5 W
Interior light . . . . 10 W
Instrument panel . . . . 3.4 W

Torque wrench settings

	lbf ft	kgf m
Magnetic switch terminal		
S114-160B, S114-163E	5 to 7	0.75 to 1.0
S114-253	8 to 11	1.1 to 1.6
Magnetic switch attachment bolts	3 to 4	0.4 to 0.5
Starter motor gear case attachment bolts	4 to 6	0.6 to 0.8
Alternator pulley nut	33 to 43	4.5 to 6.0
Alternator through bolts	4 to 5	0.6 to 0.7

1 General description

The electrical system is 12 volt negative earth and the major components comprise a 12 volt battery, an alternator which is driven from the crankshaft pulley and a starter motor.

The battery supplies a steady current for the ignition, lighting, and other electrical circuits and provides a reserve of electricity when the current consumed by the electrical equipment exceeds that being produced by the alternator.

The alternator has a regulator which ensures a high output if the battery is in a low state of charge or the demand from the electrical equipment is high, and a low output if the battery is fully charged and there is little demand for the electrical equipment.

When fitting electrical accessories to cars with a negative earth system, it is important, if they contain silicone diodes or transistors, that they are connected correctly, otherwise serious damage may result to the components concerned. Items such as radios, tape players, electronic ignition systems, automatic headlight dipping etc, should all be checked for correct polarity.

It is important that the battery positive lead is always disconnected if the battery is to be boost charged. Also if body repairs are to be carried out using electric arc welding equipment, the alternator must be disconnected otherwise serious damage can be caused to the more delicate instruments. Whenever the battery has to be disconnected, it must always be reconnected with the negative terminal earthed.

2 Battery – removal and refitting

1 The battery is situated in the engine compartment on the right-hand side at the front.
2 When removing the battery, always disconnect the negative cable first, followed by the positive cable. Then remove the nuts from the battery clamps and lift out the battery.
3 Refitting is the reverse of the removal procedure, but before fitting the terminals, smear them with a little petroleum jelly.

3 Battery – maintenance and inspection

1 Keep the top of the battery clean by wiping away dirt and moisture.
2 Remove the plugs or lid from the cells and check that the electrolyte level is just above the separator plates. If the level has fallen, add only distilled water until the electrolyte level is just above the separator plates.
3 As well as keeping the terminals clean and covered with petroleum jelly, the top of the battery, and especially the top of the cells, should be kept clean and dry. This helps prevent corrosion and ensures that the battery does not become partially discharged by leakage through dampness and dirt.
4 Once every three months, remove the battery and inspect the battery securing bolts, the battery clamp plate, tray and battery leads for corrosion (white fluffy deposits on the metal which are brittle to touch). If any corrosion is found, clean off the deposits with an ammonia or soda solution and paint over the clean metal with a fine base primer and/or underbody paint.
5 At the same time inspect the battery case for cracks. If a crack is found, clean and plug it with one of the proprietary compounds marketed for this purpose. If leakage through the crack has been excessive then it will be necessary to refill the appropriate cell with fresh electrolyte as detailed later. Cracks are frequently caused to the top of the battery cases by pouring in distilled water in the middle of winter *after* instead of *before* a run. This gives the water no chance to mix with the electrolyte and so the former freezes and splits the battery case.
6 If topping-up the battery becomes excessive and the case has been inspected for cracks that could cause leakage, but none are found, the battery is being over-charged and the voltage regulator will have to be checked and reset.
7 With the battery on the bench at the three monthly interval check, measure its specific gravity with a hydrometer to determine the state of charge and condition of the electrolyte. There should be very little variation between the different cells and if a variation in excess of 0.025 is present it will be due to either:

(a) *Loss of electrolyte from the battery at some time caused by spillage or a leak, resulting in a drop in the specific gravity of electrolyte when the deficiency was replaced with distilled water instead of fresh electrolyte*
(b) *An internal short circuit caused by buckling of the plates or a similar malady pointing to the likelihood of total battery failure in the near future*

8 The specific gravity of the electrolyte for fully charged conditions at the electrolyte temperature indicated, is listed in Table A. The specific gravity of a fully discharged battery at different temperatures of the electrolyte is given in Table B.

Table A
Specific Gravity – Battery Fully Charged
1.268 at 100°F or 38°C electrolyte temperature
1.272 at 90°F or 32°C electrolyte temperature
1.276 at 80°F or 27°C electrolyte temperature
1.280 at 70°F or 21°C electrolyte temperature
1.284 at 60°F or 16°C electrolyte temperature
1.288 at 50°F or 10°C electrolyte temperature
1.292 at 40°F or 4°C electrolyte temperature
1.296 at 30°F or −1.5°C electrolyte temperature

Table B
Specific Gravity – Battery Fully Discharged
1.098 at 100°F or 38°C electrolyte temperature
1.102 at 90°F or 32°C electrolyte temperature
1.106 at 80°F or 27°C electrolyte temperature
1.110 at 70°F or 21°C electrolyte temperature
1.114 at 60°F or 16°C electrolyte temperature
1.118 at 50°F or 10°C electrolyte temperature
1.122 at 40°F or 4°C electrolyte temperature
1.126 at 30°F or −1.5°C electrolyte temperature

4 Electrolyte replenishment

1 If the battery is in a fully charged state and one of the cells maintains a specific gravity reading which is 0.025 or more lower than

the others, and a check of each cell has been made with a battery testing meter to check for short circuits (a four to seven second test should give a steady reading of between 1.2 to 1.8 volts), then it is likely that the electrolyte has been lost from the cell with the low reading at some time.

2   Top-up the cell with a solution of 1 part of sulphuric acid to 2.5 parts water. If the cell is already fully topped up draw some electrolyte out of it with a pipette.

3   When mixing the sulphuric acid and water *never add water to sulphuric acid* – always pour the acid slowly onto the water in a glass container. *If water is added to sulphuric acid it will explode.*

4   Continue to top-up the cell with the freshly made electrolyte and then recharge the battery and check the hydrometer readings. **Note:** *If the battery is not removed from the vehicle when being charged it is essential that the cables are disconnected as described in Section 2.*

5   Battery charging

1   Under normal operating conditions there should be no need to charge a battery from an external source, and if it is found to be necessary either the battery, alternator or voltage regulator is at fault.

2   When a vehicle has not been used for a period of time (particularly in very cold conditions) and it is found that the battery condition will not allow the engine to start, it is a good idea to charge the battery for about five hours at an initial charging current of about five amps. (The amount of charge and charging time will obviously depend on the battery condition, but the charging current will fall as the battery charge builds up). Alternatively a trickle charge at an initial current of about 1.5 amps can safely be used overnight.

3   The use of rapid boost chargers, which are claimed to restore the full charge of a battery in a very short time, should be avoided if at all possible as the battery plates are likely to suffer damage.

6   Alternator – general description, maintenance and precautions

1   Briefly, the alternator comprises a rotor and stator. Current is generated in the coils of the stator as soon as the rotor revolves. This current is three-phase alternating, which is then rectified by positive and negative silicon diodes. The charging current required to maintain the battery charge is controlled by a regulator unit.

2   Maintenance consists of occasionally wiping away any oil or dirt which may have accumulated on the outside of the unit.

3   No lubrication is required, as the bearings are grease-sealed for life.

4   Check the drivebelt tension periodically to ensure that its specified deflection is correctly maintained (see Chapter 2).

5   Take extreme care when making circuit connections to a vehicle fitted with an alternator and observe the following. When making connections to the alternator from a battery, always match correct polarity. Before using electric-arc welding equipment to repair any part of the vehicle, disconnect the connector from the alternator and disconnect the battery cables. Always disconnect both battery cables before using a mains charger. If boosting from another battery, always connect in parallel using heavy cable.

7   Alternator (type LT) – testing in the vehicle

1   Where a faulty alternator is suspected, first ensure that the battery is fully charged; if necessary charge from an outside source.

2   Obtain a 0 to 30 voltmeter.

3   Disconnect the connector from the alternator terminals, then connect the 'A' terminal to the 'F' terminal.

4   Connect a test probe from the voltmeter positive terminal to the 'A' terminal of the alternator. Connect the voltmeter negative terminal

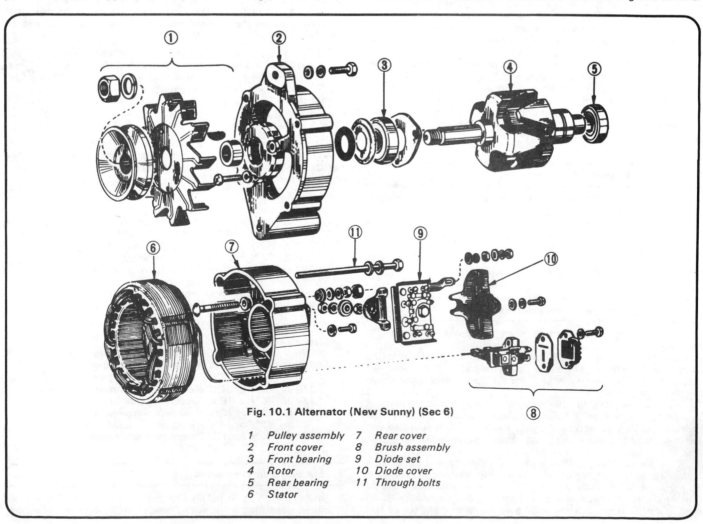

Fig. 10.1 Alternator (New Sunny) (Sec 6)

1 Pulley assembly	7 Rear cover
2 Front cover	8 Brush assembly
3 Front bearing	9 Diode set
4 Rotor	10 Diode cover
5 Rear bearing	11 Through bolts
6 Stator	

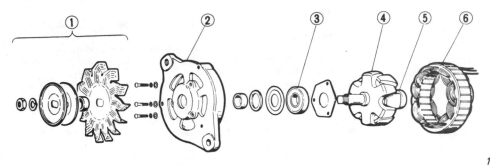

Fig. 10.2 Alternator (210) (Sec 6)

1	Pulley assembly	7	Diode set
2	Front cover	8	Brush assembly
3	Bearing (front)	9	IC voltage regulator
4	Rotor	10	Cover (rear)
5	Bearing (rear)	11	Through bolts
6	Stator		

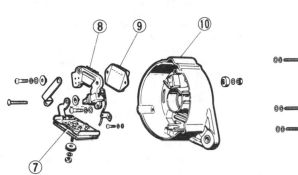

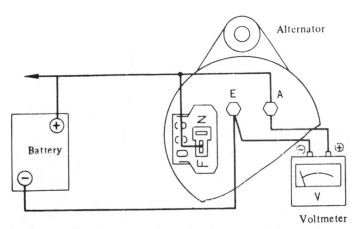

Fig. 10.3 Alternator test circuit (Sec 7)

8.3 Alternator adjustment link bolt

to earth 'E' and check that the voltmeter indicates battery voltage (12 volts).

5   Switch the headlights to main beam.

6   Start the engine and gradually increase its speed to approximately 1100 rpm and check the reading on the voltmeter. If it registers over 12.5 volts then the alternator is in good condition; if it registers below 12.5 volts then the alternator is faulty, amd must be removed and repaired. Do not exceed 1100 rpm during the test.

8   Alternator – removal and refitting

1   Detach the battery earth cable.

2   Disconnect the lead wires and connector, from the rear of the alternator.

3   Slacken the alternator pivot mounting bolts and also the adjustment link bolt (photo) sufficiently to allow the alternator to be hinged inwards towards the engine.

4   Disconnect the fan belt from the alternator pulley and then remove the pivot and adjusting link bolts whilst supporting the alternator, and

lift it clear.

5   Refitting is a reversal of the removal procedure but ensure that the fan belt tension is correctly adjusted as described in Chapter 2.

9   Alternator – brush renewal

1   These are the most likely components to require renewal, and their wear should be checked at 50 000 mile (80 000 km) intervals or whenever the alternator is suspected of being faulty (indicated by a discharged battery).

2   On the LR150–49 alternator (USA models), the brush removal necessitates the removal of the rear cover. It is therefore recommended that unless you are familiar with the circuitry and components of alternators, renewal of the brushes is best left to your local Datsun

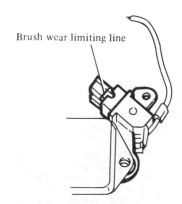

Fig. 10.4 Brush wear limit (Sec 9)

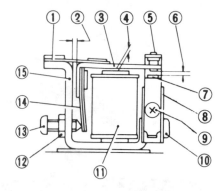

Fig. 10.5 Mechanical type voltage regulator (Sec 11)

1	Connecting spring	9	3mm (0.118 in) diameter
2	Yoke gap		screw
3	Armature	10	4 mm (0.157 in) diameter
4	Core gap		screw
5	Low speed contact	11	Coil
6	Point gap	12	Locknut
7	High speed contact	13	Adjusting screw
8	Contact set	14	Adjusting spring
		15	Yoke

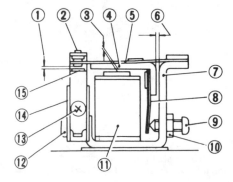

Fig. 10.6 Charging relay (Sec 11)

1	Point gap	10	Locknut
2	Charge relay circuit	11	Coil
3	Core gap	12	4 mm (0.157 in) diameter
4	Armature		screw
5	Connecting spring	13	3 mm (0.118 in) diameter
6	Yoke gap		screw
7	Yoke	14	Contact set
8	Adjusting spring	15	Voltage regulator contact
9	Adjusting screw		

dealer or auto electrician.

3   On those alternators where brushes can be renewed externally proceed as follows.

4   Remove the brush holder securing screws and withdraw the cover.

5   Remove the brush holder complete with brushes. Do not disconnect the 'N' terminal from the stator coil lead.

6   If the brushes have worn down to the limit marked on them, renew them.

7   Check that the brushes move smoothly in their holders; otherwise clean the holders free from any dust or dirt.

8   Refitting of the brushes is the reverse of the removal procedure.

10 Alternator – fault finding and repair

1   Due to the specialist knowledge and equipment required to test and service an alternator it is recommended that if the performance is suspect, the car be taken to an automobile electrician who will have the facilities for such work. Because of this recommendation no further detailed service information is given.

11 Regulator – description, testing and adjustment

New Sunny models

1   The regulator is located on the right side of the engine compartment, and incorporates a separate voltage regulator and cut-out.

2   The voltage regulator controls the output from the alternator depending upon the state of the battery and the demands of the vehicle electrical equipment, and it ensures that the battery is not overcharged. The cut-out is virtually an automatic switch which completes the charging circuit as soon as the alternator starts to rotate and isolates it when the engine stops so that the battery cannot be discharged through the alternator. One visual indication of the correct functioning of the cut-out is the ignition warning lamp. When the lamp is out, the system is charging.

3   Before testing, check that the alternator drivebelt is not broken or slack, and that all electrical leads are secure.

4   Test the regulator voltage with the unit still fitted in the vehicle. If it has been removed make sure that it is positioned with the connector plug hanging downward. Carry out the testing with the engine compartment cold, and complete the test within one minute to prevent the regulator heating up and affecting the specified voltage readings.

5   Establish the ambient temperature within the engine compartment, turn off all vehicle electrical equipment and ensure that the battery is in a fully charged state. Connect a dc (15 to 30v) voltmeter, a dc (5 to 30 A) ammeter and a 0.25 ohm 25 watt resistor, as shown (Fig. 10.7).

6   Start the engine and immediately detach the short circuit wire. Increase the engine speed to 2500 rpm and check the voltmeter reading according to the pre-determined ambient temperature table below.

7   If the voltage does not conform to that specified, continue to run the engine at 2500 rpm for several minutes and then with the engine idling check that the ammeter reads below 5 amps. If the reading is above this, the battery is not fully charged and must be removed for charging as otherwise accurate testing cannot be carried out.

Ambient temperature		Rated regulating voltage
°C	(°F)	(V)
–10	(14)	14.75 to 15.25
0	(32)	14.60 to 15.20
10	(50)	14.45 to 14.95
20	(68)	14.30 to 14.80
30	(86)	14.15 to 14.65
40	(104)	14.00 to 14.50

8   Switch off the engine, remove the cover from the voltage regulator and inspect the surfaces of the contacts. If these are rough or pitted, clean them by drawing a strip of very fine emery cloth between them.

9   Using feeler gauges, check and adjust the core gap, if necessary, to between 0.0315 to 0.0394 in (0.8 to 1.0 mm).

10 Check and adjust the contact points gap if necessary, to between 0.0118 and 0.0157 in (0.3 and 0.4 mm).

11 By now the voltage regulator will have cooled down so that the previous test may be repeated. If the voltage/temperature are still not

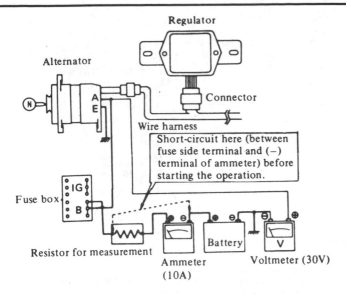

Fig. 10.7 Measuring regulated voltage (Sec 11)

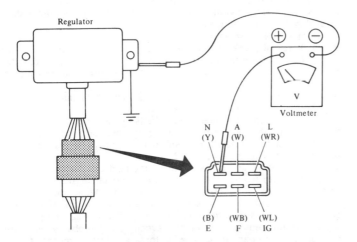

Fig. 10.8 Testing the voltage regulator (mechanical type) (Sec 11)

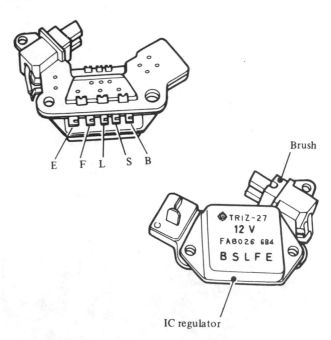

Fig. 10.9 Transistorized voltage regulator (210) (Sec 11)

correct, switch off the engine and adjust the regulator screw. Do this by loosening the locknut and turning the screw clockwise to increase the voltage reading and anti-clockwise to reduce it.

12 Turn the adjuster screw only fractionally before retesting the voltage charging rate again with the unit cold. Finally tighten the locknut.

13 If the cut-out is operating incorrectly, first check the fan belt and the ignition warning lamp bulb. Connect the positive terminal of a dc voltmeter to the 'N' socket of the regulator connector plug, and the voltmeter negative terminal to ground as shown (Fig. 10.8).

14 Start the engine and let it idle. Check the voltmeter reading. If the reading is zero volts, check for continuity between the 'N' terminals of the regulator unit and the alternator. If the reading is below 5.2 volts and the ignition warning lamp remains on, check and adjust the core gap and points gap to the specified respective clearances. Remember that this time the adjustments are carried out to the cut-out not the voltage regulator although the procedure is similar.

15 If the reading is over 5.2 volts with the ignition warning lamp on, and the core and points gap are correctly set, the complete regulator unit must be renewed.

16 The cut-out is operating correctly if the voltmeter shows a reading of more than 5.2 volts (ignition lamp out).

210 models

17 On 210 models the voltage regulator is a fully transistorized integrated circuit type. This unit is fully sealed and therefore requires no maintenance or adjustments.

18 In the unlikely event of it becoming defective, it is not repairable and must be replaced by a new unit.

19 To test the regulator, specialized knowledge and equipment is required and it should be entrusted to your Datsun dealer, or local automotive electrician.

12 Starter motor – general description

1 The starter motor incorporates a solenoid mounted on top of the starter motor body. When the ignition switch is operated, the solenoid moves the starter drive pinion, through the medium of the shift lever, into engagement with the flywheel or driveplate starter ring gear. As the solenoid reaches the end of its stroke and with the pinion by now partially engaged with the flywheel ring gear, the main fixed and moving contacts close and energize the starter motor to rotate the engine. This fractional pre-engagement of the starter drive does much to reduce the wear on the flywheel ring gear associated with inertia type starter motors.

2 On some models, the starter motor is fitted with a reduction gear, which is situated between the armature and pinion gear, and is designed to reduce the armature speed and increase the rotational torque.

3 An overrun clutch transmits drive torque from the armature or when fitted, reduction gear, to the ring gear on the flywheel (or driveplate on automatic models).

4 This system enables the mesh between the flywheel and pinion to be more positive and once the engine has started the clutch prevents the armature continuing to rotate, reducing wear and possible damage.

13 Starter motor – removal and refitting

1 Disconnect the battery earth lead.

2 Disconnect the black and yellow wire from the 'S' terminal on the solenoid, and the black cable from the 'B' terminal (also on the end cover of the solenoid).

3 Unscrew and remove the two starter motor securing bolts (photo), pull the starter forward, tilt it slightly to clear the motor shaft support from the flywheel ring gear and withdraw it.

4 Refitting is the reverse of the removal procedure.

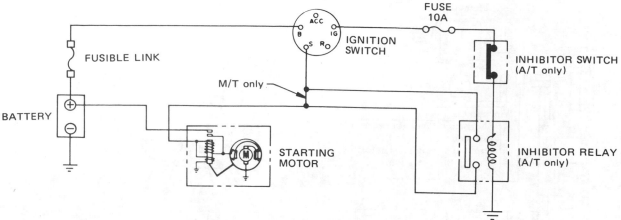

Fig. 10.10 Starter motor circuit diagram (Sec 12)

13.3 Starter motor securing bolts

14 Starter motor (non-reduction gear type) – dismantling, servicing and reassembly

1 Disconnect the lead from the 'M' terminal of the solenoid.
2 Remove the solenoid securing screws and withdraw the solenoid

from the starter motor.
3 Remove the dust cover, the E-ring and the two thrust washers from the rear cover where applicable.
4 Unscrew and remove the two screws which secure the brush holder.
5 Unscrew and remove the two tie-bolts and the rear cover.
6 Using a length of wire with a hook at its end, remove the brushes by pulling the brush springs aside.
7 Remove the brush holder.
8 Withdraw the yoke assembly and extract the armature assembly and shift lever. Push the pinion stop towards the pinion to expose the circlip. Extract the circlip and then withdraw the stop and clutch assembly.
9 Check the brushes for wear. If their length is less than that specified, renew them.
10 If an ohmmeter is available, test the field coil for continuity. To do this, connect one probe of the meter to the field coil positive terminal and the other to the positive brush holder. If no reading is indicated, the field coil circuit has a break in it.
11 Connect one probe of the meter to the field coil positive lead and the other one to the yoke. If there is a low resistance, the field coil is earthed due to a breakdown in insulation. When this fault is discovered, the field coils should be renewed by an automotive electrician, as it is very difficult to remove the field coil securing screws without special equipment. In any event, it will probably be more economical to exchange the complete starter motor for a reconditioned unit.
12 Undercut the separators of the commutator using an old hacksaw blade ground to suit to a depth of 0.02 to 0.03 in (0.5 to 0.8 mm). The commutator may be polished with a piece of very fine glass paper – never use emery cloth. as the carborundum particles will become embedded in the copper surfaces.
13 The armature may be tested for insulation breakdown, again using the ohmmeter. To do this, place one probe on the armature shaft and

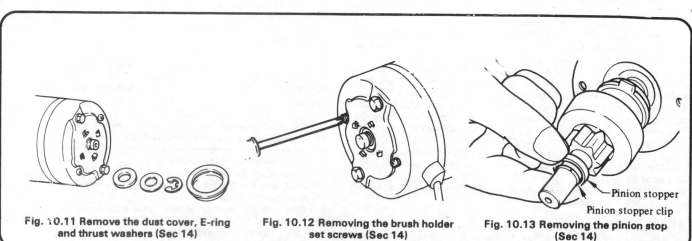

Fig. 10.11 Remove the dust cover, E-ring and thrust washers (Sec 14)

Fig. 10.12 Removing the brush holder set screws (Sec 14)

Fig. 10.13 Removing the pinion stop (Sec 14)

Pinion stopper
Pinion stopper clip

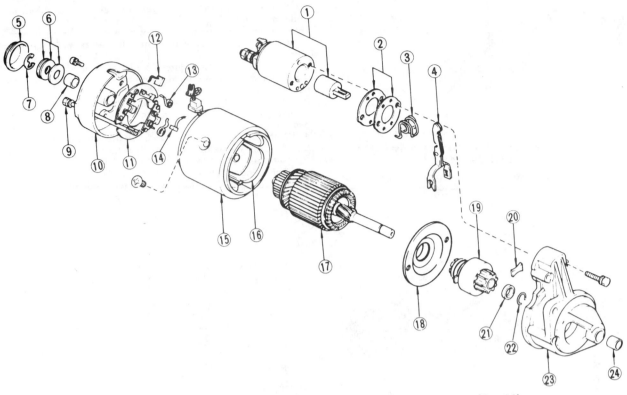

Fig. 10.14 Starter motor components – non-reduction gear type (Sec 14)

1	Magnetic switch assembly	7	E-ring	13	Brush spring	19	Pinion assembly
2	Adjusting washers	8	Rear cover bush	14	Brush (+)	20	Dust cover
3	Torsion spring	9	Through bolt	15	Yoke	21	Pinion stop
4	Shift lever	10	Rear cover	16	Field coil	22	Stop clip
5	Dust cover	11	Brush holder	17	Armature	23	Gear case
6	Thrust washer	12	Brush (-)	18	Centre bracket	24	Gear case bush

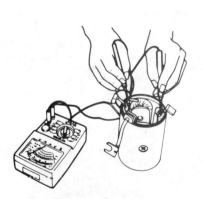

Fig. 10.15 Testing the field coils (Sec 14)

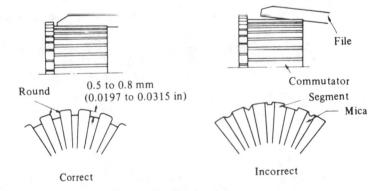

Fig. 10.16 Undercutting the commutator insulation (Sec 14)

the other on each of the commutator segments in turn. If there is a reading indicated at any time during the test, the armature must be renewed.

14 Wash the components of the drivegear in paraffin, inspect for wear or damage, particularly to the pinion teeth and renew as appropriate. Refitting is a reversal of dismantling, but stake a new stop washer in position and lubricate the sliding surfaces of the pinion assembly with a light oil, applied sparingly.

15 Reassembly of the remaining components of the starter motor is the reverse of the dismantling procedure.

16 When the starter motor has been fully reassembled, actuate the solenoid which will throw the drivegear forward into its normal flywheel engagement position. Do this by connecting jumper leads between the battery terminal and the solenoid 'M' terminal and between the battery positive terminal and the solenoid 'S' terminal.

17 Check the gap between the end face of the drive pinion and the mating face of the thrust washer. This should be between 0.012 and 0.059 in (0.3 to 1.5 mm) measured either with a vernier or feeler gauge. Adjusting washers are available in different thicknesses (Fig. 10.17).

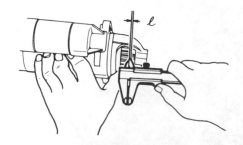

Fig. 10.17 Measuring drive pinion endface to thrust washer clearance (L) (Sec 14)

See Specifications for clearance

15 Starter motor (reduction gear types) – dismantling, servicing and reassembly

1   Detach the connection plate from the 'M' terminal on the solenoid unit.
2   Unscrew and remove the solenoid retaining screws and withdraw the solenoid unit. The torsion spring can be removed at this stage but note how it is located.
3   Unscrew the through bolts and carefully remove the rear cover– by prising it free using a screwdriver, but take care not to damage the packing.
4   Withdraw the yoke assembly and extract the armature unit.
5   The brushes and holders can now be removed, but note that the positive brush differs in that the brush is isolated from its holder and the connecting wire is attached to the field coil.
6   To extract the brushes hook back the retaining spring and pull the

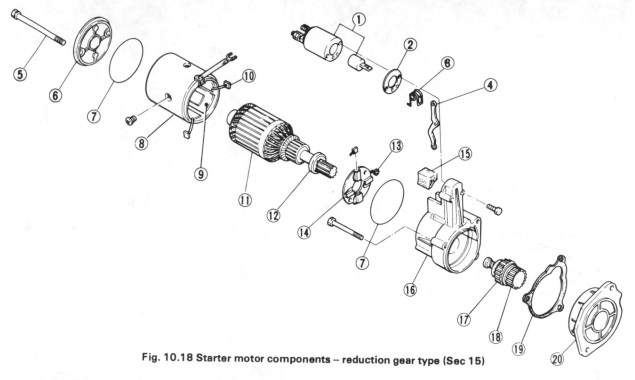

Fig. 10.18 Starter motor components – reduction gear type (Sec 15)

1	Magnetic switch assembly	6	Rear cover	11	Armature	16	Centre housing
2	Adjusting washer	7	O-ring	12	Centre bearing	17	Reduction gear
3	Torsion spring	8	Yoke	13	Brush spring	18	Pinion gear
4	Shift lever	9	Field coil	14	Brush holder	19	Packing
5	Through bolt	10	Brush	15	Dust cover	20	Gear case

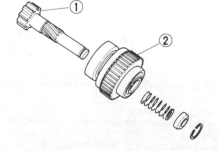

Fig. 10.19 Overrunning clutch assembly (Sec 15)

1	Pinion gear	2	Reduction gear

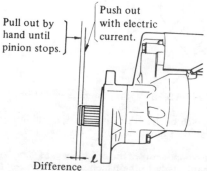

Pull out by hand until pinion stops.

Push out with electric current.

Difference

Fig. 10.20 Measuring difference in pinion length (Sec 15)

brushes from their respective holders, but keep them in order, noting their positions in case they do not require renewal.

7 To detach the centre housing from the gearcase, unscrew and remove the retaining bolts. The reduction/pinion gears can then be removed for examination.

8 The examination of the respective components closely follows that of the non-reduction gear type in Section 14, paragraphs 9 to 16, but in addition, check the condition of the pinion and reduction gear with overrun clutch components.

9 Compare the difference in length of the pinion when it is pushed out with the magnetic switch energized and when it is pulled out by hand until it touches the stopper (Fig. 6.20).

10 If necessary, adjust by changing the adjusting washer(s).

11 Any damage or signs of excessive wear in these parts will necessitate renewal. Check also that the sleeve slides freely on the shaft.

16 Fuses and fusible link

1 The fusebox is located beneath the instrument panel between the steering column and the driver's door. Fuse ratings and the circuits protected are marked on the fusebox.

2 A fusible link is incorporated in the battery-to-alternator wiring harness within the engine compartment. It provides an additional protection for the starting, charging, lighting and accessory circuits.

3 In the event of a fuse or fusible link blowing, always establish the cause before fitting a new one. This is most likely to be due to faulty

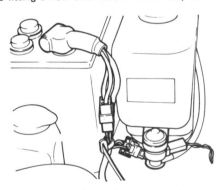

Fig. 10.21 Location of fusible link (Sec 16)

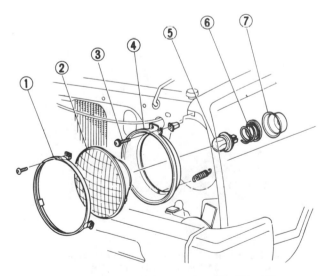

Fig. 10.22 Bulb headlamp assembly (Sec 17)

1 Retaining ring
2 Semi-sealed beam unit
3 Aiming adjusting screw
4 Mounting ring
5 Bulb
6 Retainer
7 Cover

insulation somewhere in the wiring circuit. Always carry a spare fuse for each rating, and never be tempted to substitute a piece of wire or a nail for the correct fuse as a fire may be caused or, at least, the electrical component ruined.

17 Headlight unit – removal and refitting

Headlight bulb – removal

1 The bulbs can be removed for renewal without removing the complete headlight unit, but in the following photographs, the headlamp has been removed for clarity.

2 Raise and support the bonnet and from inside the front panel, peel back the rubber cover and detach the headlight wire connector and rubber surround (photos).

3 Rotate the retaining ring to remove it and withdraw the bulb and holder (photos).

4 Refitting of the bulb is a direct reversal of the removal procedure but check operation on completion.

Headlight unit (sealed beam) – removal

5 Remove the radiator grille referring to Chapter 12 if necessary.

6 Unscrew and remove the three headlight unit retaining screws. Do not disturb the beam alignment screws or the lights will have to be readjusted.

17.2a Disconnecting the plug

17.2b Removing the rubber surround

17.3a Removing the retaining ring

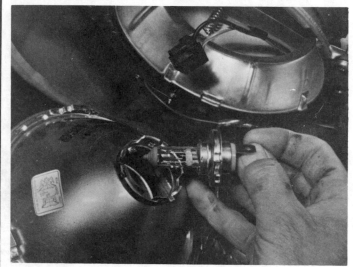

17.3b Withdrawing the bulb

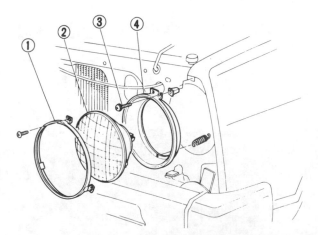

Fig. 10.23 Sealed beam headlamp assembly (Sec 17)

1   Retaining ring   3   Aiming adjusting screw
2   Sealed beam unit   4   Mounting ring

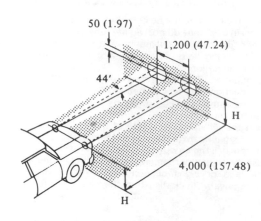

Fig. 10.24 Headlight adjustment (headlights on main beam) –
New Sunny with sealed beams (Sec 18)

H – Horizontal centre line of headlights
Dimensions given in mm (in)

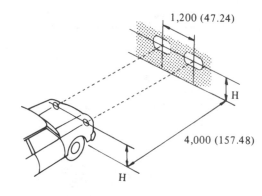

Fig. 10.25 Headlight adjustment (headlights on main beam) –
New Sunny with bulbs (Sec 18)

H – Horizontal centre line of headlights
Dimensions given in mm (in)

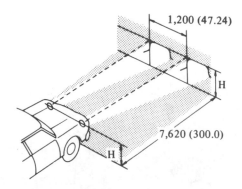

Fig. 10.26 Headlight adjustment (headlights on low beam) –
210 models (Sec 18)

H – Horizontal centre line of headlights
Dimensions given in mm (in)

7   Withdraw the headlight unit and disconnect the lead wire connectors and rubber cover to remove it completely.
8   Refit in the reverse order but ensure that the headlight unit is the correct way up and if necessary, realign the beam adjustment before refitting the grille.

18 Headlamp aiming (beam alignment)

1   The only entirely satisfactory way of checking headlamp beam alignment is by the use of special optical testers.
2   However, where this equipment is not available, the following beam aiming procedure may be used.
3   Ensure that the tyres are correctly inflated and that the vehicle is on a flat level surface facing a flat wall. Ensure that the fuel tank, radiator and oil sump are full or topped-up to the recommended levels.
4   Referring to Fig. 10.24, 25, or 26 as appropriate, position the vehicle at the prescribed distance from a wall and mark the wall to show the corresponding alignment indicator marks for your model.

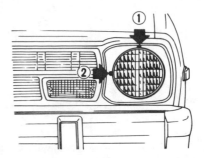

Fig. 10.27 Headlamp adjusting screws (Sec 18)

1   *Vertical adjustment*   2   *Horizontal adjustment*

18.5 Adjusting beam alignment

19.1 Removing the front combination light lens

19.3 Fitting a new bulb

Check whether you have sealed or bulb type headlight units before marking for alignment.
5   With the car positioned correctly, adjust the beam alignment screws (photo) to obtain the correct adjustment.

19 Front combination light

Bulb renewal
1   Remove the retaining screws and take off the lens (photo).
2   Press in the bulb and rotate it anti-clockwise to remove it from its socket.
3   Fit the new bulb (photo) ensuring that it is locked in the socket and check operation.
4   Position the gasket to the lamp body and fit the lens (and lamp body) using the two screws.

Lamp removal and refitting
5   Disconnect the lamp wires at the connector, and remove the grommet from the body panel.
6   Remove the lens as described in paragraph 1 then withdraw the lamp body.
7   Refitting is the reverse of the removal procedure.

20 Side marker light (front and rear)

Bulb renewal
1   Remove the retaining screws and take off the lens and rim.
2   According to the particular type, either press in the bulb and rotate it anti-clockwise to remove it, or pull the bulb and socket forward and take the bulb out (photo).
3   Fit the new bulb (and socket where applicable).
4   Position the gasket to the lamp body and refit the lens and rim.

Lamp removal and refitting
5   Disconnect the two lamp wires at the connectors, and remove the

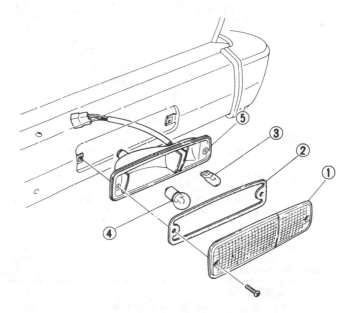

Fig. 10.28 Front combination lamp (Sec 19)

1	*Lens*	4	*Bulb (turn indicator)*
2	*Gasket*	5	*Lamp body*
3	*Bulb (park)*		

grommet (where applicable) from the body panel.
6   Remove the two retaining screws, the lens and the rim, and withdraw the lamp from the vehicle.
7   Refitting is the reverse of the removal procedure.

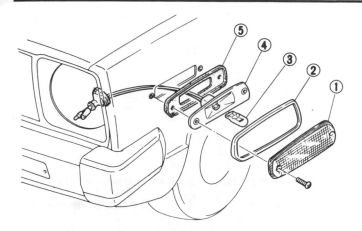

Fig. 10.29 Side marker light assembly (Sec 20)

1 Lens	4 Lamp body
2 Rim	5 Gasket
3 Bulb	

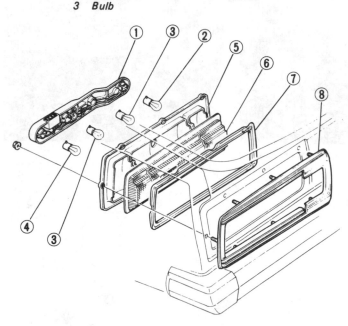

Fig. 10.30 Rear combination lamp assembly (Saloon) (Sec 21)

1 Rear cover	5 Housing
2 Bulb (reversing light)	6 Lens
3 Bulb (stop and tail)	7 Gasket
4 Bulb (turn indicator)	8 Rim

---

21 Rear combination lights

Bulb renewal – Saloon

1   Unclip the rear panel cover in the boot to gain access to the bulb holder units.
2   Remove the retaining screws and withdraw the combination bulb holder unit (photo).
3   Twist and remove the offending bulb/s. Refit in the reverse order and check the operation.

Bulb renewal – Coupe

4   Unclip the rear luggage finisher to gain access to the bulb holders.
5   Unscrew the central retaining screw and withdraw the bulb holder/s. Twist the bulb to remove it.
6   Refitting is a direct reversal of the removal process. Check operation on completion.

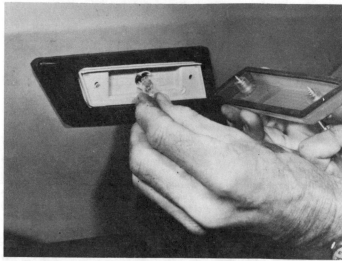

20.2 Renewing a front marker lamp

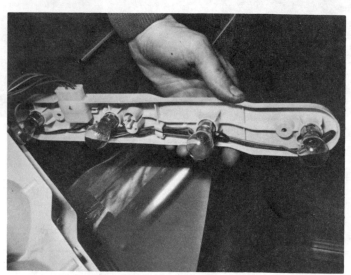

21.2 Removing the combination lamp bulbholder

Bulb renewal – Estate Car

7   Remove the lens retaining screws and withdraw the lens.
8   Pull bulb holder from lens socket.
9   Press, twist and remove the bulb to be renewed.
10   Refit in the reverse order and check operation.

Lamp removal and refitting

11   On Saloon and Coupe models remove the bulb holder unit, then unscrew the lens retaining nuts on the inside. Remove the lens retainer nuts and light unit.
12   Refit in the reverse order but check that the seals are in good condition and are not distorted during assembly.

---

22 License plate light

Saloon and Coupe (European models)

1   Unscrew and remove the lens retaining screw (photos) to gain access to the bulb. Refit in the reverse order.

Sedan and Hatchback (USA - 210 models)

2   Unclip and fold down the rear panel cover. Unscrew the unit retaining nuts, remove the lens and extract the bulb. Refit in the reverse order and check operation.

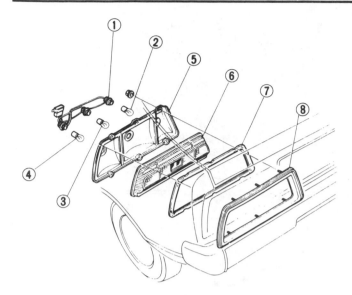

Fig. 10.31 Rear combination lamp assembly (Coupe) (Sec 21)

1	Lampholders	5	Housing
2	Bulb (reversing light)	6	Lens
3	Bulb (stop and tail)	7	Gasket
4	Bulb (turn indicator)	8	Rim

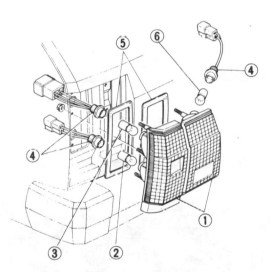

Fig. 10.32 Rear combination lamp assembly (Estate) (Sec 21)

1	Lamp body and lens	4	Lampholders
2	Bulb (turn indicator)	5	Gasket
3	Bulb (stop and tail)	6	Bulb (reversing light)

Estate Car (all markets)

3 Unscrew the lens retaining screws and remove the lens.
4 Renew the bulb and reassemble in the reverse order to removal. Check operation on completion (Fig. 10.34).

23 Interior light

1 To remove the lens, rotate it anti-clockwise. The festoon bulb can then be prised from the holder for renewal (Fig. 10.35).
2 To remove the light unit, detach the lens, unscrew the securing screws and then carefully pulling the light unit downwards, disconnect the wires.
3 Refit in the reverse order and check operation.

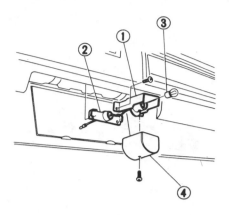

Fig. 10.33 Number plate light (Saloon and Coupe) (Sec 22)

1	Lamp body	3	Bulb
2	Gasket	4	Lens

22.1a License plate lens retaining screw

22.1b Light with lens removed

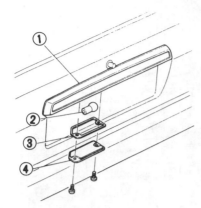

Fig. 10.34 Number plate light (Estate) (Sec 22)

1	Lamp body	3	Gasket
2	Bulb	4	Lens

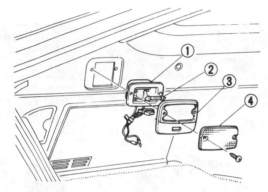

Fig. 10.36 Luggage compartment light (Coupe and Estate) (Sec 24)

1	Lamp body	3	Cover
2	Bulb	4	Lens

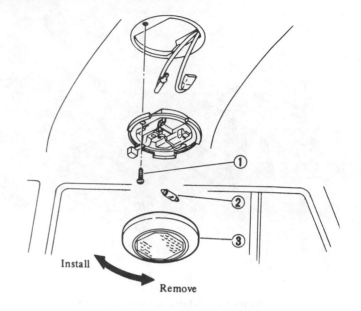

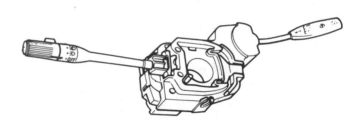

Fig. 10.35 Interior light (Sec 23)

1	Fixing screw	3	Lens
2	Bulb		

Fig. 10.37 Combination switch assembly (Sec 25)

Rear interior light – Estate Car

4   To remove the lens press the retaining clip tab upwards and detach the lens. Prise the festoon bulb free.
5   To remove the unit, unscrew the retaining screws and detach the wiring.
6   Refitting is a reversal of removal but check operation on completion.

24 Luggage compartment light

1   Unscrew and remove the lens retaining screws. Remove the lens and extract the bulb for renewal if necessary.
2   To remove the unit, pull it from the cavity (having removed the lens) and detach the wires.
3   Refitting is a reversal of removal.

25 Combination light and indicator switch – removal and refitting

1   Disconnect the battery earth cable.
2   Unscrew and remove the horn pad from the steering wheel (photo).
3   Unscrew the steering wheel retaining nut and withdraw the steering wheel.
4   Remove the steering column cover retaining screws and detach the cover.
5   Detach the combination switch wires at the connector and then loosen the switch retaining screw to remove the switch unit.
6   Refit the combination switch in the reverse sequence to removal

25.2 Removing the horn pad

but ensure that the respective circuits are fully operational before refitting the column cover. Tighten the steering wheel nut to the specified torque wrench setting given in Chapter 11.

26 Ignition switch – removal and refitting

1   Disconnect the battery earth cable.
2   Unscrew and remove the steering column cover, and then detach the wiring harness connector.
3   Unscrew the small switch body to steering lock retaining screw and remove the switch.
4   Reverse the above procedure to refit the ignition switch.

27 Light relay unit – removal and refitting

1   Disconnect the battery earth cable.
2   Detach the wiring harness at the connector.
3   Unscrew and remove the relay securing screws and remove the relay unit.
4   Refit in the reverse order and check operation.

28 Stop light switch – removal and refitting

1   The stop light switch is located above the brake pedal and can be removed as follows.
2   Detach the battery earth cable.
3   Detach the lead wires at the switch connections, slacken the locknut and then unscrew the switch unit and remove it.
4   Refit in the reverse order and retighten the locknut. Check operation on completion.

29 Reversing light switch – removal and refitting

1   This is located in the gearbox unit and can easily be removed from underneath the car. Disconnect the wires at the connector near the switch and then using a suitable spanner unscrew the switch to remove.
2   Refit in the reverse order.

30 Interior light door switch – removal and refitting

1   Disconnect the earth cable from the battery.
2   Carefully pull the switch unit from the lower door pillar and disconnect the wires at the connector (photo).
3   On Coupe models it is necessary to detach the side box from the rear armrest and then peel back the tape retaining harness to body from within the side box.
4   Refitting is a direct reversal of removal.

31 Ignition relay (California models) – removal and refitting

1   Detach the battery earth cable.
2   Detach the left-hand side dash finisher and then disconnect the wiring harness at the connector (Fig. 10.11).
3   Unscrew the relay unit retaining screw and withdraw the unit.
4   Refit in the reverse order to removal.

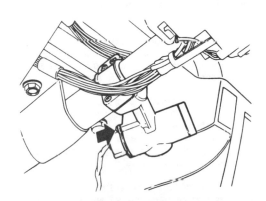

Fig. 10.38 Ignition switch with steering lock (Sec 26) Switch retaining screw arrowed

30.2 Removing the courtesy light switch

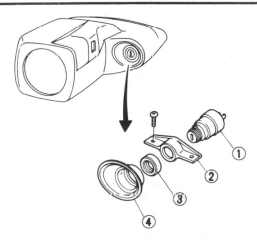

Fig. 10.39 Ignition switch without steering lock (Sec 26)

1   Ignition switch   3   Nut
2   Bracket   4   Escutcheon

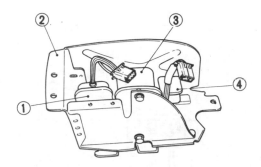

Fig. 10.40 Ignition relay location (Sec 31)

1   Automatic choke relay   3   Voltage regulator
2   Relay bracket   4   Ignition relay

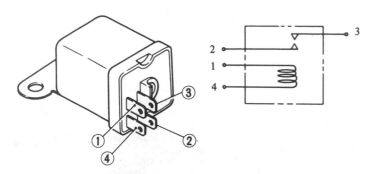

Fig. 10.41 Ignition relay connections (Sec 31)

remove the hinge cover to gain access to the switch.
3   The switch can then be carefully pulled from its retaining bracket and the wiring disconnected.
4   Reverse the above procedure to refit the switch assembly.

35 Luggage compartment light switch (Coupe) – removal and refitting

1   Detach the battery earth cable.
2   The switch is located on the side of the rear door lock. To remove the switch carefully pull it free from its bracket and disconnect the wire at the connector.
3   Refitting is a direct reversal of removal.

36 Handbrake warning switch – removal and refitting

Refer to Chapter 9, Section 4

37 Combination instrument panel – removal and refitting

1   Disconnect the battery earth cable and remove the instrument panel as described in Chapter 12, Section 30.
2   With the speedometer cable disconnected, detach the wire terminal connector and remove the panel retaining screws to withdraw the panel.
3   Refit in the reverse order of removal.

Speedometer – removal and refitting
4   Remove the combination meter as described previously.
5   Detach the reset knob of the odometer (mileage recorder).
6   Remove the screws retaining the printed circuit board.
7   Loosen the speedometer retaining screws and withdraw the speedometer.
8   Refitting is a reversal of the removal procedure.

Fuel level and water temperature gauges
9   Proceed as described in paragraphs 1 and 2.
10 Remove the retaining screws and remove the gauge.
11 Refitting is the reversal of removal.

Tachometer – removal and refitting
12 Proceed as described in paragraphs 1 and 2.
13 Detach the speedometer mileage reset knob and then the tachometer from the printed circuit board terminal.
14 Unscrew the circuit board retaining screws and loosen the tachometer securing screws to remove the tachometer.
15 Refitting is a direct reversal of the removal procedure.

32 Illumination control switch – removal and refitting

1   The switch incorporates a 35 ohm variable resistance to control the brightness of the heater control illumination lamp, wiper switch illumination lamp and lighting switch illumination lamp.
2   Detach the battery earth cable.
3   Detach the wiring harness connector from the rear of the control unit.
4   To remove the control knob, push and twist it, and withdraw with washer.
5   Use a suitable spanner and remove the control unit retaining nut. Withdraw the unit from underneath.
6   Refit in the reverse sequence.

33 Hazard warning light switch – removal and refitting

1   Detach the battery earth cable.
2   Unscrew the securing screws and remove the upper steering column cover, then detach the wiring harness connector to the switch.
3   Unscrew the retaining screw to remove the switch unit.
4   Refit in the reverse order to removal.

34 Tailgate door light switch (Estate Car) – removal and refitting

1   Detach the battery earth cable.
2   The switch is located on the right-hand tailgate hinge. First

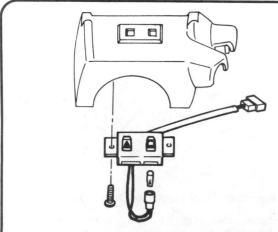

Fig. 10.42 Hazard warning light switch (Sec 33)

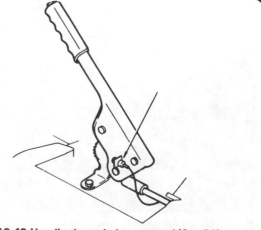

Fig. 10.43 Handbrake switch – arrowed (Sec 36)

38 Windscreen wiper and washer assembly – removal and refitting

Wiper motor

1   Disconnect the battery earth cable.
2   Pull the wire connector from the wiper motor.
3   Unscrew and remove the wiper motor securing bolts (photo).
4   Pull the motor unit carefully from the bulkhead to gain access to the wiper arm interconnecting rod securing nut. Unscrew the nut and detach the motor unit from the rod.
5   Assemble in the reverse order but ensure that the electrical connections are secure.

Windscreen wiper linkage

6   Remove the wiper motor as described previously.
7   Unscrew the central inspection cover screws (in the middle of the bulkhead), and remove the cover.
8   Detach the wiper arm from the pivot shaft. To do this lift the wiper arm from the windscreen and loosen the attachment bolt.
9   Slacken the pivot retaining nut and withdraw the link assembly.
10 Refit in the reverse order and ensure that the wiper arm is refitted at the correct operational angle on the pivot.

Wiper and washer switch

11 Detach the battery earth cable.
12 Unscrew and remove the steering column cover.

13 Unscrew the retaining screws securing the wiper switch to the combination switch and separate the two assemblies.
14 Refit in the reverse order.

Intermittent wiper amplifier

15 Detach the battery earth cable.
16 Disconnect the plug from the amplifier.
17 Remove the two screws securing the amplifier to the front bulkhead (photo).
18 The amplifier can be removed after releasing the washer pipe clip.
19 Refit in the reverse order.

Windscreen washer assembly

20 The reservoir and motor (pump) are retained on a bracket on the inner wing panel as shown, Fig. 10.48.
21 If the pipe or nozzles are to be removed, detach the pipe from the pump outlet, release the pipe from the body guide clips (bend them up) and then detach the pipe from the nozzles or T-piece connector as required.
22 The nozzles are retained by a screw which secures the bracket. If new nozzles are fitted, adjust the nozzle pipe by bending accordingly through the top grille vents to obtain the desired spray pattern.

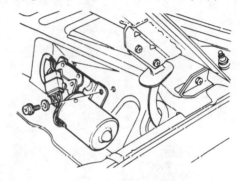

Fig. 10.44 Removing the wiper motor (Sec 38)

Fig. 10.45 Removing the wiper linkage (Sec 38)

38.3 Windscreen wiper motor

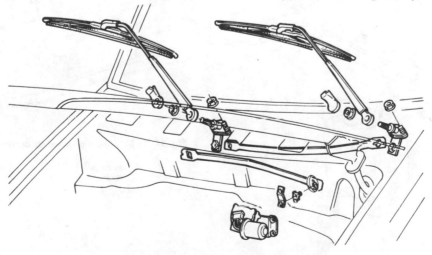

Fig. 10.46 Windscreen wiper linkage (Sec 38)

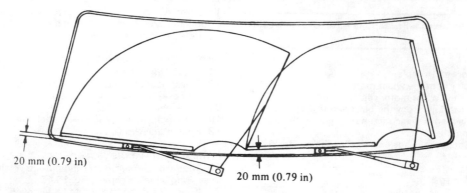

20 mm (0.79 in)

20 mm (0.79 in)

Fig. 10.47 Wiper arm setting (Sec 38)

38.17 The intermittent wipe amplifier

39 Rear window wiper (Estate Car)

1   Disconnect the earth cable from the battery.
2   Lift the wiper arm and loosen the retaining bolt, then withdraw the arm and blade assembly.
3   Detach the inner panel and sealer screen from the tailgate.
4   Detach the wire from the wiper motor connection and then unscrew the retaining bolts to remove the motor unit.
5   Refitting is a reversal of the removal procedure but check that the wiper arm is correctly positioned on the pivot shaft.

Rear windscreen washer
6   This is located in the rear side panel (left-hand side) and the inner panel must therefore be removed for access.
7   The washer nozzle is secured by a slotted clip and locknut. To remove or disconnect the nozzle the rear tailgate inner panel must be detached. The connecting pipe can then be detached and the retaining clip prised free to release the nozzle on the outside.
8   Refit in the reverse order.

Rear windscreen wiper switch
9   Detach the battery earth cable.
10 Separate the harness to switch connector and then push the switch knob and twist it to remove.
11 Unscrew the securing nut and remove the switch.
12 Refit in the reverse sequence.

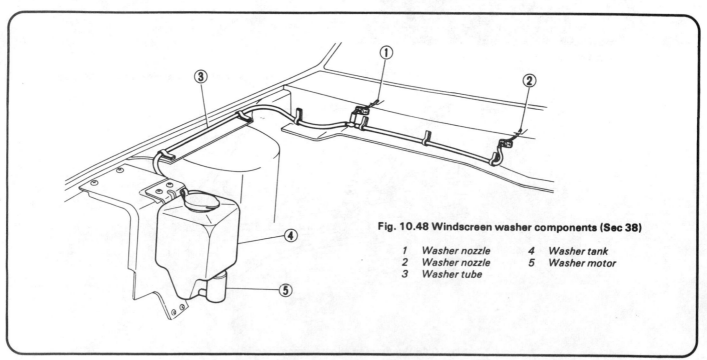

Fig. 10.48 Windscreen washer components (Sec 38)

1	Washer nozzle	4	Washer tank
2	Washer nozzle	5	Washer motor
3	Washer tube		

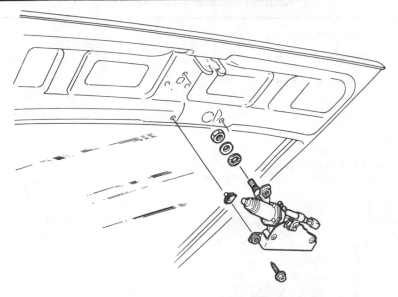

Fig. 10.49 Rear wiper motor installation (Sec 39)

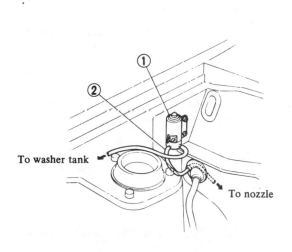

To washer tank

To nozzle

Fig. 10.50 Rear window washer installation (Sec 39)

1 Rear washer pump
2 Rear washer tube
3 Rear washer nozzle

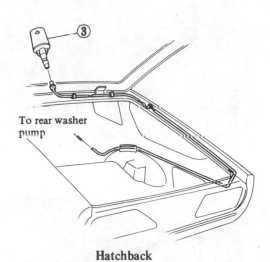

To rear washer pump

Hatchback

To rear washer pump

Wagon

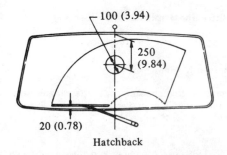

Hatchback

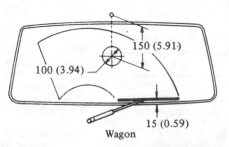

Wagon

Fig. 10.51 Rear wiper arm settings
(Sec 39)
Dimensions are in mm (inches)

40 Horns and horn relay

1　Detach the battery earth cable.
2　Detach the horn wire at the connector and then unscrew the horn retaining bolt to remove (photos).
3　Refit in the reverse order.

Horn relay

4　Detach the battery earth cable.
5　Detach the relay wire at the terminal connector of horn relay. Unscrew and remove the relay retaining screws to remove.
6　Refitting is a reversal of the removal procedure.

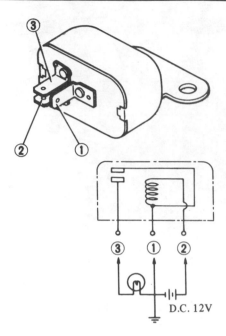

Fig. 10.52 Horn relay (Sec 40)

40.2a Horn (driver's side)

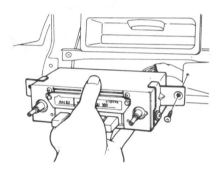

Fig. 10.53 Radio installation (Sec 41)

40.2b Horn (passenger side)

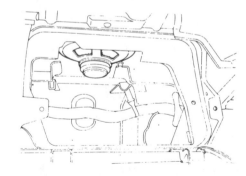

Fig. 10.54 Speaker installation (Sec 41)

41 Radio – removal and refitting

1　Disconnect the battery earth cable.
2　Remove the facia panel as described in Chapter 12, Section 29.
3　Unscrew and remove the radio bracket retaining screws. Carefully lift the radio clear complete with bracket.
4　Detach the wire connector and aerial cable.
5　Refitting is a direct reversal of the removal procedure, but check the operation before refitting the facia panel.

Radio speaker

6　Detach the battery earth cable.
7　Remove the radio.
8　Unscrew and remove the speaker unit attachment nuts and carefully remove the speaker unit, after disconnecting the leads.
9　Refitting is a direct reversal of removal.

Aerial and cable

10　To remove the aerial unscrew the upper and lower supports to the front pillar.

11 The feeder cable is accessible on removal of the front pillar moulding, then detach the facia (Chapter 12, Section 29) to disconnect the feeder cable from the receiver unit.
12 Carefully extract the cable through the front pillar.
13 Refitting is a direct reversal of the removal procedure.

Aerial adjustment
14 If a new radio receiver or aerial has been fitted it may be necessary to adjust the receiver or aerial trimmer to suit locality. This is accomplished by first raising the aerial fully.
15 Tune the radio receiver into the weakest station between 1200 to 1600 kHz. Now slowly turn the trimmer screw in each direction to adjust it to the most sensitive receiving level.

---

42 Heater unit

Heater control – removal, refitting and adjustments
1 Detach the battery earth cable.
2 Remove the facia panel as described in Chapter 12, Section 30.
3 Remove the defroster ducts.
4 Detach the door control cables and rods.
5 Detach the wiring harness connector.
6 Loosen the attachment screws and withdraw the heater control unit (and bracket).
7 Refitting is a reversal of the removal procedure but adjust the control cables and rods as follows.

Air mix door adjustment
8 With the temperature control set in the maximum position, press the air mix door lever as indicated by the arrows in Fig. 10.58. Press the temperature control cable casing (outer) towards the temperature lever and simultaneously retain the casing with the clip. Ensure that the coolant cock is fully shut when engaging the 'Temp' control lever at its maximum 'cold' position.

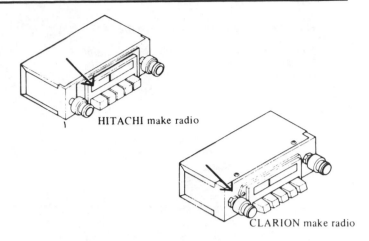

HITACHI make radio

CLARION make radio

Fig. 10.55 Position of aerial trimmer (arrowed) (Sec 41)

Ventilation door adjustment
9 Position the air lever in the 'Recirc' location and press the ventilation door as shown by the arrow in Fig. 10.59, to close the flow to the central outlet.
10 Press the ventilation door control rod to locate in the relay lever clamp. The ventilation door must be fully open whilst the air lever is positioned at the vent location.

Air intake door
11 Position the air lever to 'off' and then press the air intake door as shown in Fig. 10.60 to close the outside air flow. The air intake door cable casing is now pushed towards the air lever and simultaneously retained in the clip. Ensure that the air intake door is opened fully when

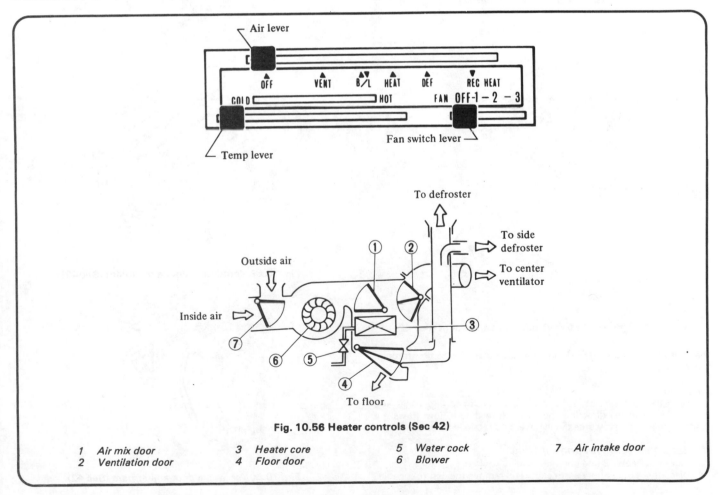

Fig. 10.56 Heater controls (Sec 42)

| 1 | Air mix door | 3 | Heater core | 5 | Water cock | 7 | Air intake door |
| 2 | Ventilation door | 4 | Floor door | 6 | Blower | | |

Fig. 10.57 Heater unit components (Sec 42)

1	Centre ventilation duct	6	Heater control
2	Side defroster duct	7	Water cock
3	Defroster nozzle	8	Water inlet hose
4	Defroster duct	9	Water outlet hose
5	Heater unit		

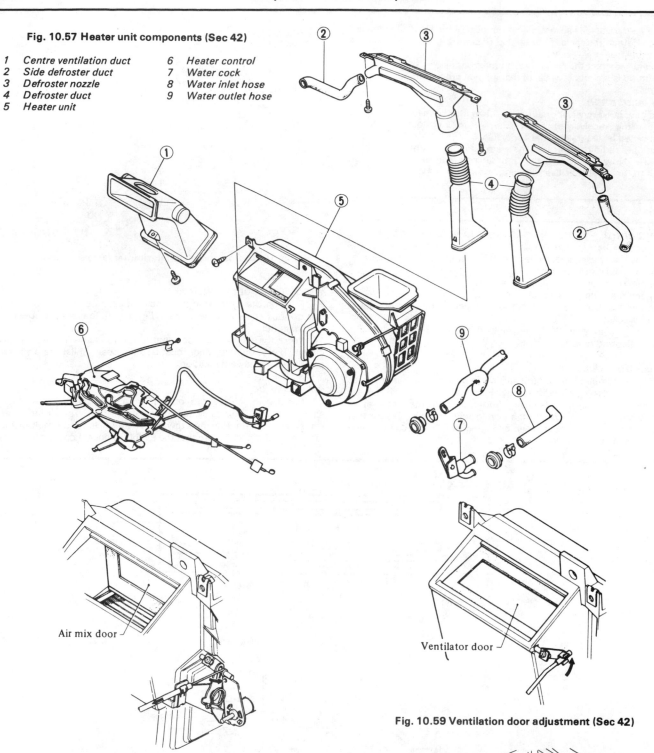

Air mix door

Fig. 10.58 Temperature control cable adjustment (Sec 42)

Ventilator door

Fig. 10.59 Ventilation door adjustment (Sec 42)

the air lever is in the Vent position (enabling outside air to flow through the intake).

Floor door

12 With the air lever set in the 'off' position refer to Fig. 10.62 and push the door in the direction shown to close the air flow. Press the control cable casing towards the air lever and retain in the clip.

Heater unit – removal and refitting

13 Refer to Chapter 2 and drain the engine coolant.
14 Disconnect the battery earth cable and remove the centre console.

Fig. 10.60 Air intake door adjustment (Sec 42)

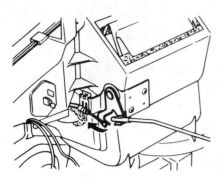

Fig. 10.61 Floor door adjustment (Sec 42) (Right-hand drive models)

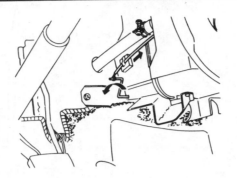

Fig. 10.62 Floor door adjustment (Sec 42) (Left-hand drive models)

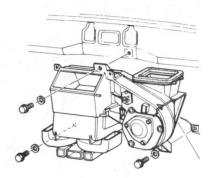

Fig. 10.63 Heater unit retaining bolts (Sec 42)

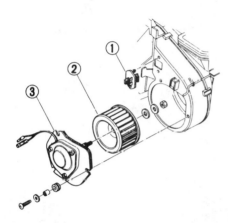

Fig. 10.64 Removing the blower motor (Sec 42)

1   Resistor   3   Blower motor
2   Blower

15   Remove the heater control unit, radio and heater ducts.
16   Unscrew and remove the defroster nozzle.
17   Detach the wiring harness from the blower motor connector.
18   Slacken the securing clips and detach the inlet and outlet coolant hoses.
19   Unscrew the retaining nuts and carefully withdraw the heater unit.
20   Refitting of the heater unit is a direct reversal of the removal procedure but readjust the controls as described in this Section.

Heater unit – dismantling and assembly

21   With the unit removed, unscrew and remove the resistor plug.
22   Unscrew and remove the blower unit retaining screws and withdraw the blower unit from the casing.
23   To remove the core unit, unclip the heater unit casing clips and split the casing. Withdraw the core.
24   Refitting is a direct reversal of the removal procedure but on completion readjust the heater controls and check for satisfactory operation.

43 Automatic transmission kickdown switch – removal and refitting

1   Disconnect the battery earth cable.
2   Detach the lead wires from the switch connector.

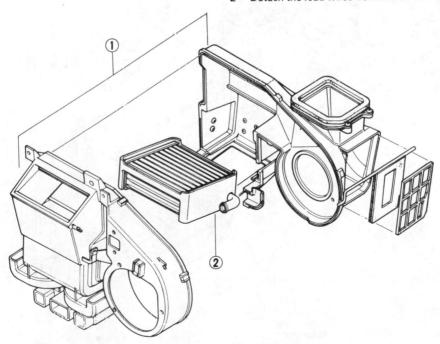

Fig. 10.65 Removing the heater core (Sec 42)

1   Heater case assembly   2   Heater core

Fig. 10.66 Seat belt switch connector (Sec 44)

Fig. 10.67 Seat belt warning system timer (Sec 44)

Fig. 10.68 Air conditioning system, showing air flow (Sec 45)

1	Heater unit	5	Cooling unit
2	Ventilation door	6	Evaporator
3	Air mix door	7	Blower motor
4	Air intake door	8	Floor door

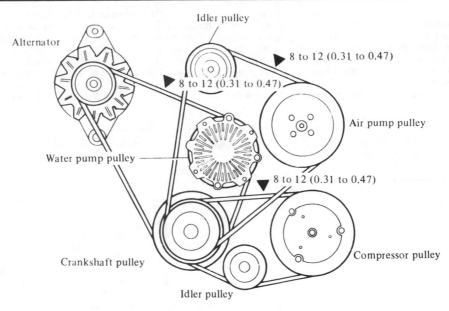

Fig. 10.69 Drivebelt layout and belt tensions (Sec 45)

Deflections are in mm (ins)

3   Slacken the locknut and then unscrew the switch unit to remove.
4   Refitting is a direct reversal of the removal procedure.

44 Seat belt warning system (210 models)

Belt switch – removal and refitting
1   If the seat belt switch is faulty it will have to be replaced as a unit with a new inner belt as they are a combined assembly.
2   Detach the battery earth cable.
3   With the seat adjusted in the forward position, separate the wiring harness at the connector (Fig. 10.66).
4   Unscrew the retaining bolt and remove the inner seat belt.
5   Refitting is a direct reversal of removal, but tighten the anchor bolt to a torque wrench setting of 14 to 27 lbf ft (2.0 to 3.8 kgf m).

Timer unit – removal and refitting
6   With the battery earth cable detached, remove the side finisher from the right dash panel.
7   Separate the wiring harness at the connector and unscrew the timing unit retaining screw to remove the timer.
8   Reverse the removal procedure to refit the timer unit.

Warning buzzer – removal and refitting
9   With the battery earth cable disconnected, separate the wire harness connector and remove the buzzer unit after unscrewing the retaining screw.
10 Refitting is a direct reversal of the removal procedure.

45 Air conditioning system – description and maintenance

1   An air conditioning system is available as an optional extra on the '210' range. The system combines heater, refrigeration and blower unit assemblies.
2   The heater system works on the normal principle in conjunction with the engine cooling system and incorporating its own booster (blower) motor.
3   The refrigeration system is shown in Fig. 10.68 and comprises five principal components, namely an evaporator, a compressor, a condenser, a receiver drier and an expansion valve.
4   Due to the nature of the refrigeration gases used in the system, no servicing other than a few basic maintenance tasks can be undertaken by the home mechanic.
5   If it is necessary to disconnect any part of the refrigeration system

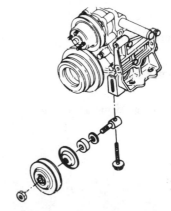

Fig. 10.70 Idler pulley adjuster (Sec 45)

in order to undertake work on other components, it is most important that the circuit be discharged prior to commencing work by a Datsun dealer or refrigeration engineer having the necessary knowledge and equipment. On completion of the particular service or overhaul the refrigeration system must be recharged again requiring specialized equipment and knowledge.
6   The maintenance tasks which can be carried out safely include checking the compressor belt tension. The drive belt layout is shown in Fig. 10.69 and the tension check points are arrowed. There should be a total deflection of 0.31 to 0.47 in (8 to 12 mm) under an average finger pressure.
7   The tension may be adjusted by moving the position of the idler pulley bolt in the desired direction. Further adjustment is obtainable by loosening the air pump mounting bolts and pivoting the unit in the direction required to tighten or loosen the pressure (in the same manner as the alternator).
8   Examine the system hoses and their connections for signs of leakage or deterioration. If evident the connection clips must be tightened or if necessary have the hose renewed by your Datsun agent or refrigeration mechanic.
9   Should the vehicle not be used regularly, the engine must be run for a period of about ten minutes once monthly at about 1500 rpm, to keep it in good condition.
10 If it is suspected that the amount of refrigerant in the system is incorrect, start the engine and hold it at a steady speed of 1500 rpm. Set the AIR lever in the A/C position and switch on the blower to maximum speed. Check the sight glass after an interval of about five minutes. The sight glass is located on the receiver drier. If a continuous

stream of bubbles or mist is observed, then there is very little refrigerant left in the system. Where some bubbles are seen at intervals of 1 or 2 seconds then there is sufficient refrigerant in the system. The system is correctly charged when conditions within the sight glass are almost transparent with a few bubbles appearing if the engine speed is raised or lowered. If the system requires recharging, this must be carried out professionally.

11 No maintenance is required for the electrical part of the system

apart from the occasional check to ensure that the wiring and connections are in good condition and securely located. A line fuse is incorporated into the circuit and in the event of this 'blowing' the cause should be located and rectified before fitting a new fuse.

12 To change the fuse, detach the battery earth cable and refer to Chapter 12 to remove the facia panel as given in Section 30. Withdraw the fuse holder from the harness and open it to remove the old fuse. Always replace with a fuse of the correct value which is 20 amp.

---

46 Fault finding chart – electrical system

Symptom	Reason/s
Starter motor fails to turn engine	Battery discharged
	Battery defective internally
	Battery terminal leads loose or earth lead not securely attached to body
	Loose or broken connections in starter motor circuit
	Starter motor switch or solenoid faulty
	Starter motor pinion jammed in mesh with flywheel gear ring
	Starter brushes badly worn, sticking, or brush wires loose
	Commutator dirty, worn or burnt
	Starter motor armature faulty
	Field coils earthed
Starter motor turns engine very slowly	Battery in discharged condition
	Starter brushes badly worn, sticking, or brush wires loose
	Loose wires in starter motor circuit
Starter motor operates without turning engine	Starter motor pinion sticking
	Pinion or flywheel gear teeth broken or worn
Starter motor noisy or excessively rough	Pinion or flywheel gear teeth broken or worn
	Starter motor retaining bolts loose
Battery will not hold charge for more than a few days	Battery defective internally
	Electrolyte level too low or electrolyte too weak due to leakage
	Plate separators no longer fully effective
	Battery plates severely sulphated
	Fan/alternator belt slipping
	Battery terminal connections loose or corroded
	Alternator not charging properly
	Short in lighting circuit causing continual battery drain
	Regulator unit not working correctly
Ignition light fails to go out, battery runs flat in a few days	Fan belt loose and slipping or broken
	Alternator faulty

Failure of individual electrical equipment to function correctly is dealt with alphabetically, item by item, under the headings listed below

Fuel gauge gives no reading	Fuel tank empty!
	Electric cable between tank sender unit and gauge earthed or loose
	Fuel gauge case not earthed
	Fuel gauge supply cable interrupted
	Fuel gauge unit broken
Fuel gauge registers full all the time	Electric cable between tank unit and gauge broken or disconnected
Horn operates all the time	Horn push either earthed or stuck down
	Horn cable to horn push earthed
Horn fails to operate	Blown fuse
	Cable or cable connection loose, broken or disconnected
	Horn has an internal fault
Horn emits intermittent or unsatisfactory noise	Cable connections loose
	Horn incorrectly adjusted
Lights do not come on	If engine not running, battery discharged
	Light bulb filament burnt out or bulbs broken
	Wire connections loose, disconnected or broken
	Light switch shorting or otherwise faulty
Lights come on but fade out	If engine not running battery discharged

Symptom	Reason/s
Lights gives very poor illumination	Lamp glasses dirty Reflector tarnished or dirty Lamps badly out of adjustment Incorrect bulb with too low wattage fitted Existing bulbs old and badly discoloured Electrical wiring too thin not allowing full current to pass
Lights work erratically — flashing on and off, especially over bumps	Battery terminals or earth connections loose Lights not earthing properly Contacts in light switch faulty
Wiper motor fails to work	Blown fuse Wire connections loose, disconnected or broken Brushes badly worn Armature worn or faulty Field coils faulty
Wiper motor works very slowly and takes excessive current	Commutator dirty, greasy or burnt Drive to wheelboxes bent or unlubricated Wheelbox spindle binding or damaged Armature bearings dry or unaligned Armature badly worn or faulty
Wiper motor works slowly and takes little current	Brushes badly worn Commutator dirty, greasy or burnt Armature badly worn or faulty
Wiper motor works but wiper blades remain static	Driving linkage disengaged or faulty Wiper motor gearbox parts badly worn

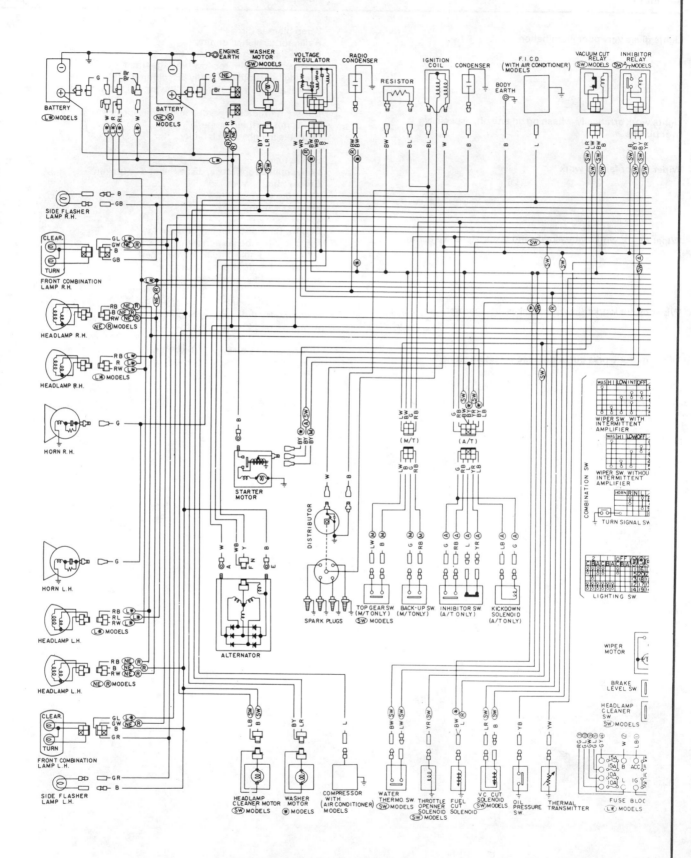

Fig. 10.71 Wiring diagram for European models

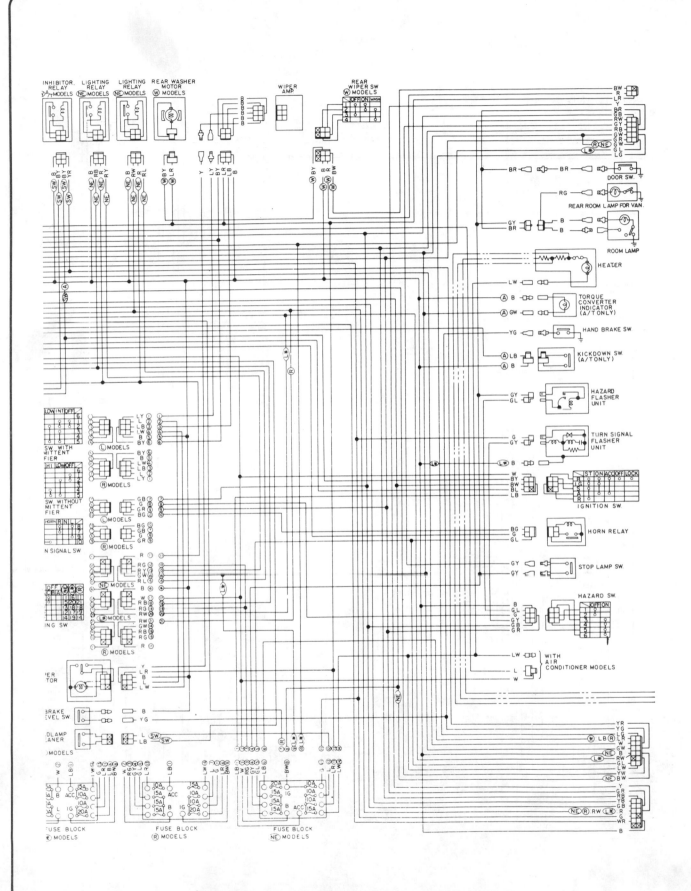

Fig. 10.71 Wiring diagram for European models – continued

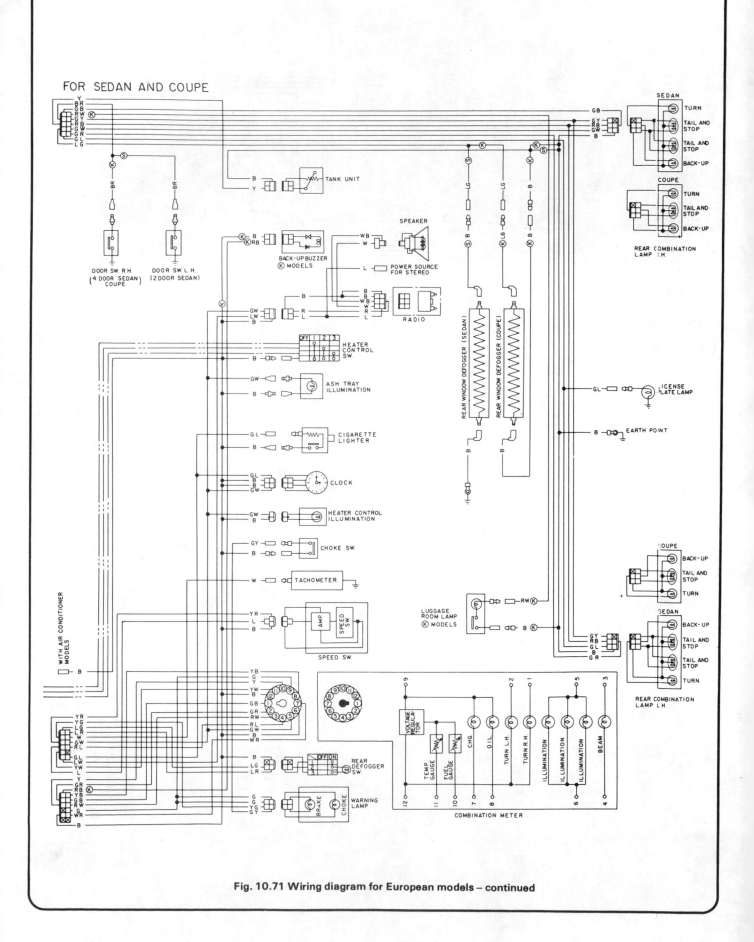

Fig. 10.71 Wiring diagram for European models – continued

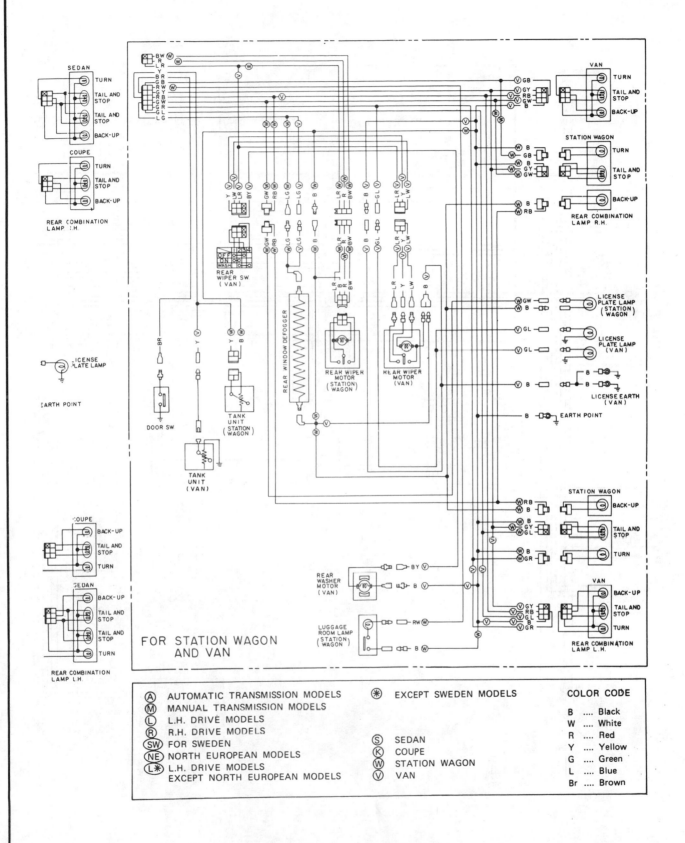

Fig. 10.71 Wiring diagram for European models – continued

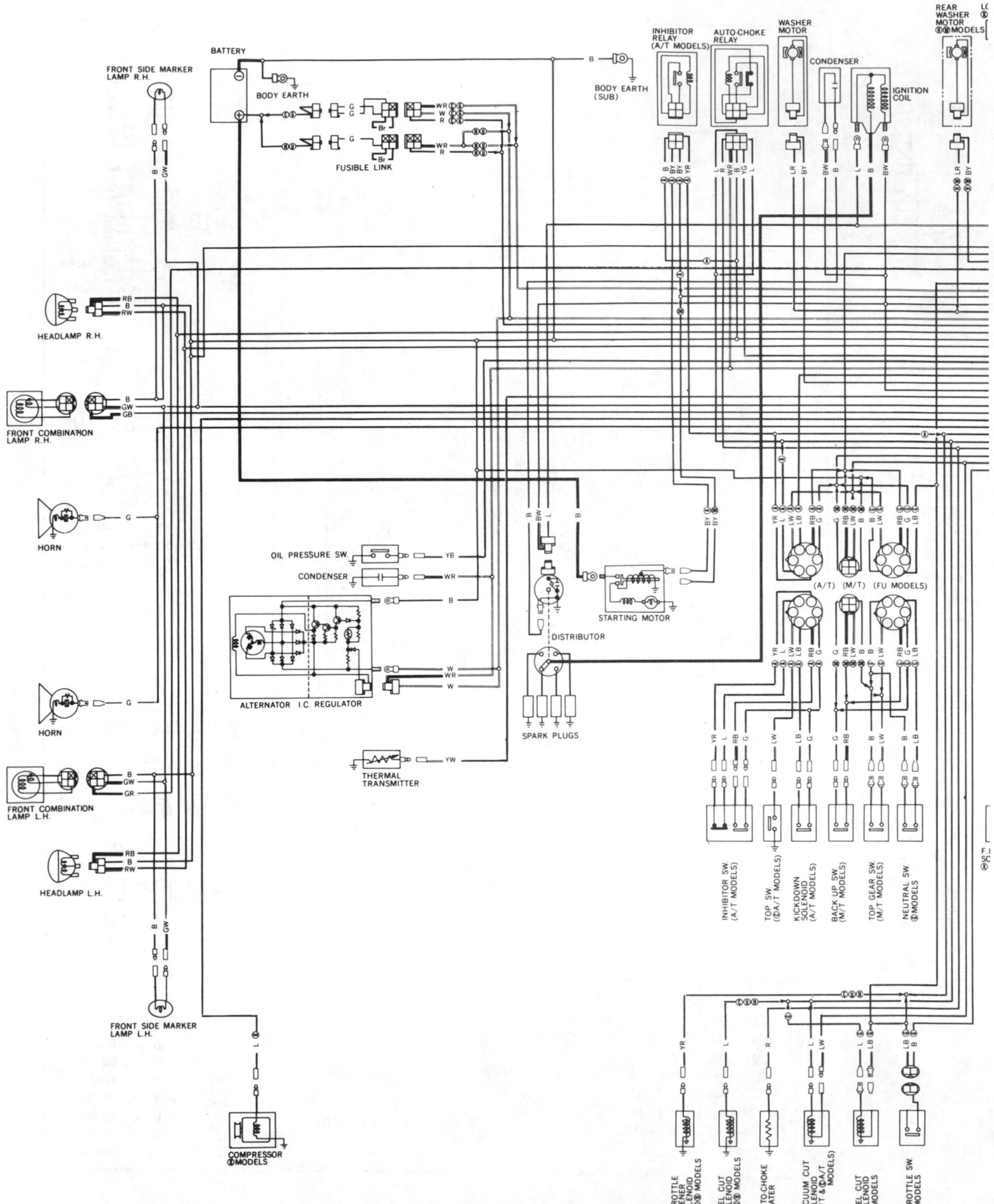

Fig. 10.72 Wiring diagram for North American models

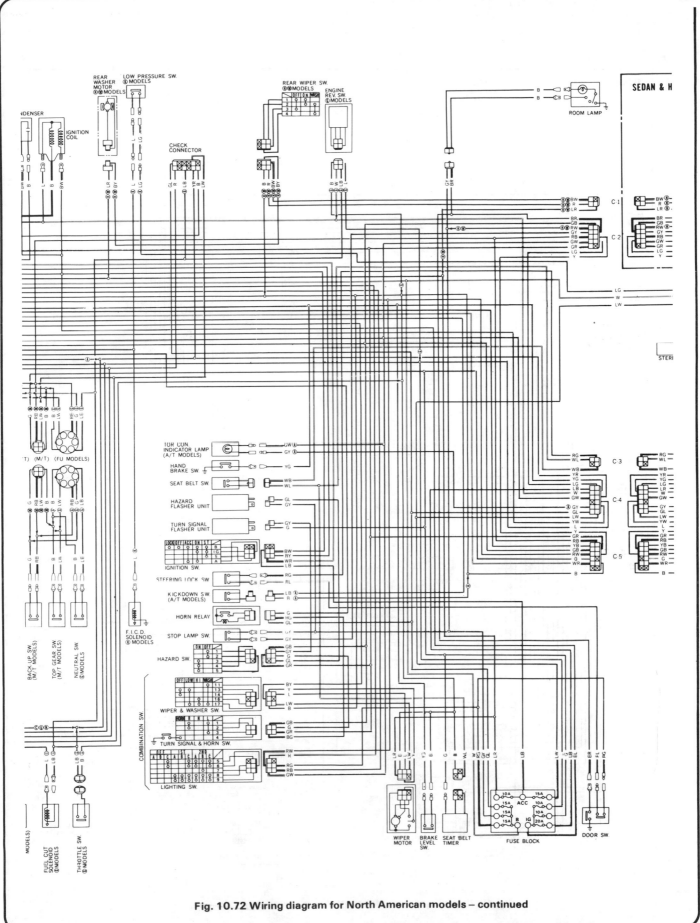

Fig. 10.72 Wiring diagram for North American models – continued

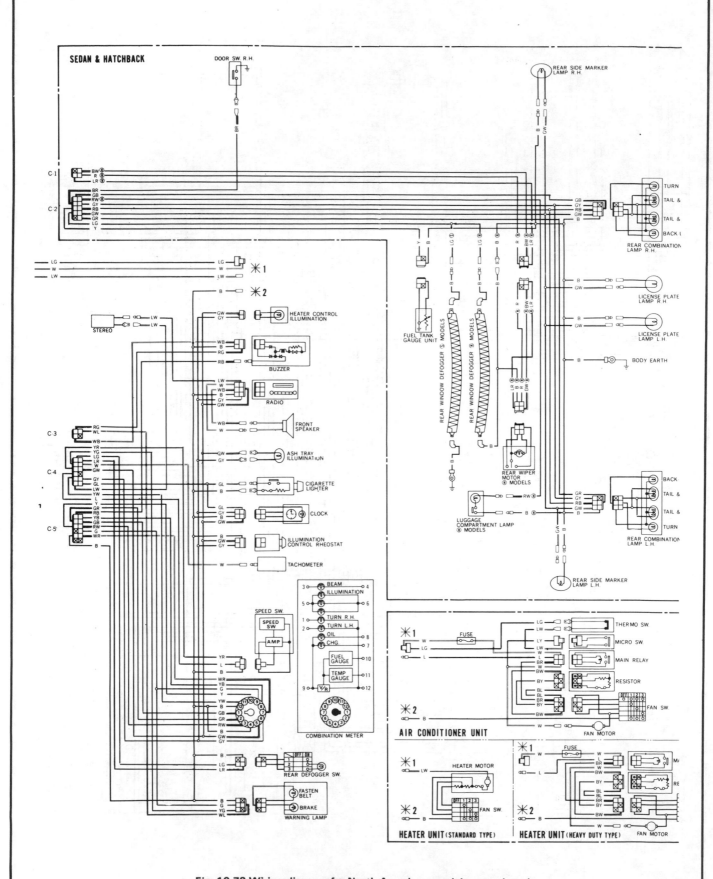

Fig. 10.72 Wiring diagram for North American models – continued

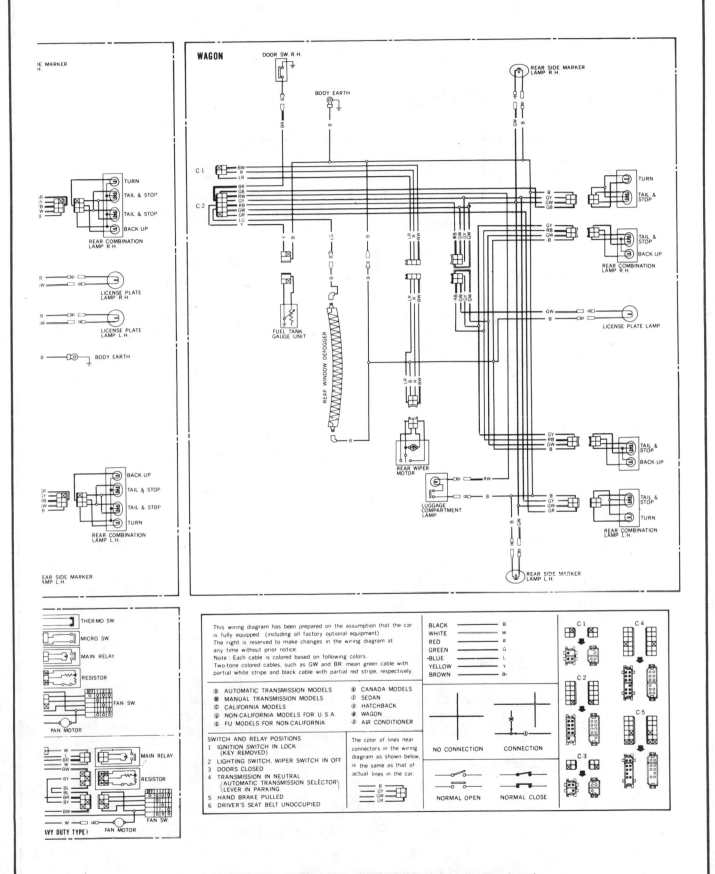

Fig. 10.72 Wiring diagram for North American models – continued

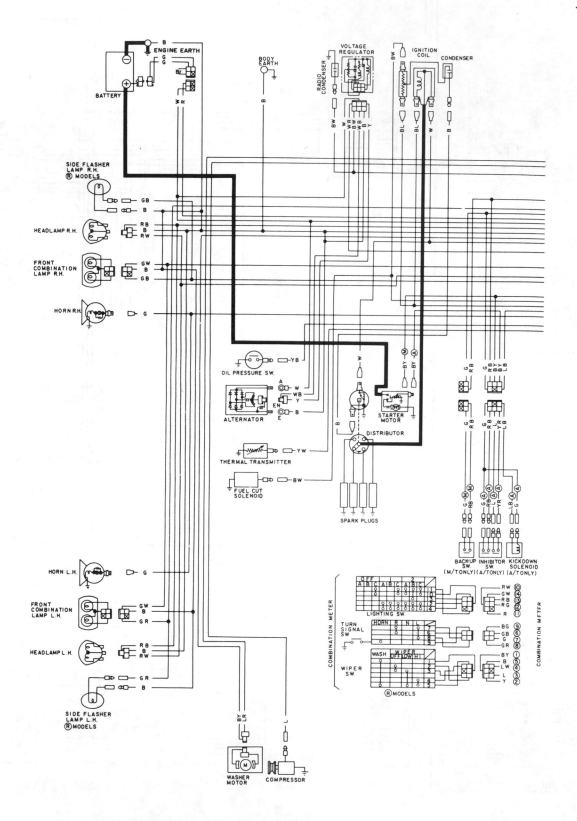

Fig. 10.73 Wiring diagram for Non-European models

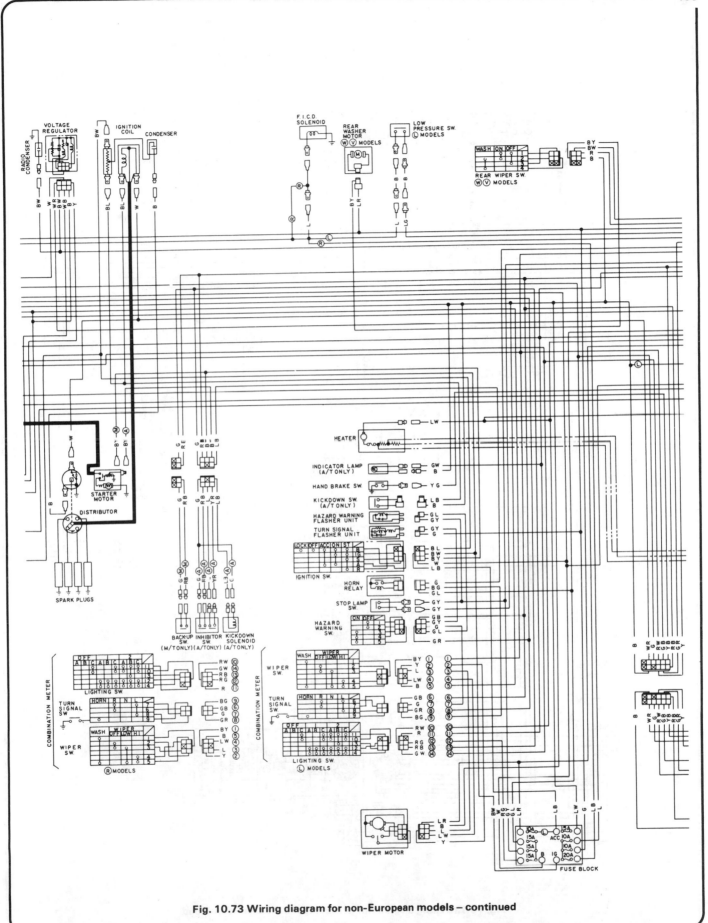

Fig. 10.73 Wiring diagram for non-European models – continued

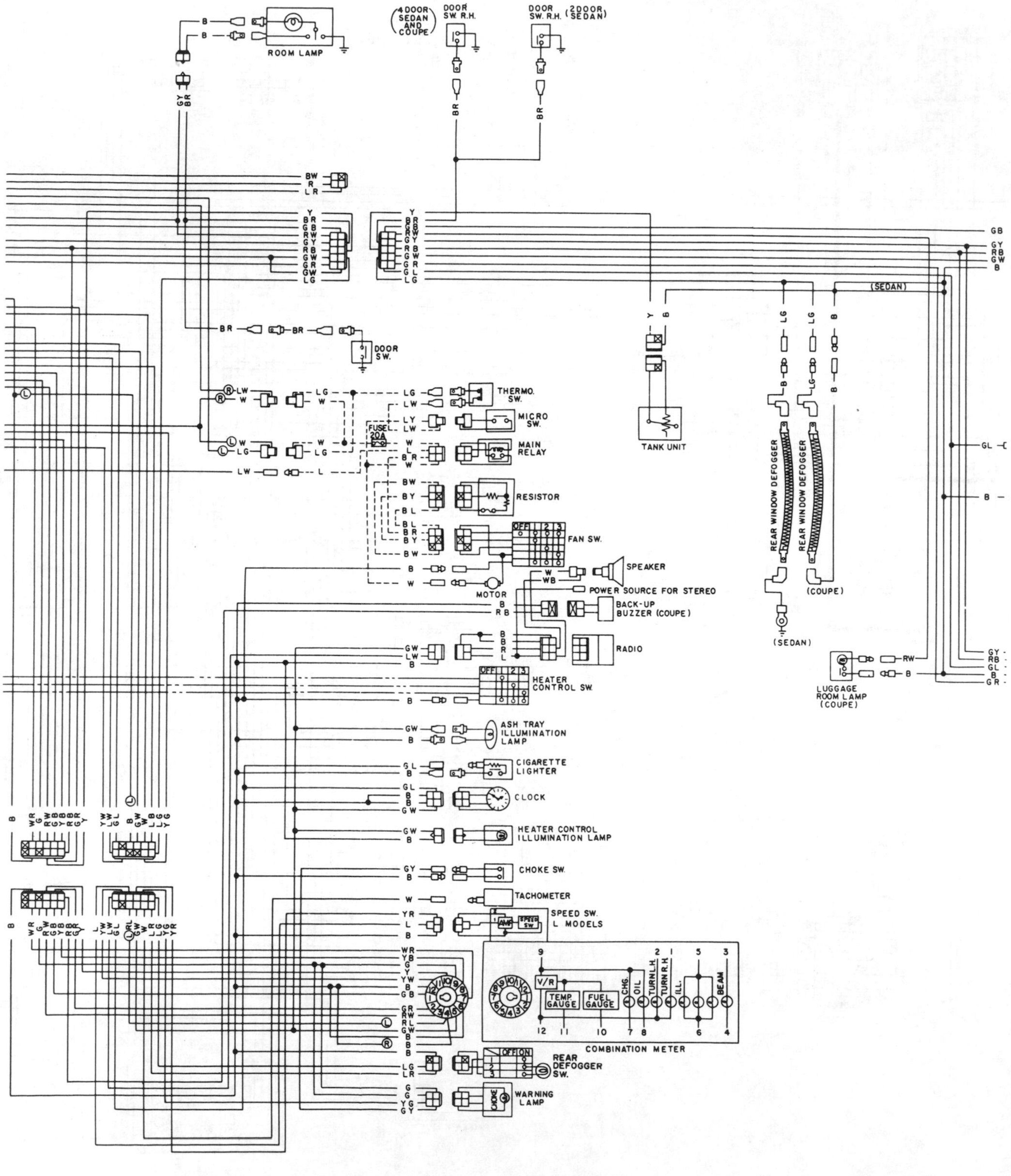

Fig. 10.73 Wiring diagram for non-European models – continued

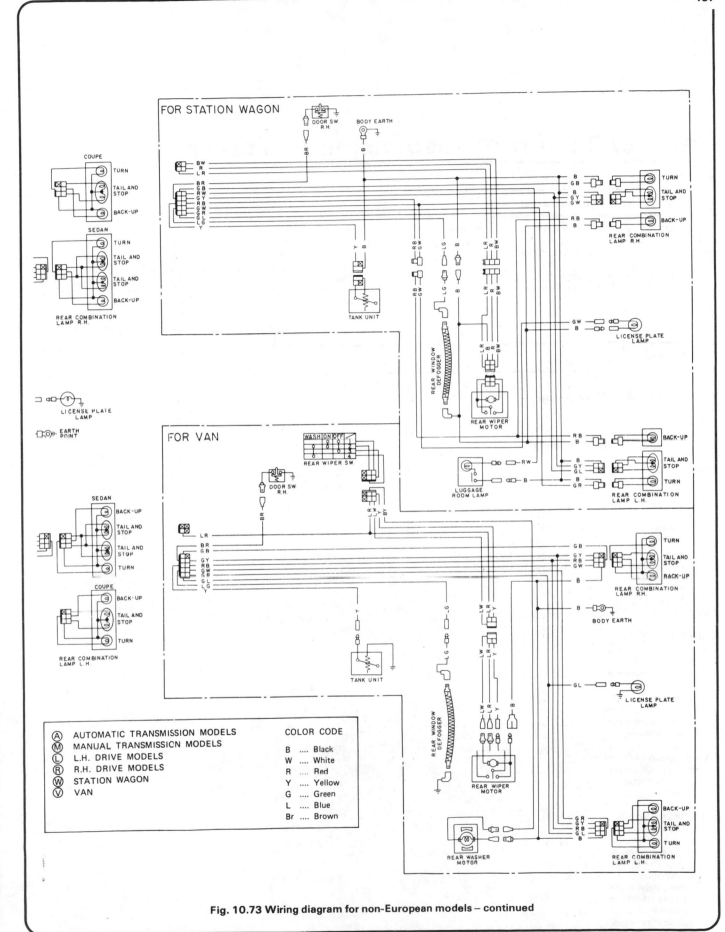

Fig. 10.73 Wiring diagram for non-European models – continued

Chapter 11   Front suspension and steering

Contents

Specifications

Front suspension (New Sunny)

Type ...... MacPherson strut

Coil spring (European models)

	Left-hand side	Right-hand side
Length	13.64 in (346.5 mm)	14.07 in (357.5 mm)
Coil diameter	3.94 in (100 mm)	3.94 in (100 mm)
Wire diameter	0.413 in (10.5 mm)	0.413 in (10.5 mm)
Number of turns	7.5	7.5
Spring constant	90.7 lbf/in (1.62 kgf/mm	90.7 lbf/in (1.62 kgf/mm)

Coil spring (non-European models)

120Y models

	Left-hand side	Right-hand side
Length	13.31 in (338.0 mm)	14.07 in (346.5 mm)
Coil diameter	3.94 in (100 mm)	3.94 in (100 mm)
Wire diameter	0.394 in (10.0 mm)	0.413 in (10.5 mm)
Number of turns	6.25	7.5
Spring constant	89.6 lbf/in (1.60 kgf/mm)	90.7 lbf/in (1.62 kgf mm)

140Y models ...... As European models

Shock absorber

Type	Double acting hydraulic
European models	
Piston rod diameter	0.79 in (20 mm)
Piston diameter	1.18 in (30 mm)
Stroke	6.46 in (164 mm)
Non-European 120Y models	
Piston rod diameter	0.71 in (18 mm)
Piston diameter	0.98 in (25 mm)
Stroke	6.46 in (164 mm)
Non-European 140Y models	
Piston rod diameter	0.79 in (20 mm)
Piston diameter	1.18 in (30 mm)
Stroke	6.46 in (164 mm)

Stabiliser bar

European models	
Bar diameter	0.79 in (20 mm)
Identification mark	Red
Non-European 120Y models	
Bar diameter	0.71 in (18 mm)
Identification mark	Pink
Non-European 140Y models	
Bar diameter	0.79 in (20 mm)
Identification mark	Red

Wheel alignment (European models)

	Saloon	Coupe	Estate
Camber	0 to 1°30'	0 to 1°30'	0 to 1°30'
Caster	1°40' to 3°10'	1°40' to 3°10'	1°55' to 3°25'
Toe-in	0.04 to 0.12 in (1 to 3 mm)	0.04 to 0.12 in (1 to 3 mm)	0.04 to 0.12 in (1 to 3 mm)

Wheel alignment (non-European models)

	Saloon	Coupe	Estate
Camber	-25' to 1°05'	-25' to 1°05'* 0 to 1°30'**	0° to 1°30'
Caster	1°40' to 3°10'	1°40' to 3°10'	1°55' to 3°25'
Toe-in	0 to 0.08 in (0 to 2 mm)	0.00 to 0.08 in (0 to 2 mm)* 0.04 to 0.12 in (1 to 3 mm)**	0.04 to 0.12 in (1 to 3 mm)

*120Y models   **140Y models*

Wheel bearings (European models)
Bearing axial play . . . . 0.0 in (0.0 mm)
Rotation torque (force at wheel stud)
    With new grease seal . . . . Less than 2.6 lbf (1.2 kgf)
    With used grease seal . . . . 0.4 to 1.7 lbf (0.17 to 0.79 kgf)

Wheel bearings (non-European models)
Bearing axial play . . . . 0.0 in (0.0 mm)
Rotation torque (force at wheel stud – 120Y models)
    With new grease seal . . . . Less than 3.1 lbf (1.4 kgf)
    With used grease seal . . . . Less than 1.5 lbf (0.7 kgf)
Rotation torque (force at wheel stud – 140Y models)
    With new grease seal . . . . Less than 2.6 lbf (1.2 kgf)
    With used grease seal . . . . 0.4 to 1.7 lbf (0.17 to 0.79 kgf)

Steering (New Sunny)

Steering gear type . . . . Recirculating ball (RB43N)

Turns of steering wheel (lock to lock) 3.5

Steering gear ratio 16.4:1

Front wheel turning angle (4J-12 wheels)
Inner wheel . . . . 41 to 45°
Outer wheel . . . . 33 to 37°

Front wheel turning angle (4½ J-13 or 5J-13 wheels)
Inner wheel . . . . 38° to 42°
Outer wheel . . . . 31½ to 35½°

Steering wheel axial play . . . . 0.0 in (0.0 mm)

Steering wheel play . . . . Less than 1.38 in (35 mm)

Wormshaft turning torque . . . . 3.5 to 7.8 lbf in (4.0 to 9.0 kgf cm)

Bearing shim
Standard thickness . . . . 0.020 in (0.5 mm)
Adjusting shim thicknesses . . . . 0.0020 in (0.05 mm)
    0.0028 in (0.07 mm)
    0.0031 in (0.08 mm)
    0.0039 in (0.10 mm)
    0.0079 in (0.20 mm)

Sector shaft
Endplay between sector shaft and adjusting screw . . . . Less than 0.0020 in (0.05 mm)
Adjusting shim thicknesses . . . . 0.0596 to 0.0604 in (1.515 to 1.535 mm)
    0.0608 to 0.0616 in (1.545 to 1.565 mm)
    0.0620 to 0.0628 in (1.575 to 1.595 mm)
    0.0632 to 0.0640 in (1.605 to 1.625 mm)
    0.0644 to 0.0652 in (1.635 to 1.655 mm)
Backlash at gear arm top end . . . . Less than 0.004 in (0.1 mm)

Steering box oil capacity . . . . ½ Imp pint; ⅝ US pint; 0.25 litre

Side rod length
Models with 4J-12 wheels	12.20 in (310 mm)
Models with 4½ J-13 or 5J-13 wheels	12.40 in (315 mm)

Wheels and tyres (New Sunny)

Wheels (European models)
4½J–13 steel or 5J–13 aluminium

Wheels (non-European models)
Saloon	4J–12 steel
120Y Coupe	4J–12 steel
140Y Coupe	4½J–13 steel
Estate	4½J–13 steel

Tyres (European models)
6·15S13–4PR crossply, 155 SR13 radial or 175/70 HR 13 radial

Tyres (non-European models)
Saloon	6·00–12–4PR crossply or 155 SR 12 radial
120Y Coupe	6·00–12–4PR crossply or 155 SR 12 radial
140Y Coupe	6·15–13–4PR crossply or 155 SR 13 radial
Estate	6·15–13–4PR crossply or 155 SR 13 radial

Tyre pressures – cold (European models)
	Front	Rear
6·15S13–4PR	24 lbf/in² (1·7 kgf/cm²)	27 lbf/in² (1·9 kgf/cm²)
155SR13	24 lbf/in² (1·7 kgf/cm²)	27 lbf/in² (1·9 kgf/cm²)
175/70 HR13	24 lbf/in² (1·7 kgf/cm²)	24 lbf/in² (1·7 kgf/cm²)

Tyre pressure – cold (non-European models)
	Front	Rear
120Y model		
6·00 12–4PR (below 60 mph)	23 lbf/in² (1·6 kgf/cm²)	23 lbf/in² (1·6 kgf/cm²)
6·00 12–4PR (over 60 mph)	27 lbf/in² (1·9 kgf/cm²)	27 lbf/in² (1·9 kgf/cm²)
155SR12	23 lbf/in² (1·6 kgf/cm²)	23 lbf/in² (1·6 kgf/cm²)
140Y model		
6·15 13–4PR (below 60 mph)	23 lbf/in² (1·6 kgf/cm²)	23 lbf/in² (1·6 kgf/cm²)
6·15 13–4PR (over 60 mph)	27 lbf/in² (1·9 kgf/cm²)	27 lbf/in² (1·9 kgf/cm²)
155SR13	23 lbf/in² (1·6 kgf/cm²)	23 lbf/in² (1·6 kgf/cm²)

Front suspension (210 models)

The specifications are the same as for the non-European 140Y New Sunny except for the following

Coil spring
	Models with air conditioning	Models without air conditioning
Length	14·76 in (375 mm)	14·76 in (375 mm)
Wire diameter	0·425 in (10·8 mm)	0·413 in (10·5 mm)
Spring constant	92·4 lbf/in (1·65 kgf/mm)	90·7 lbf/in (1·62 kgf/mm)

Wheel alignment
Camber	0 to 1° 30'
Caster	1° 40' to 3° 10' except Estate, 1° 55' to 3° 25' Estate
Toe-in	0·04 to 0·12 in (1 to 3 mm)

Wheel bearing
Bearing axial play	0·0 in (0·0 mm)
Rotation torque (force at wheel hub bolt)	
With new grease seal	Less than 2·6 lbf (1·2 kgf)
With used grease seal	0·37 to 1·74 lbf (0·17 to 0·79 kgf)

Steering (210 models)

The Specifications are the same as for the non-European 140Y New Sunny except for the following

Steering gear type
Recirculating ball (RB45L)

Turns of steering wheel (lock to lock)
3·2

Steering gear ratio
15·1

Worm bearing shim
Standard thickness	0·059 in (1·5 mm)
Adjusting shim thicknesses	0·030 in (0·762 mm)
	0·010 in (0·254 mm)
	0·005 in (0·127 mm)
	0·002 in (0·050 mm)

Sector shaft

Endplay between sector shaft and adjusting screw	0·0004 to 0·0012 in (0·01 to 0·03 mm)
Adjusting shim thicknesses	0·0620 to 0·0630 in (1·575 to 1·600 mm)
	0·0610 to 0·0620 in (1·550 to 1·575 mm)
	0·0600 to 0·0610 in (1·525 to 1·550 mm)
	0·0591 to 0·0600 in (1·500 to 1·525 mm)

Wheels and tyres (210 models)

The Specifications are the same as for the European New Sunny except for the following

Tyre pressures – cold

	Front	Rear
All tyres (except Wagon)	24 lbf/in^2 (1·7 kgf/cm^2)	24 lbf/in^2 (1·7 kgf/cm^2)
All tyres (Wagon)	24 lbf/in^2 (1·7 kgf/cm^2)	26 lbf/in^2 (1·8 kgf/cm^2)

All models

Torque wrench settings

	lbf ft	kgf m
Balljoint socket to lower arm	37 to 44	5·1 to 6·1
Balljoint to knuckle arm nut	40 to 72	5·5 to 10
Steering knuckle arm to strut	53 to 72	7·3 to 9·9
Strut to bonnet ledge	18 to 25	2·5 to 3·5
Piston rod self-locking nut	43 to 54	6·0 to 7·5
Gland packing	58 to 80	8·0 to 11·0
Disc brake rotor to hub	28 to 38	3·9 to 5·3
Side rod balljoint to knuckle arm	22 to 51	3·0 to 7·0
Lower arm bolt and nut	28 to 36	3·9 to 5·0
Side rod adjusting nut	58 to 72	8·0 to 10·0
Torsion bar installation nut	33 to 37	4·5 to 5·1
Torsion bar to lower arm	37 to 44	5·1 to 6·1
Torsion bar bracket to body	23 to 31	3·2 to 4·3
Steering wheel nut	27 to 38	3·8 to 5·2
Column clamp bolts	9 to 13	1·3 to 1·8
Jacket tube bracket to dash panel	2·5 to 3·3	0·35 to 0·45
Rubber coupling to worm shaft	29 to 36	4·0 to 5·0
Steering gear arm nut	94 to 108	13 to 15
Steering gear housing to body	51 to 58	7·0 to 8·0
Rear cover bolt	14 to 22	2·0 to 3·0
Sector shaft cover bolt	14 to 22	2·0 to 3·0
Sector shaft adjusting screw locknut	14 to 22	2·0 to 3·0
Steering idler body to frame	51 to 58	7·0 to 8·0
Ball stud nut	22 to 51	3·0 to 7·0
Side rod locknut	58 to 72	8·0 to 10·0
Idler nut	40 to 51	5·5 to 7·0
Wheel nuts	58 to 72	8·0 to 10·0
Wheel bearing nut	22 to 25	3·0 to 3·5

1 General description

The front suspension is of the MacPherson strut type, incorporating a double acting telescopic shock absorber and coil spring. A strut and torsion bar absorb any lateral and longitudinal thrust.

The stub axles on the suspension struts carry the front hubs which run on inner and outer tapered roller bearings. Bolted to the hubs are the discs of the disc brakes.

The steering gear is of the recirculating ball nut and worm type. The drop arm on the steering gear transmits motion to the roadwheels through a relay rod and two outer trackrods. The steering column is collapsible on impact.

2 Maintenance and inspection

1   Inspect the condition of all rubber balljoint covers for splits or deterioration. Renew as necessary after reference to the appropriate section of this Chapter.
2   Check the security of the locknuts on the outer trackrod ends, also the ball pin nuts.
3   Check the security of the front strut securing nuts and examine the condition of the radius rod and stabiliser bar rubber bushes and renew if necessary.
4   Every 12 000 miles (19 000 km) check the front wheel alignment (toe-in) as described in Section 17 of this Chapter.
5   Every 12 000 miles (19 000 km) remove the filler plug from the steering box and top-up as required with EP grade oil.

6   Every 24 000 miles (38 000 km) remove, clean, repack and adjust the front hub bearings, as described in Section 9 of this Chapter.
7   Every 24 000 miles (38 000 km) remove the threaded plugs from the balljoints, screw in a grease nipple and inject wheel bearing grade grease.

3 Suspension components – inspection for wear

1   The safety of a vehicle is dependent upon the correct performance of the steering and suspension and inspection of these components should be carried out regularly.
2   The front suspension should be checked by first jacking the car up so that the wheel is well clear of the ground. Place another jack under the track control arm, near to its outer end. When the arm is raised by the jack, any movement in the suspension strut balljoint will be apparent, as will any wear in the inner track control arm bush. If any movement is detected, new components should be fitted.
3   The top end of the suspension unit should have no discernible movement. To check it, grip the spring at the lower spring seat and try to push it from side to side. It should not be possible to detect movement either between the outer cylinder and the inner piston, or between the piston rod and the upper mounting.
4   Inspect the shock absorber for leaks and obvious damage. When a shock absorber is suspected of having failed, remove it from the vehicle and while holding it vertically, operate it over its full stroke several times. Any lack of resistance in either direction, or if the operation is not smooth over its entire range, the shock absorber should be renewed.

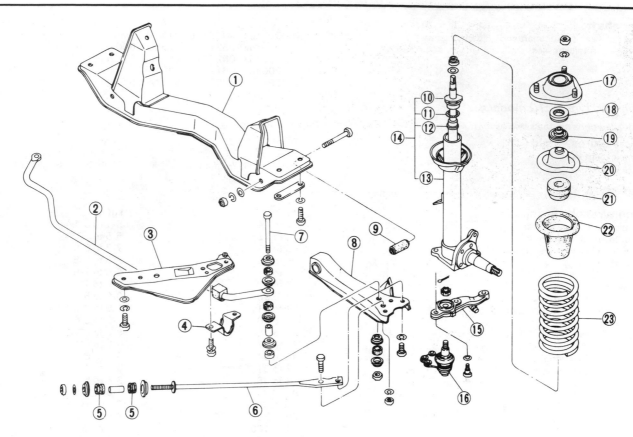

Fig. 11.1 Front suspension components (Sec 1)

1	Suspension crossmember	7	Connecting rod	13	Strut sub-assembly	19	Dust seal
2	Stabiliser bar	8	Lower arm	14	Strut assembly	20	Spring upper seal
3	Tension rod bracket	9	Lower arm bushing	15	Knuckle arm	21	Bound bumper rubber
4	Stabiliser bar bracket	10	Gland packing	16	Suspension balljoint	22	Dust cover
5	Tension rod bushing	11	O-ring	17	Strut mounting insulator	23	Coil spring
6	Tension rod	12	Shock absorber	18	Strut mounting bearing		

4   Front suspension drag strut and stabiliser bar – removal and refitting

1   Jack-up the front of the vehicle and support it securely on axle-stands. Remove the roadwheels.
2   Remove the splash shield from under the front of the engine compartment (photo).
3   Release the nut which secures the end of the drag strut to the bracket (photo).
4   Remove the bolts which secure the other end of the drag strut to the track control arm and remove the drag strut.
5   Remove the stabiliser bar drop link from the track control arm.
6   Loosen the drag strut bracket bolts and then unscrew and remove the stabiliser bracket bolts (photo) and remove the stabiliser bar from the vehicle.
7   When refitting the stabiliser bar make sure that the white marks on the bar are visible from the outer edges of the support brackets.
8   Ensure that the drag strut to bracket bushes are correctly assembled and then tighten all nuts and bolts to the specified torque, making sure that the drag strut to bracket nut is tightened before the drag strut to track control arm bolt.

5   Track control arm and balljoint – removal and refitting

1   Jack-up the front of the vehicle and support it on axle-stands. Remove the roadwheel.
2   Unscrew and remove the nut from the outer balljoint on the outer trackrod. Using a balljoint extractor or two wedges, separate the balljoint from the steering arm. Two club hammers of equal weight may be

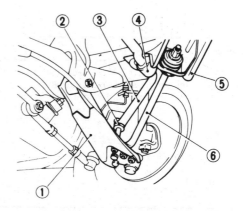

Fig. 11.2 Drag strut and stabiliser removal (Sec 4)

1	Lower arm	4	Stabiliser bar bracket
2	Stabiliser bar connecting rod	5	Tension rod bracket
3	Stabiliser bar	6	Tension rod

used to jar the balljoint taper pin from the steering arm eye. They should be used to strike the diametrically opposite edges of the eye simultaneously.

3   Unscrew and remove the two bolts which secure the steering arm and balljoint housing to the bottom of the suspension strut. Disconnect the housing from the strut.

4.2 Engine splash shield

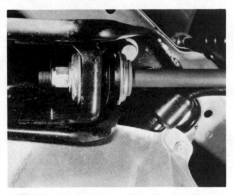

4.3 Drag strut nut

4.6 Stabiliser bar bracket

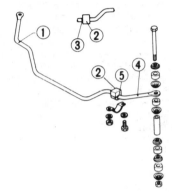

Fig. 11.3 Stabiliser centering (Sec 4)

1 Marking
2 Bushing
3 Marking
4 White painting
5 Marking

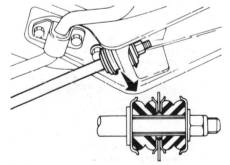

Fig. 11.4 Correct fitting of drag strut bushes (Sec 4)

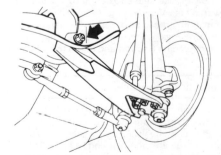

Fig. 11.5 Track control arm pivot bolt (Sec 5)

4 Disconnect the drag strut and the stabiliser bar from the track control arm.

5 Remove the pivot bolt which connects the track control arm to the front crossmember and then withdraw the track control arm complete with balljoint and steering arm.

6 Secure the track control arm in a vice and unbolt the balljoint from it.

7 Now grip the steering arm in the vice and unscrew the castellated nut from the taper pin of the balljoint. Tap the balljoint from the steering arm.

8 Clean all the dismantled components in paraffin and examine for cracks. Check the balljoints for up and down movement of the ball pin and if the taper pin moves too easily from side to side, it is worn and must be renewed. Ensure that the rubber dust excluder is not perished or torn. If the rubber bush at the inner end of the track control arm is worn or has deteriorated it must be renewed. A suitable press will be required and the new bush when correctly fitted must protrude equally either side of the arm.

9 Refitting is a reversal of removal and dismantling. Tighten all bolts and nuts to specified torque except the track control arm pivot bolt which should not be tightened until the weight of the vehicle is on the roadwheels.

10 If a new balljoint is being fitted, remove the plug, temporarily fit a nipple and inject grease. Remove the nipple and refit the plug.

6 Front suspension struts – removal and refitting

1 The strut assembly may be removed complete with hub, coil road spring and top thrust bearing unit. Removal for left and right-hand assemblies is identical.

2 Apply the handbrake and jack-up the front of the car, supporting adequately under the body side members.

3 Remove the roadwheel from the side to be dismantled.

4 Loosen the union nut which connects the rigid brake pipe to the flexible hose. Extract the lockplate which retains the flexible hose and separate the two pipes. Plug the hydraulic line to prevent loss of fluid.

5 Unscrew and remove the two caliper securing bolts and withdraw the caliper unit complete.

6 Disconnect the steering arm from the bottom of the suspension strut as described in the preceding Section. A lever can be used to carefully prise the track control arm downwards against the tension of the stabiliser bar (Figs. 11.6 and 11.7).

7 Raise the bonnet and unscrew the three upper mounting nuts.

8 Using a jack to support the strut/hub assembly, lower it carefully and then withdraw from under the front wing.

9 Using suitable coil spring compressing clamps, compress the coil springs. An alternative method of compressing the coil road springs is to make three clips from $\frac{1}{2}$ inch diameter mild steel bar, of suitable length and with bent-over ends forming hooks, to span three coils of the spring. With the weight of a person on the wing before any dismantling takes place, the clips are slipped over the coils at equidistant points around the spring circumference. Whichever method is used for spring compression, a tough encircling safety strap should be used round the clips or compressors after fixing them to the spring.

10 Remove the nut which secures the thrust bearing unit to the strut.

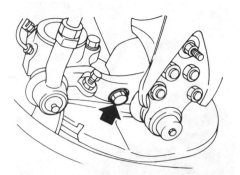

Fig. 11.6 Steering arm bolts (Sec 6)

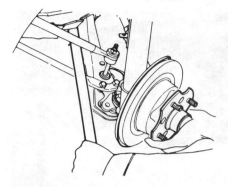

Fig. 11.7 Removing the steering arm (Sec 6)

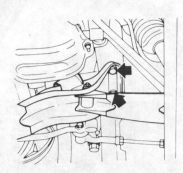

Fig. 11.8 Suspension crossmember bolts (Sec 7)

11 Remove the locating washer and bearing unit, push the damper rod into the strut and either gently release the spring compressors evenly, or remove the coil spring complete with clips for subsequent detachment. The clips can easily be removed if a centrally placed screwed rod with nuts and end plates is used to further compress the coil spring.

12 When suspension struts become damaged, soft or faulty in action, it is recommended that they are renewed as units. The procedure described in this Chapter should be followed for dismantling the hub, brake and other components as the exchange, or replacement unit, will not include anything except the bare telescopic suspension leg.

13 Refitting of the suspension strut is a reversal of removal, but the following points must be noted.

14 Where a new suspension strut is being fitted, it should be held vertically before fitting and the piston rod fully extended several times. Repeat the operation holding the strut upside down. This action will bleed the hydraulic fluid of any air which may have collected in the unit during storage.

15 Check that the coil spring is correctly located in its lower pad.

16 Make sure that the upper mounting components are fitted in their correct sequence, that grease is applied to the bearing and that the piston rod self-locking nut is tightened to the specified torque.

17 When refitting the steering arm/lower balljoint housing to the bottom of the suspension strut, apply sealing compound to the mating surfaces to prevent entry of water and subsequent corrosion of the balljoint.

18 When installation is complete, check the front wheel alignment as described later in this Chapter and bleed the brakes.

7 Front crossmember – removal and refitting

1 Jack-up the front of the vehicle and support it securely under the body side frame members.

2 Remove the roadwheels and the splash shield from under the engine.

3 Unscrew and remove the two track control arm pivot bolts, one from each side of the crossmember. Detach the track control arms from the crossmember and support them at their inner ends.

4 Using a suitable hoist take the strain of the weight of the engine and then unscrew and remove the nuts from the engine mountings.

5 Unscrew and remove the four crossmember securing bolts and lower the crossmember from the vehicle.

6 Check the condition of the engine mounting rubber insulators and renew them if necessary.

7 Refitting is a reversal of removal. Tighten all nuts and bolts to specified torque. The track control arm pivot bolts should not be tightened until the weight of the vehicle is on the roadwheels.

8 Front wheel bearings – adjustment

1 Jack-up the front of the vehicle and support it securely under the body side member

2 Remove the roadwheel, the cap from the end of the hub and then withdraw the split pin. Take off the nut retainer.

3 Using a socket spanner and a torque wrench, tighten the stub axle nut to the specified torque and at the same time rotate the hub several times in each direction to settle the bearings.

4 Unscrew the nut one quarter turn (90°), then refit the adjusting cap and align any of its slots with the hole in the spindle. If no slot aligns with the hole, tighten the locknut by an amount not exceeding 15° to achieve alignment. Do not tighten the nut by more than this amount, because this could lead to seizure of the wheel bearing

5 Attach a spring balance to one of the wheel studs and pull tangentially to measure the torque necessary to turn the wheel. The test should be carried out several times for both forward and reverse movement of the hub, to ensure that the torque is within the specification. Readjust the bearing tension if necessary. The brake pads should be removed while the tests are being made so that the brakes cannot exert any drag.

6 When the torque is satisfactory, fit a new split pin to the shaft and spread the legs of the pin away from each other against the sides of the bearing nut.

7 Check that there is no axial play of the wheel bearing. Even the slightest amount cannot be tolerated.

9 Front wheel hub and bearings – removal and refitting

1 Jack-up the front of the vehicle, remove the roadwheel and remove the friction pads. Disconnect the hydraulic brake pipe at the suspension strut bracket and plug the pipe to prevent loss of fluid. Remove the caliper unit.

2 Knock off the cap from the end of the hub, remove the split pin and unscrew and remove the retainer, nut and thrust washer.

3 Pull the hub assembly forward and extract the outer roller bearing then pull the unit from the stub axle.

4 Wash all internal grease from the hub using paraffin. If the bearings and seal are in good order, repack the interior of the hub and end cap with wheel bearing grease so that it occupies the area shown (Fig. 11.10).

5 If the bearings are worn or damaged, prise out the oil seal from the inner end of the hub and extract the inner roller race. Drift out the inner and outer bearing tracks using a thin rod.

6 Fit the new bearing tracks using a piece of tubing as a drift. If both hubs are being dismantled at the same time, ensure that the bearings are kept as matched sets and do not mix up the races and tracks.

7 Press the new grease seal squarely into the inner end of the hub, with its lip towards the roller bearing.

8 Pack the hub with grease as described in paragraph 4.

9 Refitting is a reversal of removal, adjust the bearing pre-load as described in the preceding Section and bleed the hydraulic system.

10 Steering gear linkage – inspection

1 Wear in the steering gear and linkage is indicated when there is considerable movement in the steering wheel without corresponding movement at the roadwheels. Wear is also indicated when the car tends to wander off the line one is trying to steer. There are three main steering groups to examine in such circumstances. These are the wheel bearings, the linkage joints and bushes and the steering box itself.

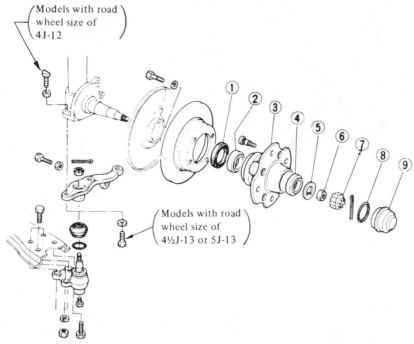

Fig. 11.9 Front hub assembly (Sec 9)

1	Grease seal	4	Outer wheel bearing	6	Wheel bearing nut	8	O-ring
2	Inner wheel bearing	5	Wheel bearing washer	7	Adjusting cap	9	Hub cap
3	Wheel hub						

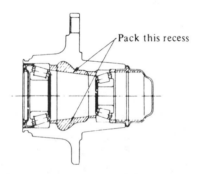

Fig. 11.10 Front hub lubrication (Sec 9)

2   First jack-up the front of the car and support it on stands under the side frame members, so that both front wheels are clear off the ground.

3   Grip the top and bottom of the roadwheel and try to rock it. It will not take any great effort to be able to feel play in the wheel bearing. If this play is very noticeable it would be as well to adjust it straight away as it could confuse further examinations. It is also possible that during this check, play may be discovered in the lower suspension track control arm balljoint (at the foot of the suspension strut). If this happens the balljoint will need renewal, as described in Section 5.

4   Next grip each side of the roadwheel and try rocking it laterally. Steady pressure will, of course, turn the steering, but an alternating back and forth pressure will reveal any loose joint. If some play is felt, it is preferable to get assistance from someone, so that while one person rocks the roadwheel from side to side, the other can look at the joints and bushes on the track rods and connections. Excluding the steering box itself, there are eight places where the play may occur. The two outer balljoints on the two outer track rods are the most likely, followed by the two inner joints on the same rods where they join the centre relay rod. Any play in these means renewal of the balljoint. Next are the two swivel bushes, one at each end of the centre relay rod. Finally check the steering box drop arm balljoint and the one on the idler arm which supports the centre relay rod on the side opposite the steering box. This unit is bolted to the side frame member and any play

calls for renewal of the unit.

5   Finally, the steering box itself is checked. First make sure that the bolts holding the steering box to the side frame member are tight. Then get another person to help examine the mechanism. One should look at, or get hold of, the drop arm at the bottom of the steering box while the other turns the steering wheel a little way from side to side. The amount of lost motion between the steering wheel and the drop arm indicates the degree of wear somewhere in the steering box mechanism. This check should be carried out with the wheels first of all in the straight ahead position and then at nearly full lock on each side. If the play only occurs noticeably in the straight ahead position, then the wear is most probably in the worm and/or nut. If it occurs at all positions of the steering, the wear is probably in the rocker shaft bush. An oil leak at this point is another indication of such wear. In either case the steering box will need removal for closer examination and repair.

11 Steering linkage and balljoints – removal and refitting

1   The balljoints on the two outer track rods and the swivel bushes on the centre relay rod are all fitted into their respective locations by means of a taper pin into a tapered hole and secured by a self-locking or castellated nut. In the case of the four ball-joints (two on each of the outer track rods) they are also screwed onto the rod and held by a locknut (photos). The two outer balljoints have left-hand threads.

2   To disconnect a balljoint taper pin, first remove the castellated nut or self-locking nut, then use an extractor, or forked tapered wedges to separate the balljoint from the attached component. Another method is to place the head of a hammer, or other solid metal article, on one side of the hole in the arm into which the pin is fitted. Then hit it smartly with a hammer on the opposite side. This has the effect of squeezing the taper out and usually works, provided one can get a good swing at it.

3   In the case of the trackrod-end balljoints, release the locknut and unscrew the trackrod-ends from the trackrods. If the lock-nut is only unscrewed by not more than one half turn, the new trackrod-end can be screwed on to take up approximately the original position, but in any event, the front wheel alignment will have to be checked and adjusted as described later in this Chapter.

4   If the balljoints of the centre relay rod require renewal then the

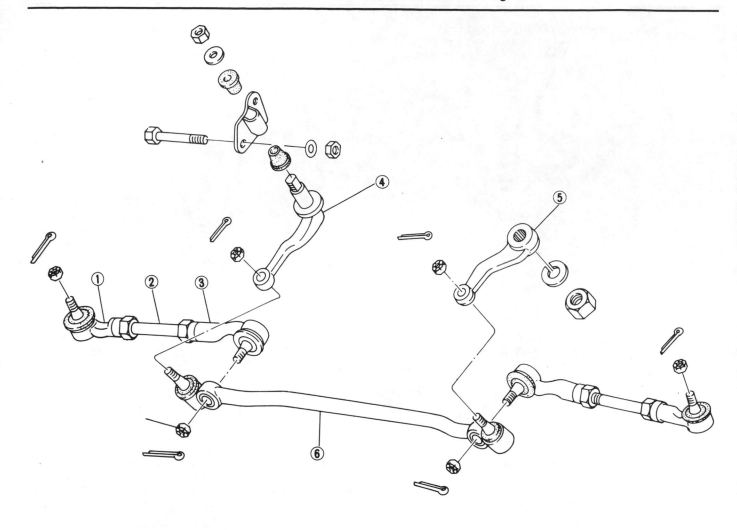

Fig. 11.11 Steering linkage components (Sec 11)

1 *Side rod outer socket*	3 *Side rod inner socket*	5 *Steering gear arm*
2 *Side rod*	4 *Idler arm*	6 *Cross rod*

complete rod assembly must be renewed after the trackrod balljoints have been disconnected from it and the steering box and idler drop arms also disconnected.

5   Any wear in the idler assembly will necessitate renewal of the split type rubber bushes. Smear a little brake fluid on them to facilitate installation.

6   Always check the front wheel alignment after any part of the steering linkage has been dismantled or renewed.

12 Steering wheel – removal and refitting

1   Disconnect the lead from the battery negative terminal.

2   Remove the pad from the steering wheel spokes. The pad is retained by screws entered from the rear of the spokes.

3   Disconnect the horn wire.

4   Unscrew the steering wheel retaining nut and then using a suitable extractor, withdraw the steering wheel. On no account jar the end of the steering column in an attempt to free the wheel otherwise serious damage may be caused to the steering column which is of the collapsible type.

5   Refitting is a reversal of removal but apply grease to the wheel and shaft mating surfaces and with the roadwheels in the straight-ahead position, align the punch marks on the end of the shaft and the steering wheel boss.

6   Tighten the steering wheel nut to the specified torque.

13 Steering column – removal and refitting

1   Remove the steering wheel, as described in the preceding Section.

2   Open the bonnet and unscrew and remove the pinch bolt which secures the flexible coupling of the steering column to the worm shaft of the steering box.

3   Remove the two halves of the steering column shroud.

4   Remove the two screws and take off the combination switch assembly.

5   Unscrew and remove the four screws which secure the column flange plate at its lower end.

6   Unscrew and remove the two bolts which secure the clamp at the upper end of the steering column.

7   Withdraw the steering column into the interior of the vehicle and then remove it.

8   The steering column bearings may be lubricated with multi-purpose grease but apart from this operation no dismantling or overhaul can be carried out. If the bearings are worn, renew the column complete.

9   In the event of a front end collision having occurred, the following dimensional checks must be carried out and the column renewed if they are outside the specified tolerances.

10   Measure the distance (A) (Fig. 11.15) between the top edge of the jacket lower tube and the column clamp. This should be 7·52 in. (191 mm). If the dimension is smaller then the column has suffered partial collapse.

11 Check that there is no gap between the end of the bolt insert and the end of the slot of the steering column clamp. If there is a measurable clearance, the jacket tube will have been crushed. In either case, renew the steering column complete.

12 Commence refitting by setting the roadwheels in the straight-ahead position. Pass the steering column from the vehicle interior and connect the flexible coupling to the worm shaft making sure that the punch mark on the upper end of the steering shaft is at the top.

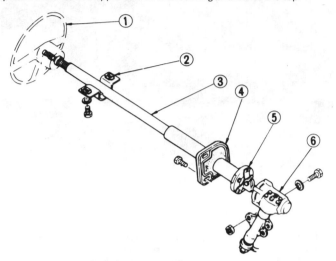

Fig. 11.12 Steering components (Sec 13)

1 Steering wheel
2 Column clamp
3 Steering column
4 Jacket tube flange
5 Rubber coupling
6 Steering gear

13 Insert the column clamp bolts finger-tight.
14 Loosen the column flange plate clamp bolt and slide the flange plate into engagement with the bulkhead. Insert the four securing bolts finger-tight.
15 Check for smooth operation of the steering wheel and column by temporarily installing the steering wheel and turning it from lock-to-lock.
16 If this proves satisfactory, tighten all bolts to the specified torque wrench settings.
17 Refit the combination switch assembly, the steering wheel and the column upper and lower shrouds.

14 Steering column lock – removal and refitting

1 The steering column lock is combined with the ignition switch.
2 The ignition switch can be withdrawn after removing the small screw which retains it to the body of the lock.
3 Removal of the lock assembly can only be carried out after removing the steering column (Section 13) and drilling out the two shear bolts (Fig. 11.17). If the lock is being renewed, it will probably be easier to remove the lock by sawing through the bolts between the two parts of the body, using a hacksaw blade.
4 Position the new lock on the steering column and insert the securing bolts finger-tight. Operate the ignition key several times to make sure that the tongue of the lock is in perfect alignment with the hole in the column tube and is operating smoothly.
5 Tighten the bolts evenly until their heads shear off.

15 Steering box – removal and refitting

1 Remove the pinch bolt which secures the flexible coupling to the steering worm shaft (photo).
2 Bend up the tab of the lockwasher and unscrew the nut which secures the drop arm to the sector shaft. Mark the relative position of the drop arm to the sector shaft, to facilitate refitting.

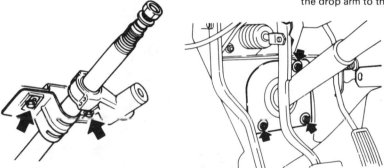

Fig. 11.13 Column clamp bolts, arrowed (Sec 13)

Fig. 11.14 Jacket tube flange bolts, arrowed (Sec 13)

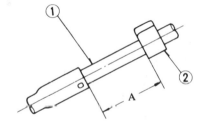

Fig. 11.16 Collapsible steering column components (Sec 13)

1 Jacket tube
2 Column clamp
For dimension A, see text

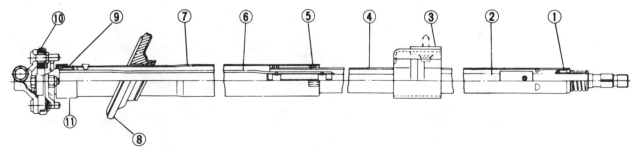

Fig. 11.15 Steering column standard dimension (Sec 13)

1 Upper bearing
2 Upper jacket shaft
3 Steering post clamp
4 Upper jacket tube
5 Steel ball
6 Lower jacket shaft
7 Lower jacket tube
8 Lower jacket tube flange
9 Lower bearing
10 Rubber coupling
11 Column dust cover

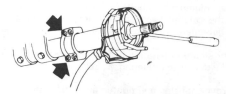

Fig. 11.17 Steering column lock bolts,
arrowed (Sec 14)

3   Using a heavy duty puller, extract the drop arm from the sector
shaft.
4   Unscrew the three bolts which secure the steering box to the body
side frame and remove the steering box from the engine compartment.
5   Refitting is a reversal of removal, but make sure that the drop arm
and sector shaft marks made before dismantling are in alignment. Do
not drive the drop arm into position, but draw it onto the sector shaft,
using the nut. Tighten all bolts to the specified torque.

16 Steering box – dismantling, adjustment and reassembly

1   After removing the steering box from the car, remove the steering
box oil filler plug and drain out all the oil.
2   Carefully secure the steering box in a vice. It is preferable to bolt
the box to a support plate and grip the plate in the vice rather than grip
the box directly.
3   Unscrew the locknut of the steering adjuster. Remove the four
bolts from the sector shaft cover and remove the cover by screwing
the adjuster clockwise.
4   Remove the four bolts from the rear cover and take off the rear
cover.

15.1 Steering box and flexible coupling pinch bolt (arrowed)

5   Remove any bearing adjusting shims which are beneath the cover
and then remove the steering worm assembly.
6   Wash all the parts in cleaning solvent and then check their condition.
7   Check the surface of the gear teeth for pitting, burrs, cracks or
other damage. If the sector shaft is damaged, a new one must be

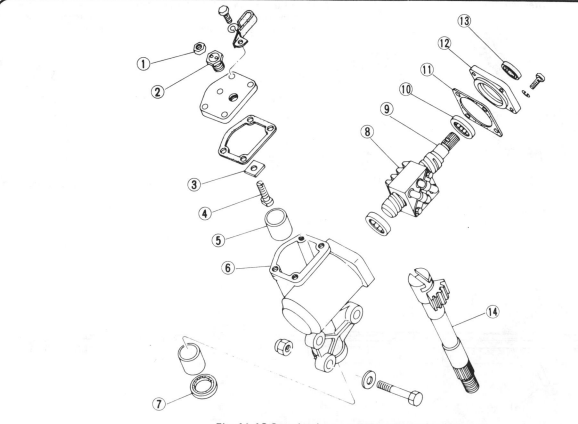

Fig. 11.18 Steering box – exploded view (Sec 16)

1 Locknut	5 Sector shaft bushing	9 Worm shaft	12 Rear cover
2 Filler plug	6 Steering gear housing	10 Worm bearing	13 Oil seal
3 Adjusting shim	7 Oil seal	11 Worm bearing adjusting shim	14 Sector shaft
4 Adjusting screw	8 Ball nut		

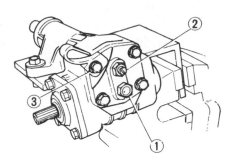

Fig. 11.19 Mounting the steering box in a vice (Sec 16)

1 Filler plug   3 Sector shaft cover bolts
2 Locknut

Fig. 11.20 Removing the steering worm assembly (Sec 16)

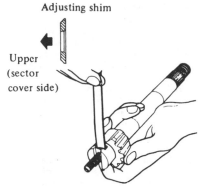

Fig. 11.21 Measuring the sector shaft endplay (Sec 16)

fitted. Examine the shaft to ensure that it is not bent and that its serrations are not damaged. If the shaft is bent or damaged, check that the gear housing and steering worm have not also been damaged.

8 Examine the gear tooth surface of the ball nut and discard it if there is evidence of pitting, burrs, or other damage. The ball nut must rotate smoothly on the worm gear and the assembly should be renewed if the movement is not smooth and free. To check that the freedom of movement is satisfactory, move the ball nut to one end of the worm gear and carefully stand the assembly on the bench with the ball nut uppermost. The nut should move down the worm under its own weight. Repeat the test with the ball nut starting from the other end of the worm. When carrying out this test, be careful not to damage the ball nut guide tube.

9 Inspect the worm bearing for wear, pitting, or any other damage. If any renewal is required, replace the bearings and outer race as a set.

10 If the sector shaft bushings in the gear housing are damaged, the bushings cannot be renewed and a new gear housing assembly is necessary.

11 Inspect the oil seals and discard any which have their sealing lips deformed or cracked. Also discard any oil seal if the spring is fatigued, or dislocated. Any oil seal which is removed from its housing should be discarded regardless of its condition and should be replaced by a new one.

12 Before starting reassembly, which is the reverse of the dismantling operations, ensure that all parts are scrupulously clean. Lubricate all moving surfaces with clean gear oil and fill the space between the sealing lips of the oil seals with the recommended multi-purpose grease. Smear the outer edge of new oil seals with gear oil before fitting them to make installation easier and insert them so that the lettered face of the seal faces outwards.

13 Fit the steering worm assembly and its bearings in the gear housing. Fit the worm bearing shims, with the thicker shim towards the worm assembly. Fit the end cover and tighten the bolts to the specified torque.

14 Rotate the worm shaft a few revolutions in each direction to settle the worm bearing and then check the bearing pre-load by measuring the torque necessary to turn the shaft. Tie a piece of cord to the splined shaft and then wind the cord a few turns round the shaft. Attach a light spring balance to the free end of the cord and increase the pull very gradually until the shaft begins to rotate. Note the spring balance reading at which the shaft begins to rotate and multiply this by the radius of the shaft to obtain the torque. To obtain the radius of the shaft, measure its diameter and halve the dimension obtained.

15 If the bearing pre-load is outside the specification it must be corrected by removing the cover and decreasing the thickness of shims if the pre-load is too high, or increasing shim thickness if the pre-load is too low. The different shim thicknesses available are given in the Specification.

16 When the correct worm bearing pre-load has been obtained, remove the rear cover again and apply sealant to the end of the housing and to the cover side of the shims. Attach the shims to the inside face of the cover and refit the cover.

17 Insert the adjuster screw into the T-shaped groove in the top of the sector shaft and use feeler gauges to measure the clearance between the sector shaft and the adjusting screw. Select a shim of a size which will give the specified clearance. Available thicknesses of

shim are given in the Specification. When fitting the adjusting shim, ensure that it is fitted with its chamfered face towards the screw.

18 Turn the worm shaft until the nut is in the middle of its travel and then insert the sector shaft so that the centre tooth of the shaft engages in the centre groove of the nut. When inserting the sector shaft be careful not to damage the lip of the shaft oil seal.

19 Apply sealant to each side of a new sector shaft cover gasket and locate the gasket on the housing. Position the end cover over the housing so that the end of the adjuster screw is aligned with its hole in the cover, then fit the cover by turning the adjuster screw anti-clockwise.

20 Insert the cover fixing bolts to secure the cover temporarily.

21 Turn the adjusting screw anti-clockwise about three turns to pull the sector shaft towards the cover and then tighten the sector shaft cover bolts to the specified torque.

22 Turn the adjusting screw clockwise until any end movement of the sector shaft just disappears and temporarily secure the adjuster screw in this position with the locknut.

23 Fit the gear arm on to the sector shaft and move the sector shaft from side to side several times, making sure that it turns smoothly.

24 With the steering gear in its central position adjust the backlash in the steering gear by turning the adjusting screw in or out until the movement of the top end of the gear arm does not exceed 0·004 in (0·1 mm). Move the sector shaft over its entire range several times before making the final adjustment and then tighten the locknut.

25 Using a spring balance and a piece of cord attached to the end of the gear arm, measure the initial turning torque of the worm assembly with the arm in its central position and at each end of its stroke. If either of the values obtained is outside the specified figures, readjust the adjusting screw until the correct turning torque is obtained.

26 Fill the steering box with oil of the recommended grade and fit the filler plug.

17 Front wheel alignment

1 Accurate front wheel alignment is essential for good steering and minimum tyre wear. Before adjusting wheel alignment, check that the tyres are at their correct pressures and that the wheels are balanced. Examine all components of the steering gear to ensure that there is no looseness. Check the tightness of the front wheel bearings and the efficiency of the front shock absorbers.

2 Wheel alignment consists of three different measurements.

Camber is the angle to the vertical of the front wheels when viewed from the front of the car. Positive camber is when the tops of the wheels are tilted outwards.

Caster is the inclination of the steering axis to the vertical when viewed from the side of the car. Positive caster is when the steering axis is inclined rearwards.

Toe-in is the amount by which the front edges of the front wheels are nearer to each other than the diametrically opposite points of the wheel rim. The measurement is made on the horizontal line through the wheel centre.

3 Camber and caster are pre-set at the factory and do not normally require adjustment unless the vehicle has been damaged in a collision. If the camber, or caster are not within the specified limits, the relevant

parts of the steering gear must be checked and then repaired, or renewed as necessary.

4 Toe-in should be checked when the vehicle is unladen. The fuel tank should be full and the level of coolant in the radiator and oil in the sump should be at their maximum. All tyres should be inflated to their specified pressures and the vehicle should be free from excessive accumulations of mud and dirt.

5 To adjust the toe-in place the vehicle on level ground with the wheels in the straight ahead position.

6 Obtain or make a toe-in gauge. One may be easily made from tubing, cranked to clear the sump having an adjustable nut and setscrew at one end.

7 Using the gauge, measure the distance between the two inner wheel rims at hub height at the rear of the wheels.

8 Rotate the wheels (by pushing the car backwards or forwards) through 180° (half a turn) and again using the gauge, measure the distance of hub height between the two inner wheel rims at the front of the wheels. This measurement should be less than that previously taken at the rear of the wheel by the amount given in the Specifications, and represents the correct toe-in.

9 Where the toe-in is found to be incorrect, slacken the locknuts on each end of the steering rod, and rotate the rod until the correct toe-in is obtained. Tighten the locknuts, ensuring that the balljoints are held in the centre of their arc of travel during tightening.**Note**: *Toe-in is increased by rotating the steering rod forwards (ie, clockwise when viewed from the right side of the vehicle), and vice versa.*

10 If the steering rods have been dismantled, set the length between the two ball rod centres (dimension A in Fig. 11.23) to the specified length when reassembling and ensure that each rod end is screwed at least 0·8 in (20 mm) into its balljoint socket.

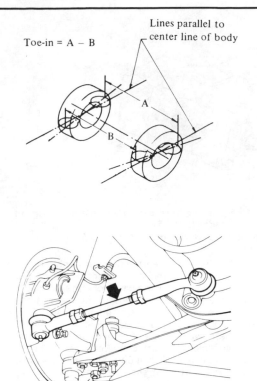

Toe-in = A − B   Lines parallel to center line of body

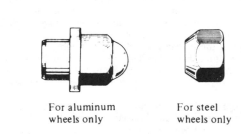

Fig. 11.22 Adjusting toe-in. Steering side rod arrowed (Sec 17)

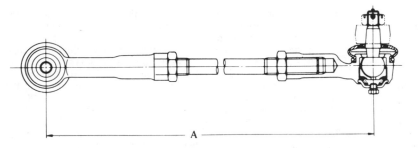

Fig. 11.23 Steering side rod length (Sec 17)
See Specification for dimension A

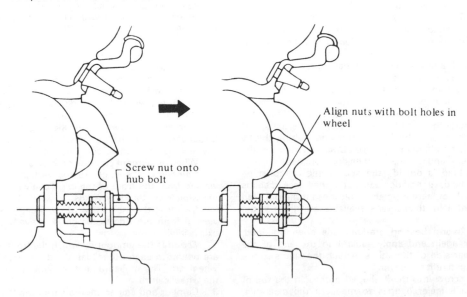

For aluminum wheels only   For steel wheels only

Fig. 11.24 The different types of wheel nut (Sec 18)

Screw nut onto hub bolt

Align nuts with bolt holes in wheel

Fig. 11.25 Installing aluminium wheels (Sec 18)

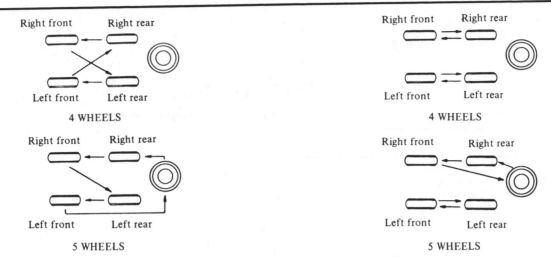

Fig. 11.26 Tyre rotation – crossply tyres (Sec 18)

Fig. 11.27 Tyre rotation – radial tyres (Sec 18)

bolts and the seats of the wheel nuts are kept free from oil and grease.

18 Wheels and tyres

Wheels

1   The roadwheels normally fitted are of pressed steel, but aluminium alloy wheels are fitted to some models. It is important to note that there are different wheel nuts for pressed steel and aluminium wheels, the ones for aluminium wheels being longer. It is essential that the correct nuts are used for the particularly type of wheels fitted.

2   When fitting a steel wheel, screw the nuts on finger tight and then tighten them in diagonal pairs to the recommended torque.

3   When fitting aluminium alloy wheels, screw each nut onto the end of the hub bolt. Align the nuts with the bolt holes in the wheel and then pull the wheel forward so that the nuts engage in the holes in the wheel. Tighten the nuts evenly, turning each one a little at a time in diagonal sequence until the recommended torque is achieved.

4   In order to lessen the risk of wheel nuts becoming loose due to vibration, it is recommended that the threaded portion of the wheel

Tyres

5   Radial ply tyres are fitted to the vehicle as standard equipment and if any other types are fitted subsequently it is important that different types of tyre such as radial ply, crossply and bias belted are not mixed. Mixed use of different types of tyres can affect car handling adversely and may result in the driver losing control. The use of a mixture of tyres may also be illegal.

6   The tyres may wear unevenly and become unbalanced. To equalise wear it is necessary to fit each wheel on a different axle. If radial tyres are fitted, do not move wheels from one side of the car to the other, but only interchange front and rear wheels on the same side. Patterns of tyre rotation are shown in Figs 11.26 and 11.27.

7   Balancing of wheels and tyres is an essential factor for good steering and road holding and they should be balanced both statically and dynamically. Rebalancing is required when the tyres have worn to about half their tread depth and also if a tyre has been punctured and repaired.

19 Fault diagnosis – front suspension and steering

Before diagnosing faults from the following chart, check that irregularities are not caused by:

1   Binding brakes
2   Incorrect mix of radial and crossply tyres
3   Incorrect tyre pressures
4   Misalignment of the bodyframe

Symptom	Reason(s)
Steering wheel can be moved considerably before any movement of the wheels is apparent	Wear in steering gear linkages
Vehicle difficult to steer in a straight line continuously	Wear in steering gear linkages Wheel alignment incorrect Front hub bearings loose, or worn Worn suspension unit swivel joints
Steering stiff and heavy	Tyre pressures too low Lack of lubrication in steering gear Steering box adjustment incorrect
Wheel wobble and vibration	Front hub bearing loose Wheels unbalanced Wheel buckled Wear in suspension unit bearings, or track control arm bushes Broken front spring
Excessive pitching and rolling when cornering or braking	Defective shock absorbers Broken front spring

Chapter 12 Bodywork and fittings

For modifications, and information applicable to later models, see Supplement at end of manual

Contents

1 General description

The body and underframe are of unitary, all welded construction on all models and the front wings are bolt on to give economical repair or renewal in the event of damage.

The wide choice of body styles comprises a saloon with 2 door or 4 door alternatives, an estate version with a fastback variant and a coupe with liftback.

The availability of the wide range of body styles, the alternative engine sizes and different standards of equipment make it essential that the car's year of manufacture, its chassis number and engine number are quoted when ordering spares. The position of the engine and chassis number are given in the Introduction and Maintenance Section.

2 Maintenance – bodywork and underframe

The general condition of a vehicle's bodywork is the one thing that significantly affects its value. Maintenance is easy but needs to be regular. Neglect, particularly after minor damage, can lead quickly to further deterioration and costly repair bills. It is important also to keep watch on those parts of the vehicle not immediately visible, for instance the underside, inside all the wheel arches and the lower part of the engine compartment.

The basic maintenance routine for the bodywork is washing – preferably with a lot of water, from a hose. This will remove all the loose solids which may have stuck to the vehicle. It is important to flush these off in such a way as to prevent grit from scratching the finish. The wheel arches and underframe need washing in the same way to remove any accumulated mud which will retain moisture and tend to encourage rust. Paradoxically enough, the best time to clean the underframe and wheel arches is in wet weather when the mud is thoroughly wet and soft. In very wet weather the underframe is usually cleaned of large accumulations automatically and this is a good time for inspection.

Periodically, except on vehicles with a wax-based underbody protective coat, it is a good idea to have the whole of the underframe of the vehicle steam cleaned, engine compartment included, so that a thorough inspection can be carried out to see what minor repairs and renovations are necessary. Steam cleaning is available at many garages and is necessary for removal of the accumulation of oily grime which sometimes is allowed to become thick in certain areas. If steam cleaning facilities are not available, there are one or two excellent grease solvents available which can be brush applied. The dirt can then be simply hosed off. Note that these methods should not be used on vehicles with wax-based underbody protective coating or the coating will be removed. Such vehicles should be inspected annually, preferably just prior to winter, when the underbody should be washed down and any damage to the wax coating repaired. Ideally, a completely fresh coat should be applied. It would also be worth considering the use of such wax-based protection for injection into door panels, sills, box sections etc, as an additional safeguard against rust damage.

After washing paintwork, wipe off with a chamois leather to give an unspotted clear finish. A coat of clear protective wax polish will give added protection against chemical pollutants in the air. If the paintwork sheen has dulled or oxidised, use a cleaner/polisher combination to restore the brilliance of the shine. This requires a little effort, but such dulling is usually caused because regular washing has been neglected. Care needs to be taken with metallic paintwork, as special non-abrasive cleaner/polisher is required to avoid damage to the finish. Always check that the door and ventilator opening drain holes and pipes are completely clear so that water can be drained out. Bright work should be treated in the same way as paintwork. Windscreens and windows can be kept clear of the smeary film which often appears by the use of a proprietary glass cleaner. Never use any form of wax or other body or chromium polish on glass.

3 Maintenance – upholstery and carpets

Mats and carpets should be brushed or vacuum cleaned regularly to keep them free of grit. If they are badly stained remove them from the vehicle for scrubbing or sponging and make quite sure they are dry before refitting. Seats and interior trim panels can be kept clean by wiping with a damp cloth. If they do become stained (which can be more apparent on light coloured upholstery) use a little liquid detergent and a soft nail brush to scour the grime out of the grain of the material. Do not forget to keep the headlining clean in the same way as the upholstery. When using liquid cleaners inside the vehicle do not over-wet the surfaces being cleaned. Excessive damp could get into the seams and padded interior causing stains, offensive odours or even rot. If the inside of the vehicle gets wet accidentally it is worthwhile taking some trouble to dry it out properly, particularly where carpets are involved. *Do not leave oil or electric heaters inside the vehicle for this purpose.*

4 Minor body damage – repair

The photographic sequences on pages 206 and 207 illustrate the operations detailed in the following sub-sections.

Repair of minor scratches in bodywork

If the scratch is very superficial, and does not penetrate to the metal of the bodywork, repair is very simple. Lightly rub the area of the scratch with a paintwork renovator, or a very fine cutting paste, to remove loose paint from the scratch and to clear the surrounding bodywork of wax polish. Rinse the area with clean water.

Apply touch-up paint to the scratch using a fine paint brush; continue to apply fine layers of paint until the surface of the paint in the scratch is level with the surrounding paintwork. Allow the new paint at least two weeks to harden: then blend it into the surrounding paintwork by rubbing the scratch area with a paintwork renovator or a very fine cutting paste. Finally, apply wax polish.

Where the scratch has penetrated right through to the metal of the bodywork, causing the metal to rust, a different repair technique is required. Remove any loose rust from the bottom of the scratch with a penknife, then apply rust inhibiting paint to prevent the formation of rust in the future. Using a rubber or nylon applicator fill the scratch with bodystopper paste. If required, this paste can be mixed with cellulose thinners to provide a very thin paste which is ideal for filling narrow scratches. Before the stopper-paste in the scratch hardens, wrap a piece of smooth cotton rag around the top of a finger. Dip the finger in cellulose thinners and then quickly sweep it across the surface of the stopper-paste in the scratch; this will ensure that the surface of the stopper-paste is slightly hollowed. The scratch can now be painted over as described earlier in this Section.

Repair of dents in bodywork

When deep denting of the vehicle's bodywork has taken place, the first task is to pull the dent out, until the affected bodywork almost attains its original shape. There is little point in trying to restore the original shape completely, as the metal in the damaged area will have stretched on impact and cannot be reshaped fully to its original contour. It is better to bring the level of the dent up to a point which is about $\frac{1}{8}$ in (3 mm) below the level of the surrounding bodywork. In cases where the dent is very shallow anyway, it is not worth trying to pull it out at all. If the underside of the dent is accessible, it can be hammered out gently from behind, using a mallet with a wooden or plastic head. Whilst doing this, hold a suitable block of wood firmly against the outside of the panel to absorb the impact from the hammer blows and thus prevent a large area of the bodywork from being 'belled-out'.

Should the dent be in a section of the bodywork which has a double skin or some other factor making it inaccessible from behind, a different technique is called for. Drill several small holes through the metal inside the area – particularly in the deeper section. Then screw long self-tapping screws into the holes just sufficiently for them to gain a good purchase in the metal. Now the dent can be pulled out by pulling on the protruding heads of the screws with a pair of pliers.

The next stage of the repair is the removal of the paint from the damaged area, and from an inch or so of the surrounding 'sound' bodywork. This is accomplished most easily by using a wire brush or abrasive pad on a power drill, although it can be done just as effectively by hand using sheets of abrasive paper. To complete the preparation for filling, score the surface of the bare metal with a screwdriver or the tang of a file, or alternatively, drill small holes in the affected area. This will provide a really good 'key' for the filler paste.

To complete the repair see the Section on filling and re-spraying.

Repair of rust holes or gashes in bodywork

Remove all paint from the affected area and from an inch or so of the surrounding 'sound' bodywork, using an abrasive pad or a wire brush on a power drill. If these are not available a few sheets of abrasive paper will do the job just as effectively. With the paint removed you will be able to gauge the severity of the corrosion and therefore decide whether to renew the whole panel (if this is possible) or to repair the affected area. New body panels are not as expensive as most people think and it is often quicker and more satisfactory to fit a new panel than to attempt to repair large areas of corrosion.

Remove all fittings from the affected area except those which will act as a guide to the original shape of the damaged bodywork (eg headlamp shells etc). Then, using tin snips or a hacksaw blade, remove all loose metal and any other metal badly affected by corrosion. Hammer the edges of the hole inwards in order to create a slight depression for the filler paste.

Wire brush the affected area to remove the powdery rust from the surface of the remaining metal. Paint the affected area with rust inhibiting paint; if the back of the rusted area is accessible treat this also.

Before filling can take place it will be necessary to block the hole in some way. This can be achieved by the use of aluminium or plastic mesh, or aluminium tape.

Aluminium or plastic mesh is probably the best material to use for a large hole. Cut a piece to the approximate size and shape of the hole to be filled, then position it in the hole so that its edges are below the level of the surrounding bodywork. It can be retained in position by several blobs of filler paste around its periphery.

Aluminium tape should be used for small or very narrow holes. Pull a piece off the roll and trim it to the approximate size and shape required, then pull off the backing paper (if used) and stick the tape over the hole; it can be overlapped if the thickness of one piece is insufficient. Burnish down the edges of the tape with the handle of a screwdriver or similar, to ensure that the tape is securely attached to the metal underneath.

Bodywork repairs – filling and re-spraying

Before using this Section, see the Sections on dent, deep scratch, rust holes and gash repairs.

Many types of bodyfiller are available, but generally speaking those proprietary kits which contain a tin of filler paste and a tube of resin hardener are best for this type of repair. A wide, flexible plastic or nylon applicator will be found invaluable for imparting a smooth and well contoured finish to the surface of the filler.

Mix up a little filler on a clean piece of card or board – measure the hardener carefully (follow the maker's instructions on the pack) otherwise the filler will set too rapidly or too slowly.

Using the applicator apply the filler paste to the prepared area; draw the applicator across the surface of the filler to achieve the correct contour and to level the filler surface. As soon as a contour that approximates to the correct one is achieved, stop working the paste – if you carry on too long the paste will become sticky and begin to 'pick up' on the applicator. Continue to add thin layers of filler paste at twenty-minute intervals until the level of the filler is just proud of the surrounding bodywork.

Once the filler has hardened, excess can be removed using a metal plane or file. From then on, progressively finer grades of abrasive paper should be used, starting with a 40 grade production paper and finishing with 400 grade wet-and-dry paper. Always wrap the abrasive paper around a flat rubber, cork, or wooden block – otherwise the surface of the filler will not be completely flat. During the smoothing of the filler surface the wet-and-dry paper should be periodically rinsed in water. This will ensure that a very smooth finish is imparted to the filler at the final stage.

At this stage the 'dent' should be surrounded by a ring of bare metal, which in turn should be encircled by the finely 'feathered' edge of the good paintwork. Rinse the repair area with clean water, until all of the dust produced by the rubbing-down operation has gone.

Spray the whole repair area with a light coat of primer – this will show up any imperfections in the surface of the filler. Repair these imperfections with fresh filler paste or bodystopper, and once more smooth the surface with abrasive paper. If bodystopper is used, it can be mixed with cellulose thinners to form a really thin paste which is ideal for filling small holes. Repeat this spray and repair procedure until you are satisfied that the surface of the filler, and the feathered edge of the paintwork are perfect. Clean the repair area with clean water and allow to dry fully.

The repair area is now ready for final spraying. Paint spraying must be carried out in a warm, dry, windless and dust free atmosphere. This condition can be created artificially if you have access to a large indoor working area, but if you are forced to work in the open, you will have to pick your day very carefully. If you are working indoors, dousing the floor in the work area with water will help to settle the dust which would otherwise be in the atmosphere. If the repair area is confined to one body panel, mask off the surrounding panels; this will help to minimise the effects of a slight mis-match in paint colours. Bodywork fittings (eg chrome strips, door handles etc) will also need to be masked off. Use genuine masking tape and several thicknesses of newspaper for the masking operations.

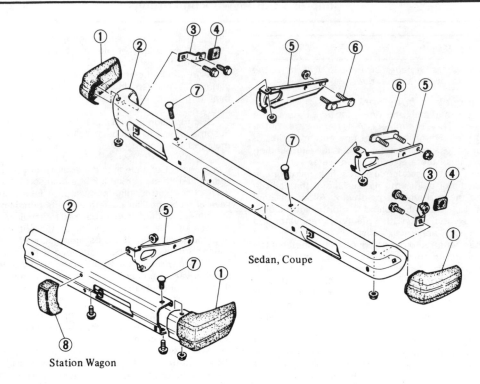

Sedan, Coupe

Station Wagon

Fig. 12.1 Front bumper components – European models (Sec 6)

1 Side bumper rubber	3 Side bumper bracket	5 Bumper stay	7 Carriage bolt
2 Bumper	4 Side bumper bracket shim	6 Bolt plate	8 Overrider

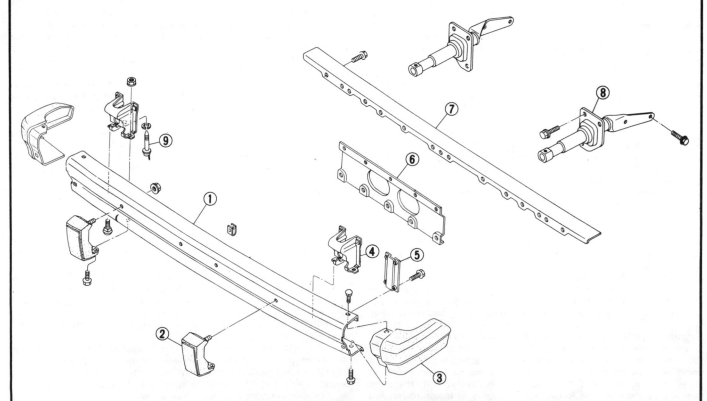

Fig. 12.2 Front bumper components – 210 models (Sec 6)

1 Front centre bumper	4 Bumper mounting bracket	6 Bumper reinforcement	8 Shock absorber
2 Overrider	5 Centre bumper brace	7 Cover strip	9 Bumper bolt
3 Side bumper rubber			

Before commencing to spray, agitate the aerosol can thoroughly, then spray a test area (an old tin, or similar) until the technique is mastered. Cover the repair area with a thick coat of primer; the thickness should be built up using several thin layers of paint rather than one thick one. Using 400 grade wet-and-dry paper, rub down the surface of the primer until it is really smooth. While doing this, the work area should be thoroughly doused with water, and the wet-and-dry paper periodically rinsed in water. Allow to dry before spraying on more paint.

Spray on the top coat, again building up the thickness by using several thin layers of paint. Start spraying in the centre of the repair area and then, using a circular motion, work outwards until the whole repair area and about 2 inches of the surrounding original paintwork is covered. Remove all masking material 10 to 15 minutes after spraying on the final coat of paint.

Allow the new paint at least two weeks to harden, then, using a paintwork renovator or a very fine cutting paste, blend the edges of the paint into the existing paintwork. Finally, apply wax polish.

5 Major body damage – repair

1   Because the car is built without a separate chassis frame and the body is therefore integral with the underframe, major damage must be repaired by competent mechanics with the necessary welding and hydraulic straightening equipment.
2   If the damage has been serious it is vital that the body is checked for correct alignment as otherwise the handling of the car will suffer and many other faults such as excessive tyre wear and wear in the transmission and steering may occur.
3   There is a special body jig which most large body repair shops have, and to ensure that all is correct it is important that the jig be used for all major repair work.

6 Front bumper – removal and refitting

European models
1   For safety reasons disconnect the battery positive terminal.

2   Disconnect the front direction indicator light cable connectors.
3   Undo and remove the bolts and washers securing the front bumper side bracket to the lower side of the front wing.
4   Undo and remove the bolts that secure the front bumper stay to body side member and draw the front bumper forward from the body. Take care not to scratch the paintwork.
5   Refitting the front bumper is the reverse sequence to removal, but align the bumper correctly prior to tightening the securing bolts.

USA models
6   The bumper assembly on these models incorporates shock absorbers and side bumper units to assist in the event of a sudden impact – see Fig. 12.2.
7   The removal procedure follows that of the European model bumper given previously. Under no circumstances should the shock absorber units be dismantled if they are removed, but if faulty renew them.
8   Refitting is a reversal of the removal procedure but check the bumpers for correct alignment on completion. The ground clearance from the lower edge of the bumpers should be 14.17 to 16.06 in (360 to 408 mm).

7 Rear bumper – removal and refitting

European models
1   If your model incorporates the number plate light into the rear bumper, detach the battery earth cable and then disconnect the rear number plate light cable connections.
2   Unscrew and remove the bolts securing the bumper stay to the body side member.
3   Unscrew and remove the bolts securing the rear bumper side bracket to the rear lower wing section.
4   Carefully withdraw the bumper from the car taking care not to scratch the paintwork.
5   Refit the bumper in the reverse sequence but ensure that the bumper is correctly aligned before fully tightening the securing bolts.

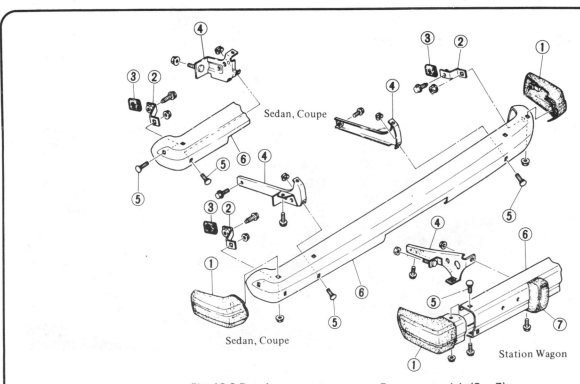

Fig. 12.3 Rear bumper components – European models (Sec 7)

1 Side bumper rubber	3 Side bumper bracket shim	5 Carriage bolt	7 Overrider
2 Side bumper bracket	4 Bumper stay	6 Bumper	

This sequence of photographs deals with the repair of the dent and paintwork damage shown in this photo. The procedure will be similar for the repair of a hole. It should be noted that the procedures given here are simplified — more explicit instructions will be found in the text

In the case of a dent the first job — after removing surrounding trim — is to hammer out the dent where access is possible. This will minimise filling. Here, the large dent having been hammered out, the damaged area is being made slightly concave

Now all paint must be removed from the damaged area, by rubbing with coarse abrasive paper. Alternatively, a wire brush or abrasive pad can be used in a power drill. Where the repair area meets good paintwork, the edge of the paintwork should be 'feathered', using a finer grade of abrasive paper

In the case of a hole caused by rusting, all damaged sheet-metal should be cut away before proceeding to this stage. Here, the damaged area is being treated with rust remover and inhibitor before being filled

Mix the body filler according to its manufacturer's instructions. In the case of corrosion damage, it will be necessary to block off any large holes before filling — this can be done with aluminium or plastic mesh, or aluminium tape. Make sure the area is absolutely clean before ...

... applying the filler. Filler should be applied with a flexible applicator, as shown, for best results; the wooden spatula being used for confined areas. Apply thin layers of filler at 20-minute intervals, until the surface of the filler is slightly proud of the surrounding bodywork

Initial shaping can be done with a Surform plane or Dreadnought file. Then, using progressively finer grades of wet-and-dry paper, wrapped around a sanding block, and copious amounts of clean water, rub down the filler until really smooth and flat. Again, feather the edges of adjoining paintwork

The whole repair area can now be sprayed or brush-painted with primer. If spraying, ensure adjoining areas are protected from over-spray. Note that at least one inch of the surrounding sound paintwork should be coated with primer. Primer has a 'thick' consistency, so will find small imperfections

Again, using plenty of water, rub down the primer with a fine grade wet-and-dry paper (400 grade is probably best) until it is really smooth and well blended into the surrounding paintwork. Any remaining imperfections can now be filled by carefully applied knifing stopper paste

When the stopper has hardened, rub down the repair area again before applying the final coat of primer. Before rubbing down this last coat of primer, ensure the repair area is blemish-free — use more stopper if necessary. To ensure that the surface of the primer is really smooth use some finishing compound

The top coat can now be applied. When working out of doors, pick a dry, warm and wind-free day. Ensure surrounding areas are protected from over-spray. Agitate the aerosol thoroughly, then spray the centre of the repair area, working outwards with a circular motion. Apply the paint as several thin coats

After a period of about two weeks, which the paint needs to harden fully, the surface of the repaired area can be 'cut' with a mild cutting compound prior to wax polishing. When carrying out bodywork repairs, remember that the quality of the finished job is proportional to the time and effort expended

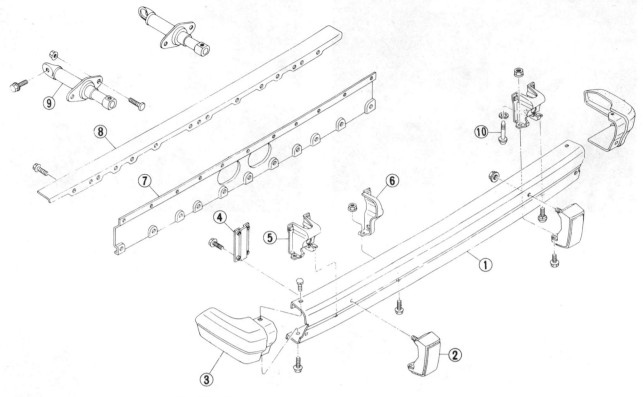

Fig. 12.4 Rear bumper components – 210 models (Sec 7)

1 Rear centre bumper	4 Centre bumper brace	7 Bumper reinforcement	9 Shock absorber
2 Overrider	5 Bumper mounting bracket	8 Cover strip (Estate only)	10 Bumper bolt
3 Side bumper	6 Baffle plate		

USA models

6   The bumper assemblies on these models incorporate shock absorbers and side bumpers to assist in the event of a sudden impact – see Fig. 12.4.

7   The removal procedure is similar to that of the European models given previously but note the following. Under no circumstances should the shock absorber units be dismantled if they are removed. If they are defective, renew them.

8   Refitting is the reversal of the removal procedure but check the bumpers for correct alignment on completion. The ground clearance from the lower edge of the bumpers should be 15.39 to 17.05 in (391 to 433 mm) for Saloon and Coupe models and 14.80 to 16.46 in (376 to 418 mm) for Estate Car models.

8   Windscreen – removal and refitting

1   Where a windscreen is to be renewed then if it is due to shattering, the facia air vents should be covered before attempting removal. Adhesive sheeting is useful to stick to the outside of the glass to enable large areas of crystallised glass to be removed.

2   Where the screen is to be removed intact then an assistant will be required. First release the rubber surround from the bodywork by running a blunt, small screwdriver around and under the rubber weatherstrip both inside and outside the car. This operation will break the adhesive of the sealer originally used. Take care not to damage the paintwork or cut the rubber surround with the screwdriver. Remove the windscreen wiper arms and interior mirror and place a protective cover on the bonnet.

3   Have your assistant push the inner lip of the rubber surround off the flange of the windscreen body aperture. Once the rubber surround starts to peel off the flange, the screen may be forced gently outwards by careful hand pressure. The second person should support and remove the screen complete with rubber surround and metal trim as it comes out.

4   Remove the beading from the rubber surround.

5   Before fitting a windscreen, ensure that the rubber surround is completely free from old sealant, glass fragments and has not hardened or cracked. Fit the rubber surround to the glass and apply a bead of suitable sealant between the glass outer edge and the rubber.

6   Refit the bright trim to the rubber surround.

7   Cut a piece of strong cord greater in length than the periphery of the glass and insert it into the body flange locating channel of the rubber surround.

8   Apply a thin bead of sealant to the face of the rubber channel which will eventually mate with the body.

9   Offer the windscreen to the body aperture and pass the ends of the cord, previously fitted and located at bottom centre into the vehicle interior.

10   Press the windscreen into place, at the same time have an assistant pulling the cords to engage the lip of the rubber channel over the body flange.

11   Remove any excess sealant with a paraffin soaked rag.

12   Removal and refitting of the rear window glass is carried out in an identical manner but (if fitted) disconnect the leads to the heating element in the glass.

9   Radiator grille – removal and refitting

1   Open and secure the bonnet in the raised position with the stay.

2   Unscrew and remove the radiator grille screws at the top (to front body crossmember).

3   To remove the clips at the bottom, use a screwdriver and insert the blade between the clips and grille and twist. Lift the grille clear.

4   Refitting is the reverse of the removal procedure.

10   Front apron – removal and refitting

1   Refer to Sections 6 and 9 and remove the front bumper and the radiator grille.

2   Unscrew and remove the front apron attachment screws from the positions arrowed in Fig. 12.6 and lift the panel clear.

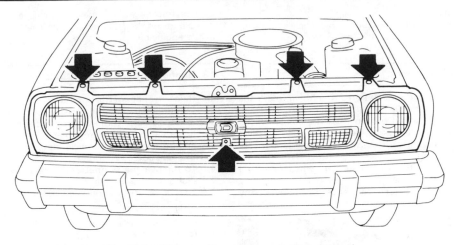

Fig. 12.5 Radiator grille attachment points (Sec 9)

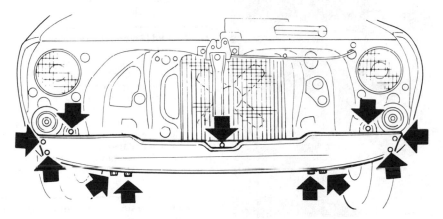

Fig. 12.6 Front apron attachment points (Sec 10)

Fig. 12.7 Front wing attachment points (Sec 11)

3   Refit in the reverse order.

11 Front wing – removal and refitting

1   Disconnect the battery earth terminal.
2   Refer to Sections 6 and 9 and remove the front bumper and radiator grille.

3   Disconnect and remove the side turn indicator light from the wing panel (see Chapter 10).
4   Unscrew the wing to inner panel retaining bolts, also the front apron, inner sill and moulding and front pillar bolts to wing panel – see Fig. 12.7.
5   Prior to removing the wing, check that there are no other fittings

still attached, then lift the panel away.

6   Refit the wing panel in the reverse sequence but apply some suitable body sealant between the wing and inner panel.

12 Bonnet – removal and refitting

1   Open the bonnet and, to act as a datum for refitting, mark the position of the hinges on the bonnet using a soft pencil.

2   With the assistance of a second person hold the bonnet in the open position, undo and remove the bolts, spring and plain washers that hold each hinge to the bonnet. Lift away the bonnet taking care not to scratch the top of the wing.

3   Whilst the bonnet is being lifted away take care when detaching the bonnet support rod.

4   Refitting the bonnet is the reverse sequence to removal. Any

13.4 Bonnet catch

adjustments necessary may be made at the hinge, catch or rubber bump pads on the front panel. Lubricate the hinge pivots and lock with a little engine oil.

13 Bonnet lock and control cable – removal and refitting

1   Raise and secure the bonnet.

2   Compress the catch and detach the cable nipple from its location slot. Prise the outer cable clip free at the catch.

3   If the cable is to be removed, unclip the cable from the location clip and from inside the vehicle, detach the cable bracket by removing the retaining bolts. Withdraw the cable through the interior.

4   To remove the bonnet catch, unscrew and remove the securing bolts (photo).

5   To refit, reverse the removal instructions but note the following:

(a) *Lubricate the safety catch lever, spring and pivot on assembly*
(b) *Do not refit any defective parts – always renew them*
(c) *Check the operation of the catch before closing the bonnet*
(d) *Check the operation of the catch when the bonnet is closed and adjust if necessary (Fig. 12.9).*

14 Boot lid (Saloons) – removal and refitting

1   Open the boot lid and, using a soft pencil, mark the outline of the hinges on the lid to act as a datum for refitting.

2   With the assistance of a second person hold the boot lid in the open position and then remove the two bolts from each hinge.

3   Lift away the boot lid.

4   Refiting the boot lid is the reverse sequence to removal. If necesary adjust the position of the hinges relative to the lid until the lid is centralised in the aperture.

5   To obtain a watertight fit between the boot lid and weatherstrip move the striker up and down or side to side as necessary.

15 Boot lid torsion bar assembly (Saloon) – removal and refitting

1   Open the boot lid and then remove the luggage compartment finisher panel securing screws. Lift away the finisher panel.

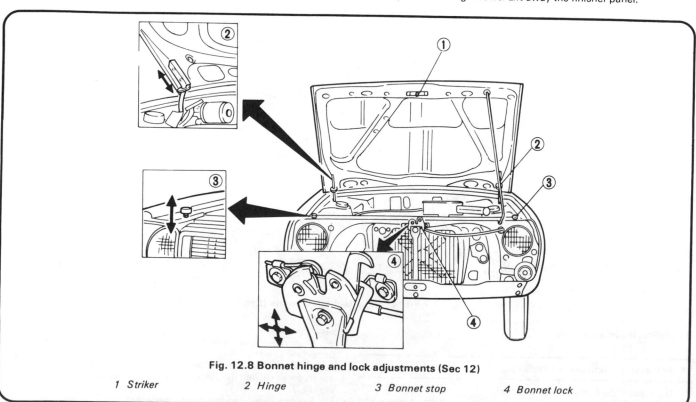

Fig. 12.8 Bonnet hinge and lock adjustments (Sec 12)

1 Striker   2 Hinge   3 Bonnet stop   4 Bonnet lock

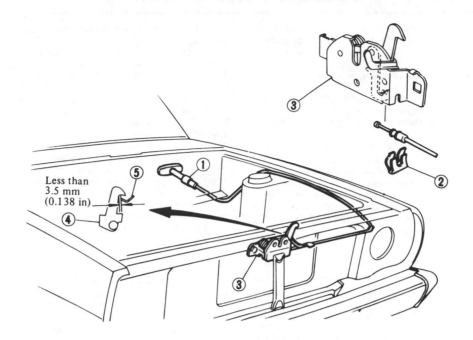

Less than
3.5 mm
(0.138 in)

Fig. 12.9 Bonnet lock mechanism (Sec 13)

1 Cable bracket   3 Bonnet lock   4 Safety catch   5 Striker
2 Cable clip

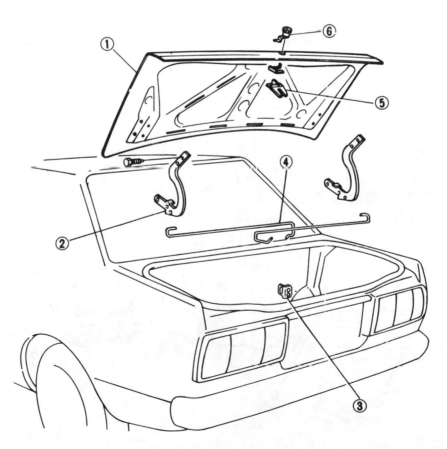

Fig. 12.10 Boot lid components (Saloon) (Sec 14)

1 Boot lid   3 Striker   5 Lock
2 Hinge   4 Torsion bar   6 Lock cylinder

2   Support the boot lid with a piece of wood and carefully draw the end of the left torsion bar out of the hole drilled in the side panel – Watch your fingers!

3   Detach the torsion bar from the bracket and hinge.

4   The right-hand torsion bar is now removed in a similar manner to the left-hand torsion bar.

5   To refit the assembly first position the end of the right-hand torsion bar onto the right boot lid hinge.

6   Twist the torsion bar rearward and engage the bar in the torsion bar bracket.

7   Fit the left-hand torsion bar in a similar manner to the right.

16 Tailgate (Estate) – removal and refitting

1   Open the tailgate and support it in the open position with a piece of wood. The assistance of a second person is required to hold the tailgate as it is detached from the hinges.

2   Using a soft pencil, mark the outline of the hinge on the tailgate to act as a datum for refitting.

3   Detach the rear screen demister wires.

4   Undo and remove the three bolts and washers securing each hinge to the tailgate and carefully lift away the tailgate. Refitting the tailgate is the reverse sequence to removal.

5   Should it be necessary to adjust the position of the tailgate in the aperture, it may be moved up or down and side to side at the tailgate to hinge securing bolts. The fore and aft movement adjustment is obtained by slackening the bolts securing the tailgate hinges to the body.

17 Tailgate torsion bar assembly (Estate) – removal and refitting

1   Open the tailgate and support it in the open position with a piece of wood.

2   Undo and remove the fixing that secures the tailgate hinge cover to body, lift away the cover.

3   Undo and remove the screws fixing the head-lining rear end to the tailgate aperture rail panel (clean hands). Detach the head-lining.

4   Using a suitable pry bar detach the left torsion bar from the bracket.

5   Remove the right-hand torsion bar (painted yellow) from the bracket in a similar manner to the left-hand torsion bar.

6   Refitting the assembly is the reverse sequence to removal, but always refit the yellow bar first.

7   To adjust the tailgate, loosen the tailgate/hinge bolts and adjust the tailgate accordingly, then retighten the bolts. If the tailgate needs to be adjusted in the fore and aft direction, first remove the hinge cover, then the rear welt. Detach the rear end of the headlining and slacken the tailgate hinge bolts to the body. The tailgate can now be adjusted to enable it to fit evenly with equal clearances between it and the roof on each side. Retighten the bolts when the correct position has been located. Reverse the dismantling instructions to complete but check the tailgate action and security when closed.

18 Coupe rear door – removal and refitting

1   Raise the door and using a soft lead pencil, mark the outline of the hinge on the rear door to act as a guide when refitting.

2   With the aid of an assistant, support the door and unscrew the stay bolts.

3   Unscrew and remove the door to hinge bolts and lift the door clear.

4   Refit in the reverse order but check the door adjustment before fully tightening the hinge bolts. Note the respective positions of the stay bolt components and refit as shown in Fig. 12.13.

5   To adjust the catch, loosen the bolts and move the catch in the desired direction, then retighten the bolts.

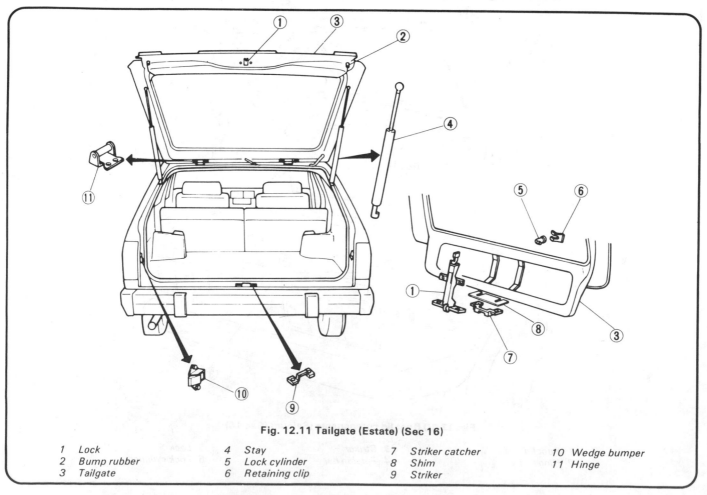

Fig. 12.11 Tailgate (Estate) (Sec 16)

1	Lock	4	Stay	7	Striker catcher
2	Bump rubber	5	Lock cylinder	8	Shim
3	Tailgate	6	Retaining clip	9	Striker

10 Wedge bumper
11 Hinge

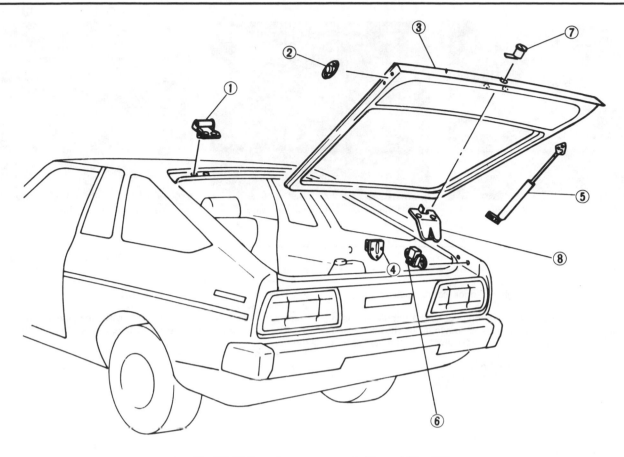

Fig. 12.12 Rear door components (Coupe) (Sec 18)

1 Hinge   3 Rear door   5 Stay   7 Lock cylinder
2 Side stop striker 4 Striker   6 Side stopper   8 Back door lock

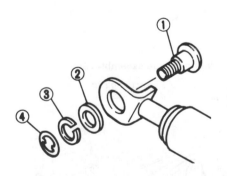

Fig. 12.13 Stay bolt assembly (Sec 18)

1 Bolt   3 Spring washer
2 Rubber spacer   4 Stopper ring

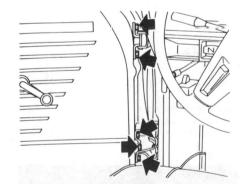

Fig. 12.14 Front door bolt position (Sec 19)

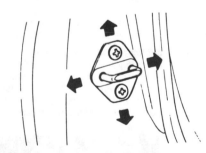

Fig. 12.15 Door latch striker adjustment (Sec 19)

19 Front and rear doors – removal, refitting and adjustment

1   Open the door to be removed and position a support under it to take its weight. An assistant should be enlisted to hold the door.
2   Unscrew and remove the respective bolts that secure the door hinges to the body.
3   Carefully lift the door clear from the side of the car.
4   Refit in the reverse order and if necessary adjust as follows.

5   Any adjustment to be made to either the front or rear doors can be made by slackening the hinge bolts and repositioning the hinges on the body mounting locations. The door should be adjusted to give an even clearance from its periphery to the body aperture on all faces.
6   Further adjustment will probably be needed to the door lock striker plate and this can be moved in the direction required by simply loosening the two retaining screws. Make sure that both the hinge bolts and lock striker plate screws are securely tightened on completion.

20.2 Removing the door handle escutcheon plate

20.3 Window winder handle and fixing clip

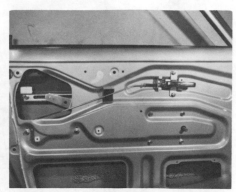

20.4 Door with trim removed

20 Door trim – removal and refitting

1   Unscrew the lock knob and door pull.
2   Unscrew and remove the inner door catch escutcheon plate (photo).
3   To remove the window winder handle, prise the handle and trim apart, and with a suitable wire hook reach down inside the handle and pull free the release spring from the winder pivot. Pull the handle free (photo).
4   Prise the trim carefully away from the door around the edges which is retained by plastic clips. The trim can now be lifted clear of the door (photo).
5   Refitment of the trim is a direct reversal of the removal sequence but ensure that the spring clip is correctly located to retain the window winder handle.

21 Front door lock and control unit – removal, refitting and adjustment

1   First remove the inner door trim panel as described in Section 20 and peel back the dust sheet.
2   Refer to Fig. 12.16 and turn the lock cylinder clip in the direction indicated by the arrow, and detach the rod.
3   Unscrew and remove the inside door handle and lock screws (photo). Remove the lock unit (photo).
4   The outer door handle can be removed by unscrewing the securing nuts.
5   The lock cylinder can be removed by prising free the retaining clip.
6   Refit in the reverse order but note the following:

    (a)   *Lubricate the springs and levers with grease prior to final assembly*
    (b)   *If adjustment is necessary, refer to the adjustment clearance shown in Fig. 12.17 which shows the free play necessary. Adjustment can be made by turning the adjuster nut to obtain the specified clearance*

22 Rear door lock and control unit – removal, refitting and adjustment

1   Remove the inner trim panel as given in Section 20.
2   Unscrew the inner door handle retaining screws. Detach the bell crank and remove the door lock unit through the inner door.
3   The outer handle can now be removed by unscrewing the retaining nuts.
4   Refit in the reverse order.

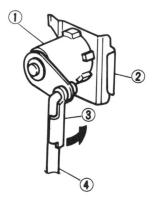

Fig. 12.16 Lock cylinder and rod assembly (Sec 21)

  1 Door lock cylinder   3 Securing clip
  2 Retaining clip   4 Rod

21.3a Door lock screws

21.3b Door lock assembly

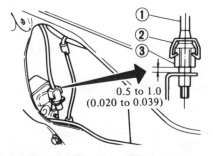

0.5 to 1.0
(0.020 to 0.039)

Fig. 12.17 Lock adjustment (Sec 21)
Dimensions in mm (in)

1 Exterior handle rod 3 Nylon adjustment nut
2 Clip

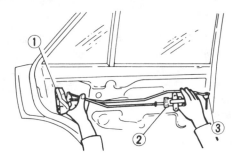

Fig. 12.18 Removing the door lock (Sec 22)

1 Door lock   3 Bell crank
2 Inside door handle

23 Front door glass and regulator (Saloon and Estate) – removal, refitting and adjustment

1   Remove the inner trim panel (Section 20).
2   Use a screwdriver blade and turn the outer moulding retainer clips 90° and remove. Do not use excessive force.
3   Relocate the regulator handle and lower the door glass to gain access to the regulator/glass securing screws. Support the glass in this position and remove the screws.
4   Lift the glass and remove the regulator unit through the inner panel aperture.
5   Refitting is a direct reversal of the removal procedure.
6   To adjust the glass alignment, loosen the guide channel just sufficiently to enable it to be repositioned to suit. Retighten the bolts on achieving the correct alignment.
7   Check that the glass can be raised or lowered without binding before refitting the trim panel.

24 Rear door glass and regulator (Saloon and Estate) – removal, refitting and adjustment

1   Remove the inner door trim (Section 20).
2   Using the regulator handle, lower the glass sufficiently to gain access to the regulator/glass attachment screws through the inner door panel aperture.
3   Unscrew and remove the glass/regulator attachment screws and also the sash (rear window channel) retaining bolts. Lower the glass.
4   Detach the clip from the front of the centre sash and prise the outside moulding back to gain access to the sash retaining screw at the top (Fig. 12.22).
5   Remove the sash screw, tilt the sash forward, slide it free and then lift the door glass out (Fig. 12.23).
6   To remove the regulator unscrew the attachment bolts, and withdraw the regulator through the inner panel aperture (Fig. 12.24).
7   Refit in the reverse sequence to removal. Any adjustment to the glass fitting can be made by resetting the sash position to suit. Loosen the retaining bolts/screws, adjust sash and retighten the bolts/screws.
8   Check that the glass can be raised and lowered without binding before refitting the trim panel.

25 Door glass and regulator (Coupe) – removal, refitting and adjustment

1   Refer to Section 20 and remove the door trim.
2   Use a screwdriver blade and turn the outer moulding retainer clips 90° to remove. Do not use excessive force.
3   Relocate the regulator handle and lower the glass sufficiently to enable the upper stoppers to be visible through the aperture in the inner panel.
4   Support the glass and remove the glass/regulator attachment bolts, and the rear and front stoppers.
5   The glass can now be lifted clear.

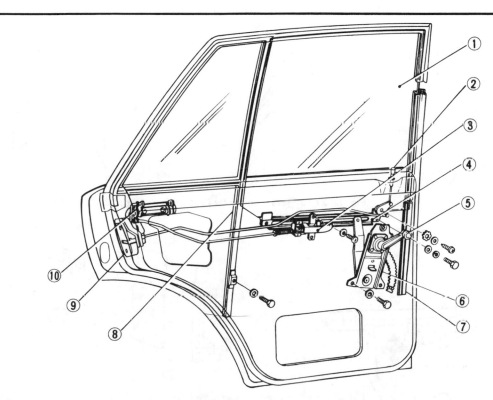

Fig. 12.19 Rear door components (Saloon and Estate) (Sec 24)

1	Door glass	4	Guide channel A	7	Lower sash	9	Door lock assembly
2	Inside door lock knob	5	Regulator handle	8	Centre sash	10	Outside door handle
3	Inside door handle	6	Regulator assembly				

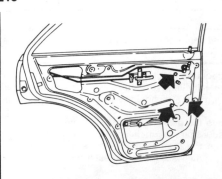

Fig. 12.20 Rear door regulator attachment bolts (Sec 24)

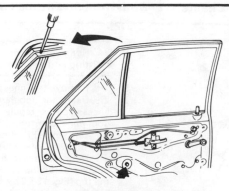

Fig. 12.21 Centre sash retaining bolts (Sec 24)

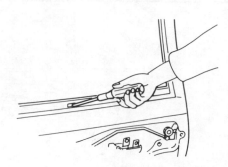

Fig. 12.22 Removing the outer door moulding (Sec 24)

Fig. 12.23 Door glass removal (Sec 24)

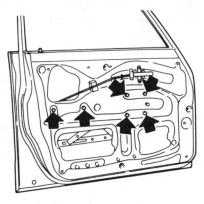

Fig. 12.24 Regulator attachment bolts (Sec 24)

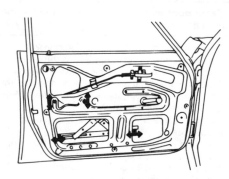

Fig. 12.25 Guide rail adjustment (Sec 24)

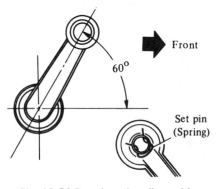

Fig. 12.26 Regulator handle position (Sec 24)

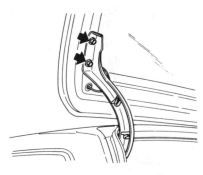

Fig. 12.27 Tailgate hinge bolts (Sec 26)

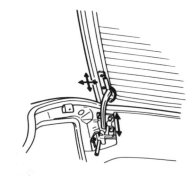

Fig. 12.28 Tailgate adjustment (Sec 26)

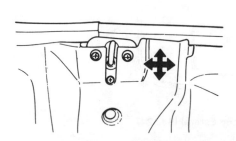

Fig. 12.29 Coupe rear door latch adjustment (Sec 27)

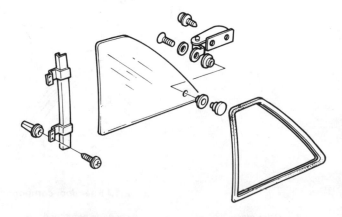

Fig. 12.30 Coupe rear quarter light (Sec 28)

6 To remove the regulator, unscrew the retaining bolts and withdraw the unit through the inner panel aperture.

7 Refit in the reverse order and if necessary, adjust the glass.

8 To adjust the glass horizontally or vertically, loosen the upper stopper and adjust accordingly. The front height alignment can be adjusted by loosening the upper stopper and repositioning it to suit. If adjustment needs to be made inwards or outwards, loosen and reposition the guide rail to suit. The correct position is gained when the clearance between the upper side of the door panel (outside) and the glass is set as 0.43 in (11 mm). Turn the upper adjustment bolts accordingly to achieve this clearance. The clearance for the glass upper edge is adjusted via the lower adjusting bolts.

9 Check all bolts/screws for security and ensure that the window operates freely and correctly before refitting the trim panel.

26 Tailgate lock and cylinder (Estate) – removal and refitting

1 Raise the tailgate and remove the trim, carefully prising it free and then peel back the dust sheet.

2 Slacken the tailgate lock retaining bolts and remove the lock and striker plate.

3 Remove the cylinder by prising the retaining clip free and withdrawing the lock cylinder from the outside.

4 Refit in the reverse sequence.

5 Tailgate adjustment can be made by loosening the hinge to lid bolts and re-aligning the tailgate as required or alternatively by loosening the hinge to body bolts which will necessitate removing the rear portion of the headlining for access. The tailgate striker and catch plates can be adjusted to suit.

27 Back door lock and cylinder (Coupe) – removal and refitting

1 Open and support the back door.

2 Detach the finisher in the boot.

3 Unscrew and remove the door lock retaining bolts and detach the lock unit.

4 The lock cylinder can be removed by prising out the lock plate and pushing the cylinder free from inside.

5 Refitting of both units is a direct reversal of the removal sequence, although the back door may have to be readjusted as described earlier.

28 Rear quarter window (Coupe and Two door Saloon) – removal and refitting

Coupe

1 Open the quarter window and prise free the weatherstrip from the sash/retainer.

2 Unscrew and remove the sash and retainer.

3 Loosen the quarter window handle retaining screws and withdraw

the window.

4 Refit in the reverse sequence but renew the retainer sponge seal if it is defective.

Two door Saloon

5 Open the rear side window, unscrew the glass and handle retaining screws and withdraw the window.

6 Refitting is a reversal of the removal procedure.

Hatchback (210)

7 Open the rear side window, remove the blind rivets, and withdraw the pillar cover.

8 Unscrew the retaining screws and withdraw the window.

9 Refitting is a reversal of removal.

29 Facia panels – removal and refitting

1 The facia panel is divided into two sections these being on the driving side 'A' and the passenger side 'B', see Fig. 12.32.

Driver's side 'A'

2 To remove the driving side 'A', first detach the battery earth cable.

3 Unscrew the wiper switch retaining screws and remove the switch.

4 Pull out the ashtray from its location.

5 Pull the heater control knobs off the levers and then withdraw the control facia panel. This is best removed by inserting a thin screwdriver blade into the fan lever slot and prising out the right-hand side of the heater facia panel but take care not to mark the panel facia.

6 Pull the radio knobs free and remove the nuts and washers.

7 Detach the manual choke knob and the side defroster control knob.

8 Remove the finisher 'A' (Fig. 12.32).

9 Unscrew and remove the facia retaining screws.

10 Detach the wire harness connectors as follows:

    (a) Indicator switch
    (b) Cigarette lighter
    (c) Clock
    (d) Rear window demister switch
    (e) Centre illumination

11 Withdraw the driving side facia panel.

12 Refit in the reverse order but check that all electrical connections are good on reassembly and check operation of each component on completion.

Passenger side 'B'

13 To detach the passenger side facia, open the glove box lid and remove the lid stopper screw.

14 Unscrew and remove the passenger facia securing screws. Their positions are shown in Fig. 12.32.

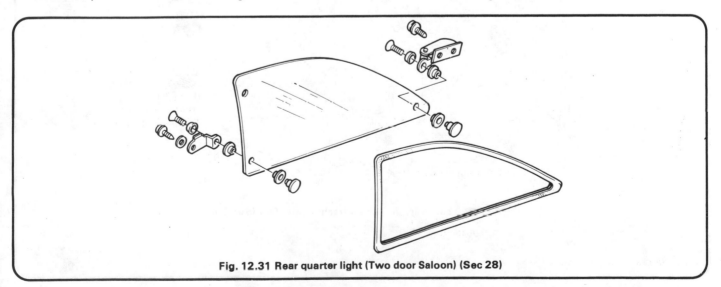

Fig. 12.31 Rear quarter light (Two door Saloon) (Sec 28)

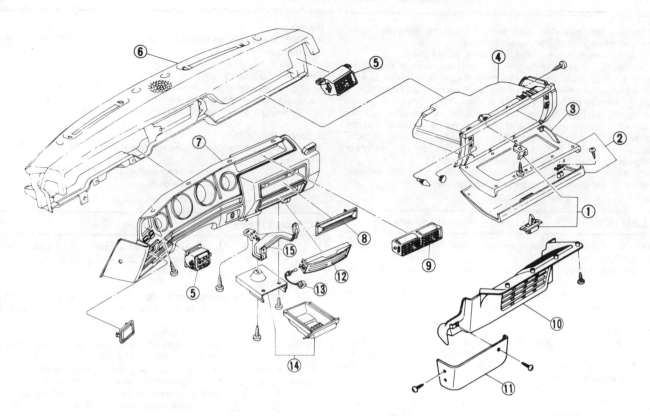

Fig. 12.32 Instrument panel assembly (Sec 30)

1	Lock and striker	5	Side vent grille	9	Centre vent grille	13	Illumination lamp
2	Lid finisher	6	Instrument panel assembly	10	Instrument lower assist cover	14	Ash tray
3	Lid stopper	7	Cluster lid A	11	Instrument lower centre cover	15	Heater control lever bracket
4	Cluster lid B compartment	8	Radio mask	12	Heater control finisher		

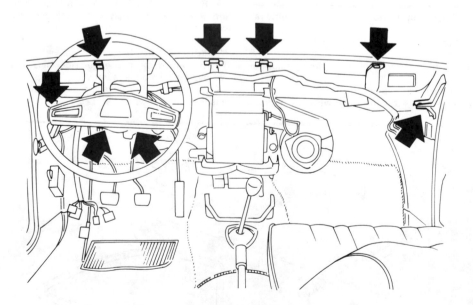

Fig. 12.33 Instrument panel attachment points (Sec 30)

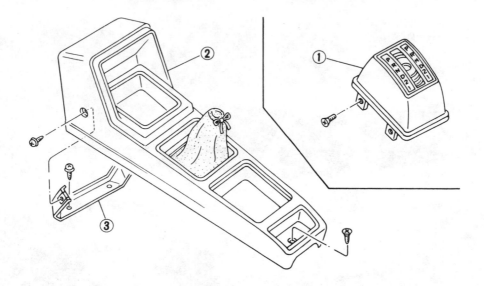

Fig. 12.34 Console box (Sec 31)

1 Automatic control indicator   *2 Console box*   *3 Console box bracket*

15 Remove the two driving side facia securing screws from their central positions. Withdraw the passenger side facia.
16 Refit in the reverse sequence to removal.

30 Instrument panel – removal and refitting

1   Refer to the previous Section and remove the right and left-hand facia panels.
2   Detach the speedometer cable from its location at the rear of the speedometer.
3   Detach the radio aerial cable.
4   Disconnect the respective body/instrument harness connectors.
5   Disconnect the heater control cables, and the heater earth harness connection.

6   Unscrew the respective instrument panel retaining screws and withdraw the panel – carefully.
7   Refitting is the direct reversal of removal but make sure that all electrical connections are fully secure.

31 Central console – removal and refitting

1   Refer to the illustration (Fig. 12.34), unscrew and remove the retaining screws at the front side faces.
2   Prise the tray from the rear section to expose the rear retaining screw, and remove it.
3   Engage 4th gear and pull the handbrake lever back. Lift the console unit clear of the gear lever and handbrake.
4   Refit in the reverse sequence.

The Datsun Sunny Estate/Van

The redesigned Datsun Sunny Saloon; available from April 1980

Chapter 13 Supplement:
Revisions and information on later models

Contents

1 Intoduction

This Chapter contains information which has become available since this manual was first written.

It also contains additional information about Estate/Van models. In an attempt to avoid too much confusion Fastback Estate models are referred to as 'Estates' and Estate/Van models are called 'Vans'.

The Sections in this Chapter follow the same order as the first twelve Chapters of the book. The Specifications are all grouped together for convenience, but they too are arranged in Chapter order.

It is suggested that before undertaking a particular job, reference be made first to this Supplement for the latest information, then to the appropriate Chapter earlier in the book. In this way any revisions can be noted before the job begins.

2 Specifications

These Specifications are revisions of, or supplementary to, the figures given in the preceding Chapters. To avoid confusion Fastback Estate models are referred to as 'Estates' and Estate/Van models are called 'Vans'.

Engine – A15 (UK market)
The UK A15 engine is identical to the A15 engine for USA in all but the following respects

General

Compression ratio .... 9.0 : 1
Idle speed:
  Manual transmission .... 650 rpm
  Automatic transmission .... 700 rpm in N

Valves
Valve length .... 4.030 to 4.041 in (102.35 to 102.65 mm)

Connecting rods and bearings
Bearing clearance .... 0.0008 to 0.0020 in (0.020 to 0.050 mm)

Cooling system – A15 (UK engine)
Capacity (with heater)
Manual transmission .... 8.4 pints (4.8 litres)
Automatic transmission .... 8.6 pints (4.9 litres)

Fuel system – A15 (UK) engine
Carburettor
Type .... Hitachi DCF306-11

	Primary	Secondary
Venturi diameter	0.83 in (21 mm)	1.06 in (27 mm)
Main jet	100	145
Compensating jet	70	80
Slow running jet	43	70
Slow running air bleed	170	100
Power jet	40	–
Float level	0.75 in (19 mm)	
Exhaust gas CO content	1.0 to 2.0% at idle	

Ignition system – A15 (UK) engine
Ignition timing .... 7° BTDC at idle

Distributor
Type .... Hitachi D4A6 – 11 or Mitsubishi T3T03574

Ignition coil
Type .... Hitachi C6R – 206 or Hanshin HP5 – 13E

Spark plugs
Type .... NGK BPR5ES or Hitachi L46PW
Plug gap .... 0.031 to 0.035 in (0.8 to 0.9 mm)

Clutch
Pedal adjustments
Models with double nut cable adjustment
Pedal height .... 6.42 to 6.65 in (163 to 169 mm)
Withdrawal lever free play .... 0.098 to 0.197 in (2.5 to 5.0 mm)
Pedal free travel .... 0.43 to 0.83 in (11 to 21 mm)

Manual gearbox (FS5W60A)
All figures are as for gearbox FS5W60L (Chapter 6) except for the following
Gear endplay
1st .... 0.0059 to 0.0098 in (0.15 to 0.25 mm)
2nd .... 0.0118 to 0.0157 in (0.30 to 0.40 mm)
3rd .... 0.0059 to 0.0138 in (0.15 to 0.35 mm)
5th .... 0.0118 to 0.0157 in (0.30 to 0.40 mm)
Reverse .... 0.0118 to 0.0217 in (0.30 to 0.55 mm)
Countershaft .... 0.0039 to 0.0079 in (0.10 to 0.20 mm)
Reverse idler gear .... 0 to 0.0079 in (0 to 0.20 mm)

Baulk ring-to-gear clearance .... 0.0433 to 0.0551 in (1.10 to 1.40 mm)

Selective circlip thicknesses   **Available circlips**
3rd/4th synchronizer-to-mainshaft front end .... 0.0610 to 0.0630 in (1.55 to 1.60 mm),
0.0630 to 0.0650 in (1.60 to 1.65 mm) and
0.0650 to 0.0669 in (1.65 to 1.70 mm)

Main drive bearing spacer .... 0.0528 to 0.0551 in (1.34 to 1.40 mm),
0.0551 to 0.0575 in (1.40 to 1.46 mm),
0.0575 to 0.0598 in (1.46 to 1.52 mm),
0.0598 to 0.0622 in (1.52 to 1.58 mm),
0.0622 to 0.0646 in (1.58 to 1.64 mm),
0.0646 to 0.0669 in (1.64 to 1.70 mm) and
0.0669 to 0.0693 in (1.70 to 1.76 mm)

Reverse idler gear .... 0.043 in (1.1 mm) and 0.047 in (1.2 mm)
Reverse main gear .... 0.0520 in (1.32 mm),
0.0543 in (1.38 mm),
0.0575 in (1.46 mm),
0.0606 in (1.54 mm) and
0.0638 in (1.62 mm)

Mainshaft end bearing .... 0.0453 in (1.15 mm) and
0.047 in (1.20 mm)

Thrust washer thicknesses

Countershaft ....

Available thickness
0.0866 to 0.0886 in (2.20 to 2.25 mm),
0.0886 to 0.0906 in (2.25 to 2.30 mm),
0.0906 to 0.0925 in (2.30 to 2.35 mm),
0.0925 to 0.0945 in (2.35 to 2.40 mm),
0.0945 to 0.0965 in (2.40 to 2.45 mm),
0.0965 to 0.0984 in (2.45 to 2.50 mm),
0.0984 to 0.1004 in (2.50 to 2.55 mm) and
0.1004 to 0.1024 in (2.55 to 2.60 mm)

5th gear ....
0.3098 in (7.87 mm),
0.3126 in (7.94 mm),
0.3154 in (8.01 mm),
0.3181 in (8.08 mm),
0.3209 in (8.15 mm) and
0.3236 in (8.22 mm)

Torque wrench settings

	lbf ft	kgf m
Clutch withdrawal lever ball pin	14 to 22	2.0 to 3.0
Striking lever locknut	6.5 to 8.7	0.9 to 1.2
Mainshaft bearing retainer screw	5.1 to 7.2	0.7 to 1.0
Countershaft nut (requires the use of a special tool) ...	36 to 43	5.0 to 6.0
Rear extension through bolt	12 to 16	1.6 to 2.2
Rear extension return spring plug	3.6 to 7.2	0.5 to 1.0

Propeller shaft
Centre bearing type

Length ....
17.32 and 28.94 in (440 and 735 mm)

Outer diameter ....
2.50 in (63.5 mm)

Torque wrench settings

	lbf ft	kgf m
Centre bearing locking nut:		
Flange nut type	181 to 217	25 to 30
Nut and washer type	145 to 174	20 to 24

Rear axle and rear suspension
Differential

Ratio (models with centre bearing propeller shaft) ....
4.111 : 1

Rear suspension

Type ....
Leaf spring

Spring dimensions:
Length ....
45.87 in (1165 mm)

Width ....
1.97 in (50 mm)

Leaf thicknesses ....
0.24 in (6 mm) — one leaf,
0.28 in (7 mm) — two leaves and
0.51 in (13 mm) — one leaf

Free camber(s) ....
6.161 in (156.5 mm)

Laden camber — 650 lb (295 kg) load ....
1.50 to 1.93 in (38 to 49 mm)

Shock absorber:
Maximum length ....
18.82 in (478 mm)

Stroke ....
7.28 in (185 mm)

Torque wrench settings

Leaf spring suspension	lbf ft	kgf m
Shock absorber upper end nut	26 to 33	3.6 to 4.5
Shock absorber lower end nut	26 to 33	3.6 to 4.5
U-bolt	33 to 40	4.5 to 5.5
Front pin nut	23 to 29	3.2 to 4.0
Front plate bolt	12 to 15	1.6 to 2.1
Shackle nut	12 to 14	1.6 to 2.0

Electrical system
Battery — A15 (UK) engine

Capacity ....
12 volt, 50 Amp hour

Bulbs (UK models)

	Wattage
Headlights:	
Sealed beam	65/55
Semi-sealed beam	45/40
Halogen	60/55
Rear compartment lamp (Van)	10
Meter illumination lamp	3.4
High beam pilot lamp	3.4
Charge warning lamp	3.4
Oil pressure warning lamp	3.4
Brake warning lamp	3.4

Bulbs (UK models)

	Wattage
Choke warning lamp	3.4
Turn signal pilot lamp	3.4
Clock illumination lamp	3.4
Heater panel illumination lamp	3.4
Ashtray illumination lamp	2
Cigarette lighter illumination lamp	1.7
Rear window defogger switch	1.4
Hazard warning indicator lamp	1.4
Automatic transmission lever illumination lamp	3.4

Front suspension and steering

Tyre pressures – Van models

	Partial load	Full load
6.15S13–4PR tyres:		
Front	24 lbf/in^2 (1.7 kgf/cm^2)	24 lbf/in^2 (1.7 kgf/cm^2)
Rear	24 lbf/in^2 (1.7 kgf/cm^2)	33 lbf/in^2 (2.3 kgf/cm^2)
155SR13 tyres:		
Front	27 lbf/in^2 (1.9 kgf/cm^2)	27 lbf/in^2 (1.9 kgf/cm^2)
Rear	27 lbf/in^2 (1.9 kgf/cm^2)	34 lbf/in^2 (2.4 kgf/cm^2)

Capacities, dimensions and weights

These values are for Vans and all other later models (including UK A15 engine). Figures for early models are tabulated at the beginning of the manual.

Refill capacities

Fuel tank (Van)	10.4 gallons (47 litre)

Dimensions

	Saloon	Coupe	Estate	Van
Length	160.6 in (4080 mm)	106.6 in (4080 mm)	165.9 in (4215 mm)	159.4 in (4050 mm)
Width:				
With side moulding	63.0 in (1600 mm)	–	63.0 in (1600 mm)	–
Without side moulding	62.6 in (1590 mm)	63.0 in (1600 mm)	62.2 in (1580 mm)	62.2 in (1580 mm)
Ground clearance:				
With 4J-12 wheels	7.0 in (177 mm)	7.0 in (177 mm)	–	6.0 in (152 mm)
All other models	7.5 in (190 mm)	7.5 in (190 mm)	7.5 in (190 mm)	6.5 in (165 mm)
Wheelbase	92.1 in (2340 mm)			
Height (Van)	54.7 in (1390 mm)			
Turning circle (wall to wall):				
With 4J-12 wheels	31.5 ft (9.6 m)			
All other models	32.8 ft (10 m)			

Kerb weights

A12 engine:

Van:	
Two-door	1865 lb (845 kg)
Four-door	1940 lb (880 kg)

A14 engine:

Van:	
Two-door	1895 lb (860 kg)
Four-door	1975 lb (895 kg)

A15 engine:

	Saloon	Coupe	Estate	Van
Two-door	1905 lb (865 kg)	1960 lb (890 kg)	–	1895 lb (860 kg)
Four-door	1930 lb (875 kg)	–	2040 lb (925 kg)	1975 lb (895 kg)

3 Engine

1.5 litre engine

1   The 1488 cc A15 engine used for later UK models is essentially the same as the earlier UK A12 and A14 engines (and the US A15 engine). The only changes are to the specifications, otherwise all procedures are as described in Chapter 1.

4 Fuel system

Crankcase ventilation system valve – checking

1   With the engine idling, remove the ventilator hose from the PCV valve. If the valve is operating correctly a hissing noise will be heard as air passes through the valve, and it should be possible to feel a strong vacuum if a finger is placed over the inlet.

2   If the valve is not operating correctly it must be renewed, as repair is not possible.

5 Clutch

Clutch pedal – adjustment

1   The cable adjustment E-ring has been superseded by two nuts on later models.

2   Adjustment procedures are similar to those given in Chapter 5, but the setting dimensions have changed; see Specifications. Adjustment in this case is by effectively altering the length of the outer cable by screwing the adjuster nut along the cable screw thread, then locking it in position with the second nut.

6 Manual gearbox

Countershaft needle bearing – installation

1   The fitted position of this bearing has been revised (see Fig. 13.2). The new location applies to all gearboxes.

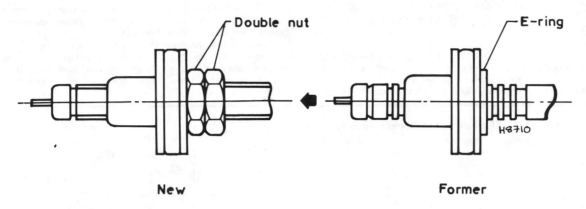

Fig. 13.1 Revised clutch cable adjustment (Sec 5)

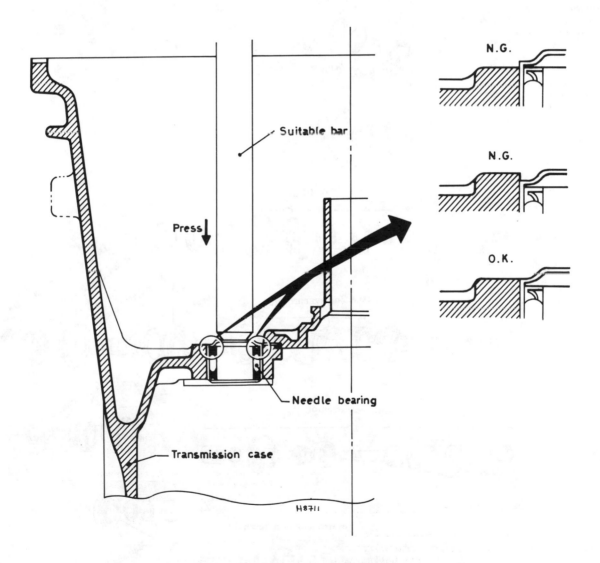

Fig. 13.2 Fitted position of a new countershaft needle roller bearing (Sec 6)

Five-speed gearbox FS5W60A — general
2   Removal and refitting procedures for this gearbox are as described in Chapter 6, Section 2.

Gearbox FS5W60A — dismantling into major assemblies
3   Before commencing work on the gearbox, clean off its external surfaces using a water soluble solvent or paraffin.
4   If not already done on removal, drain the transmission lubricant.

5   Refer to Chapter 5 and remove the clutch release mechanism.
6   If still attached, remove the crossmember mounting support bracket from the extension housing.
7   Unscrew and withdraw the reverse light switch.
8   Unscrew and remove the retaining bolt from the speedometer drivegear retaining housing flange and withdraw the unit.
9   Unscrew and remove the nut and stopper pin-bolt from the rear extension.

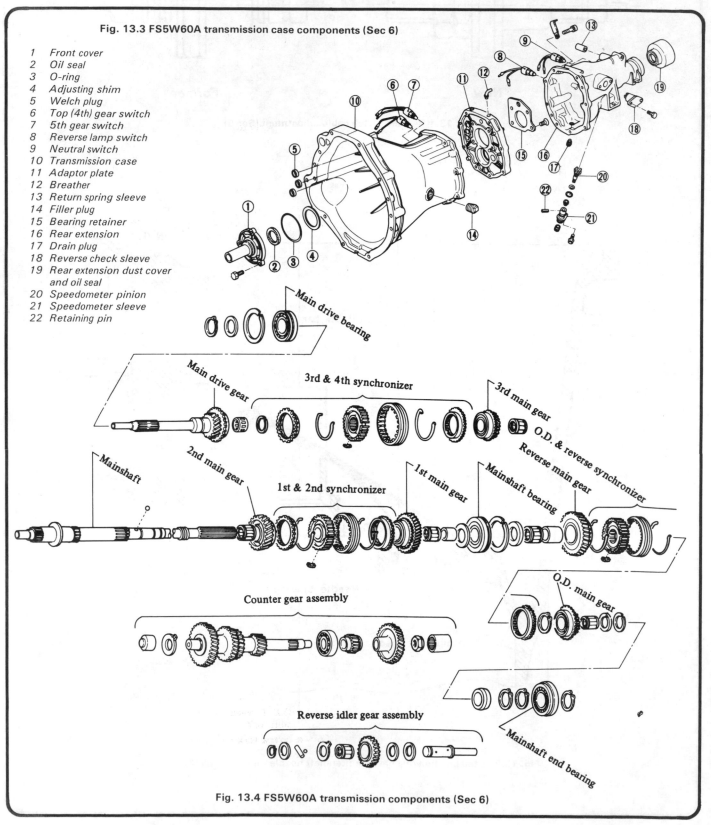

Fig. 13.3 FS5W60A transmission case components (Sec 6)

1   Front cover
2   Oil seal
3   O-ring
4   Adjusting shim
5   Welch plug
6   Top (4th) gear switch
7   5th gear switch
8   Reverse lamp switch
9   Neutral switch
10   Transmission case
11   Adaptor plate
12   Breather
13   Return spring sleeve
14   Filler plug
15   Bearing retainer
16   Rear extension
17   Drain plug
18   Reverse check sleeve
19   Rear extension dust cover
     and oil seal
20   Speedometer pinion
21   Speedometer sleeve
22   Retaining pin

Fig. 13.4 FS5W60A transmission components (Sec 6)

10 The return spring plug, spring, reverse check spring and plunger can now be carefully removed from the rear extension unit. Remove the reverse check sleeve assembly.

11 Unscrew the retaining bolts from the front cover and withdraw it together with the O-ring and adjustment shim over the input shaft. Keep the shim with the O-ring and cover.

12 Using a suitable pair of circlip pliers, extract the front main drive bearing retaining circlip from the bearing orifice.

13 Unscrew and remove the rear extension unit retaining bolts, and note the position of the cable retainer clip.

14 Turn the striking rod clockwise and then using a standard puller, draw the rear extension off. Do not attempt to remove the rear extension by prising it off the adaptor plate.

15 Hold the mainshaft and then separate the transmission case from the adaptor plate by tapping round the case evenly with a soft headed hammer. Do not attempt to prise the transmission case off the adaptor plate.

16 With the gear assembly removed, make an initial inspection of the components. If it is decided to dismantle the entire assembly, it is desirable to devise a method of supporting the adaptor plate assembly. An adaptor plate mounting can easily be fabricated and bolted to the adaptor plate so that it can be supported in a vice securely for convenience when working. Fig. 13.5 shows the special adaptor plate setting tool manufactured by Datsun (Tool No. KV 32100300).

17 Note which way round the countershaft thrust washer is fitted and then remove it.

Gearbox FS5W60A – dismantling the gear assemblies
Shift forks and rods – removal

18 Use a suitable pin punch to drive the selector fork retaining pins from the respective fork rods.

19 Unscrew and remove the check ball plugs and extract the detent balls and springs. Drive the selector rods out of the adaptor plate by tapping them lightly on the front end. When the rods are removed, take care to recover the two interlock plungers. Having removed the shift rods, remove the shift forks and place them with their respective rods.

Gearshafts – removal

20 Before removing any shaft components measure the endplay of each gear. Note the measured endplay of every gear listed in the Specifications.

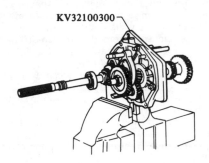

Fig. 13.5 Adaptor plate bolted to support plate (Sec 6)

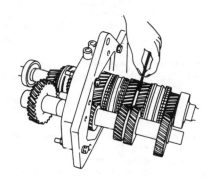

Fig. 13.6 Measure gear endplay (Sec 6)

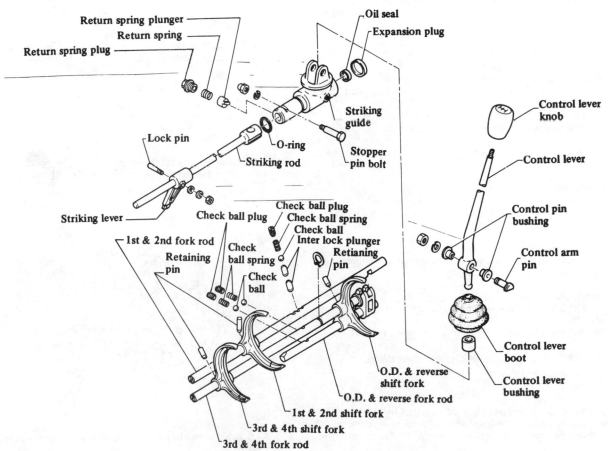

Fig. 13.7 Shift fork and rod components – gearbox FS5W60A
(Sec 6)

21 Using suitable circlip pliers, remove the circlip from the rear end of the mainshaft. The bearing must now be pulled off and this can be achieved with a suitable puller. Remove the second circlip from its position on the shaft behind the bearing.

22 Position the 1st and reverse gears so that they are both in engagement and the transmission is locked, then relieve the staking of the countershaft nut, unscrew the nut and remove it.

23 Remove the components from the mainshaft and, as they are removed, note which way round they are fitted and their sequence of removal so that they can be refitted correctly.

24 Remove the mainshaft C-ring holder circlip, C-ring holder, C-ring and thrust washer.

25 Remove 5th gear and its needle bearing. At the same time remove 5th gear from the countershaft.

26 From the mainshaft remove the circlip, baulk ring and synchronizer. Simultaneously remove reverse main gear, along with its needle bearing and sleeve, from the mainshaft and reverse gear from the countershaft.

27 Remove the thrust washer from the mainshaft.

28 Use an impact driver to remove the four screws from the bearing retainer and remove the bearing retainer.

29 Remove the circlip from the mainshaft rear bearing.

30 Support the mainshaft and the countershaft assembly and gently tap the rear end of the mainshaft with a soft headed hammer to drive out the gear assembly.

31 Remove the countershaft assembly, the main drive gear and then the mainshaft assembly in that order, taking care not to drop any of the gears.

32 Remove the circlip and thrust washer from the reverse idler shaft. Tap the end of the shaft with a hammer and suitable rod (Fig. 13.9) to release it from the adaptor plate.

33 Using a pin punch, drive out the retaining pin from the reverse idler shaft and remove the shaft.

34 Remove the thrust washers, spacer and reverse idler gear with its needle bearing, taking note of the components fitted order.

35 The gearbox major components have now been removed and can be inspected. If further dismantling is necessary the use of a press is required and a precision measuring instrument such as a micrometer is also necessary.

Mainshaft – dismantling the remaining components

36 Remove the circlip from the front end of the mainshaft.

37 Remove the 3rd/4th synchronizer assembly, baulk rings, 3rd gear and needle bearing.

38 Press/pull the mainshaft bearing off the shaft.

39 Remove the thrust washer with 1st gear, its needle bearing and sleeve.

40 Remove the baulk rings, coupling sleeve, 1st/2nd synchronizer, 2nd gear and needle bearing.

Main drive gear (input shaft) – dismantling

41 Using suitable circlip pliers, remove the circlip and withdraw the spacer. Use a puller or press to remove the bearing from the shaft. Take care not to drop the components.

Countershaft – dismantling

42 This shaft is partially dismantled as part of its removal procedure. The rear bearing should be pressed out.

Synchronizers – dismantling

43 Refer to Fig.13.11, remove spread spring (1) and take out the shifting insert (2).

44 Separate the coupling sleeve (3) from the synchro hub (4).

Gearbox FS5W60A rear extension – dismantling, inspection and reassembly

45 Refer to Chapter 6, Section 16.

Gearbox FS5W60A – inspection of components

46 Wash all parts in a suitable solvent and check for wear, damage or other faults. **Note**: *be careful not to damage any parts if scraping them clean.*

47 All oil seals and O-rings should be renewed. Be sure not to allow new sealing components to come into contact with any solvent.

Transmission casing and rear extension

48 Check for cracks or other faults in the casings.

49 Remove all nicks, projections or hardened sealant from the mating faces using a very fine stone.

50 If the rear extension bushing is worn or cracked the whole rear extension assembly must be renewed.

Bearings

51 Clean all bearings thoroughly and blow dry with compressed air, if available.

52 Do not spin unlubricated bearings, as this will damage the race and balls. Turn them slowly by hand.

53 If the race and ball surfaces are worn, or if the bearing action feels rough the bearing should be renewed.

54 Renew needle bearings if they feel rough.

Gears and shafts

55 Check all components for wear, chips or cracks. Renew as necessary.

56 Check the shafts for bends and worn splines. Renew as necessary.

57 Compare the gear endplay values measured before dismantling the shafts with the tolerances given in Specifications. If any of 1st, 2nd or 3rd gears are outside the given range renew the gear.

58 Check the speedometer pinion for stripped or damaged teeth. Renew if necessary.

Synchronizers

59 Examine all components for cracks or deformation. Renew as necessary.

60 Position the baulk ring on the gear cone and measure the baulk ring-to-gear clearance with the baulk ring pushed towards the gear. If the clearance is smaller than specified, renew the baulk ring.

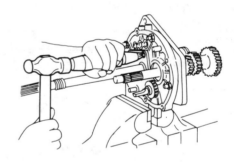

Fig. 13.8 Use an impact driver to remove the mainshaft rear bearing retainer screws (Sec 6)

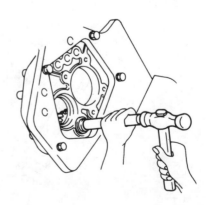

Fig. 13.9 Tap the end of the reverse idler shaft with a suitable rod (Sec 6)

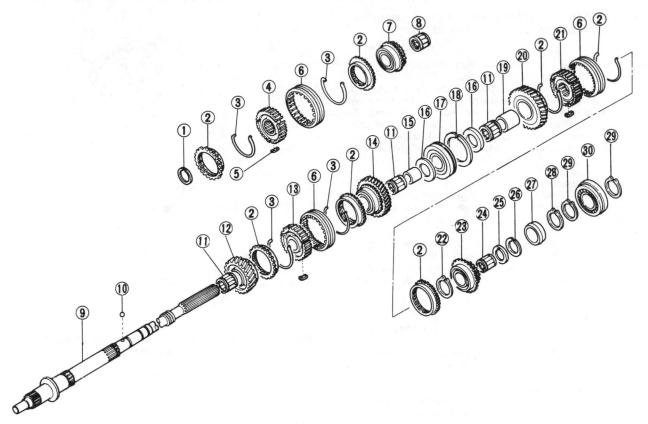

Fig. 13.10 Mainshaft components – gearbox FS5W60A (Sec 6)

1	Circlip	9	Mainshaft	17	Mainshaft bearing	25	Thrust washer
2	Baulk ring	10	Steel ball	18	Circlip	26	C-ring
3	Spread spring	11	Needle bearing	19	Reverse gear sleeve	27	C-ring holder
4	3rd/4th synchro hub	12	2nd gear	20	Reverse gear	28	Mainshaft holder circlip
5	Shifting insert	13	1st/2nd synchro hub	21	5th/reverse synchro hub	29	Mainshaft end bearing circlip
6	Coupling sleeve	14	1st gear	22	Circlip	
7	3rd gear	15	1st gear sleeve	23	5th gear	30	Mainshaft end bearing
8	3rd gear bearing	16	Thrust washer	24	Needle bearing	

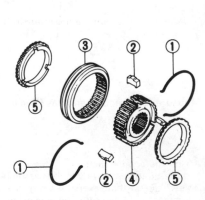

Fig. 13.11 Synchronizer components (Sec 6)

1	Spread spring	4	Synchro hub
2	Shifting insert	5	Baulk ring
3	Coupling sleeve		

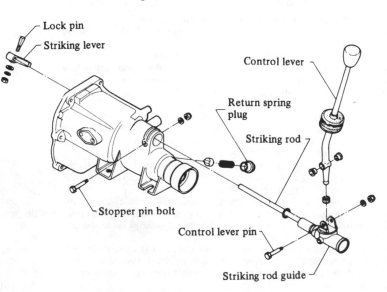

Fig. 13.12 Rear extension components – gearbox FS5W60A (Sec 6)

Gearbox FS5W60A – reassembling the gear assemblies

61 Lubricate all components with gear oil prior to assembly.

Synchronizers

62 Insert a synchro hub into its respective coupling sleeve and then locate the three shift inserts into their grooves.

63 Refit the spread spring with its protrusion located in the groove to retain the insert on the inside of the coupling sleeve. Fit the second spread spring to the opposing side of the hub. When fitting the synchromesh springs they must be located so that their respective opposing positions are offset to each other (Fig. 13.13).

64 Operate the hub and sleeve by hand to ensure that they function correctly.

Mainshaft (initial reassembly)

65 Assemble 2nd gear needle bearing, 2nd gear, 2nd gear baulk ring, 1st/2nd gear synchronizer, 1st gear baulk ring, 1st gear sleeve and needle bearing, 1st gear and the thrust washer on the mainshaft.

66 Press the mainshaft bearing onto the shaft.

67 Fit 3rd gear needle bearing, 3rd gear, 3rd gear baulk ring and 3rd/4th synchronizer to the front end of the mainshaft.

68 Fit a suitable circlip so there is minimum clearance between the baulk ring and the circlip. The thickness of available circlips is given in the Specifications.

Main drivegear (input shaft)

69 Press the bearing onto the shaft. Make sure the bearing clears the circlip groove.

70 Place the bearing spacer on the bearing and fit a circlip that will eliminate all endplay. Available circlips are listed in the Specifications.

Countershaft (initial reassembly)

71 Fit a countershaft thrust washer in the transmission case and then, with the transmission case resting on the bellhousing end, insert the countershaft.

72 Place a straight edge across the top face of the transmission case and use feeler gauges to measure the gap between the straight edge and the face of the gear (Fig. 13.14). Move the straight edge to at least two other positions across the gear and again measure the clearance.

73 Select a thrust washer to ensure that the endplay of the countershaft will be the specified amount. Available thicknesses are listed in Specifications.

74 Remove the countershaft from the transmission case and fit the rear bearing, using a suitable press.

75 Keep the countershaft and thrust washers together for refitting.

Refitting the gear assemblies to the adaptor plate

76 Refit the components from the reverse idler shaft in the reverse order to removal.

77 Tap the shaft assembly into the adaptor plate.

78 Compare the reverse idler gear endplay value recorded before dismantling with the tolerance in the Specifications. The circlip fitted to the reverse idler shaft is available in varying thicknesses to bring the idler gear endplay within the specified limits.

79 Fit the thrust washer and a circlip of suitable thickness.

80 Install a baulk ring on the main drive gear and combine the main drive gear and mainshaft to make one assembly. Be sure to fit the pilot bearing between the sub-assemblies.

81 With the adaptor plate mounted and supported firmly, fit the mainshaft assembly as follows. First check that the main drive gear is located correctly with the mainshaft.

82 Mesh the gears of the mainshaft assembly with those of the countershaft assembly and insert the two gear trains into the adaptor plate simultaneously, having first fitted a thrust washer on to the end of the countershaft assembly.

83 While still holding the gears in mesh, carefully tap the shaft ends with a soft-headed hammer until the countershaft assembly is fully home and the circlip groove of the mainshaft bearing is clear of the rear face of the adaptor plate.

84 Fit the circlip in the external groove of the main bearing outer track, making sure that the circlip is properly fitted to the groove.

85 Fit the bearing retainer on the adaptor plate, tighten the four screws to the specified torque and then stake the screw by centre punching their heads at two points.

86 Position the thrust washer, reverse gear sleeve, needle bearing and reverse main gear on the mainshaft.

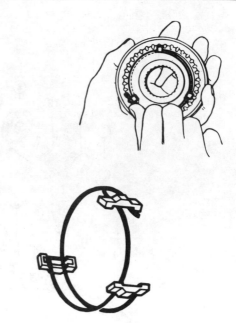

Fig. 13.13 Fit the synchromesh spread springs offset from each other (Sec 6)

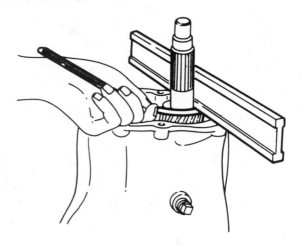

Fig. 13.14 Measure countershaft endplay (Sec 6)

87 Install reverse gear on the countershaft.

88 Install 5th gear and the 5th/reverse synchronizer assembly on the mainshaft. Fit a suitable circlip so that reverse main gear endplay is within the specified tolerances. Make sure the circlip seats in its groove.

89 Position the baulk ring, 5th gear needle bearing and 5th gear steel ball on the end of the mainshaft.

90 Install 5th gear on the countershaft.

91 Position the thrust washer, C-ring and C-ring holder on the mainshaft. Select the thrust washer so the 5th gear endplay is within the specified tolerances.

92 Fit the C-ring holder circlip. Make sure the circlip seats in its groove.

93 Engage 1st and reverse gears and refit the countershaft nut. Tighten the nut to the specified torque using a torque wrench and

adaptor tool, see Fig. 13.15. The torque conversion graph only applies when using an adaptor tool 0.33 ft (0.1 m) long. When using an adaptor of different length use this formula:

$$C = \text{Specified torque (at nut)} \times \left(\frac{L}{L + A}\right)$$

Where: A = Length of adaptor
        C = Torque measured on wrench
        L = Effective length of torque wrench

Thus, when using a torque wrench 1.31 ft (0.4 m) long with a 0.33 ft (0.1 m) adaptor, the torque range read off the wrench should be 29 to 35 lbf ft (4.0 to 4.8 kgf m).
94 Stake the countershaft nut to the shaft.
95 Measure the endplay of 1st, 2nd and 3rd gears and compare the values to that specified. If any are outside the tolerances the gear(s) will have to be renewed.
96 Fit a 0.0453 in (1.15 mm) thick circlip to the front side of the mainshaft bearing. Install the bearing, using a suitable drift.
97 Fit a thick circlip after the bearing to eliminate all endplay.

Shift forks and rods
98 **Note**: *When installing all shift forks ensure that they align with the groove on their respective coupling sleeves.*
99 Install the 5th and reverse fork rod into its shift fork and through the adaptor plate.
100 With the 5th and reverse fork rod set in neutral, insert the interlock plunger into the adaptor plate. Be sure to align the groove in the fork rod with the plunger.
101 Insert the 3rd and 4th fork rod into the 5th and reverse fork and

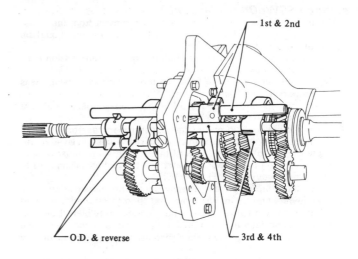

Fig. 13.16 Shift forks and rods in position – gearbox FS5W60A (Sec 6)

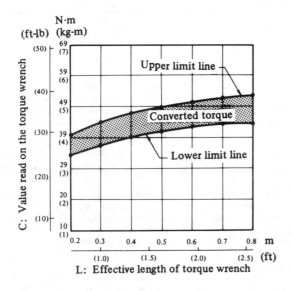

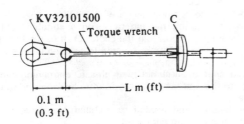

Fig. 13.15 Special tool for tightening the countershaft nut and conversion graph for alternative torque wrenches (Sec 6)

The graph is for an adaptor 0.33 ft (0.1 m) long

fit a new circlip to the 3rd and 4th fork rod.
102 Insert the 3rd and 4th fork rod into the adaptor plate and its shift fork.
103 With the 3rd and 4th fork rod set in neutral, insert the interlock plunger into the adaptor plate. Be sure to align the groove in the fork rod with the plunger.
104 Insert the 1st and 2nd fork rod into the adaptor plate and its shift fork.
105 With the holes of the selector forks and shift rods in exact alignment, locate and drive new retaining pins into position, so that the ends of the pins are flush with the outside surface of the forks.
106 Fit the check balls and the check ball springs, ensuring that the ball is aligned with the centre notch in each of the fork rods.
107 Apply locking compound to the threads of the ball plugs and screw the plugs in flush. Note that the plug for the 1st and 2nd fork rod is longer than the plugs for the other two rods.
108 To ensure that the interlock plungers have been fitted correctly, slide the 1st and 2nd fork rod to engage either gear. With the gear engaged, slide the other two shift rods to ensure that no other gear can be engaged at the same time.
109 Lubricate all sliding surfaces with gear oil and then check that all three shift rods move smoothly and that the gears engage easily and correctly.

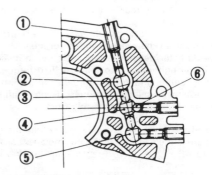

Fig. 13.17 Cross-section of the shift forks and interlock plunger – gearbox FS5W60A (Sec 6)

1 Ball plug   4 3rd/4th fork rod
2 1st/2nd fork rod   5 5th/reverse fork rod
3 Interlock plunger   6 Check ball

Gearbox FS5W60A – reassembly

110 If the countershaft needle bearing was removed from the transmission casing it should be renewed. The new bearing should be installed as shown in Fig. 13.2.

111 Fit the clutch withdrawal lever ball pin to the transmission case and tighten the screw.

112 Remove the adaptor plate from the mounting fixture which was used to support it during assembly.

113 Clean the mating surfaces of the adaptor plate and the transmission case and apply sealant to them.

114 Stand the bellhousing end of the transmission case on blocks of wood at least 0.79 in (20 mm) thick so that the case is level.

115 Apply grease to the two faces of the countershaft thrust washer which was selected (paragraph 73) and fit the washer, taking care to fit it the correct way round (Fig. 13.18).

116 Lower the adaptor plate assembly on to the transmission case. Align the dowels and the dowel holes and then tap the adaptor plate lightly, but evenly with a soft-headed hammer until the plate is bearing against its mating face on the transmission case and the main drive bearing and the countershaft front needle bearing are positioned correctly.

117 Make certain that the mainshaft rotates freely and then fit the circlip in the groove in the outer track of the main drive bearing, ensuring that the circlip is fitted into the groove properly.

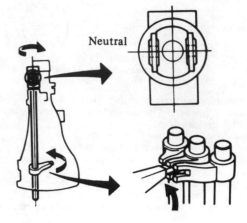

Fig. 13.19 Setting the striking lever and fork rod before refitting the rear extension – gearbox FS5W60A (Sec 6)

 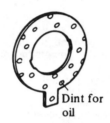

Front (Oil groove side)   Rear (Thrust side)

Fig. 13.18 Be sure to fit the countershaft thrust washer the correct way round (Sec 6)

Rear extension – refitting

118 Clean the mating surfaces of the adaptor plate and the rear extension and apply sealant to them.

119 Set the gears in neutral and turn the striking rod anti-clockwise. Set the striking lever and fork rod as shown in Fig. 13.19.

120 With the components in these positions lower the rear extension on to the adaptor plate. While doing this, take care that the shift arm does not come out of the striking lever.

121 Fit the through bolts and washers and tighten the bolts evenly until the recommended torque is achieved.

122 Smear grease on to the rear extension plunger and insert it in its hole, then insert its spring.

123 Apply locking compound to the threads of the return spring plug and screw the plug in to the recommended torque.

124 Fit the speedometer pinion assembly. Screw in its securing bolt on the locking plate, tightening it to the specified torque.

125 Apply locking compound to the threads of the reversing light switch and the top gear selecting switch, if the gearbox has one. Screw the switches in until they are firmly fitted.

Front cover – refitting

126 This procedure is the same as that given in Chapter 6, Section 13, paragraphs 46 to 48.

General

127 Temporarily refit the gear shift lever and check for smooth, positive gear engagement. Make sure that the main drive gear (input) shaft rotates freely in neutral.

128 Coat the drain plug with sealant and refit it to the transmission case.

129 Refitting the gearbox is as described in Chapter 6, Section 2.

7   Propeller shaft

Two-piece shaft with centre bearing

1   Later models are fitted with a two-piece propeller shaft which has a centre bearing.

Removal and refitting

2   Removal of this shaft is the same as that given in Chapter 7, except that it will be necessary to remove the centre bearing bracket.

3   When refitting the shaft the centre bearing must be positioned on the bracket with the cushion contact surface facing upwards (see Fig. 13.21).

Centre bearing – renewal

4   If the centre bearing is noisy or damaged it cannot be repaired, it must be renewed.

5   Remove the propeller shaft from the car.

6   Mark the companion flange on the front section and the corresponding flange on the rear section so they can be refitted in the same relative position.

7   Undo the bolts and separate the two shaft sections.

8   Mark the flange on the front section and the shaft so they can also be reassembled in the same relative positions.

9   Unstake the nut on the shaft and remove it. It will be necessary to hold the shaft still when undoing the nut. If possible, use Datsun tool ST31530000, otherwise a suitable alternative method for holding the shaft will have to be devised.

10   Remove the companion flange with a puller.

11   Remove the centre bearing by using a suitable support collar under the bearing and pressing the shaft out. If using a support collar of the type shown in Fig. 13.25 be sure to position it correctly to avoid damage.

12   Apply a coat of lithium based grease, containing molybdenum disulphide, to the end face of a new centre bearing and both sides of the washer.

13   Fit the bearing and washer to the shaft. Be sure the F mark is towards the front of the car.

14   Align the companion flange-to-shaft marks made at removal and refit the flange.

15   Refit the retaining nut and tighten it to the specified torque. Restake the nut.

16   Align the flange marks made before separation and reconnect the two shaft sections. Tighten the bolts to the specified torque.

17   Refit the propeller shaft, as described earlier in this Section and in Chapter 7.

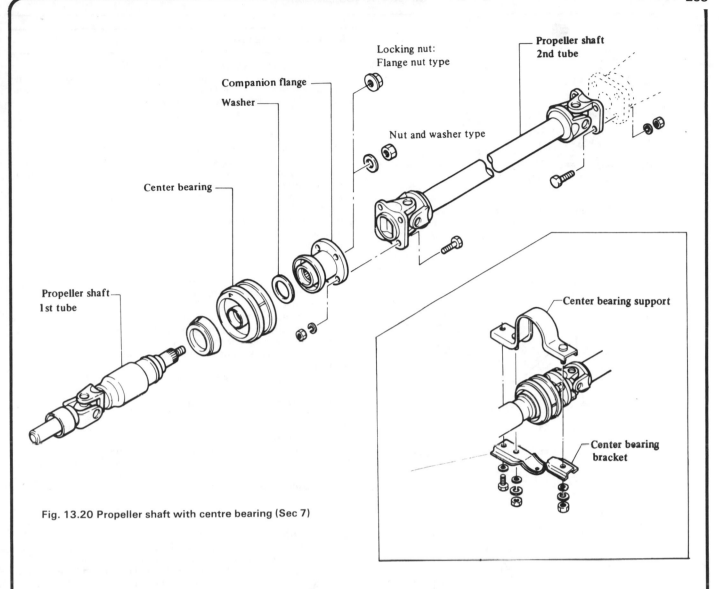

Fig. 13.20 Propeller shaft with centre bearing (Sec 7)

Locking nut:
Flange nut type

Companion flange

Washer

Nut and washer type

Center bearing

Propeller shaft
2nd tube

Propeller shaft
1st tube

Center bearing support

Center bearing
bracket

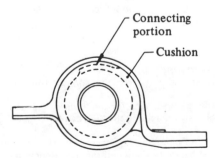

Connecting
portion

Cushion

Fig. 13.21 When refitting the shaft the centre bearing cushion
must be uppermost (Sec 7)

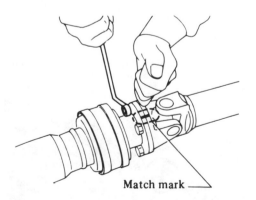

Match mark

Fig. 13.22 Make a match mark on the shaft joint flanges (Sec 7)

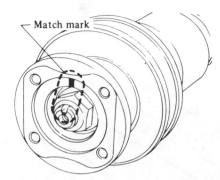

Fig. 13.23 Flange-to-shaft match mark (Sec 7)

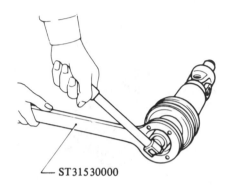

Fig. 13.24 Holding the shaft still while undoing the nut (Sec 7)

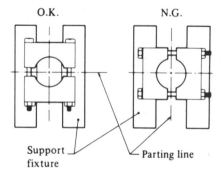

Fig. 13.25 Correct positioning of the support when removing the centre bearing (Sec 7)

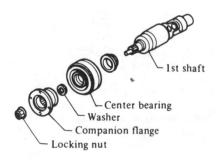

Fig. 13.26 Centre bearing and front shaft section components (Sec 7)

8   Rear axle and rear suspension

Leaf spring rear suspension – general
1   Some Sunny models are fitted with leaf spring type rear suspension. Any removal and refitting procedures which differ from those in Chapter 8 are described here.

Leaf sprung rear axle – removal and refitting
2   Block the front wheels with chocks, loosen the nuts of the rear wheels and raise the rear of the car high enough to permit working underneath. Place securely based stands under the body member at each side of the vehicle, or support the bodymember on substantial baulks of timber.
3   Support the centre of the differential carrier with a wheeled jack, but place a block of wood between the head of the jack and the carrier to spread the load.
4   Remove the rear road wheels.
5   Mark a line across the edge of the two flanges of the differential to propeller shaft joint. Remove the four bolts from the joint flange, separate the two flanges and lower the free end of the propeller shaft to the ground.
6   Disconnect the brake hose from its connection to the brake pipe on the car body and plug the open ends of the pipe and the hose to prevent loss of fluid and the entry of dirt.
7   Slacken the locknut of the brake cable adjuster and disconnect the cable from the adjuster.
8   Remove the bolt from the lower end of each of the rear shock absorbers and push them up out of the way.
9   Remove the U-bolt nuts securing the axle case ot the leaf spring.
10   Remove the axle from one side of the car by rolling it sideways and passing it between the leaf springs and car body. Raise or lower the jack as necessary.
11   Refitting is the reversal of removal. After reconnecting the brake pipe bleed the hydraulic system, as described in Chapters 9 and 13. **Note**: *the weight of the car must be on its wheels when tightening the shock absorber lower end bolts.*

Leaf spring – removal and refitting
12   Chock the front wheels, raise the rear of the car and support it securely on axle stands positioned beneath the body members.
13   Disconnect the shock absorber(s) at their lower ends and remove the U-bolt nuts securing the axle to the leaf springs.
14   Position a jack, with an interposed block of wood, beneath the differential carrier and raise the axle from the leaf spring.
15   Disconnect the rear spring shackle.
16   Undo the front pin and remove the leaf spring from the car.
17   Refitting is a reversal of removal, but coat the front pin, shackle and rubber bushing with a soap solution to aid assembly. **Note**: *the weight of the car must be on the wheels when tightening the securing nuts and bolts.*

Leaf spring – inspection
18   Clean all rust and dirt from the spring; using a wire brush if necessary.
19   Examine the spring leaves for fractures or cracks and check for excessive sagging by measuring the 'free camber' – see Fig. 13.28 and Specifications.
20   Check the front pin, shackle, shackle pin, U-bolts and spring seat for wear, cracks, bends or damaged threads. Renew any faulty parts.
21   Inspect all rubber parts for wear, damage, separation or deformation. Renew any faulty parts.

Leaf spring shock absorbers – removal and refitting
22   Undo and remove the upper and lower securing nuts; remove the shock absorber.
23   Refitting is a reversal of removal, but tighten the securing nuts when the vehicle weight is on its wheels.

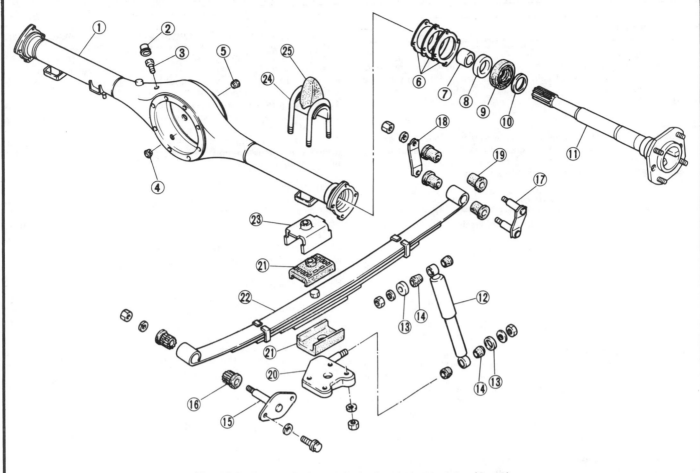

Fig. 13.27 Exploded view of the leaf spring suspension (Sec 8)

1	Rear axle case	8	Oil seal
2	Breather cap	9	Rear axle bearing (wheel bearing)
3	Breather	10	Bearing spacer
4	Drain plug	11	Rear axle shaft
5	Filler plug	12	Shock absorber
6	Rear axle case end shim	13	Special washer
7	Bearing collar		

14	Shock absorber bushing
15	Front pin
16	Spring bushing
17	Shackle pin
18	Shackle
19	Spring bushing

20	Lower spring seat
21	Spring seating pad
22	Leaf spring
23	Location plate
24	U-bolt
25	Rear axle bumper

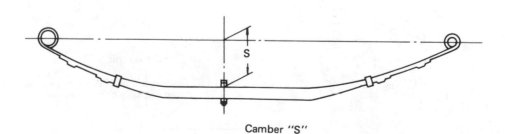

Camber "S"

Fig. 13.28 Leaf spring camber measurement (Sec 8)

9 Braking system

Front brake caliper

1 Some models are fitted with an alternative type of caliper (Fig. 13.29). Note that this type of caliper has no bias springs on the yoke and has shims behind the pads which must be refitted the correct way round (see Fig. 13.30).

Removal and refitting

2 The procedure is the same as that described in Chapter 9, except that the knuckle arm will have to be separated from the strut before the caliper can be detached. Be sure to tighten all nuts and bolts to the specified torque on reassembly (Chapters 9 and 11).

Bleeding the hydraulic system

3 Bleeding the hydraulic system can be performed adequately using the procedure given in Chapter 9, but the operation is simpler using a one-way valve kit or a pressure bleeding kit.

4 The sequence for bleeding remains the same:

1st master cylinder bleed valve
2nd master cylinder bleed valve
Left rear brake
Right rear brake
Left front brake
Right front brake

Using a one-way valve kit

5 There are a number of one-man, one-way brake bleeding kits available from motor accessory shops. It is recommended that one of these kits is used wherever possible, rather than just a tube, as it will greatly simplify the bleeding operation and reduce the risk of air or fluid being drawn back into the system, quite apart from being able to do the work without the help of an assistant.

6 To use the kit, connect the tube to the bleed valve and open the screw one half turn.

7 Depress the brake pedal fully and slowly release it. The one-way valve in the kit will prevent expelled air from returning at the end of each pedal downstroke. Repeat this operation several times to be sure of ejecting all air from the system. Some kits include a translucent container which can be positioned so that the air bubbles can actually be seen being ejected from the system.

8 During the bleeding operation ensure that the master cylinder reservoir is topped-up as necessary, otherwise air will be introduced into the system.

9 Tighten the bleed valve, remove the tube and repeat the operations on the remaining brakes.

10 On completion, depress the brake pedal. If it still feels spongy repeat the bleeding operations as air must still be trapped in the system.

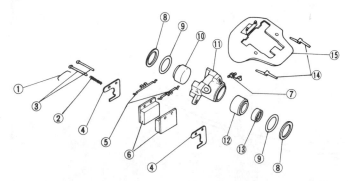

Fig. 13.29 Alternative brake caliper components (Sec 9)

1	Clip	9	Boot
2	Spring	10	Piston B
3	Clevis pin	11	Cylinder body
4	Shim	12	Piston A
5	Hanger spring	13	Bias ring
6	Brake pad	14	Yoke spring
7	Bleed valve	15	Yoke
8	Retaining ring		

Using a pressure bleeding kit

11 These kits are available from motor accessory shops and are usually operated by air pressure from the spare tyre.

12 By connecting a pressurised container to the master cylinder fluid reservoir, bleeding is then carried out by simply opening each bleed screw in turn and allowing the fluid to run out, rather like turning on a tap, until no air is visible in the expelled fluid.

13 By using this method the large reserve of hydraulic fluid provides a safeguard against air bring drawn into the system during bleeding which often occurs if the fluid level in the reservoir is not maintained.

14 Pressure bleeding is particularly effective when bleeding 'difficult' systems or when bleeding the complete system at a time of routine fluid renewal.

All methods

15 When bleeding is completed, check and top up the fluid level in the master cylinder reservoir.

16 Check the feel of the brake pedal. If it feels at all spongy, air must still be present in the system and further bleeding is indicated. Failure to bleed satisfactorily after a reasonable repetition of the bleeding operations may be due to worn master cylinder seals.

17 Discard brake fluid which has been expelled. It is almost certain to be contaminated with moisture, air and dirt, making it unsuitable for further use. Clean fluid should always be stored in an airtight container as it absorbs moisture readily (hygroscopic) which lowers its boiling point and could affect braking performance under severe conditions.

Brake pedal – removal and refitting

18 On some models the clevis pin which secures the brake pushrod to the pedal is fitted with a resin clip, as well as the split pin.

19 Removal and refitting procedures are unchanged, but be careful not to damage the clip.

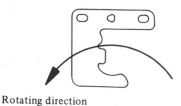

Rotating direction

Fig. 13.30 Be sure to fit the brake caliper shims correctly (Sec 9)

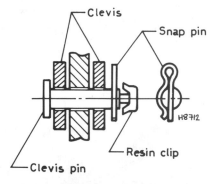

Fig. 13.31 Cross-section of the brake pedal clevis pin. Note the fitted position of the new resin clip (Sec 9)

10 Electrical system

Maintenance-free battery

1 Later models are fitted with a battery which does not require periodical fluid level checks or topping-up. The condition of the battery is indicated by the colour of an indicator sign on top of the battery.

2 If the indicator sign shows that charging is necessary disconnect the battery earth lead and charge it for at least four hours using a 6 Amp DC flow.

3 If the car will still not start after recharging, the battery has

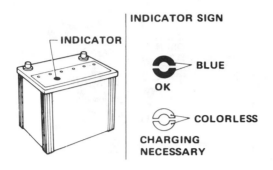

Fig. 13.32 Maintenance-free battery indicator sign (Sec 10)

reached the end of its useful life and should be renewed.
4   Do not use more than a 10 amp current flow to charge the battery quickly, as this will shorten its service life.

Headlamps (rectangular)

5   The circular headlamp has been superseded by a rectangular unit.
6   The procedure for renewing the bulb in a semi-sealed type lamp is the same as given in Chapter 10. Removing a rectangular sealed beam unit is slightly different.
7   Remove the bolt securing the headlight finisher trim. Pull off the finisher trim while pressing down on its protruding portion with a screwdriver.
8   Remove the four screws securing the headlamp retaining ring. This will allow removal of the lamp unit. Disconnect the wiring from the rear of the lamp.
9   Refitting is the reversal of the removal procedure. Be sure that the word TOP on the lens is on the upper side.

Headlamp aiming (beam alignment)

10   The general procedure for cars with rectangular headlamps is the same as that given in Chapter 10. The adjusting screws are in slightly different positions and the beam aiming patterns are also different (see Figs. 13.36 and 13.37).

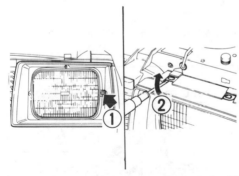

Fig. 13.33 Remove the bolt securing the finisher trim (1). Pull off the trim while pressing down on its protruding portion (2) (Sec 10)

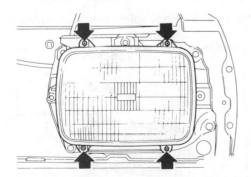

Fig. 13.34 Remove the screws securing the headlamp retaining ring (Sec 10)

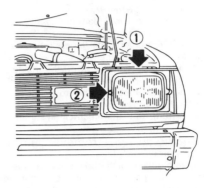

Fig. 13.35 Rectangular headlamp aim adjusting screws (Sec 10)

1   Vertical aim   *2   Horizontal aim*

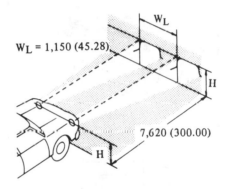

$W_L = 1,150 (45.28)$

7,620 (300.00)

"H":   Horizontal center line of headlamps

Unit: mm (in)

Fig. 13.36 Headlamp adjustment – rectangular sealed beam units (Sec 10)

Headlamps on low beam
LHD pattern – for RHD the pattern is reversed

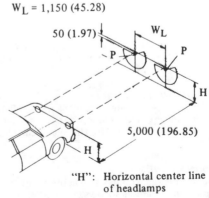

$W_L = 1,150 (45.28)$

50 (1.97)

5,000 (196.85)

"H":   Horizontal center line of headlamps

Unit: mm (in)

Fig. 13.37 Headlamp adjustment – rectangular semi-sealed type (Sec 10)

Headlamps on low beam
LHD pattern – for RHD the pattern is reversed

Heated rear window – general

11 Care should be taken to avoid damage to the element for the heated rear window or tailgate.
12 Avoid scratching with rings on the fingers when cleaning, and do not allow luggage to rub against the glass.
13 Do not stick labels over the element on the inside of the glass.
14 If the element grids do become damaged, a special conductive paint is available from most motor factors to repair it.
15 Do not leave the heated rear window switched on unnecessarily as it draws a high current from the electrical system.

Heated rear window switch – removal and refitting

16 Disconnect the battery earth lead.
17 Use a suitable screwdriver or flat blade tool and lever the switch unit from its aperture in the panel. Take care not to damage the plastic.
18 Withdraw the switch sufficiently to disconnect the wiring connector for switch removal or bulb removal.
19 Refit in the reverse order and check operation of the switch.

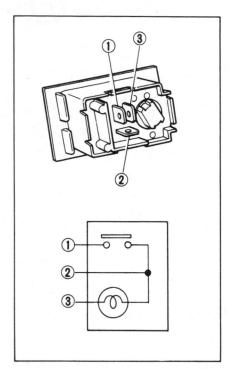

Fig. 13.38 Heated rear window switch (Sec 10)

1 Live feed   2 To window element   3 To earth

Windscreen wiper switch

20 The wiper switch on later models is of a slightly modified design. The removal and refitting procedures remain as described in Chapter 10.

Combination instrument panel

21 The instrument cluster on later models is of modified design. The procedures for removing and refitting the individual instruments remain as described in Chapter 10. The electrical circuitry is also unchanged.

Rear combination lights

22 On later models the rear combination lights are of modified design. Bulb renewal procedures are as follows.

Saloon models

23 The bulb holders are readily accessible from the luggage compartment. Loosen and remove the bulb holder and bulb from the light assembly by turning anti-clockwise and pulling.
24 The bulbs are of bayonet-type fitting: push in and turn anti-clockwise to remove. Renew with a bulb of the same wattage.

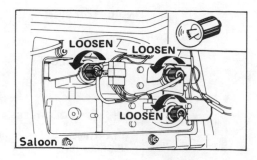

Fig. 13.39 Bulb removal – Saloon models (Sec 10)

Coupe models

25 Unclip the luggage compartment finisher to gain access to the bulb holders. Remove the bulb holders from the light assembly by turning anti-clockwise and pulling.
26 The bulbs are of bayonet-type fitting: push in and turn anti-clockwise to remove. Renew with a bulb of the same wattage.

Estate models

27 Bulb removal on Estate models is essentially the same as for Coupe models.

Van models

28 Bulb renewal on Vans is essentially the same as for Coupe models.

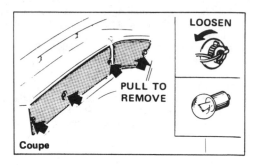

Fig. 13.40 Bulb removal – Coupe models (Sec 10)

Fig. 13.41 Bulb removal – Estate models (Sec 10)

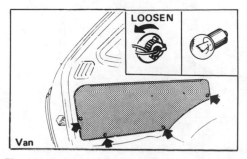

Fig. 13.42 Bulb removal – Van models (Sec 10)

All models

29 Refitting is the reverse of removal. Check that all lights work on completion.

Rear foglamps

30 Later models have twin rear foglamps fitted, bolted on below the bumper.

Bulb renewal

31 Unscrew the screws securing the lens to the foglamp body and remove the lens. The bulb is of bayonet-type fitting: push in and turn anti-clockwise to remove.

32 Renew the inoperative bulb with one of the same wattage and refit the lens. Check for correct operation on completion.

Switch – removal and refitting

33 Disconnect the battery earth lead.

34 Pull off the switch knob.

35 Unscrew the threaded collar securing the switch to the facia and push the switch out of its mounting hole.

36 Unplug the switch multi-plug and remove it from the car.

37 Refitting is a reversal of removal. Check for correct operation on completion.

Headlamp washer

38 Some later models are fitted with headlamp washers. The location of the washer reservoir varies from model to model (see Fig. 13.44).

39 Do not use radiator antifreeze in the reservoir, as it damages paintwork. A suitable proprietary preparation should be available from motor accessory shops.

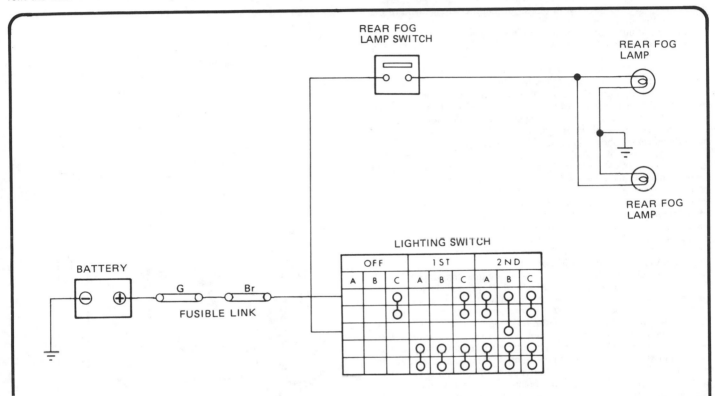

Fig. 13.43 Schematic wiring diagram for rear foglamps (Sec 10)

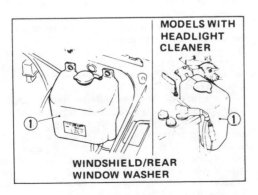

Fig. 13.44 Windscreen/rear window/headlamp washer reservoir locations (Sec 10)

1 All models (except Van) 2 Van models 3 Van models

11   Mobile radio equipment – interference-free installation

A radio and aerial are generally fitted as standard equipment to this range of vehicles. This section is of a general nature, but will provide useful information should it be decided to upgrade or change the equipment for any reason.

Aerials – selection and fitting

The choice of aerials is now very wide. It should be realised that the quality has a profound effect on radio performance, and a poor, inefficient aerial can make suppression difficult.

A wing-mounted aerial is regarded as probably the most efficient for signal collection, but a roof aerial is usually better for suppression purposes because it is away from most interference fields. Stick-on wire aerials are available for attachment to the inside of the windscreen, but are not always free from the interference field of the engine and some accessories.

Motorised automatic aerials rise when the equipment is switched on and retract at switch-off. They require more fitting space and supply leads, and can be a source of trouble.

There is no merit in choosing a very long aerial as, for example, the type about three metres in length which hooks or clips on to the rear of the car, since part of this aerial will inevitably be located in an interference field. For VHF/FM radios the best length of aerial is about one metre. Active aerials have a transistor amplifier mounted at the base and this serves to boost the received signal. The aerial rod is sometimes rather shorter than normal passive types.

A large loss of signal can occur in the aerial feeder cable, especially over the Very High Frequency (VHF) bands. The design of feeder cable is invariably in the co-axial form, ie a centre conductor surrounded by a flexible copper braid forming the outer (earth) conductor. Between the inner and outer conductors is an insulator material which can be in solid or stranded form. Apart from insulation, its purpose is to maintain the correct spacing and concentricity. Loss of signal occurs in this insulator, the loss usually being greater in a poor quality cable. The quality of cable used is reflected in the price of the aerial with the attached feeder cable.

The capacitance of the feeder should be within the range 65 to 75 picofarads (pF) approximately (95 to 100 pF for Japanese and American equipment), otherwise the adjustment of the car radio aerial trimmer may not be possible. An extension cable is necessary for a long run between aerial and receiver. If this adds capacitance in excess of the above limits, a connector containing a series capacitor will be required, or an extension which is labelled as 'capacity-compensated'.

Fitting the aerial will normally involve making a $\frac{7}{8}$ in (22 mm) diameter hole in the bodywork, but read the instructions that come with the aerial kit. Once the hole position has been selected, use a centre punch to guide the drill. Use sticky masking tape around the area for this helps with marking out and drill location, and gives protection to the paintwork should the drill slip. Three methods of making the hole are in use:

(a)   Use a hole saw in the electric drill. This is, in effect, a circular hacksaw blade wrapped round a former with a centre pilot drill.

(b)   Use a tank cutter which also has cutting teeth, but is made to shear the metal by tightening with an Allen key.

(c)   The hard way of drilling out the circle is using a small drill, say $\frac{1}{8}$ in (3 mm), so that the holes overlap. The centre metal drops out and the hole is finished with round and half-round files.

Whichever method is used, the burr is removed from the body metal and paint removed from the underside. The aerial is fitted tightly ensuring that the earth fixing, usually a serrated washer, ring or clamp, is making a solid connection. *This earth connection is important in reducing interference.* Cover any bare metal with primer paint and topcoat, and follow by underseal if desired.

Aerial feeder cable routing should avoid the engine compartment and areas where stress might occur, eg under the carpet where feet will be located. Roof aerials require that the headlining be pulled back and that a path is available down the door pillar. It is wise to check with the vehicle dealer whether roof aerial fitting is recommended.

Loudspeakers

Speakers should be matched to the output stage of the equipment, particularly as regards the recommended impedance.

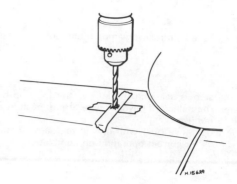

Fig. 13.45 Drilling the bodywork for aerial mounting (Sec 11)

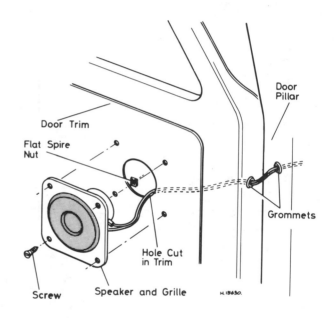

Fig. 13.46 Door-mounted speaker installation (Sec 11)

Power transistors used for driving speakers are sensitive to the loading placed on them.

Before choosing a mounting position for speakers, check whether the vehicle manufacturer has provided a location for them. Generally door-mounted speakers give good stereophonic reproduction, but not all doors are able to accept them. The next best position is the rear parcel shelf, and in this case speaker apertures can be cut into the shelf, or pod units may be mounted.

For door mounting, first remove the trim, which is often held on by 'poppers' or press studs, and then select a suitable gap in the inside door assembly. Check that the speaker would not obstruct glass or winder mechanism by winding the window up and down. A template is often provided for marking out the trim panel hole, and then the four fixing holes must be drilled through. Mark out with chalk and cut cleanly with a sharp knife or keyhole saw. Speaker leads are then threaded through the door and door pillar, if necessary drilling 10 mm diameter holes. Fit grommets in the holes and connect to the radio or tape unit correctly. Do not omit a waterproofing cover, usually supplied with door speakers. If the speaker has to be fixed into the metal of the door itself, use self-tapping screws, and if the fixing is to the door trim use self-tapping screws and flat spire nuts.

Rear shelf mounting is somewhat simpler but it is necessary to find gaps in the metalwork underneath the parcel shelf. However, remember that the speakers should be as far apart as possible to give a good stereo effect. Pod-mounted speakers can be screwed into position through the parcel shelf material, but it is worth testing for the best position. Sometimes good results are found by reflecting sound off the rear window.

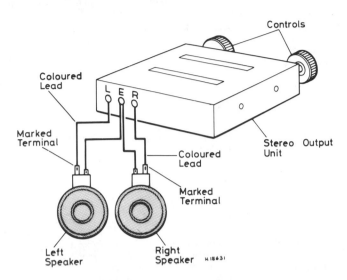

Fig. 13.47 Speaker connections must be correctly made (Sec 11)

Unit installation

Many vehicles have a dash panel aperture to take a radio/audio unit, a recognised international standard being 189.5 mm x 60 mm. Alternatively a console may be a feature of the car interior design and this, mounted below the dashboard, gives more room. If neither facility is available a unit may be mounted on the underside of the parcel shelf; these are frequently non-metallic and an earth wire from the case to a good earth point is necessary. A three-sided cover in the form of a cradle is obtainable from car radio dealers and this gives a professional appearance to the installation; in this case choose a position where the controls can be reached by a driver with his seat belt on.

Installation of the radio/audio unit is basically the same in all cases, and consists of offering it into the aperture after removal of the knobs (not push buttons) and the trim plate. In some cases a special mounting plate is required to which the unit is attached. It is worthwhile supporting the rear end in cases where sag or strain may occur, and it is usually possible to use a length of perforated metal strip attached between the unit and a good support point nearby. In general it is recommended that tape equipment should be installed at or nearly horizontal.

Connections to the aerial socket are simply by the standard plug terminating the aerial downlead or its extension cable. Speakers for a stereo system must be matched and correctly connected, as outlined previously.

Note: *While all work is carried out on the power side, it is wise to disconnect the battery earth lead.* Before connection is made to the vehicle electrical system, check that the polarity of the unit is correct. Most vehicles use a negative earth system, but radio/audio units often have a reversible plug to convert the set to either + or – earth. *Incorrect connection may cause serious damage.*

The power lead is often permanently connected inside the unit and terminates with one half of an in-line fuse carrier. The other half is fitted with a suitable fuse (3 or 5 amperes) and a wire which should go to a power point in the electrical system. This may be the accessory terminal on the ignition switch, giving the advantage of power feed with ignition or with the ignition key at the 'accessory' position. Power to the unit stops when the ignition key is removed. Alternatively, the lead may be taken to a live point at the fusebox with the consequence of having to remember to switch off at the unit before leaving the vehicle.

Before switching on for initial test, be sure that the speaker connections have been made, for running without load can damage the output transistors. Switch on next and tune through the bands to ensure that all sections are working, and check the tape unit if

applicable. The aerial trimmer should be adjusted to give the strongest reception on a weak signal in the medium wave band, at say 200 metres.

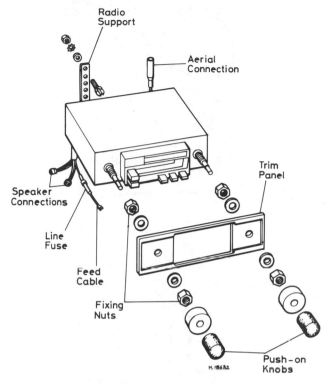

Fig. 13.48 Mounting component details for radio/cassette unit (Sec 11)

Interference

In general, when electric current changes abruptly, unwanted electrical noise is produced. The motor vehicle is filled with electrical devices which change electric current rapidly, the most obvious being the contact breaker.

When the spark plugs operate, the sudden pulse of spark current causes the associated wiring to radiate. Since early radio transmitters used sparks as a basis of operation, it is not surprising that the car radio will pick up ignition spark noise unless steps are taken to reduce it to acceptable levels.

Interference reaches the car radio in two ways:

(a) by conduction through the wiring.
(b) by radiation to the receiving aerial.

Initial checks presuppose that the bonnet is down and fastened, the radio unit has a good earth connection (not through the aerial downlead outer), no fluorescent tubes are working near the car, the aerial trimmer has been adjusted, and the vehicle is in a position to receive radio signals, ie not in a metal-clad building.

Switch on the radio and tune it to the middle of the medium wave (MW) band off-station with the volume (gain) control set fairly high. Switch on the ignition (but do not start the engine) and wait to see if irregular clicks or hash noise occurs. Tapping the facia panel may also produce the effects. If so, this will be due to the voltage stabiliser, which is an on-off thermal switch to control instrument voltage. It is located usually on the back of the instrument panel, often attached to the speedometer. Correction is by attachment of a capacitor and, if still troublesome, chokes in the supply wires.

Switch on the engine and listen for interference on the MW band. Depending on the type of interference, the indications are as follows.

A harsh crackle that drops out abruptly at low engine speed or when the headlights are switched on is probably due to a voltage regulator.

A whine varying with engine speed is due to the dynamo or alternator. Try temporarily taking off the fan belt — if the noise goes this is confirmation.

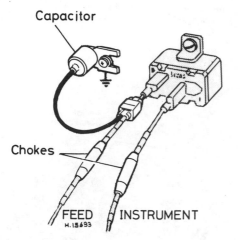

Fig. 13.49 Voltage stabiliser interference suppression (Sec 11)

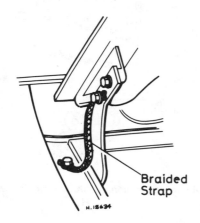

Fig. 13.50 Braided earth strap between bonnet and body (Sec 11)

Regular ticking or crackle that varies in rate with the engine speed is due to the ignition system. With this trouble in particular and others in general, check to see if the noise is entering the receiver from the wiring or by radiation. To do this, pull out the aerial plug, (preferably shorting out the input socket or connecting a 62 pF capacitor across it). If the noise disappears it is coming in through the aerial and is *radiation noise*. If the noise persists it is reaching the receiver through the wiring and is said to be *line-borne*.

Interference from wipers, washers, heater blowers, turn-indicators, stop lamps, etc is usually taken to the receiver by wiring, and simple treatment using capacitors and possibly chokes will solve the problem. Switch on each one in turn (wet the screen first for running wipers!) and listen for possible interference with the aerial plug in place and again when removed.

Electric petrol pumps are now finding application again and give rise to an irregular clicking, often giving a burst of clicks when the ignition is on but the engine has not yet been started. It is also possible to receive whining or crackling from the pump.

Note that if most of the vehicle accessories are found to be creating interference all together, the probability is that poor aerial earthing is to blame.

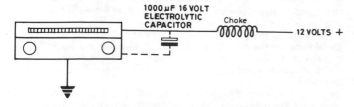

Fig. 13.51 Line-borne interference suppression (Sec 11)

Component terminal markings

Throughout the following sub-sections reference will be found to various terminal markings. These will vary depending on the manufacturer of the relevant component. If terminal markings differ from those mentioned, reference should be made to the following table, where the most commonly encountered variations are listed.

Alternator	Alternator terminal (thick lead)	Exciting winding terminal
DIN/Bosch	B+	DF
Delco Remy	+	EXC
Ducellier	+	EXC
Ford (US)	+	DF
Lucas	+	F
Marelli	+B	F

Ignition coil	Ignition switch terminal	Contact breaker terminal
DIN/Bosch	15	1
Delco Remy	+	–
Ducellier	BAT	RUP
Ford (US)	B/+	CB/–
Lucas	SW/+	–
Marelli	BAT/+B	D

Voltage regulator	Voltage input terminal	Exciting winding terminal
DIN/Bosch	B+/D+	DF
Delco Remy	BAT/+	EXC
Ducellier	BOB/BAT	EXC
Ford (US)	BAT	DF
Lucas	+/A	F
Marelli		F

Suppression methods – ignition

Suppressed HT cables are supplied as original equipment by manufacturers and will meet regulations as far as interference to neighbouring equipment is concerned. It is illegal to remove such suppression unless an alternative is provided, and this may take the form of resistive spark plug caps in conjunction with plain copper HT cable. For VHF purposes, these and 'in-line' resistors may not be effective, and resistive HT cable is preferred. Check that suppressed cables are actually fitted by observing cable identity lettering, or measuring with an ohmmeter – the value of each plug lead should be 5000 to 10 000 ohms.

A 1 microfarad capacitor connected from the LT supply side of the ignition coil to a good nearby earth point will complete basic ignition interference treatment. *NEVER fit a capacitor to the coil terminal to the contact breaker – the result would be burnt out points in a short time.*

If ignition noise persists despite the treatment above, the following sequence should be followed:

(a) Check the earthing of the ignition coil; remove paint from fixing clamp.

(b) If this does not work, lift the bonnet. Should there be no change in interference level, this may indicate that the bonnet is not electrically connected to the car body. Use a proprietary braided strap across a bonnet hinge ensuring a first class electrical connection. If, however, lifting the bonnet increases the interference, then fit resistive HT cables of a higher ohms-per-metre value.

(c) If all these measures fail, it is probable that re-radiation from metallic components is taking place. Using a braided strap between metallic points, go round the vehicle systematically – try the following: engine to body, exhaust system to body, front suspension to engine and to body, steering column to body (especially French and Italian cars), gear lever to engine and to body (again especially French and Italian cars), Bowden cable to body, metal parcel shelf to body. When an offending component is located it should be bonded with the strap permanently.

(d) As a next step, the fitting of distributor suppressors to each lead at the distributor end may help.

(e) Beyond this point is involved the possible screening of the distributor and fitting resistive spark plugs, but such advanced treatment is not usually required for vehicles with entertainment equipment.

Electronic ignition systems have built-in suppression components, but this does not relieve the need for using suppressed HT leads. In some cases it is permitted to connect a capacitor on the low tension supply side of the ignition coil, but not in every case. Makers' instructions should be followed carefully, otherwise damage to the ignition semiconductors may result.

Suppression methods – generators

For older vehicles with dynamos a 1 microfarad capacitor from the D (larger) terminal to earth will usually cure dynamo whine. Alternators should be fitted with a 3 microfarad capacitor from the B+ main output terminal (thick cable) to earth. Additional suppression may be obtained by the use of a filter in the supply line to the radio receiver.

It is most important that:

(a) Capacitors are never connected to the field terminals of either a dynamo or alternator.
(b) Alternators must not be run without connection to the battery.

Suppression methods – voltage regulators

Voltage regulators used with DC dynamos should be suppressed by connecting a 1 microfarad capacitor from the control box D terminal to earth.

Alternator regulators come in three types:

(a) Vibrating contact regulators separate from the alternator. Used extensively on continental vehicles.
(b) Electronic regulators separate from the alternator.
(c) Electronic regulators built-in to the alternator.

In case (a) interference may be generated on the AM and FM (VHF) bands. For some cars a replacement suppressed regulator is available. Filter boxes may be used with non-suppressed regulators. But if not available, then for AM equipment a 2 microfarad or 3 microfarad capacitor may be mounted at the voltage terminal marked D+ or B+ of the regulator. FM bands may be treated by a feed-through capacitor of 2 or 3 microfarad.

Electronic voltage regulators are not always troublesome, but where necessary, a 1 microfarad capacitor from the regulator + terminal will help.

Integral electronic voltage regulators do not normally generate much interference, but when encountered this is in combination with alternator noise. A 1 microfarad or 2 microfarad capacitor from the warning lamp (IND) terminal to earth for Lucas ACR alternators and Femsa, Delco and Bosch equivalents should cure the problem.

Suppression methods – other equipment

Wiper motors – Connect the wiper body to earth with a bonding strap. For all motors use a 7 ampere choke assembly inserted in the leads to the motor.

Heater motors – Fit 7 ampere line chokes in both leads, assisted if necessary by a 1 microfarad capacitor to earth from both leads.

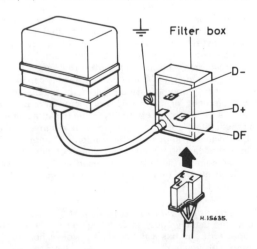

Fig. 13.52 Typical filter box for vibrating contact voltage regulator (alternator equipment) (Sec 11)

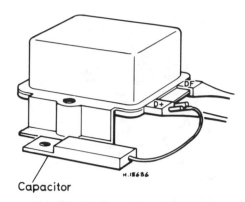

Fig. 13.53 Suppression of AM interference by vibrating contact voltage regulator (alternator equipment) (Sec 11)

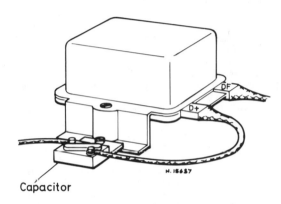

Fig. 13.54 Suppression of FM interference by vibrating contact voltage regulator (alternator equipment) (Sec 11)

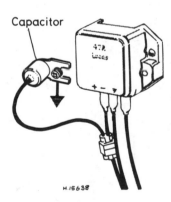

Fig. 13.55 Electronic voltage regulator suppression (Sec 11)

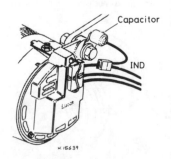

Fig. 13.56 Suppression of interference from electronic voltage regulator when integral with alternator (Sec 11)

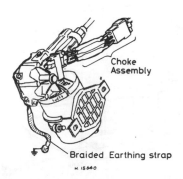

Fig. 13.57 Wiper motor suppression (Sec 11)

Electronic tachometer — The tachometer is a possible source of ignition noise – check by disconnecting at the ignition coil CB terminal. It usually feeds from ignition coil LT pulses at the contact breaker terminal. A 3 ampere line choke should be fitted in the tachometer lead at the coil CB terminal.

Horn — A capacitor and choke combination is effective if the horn is directly connected to the 12 volt supply. The use of a relay is an alternative remedy, as this will reduce the length of the interference-carrying leads.

Electrostatic noise — Characteristics are erratic crackling at the receiver, with disappearance of symptoms in wet weather. Often shocks may be given when touching bodywork. Part of the problem is the build-up of static electricity in non-driven wheels and the acquisition of charge on the body shell. It is possible to fit spring-loaded contacts at the wheels to give good conduction between the rotary wheel parts and the vehicle frame. Changing a tyre sometimes helps – because of tyres' varying resistances. In difficult cases a trailing flex which touches the ground will cure the problem. If this is not acceptable it is worth trying conductive paint on the tyre walls.

Fuel pump — Suppression requires a 1 microfarad capacitor between the supply wire to the pump and a nearby earth point. If this is insufficient a 7 ampere line choke connected in the supply wire near the pump is required.

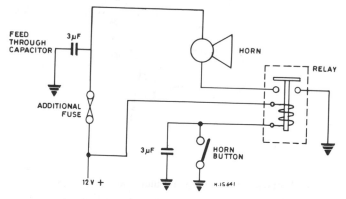

Fig. 13.58 Use of relay to reduce horn interference (Sec 11)

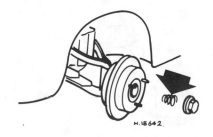

Fig. 13.59 Use of spring contacts at wheels (Sec 11)

Fluorescent tubes — Vehicles used for camping/caravanning frequently have fluorescent tube lighting. These tubes require a relatively high voltage for operation and this is provided by an inverter (a form of oscillator) which steps up the vehicle supply voltage. This can give rise to serious interference to radio reception, and the tubes themselves can contribute to this interference by the pulsating nature of the lamp discharge. In such situations it is important to mount the aerial as far away from a fluorescent tube as possible. The interference problem may be alleviated by screening the tube with fine wire turns spaced an inch (25 mm) apart and earthed to the chassis. Suitable chokes should be fitted in both supply wires close to the inverter.

Radio/cassette case breakthrough

Magnetic radiation from dashboard wiring may be sufficiently intense to break through the metal case of the radio/cassette player. Often this is due to a particular cable routed too close and shows up as ignition interference on AM and cassette play and/or alternator whine on cassette play.

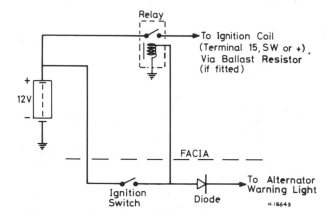

Fig. 13.60 Use of ignition coil relay to suppress case breakthrough (Sec 11)

The first point to check is that the clips and/or screws are fixing all parts of the radio/cassette case together properly. Assuming good earthing of the case, see if it is possible to re-route the offending cable – the chances of this are not good, however, in most cars.

Next release the radio/cassette player and locate it in different positions with temporary leads. If a point of low interference is found, then if possible fix the equipment in that area. This also confirms that local radiation is causing the trouble. If re-location is not feasible, fit the radio/cassette player back in the original position.

Alternator interference on cassette play is now caused by radiation from the main charging cable which goes from the battery to the output terminal of the alternator, usually via the + terminal of the starter motor relay. In some vehicles this cable is routed under the dashboard, so the solution is to provide a direct cable route. Detach the original cable from the alternator output terminal and make up a new cable of at least 6 mm² cross-sectional area to go from alternator to battery with the shortest possible route. *Remember – do not run the engine with the alternator disconnected from the battery.*

Ignition breakthrough on AM and/or cassette play can be a difficult problem. It is worth wrapping earthed foil round the offending cable run near the equipment, or making up a deflector plate well screwed down to a good earth. Another possibility is the use of a suitable relay to switch on the ignition coil. The relay should be mounted close to the ignition coil; with this arrangement the ignition coil primary current is not taken into the dashboard area and does not flow through the ignition switch. A suitable diode should be used since it is possible that at ignition switch-off the output from the warning lamp alternator terminal could hold the relay on.

Connectors for suppression components

Capacitors are usually supplied with tags on the end of the lead, while the capacitor body has a flange with a slot or hole to fit under a nut or screw with washer.

Connections to feed wires are best achieved by self-stripping connectors. These connectors employ a blade which, when squeezed down by pliers, cuts through cable insulation and makes connection to the copper conductors beneath.

Chokes sometimes come with bullet snap-in connectors fitted to the wires, and also with just bare copper wire. With connectors, suitable female cable connectors may be purchased from an auto-accessory shop together with any extra connectors required for the cable ends after being cut for the choke insertion. For chokes with bare wires, similar connectors may be employed together with insulation sleeving as required.

VHF/FM broadcasts

Reception of VHF/FM in an automobile is more prone to problems than the medium and long wavebands. Medium/long wave transmitters are capable of covering considerable distances, but VHF transmitters are restricted to line of sight, meaning ranges of 10 to 50 miles, depending upon the terrain, the effects of buildings and the transmitter power.

Because of the limited range it is necessary to retune on a long journey, and it may be better for those habitually travelling long distances or living in areas of poor provision of transmitters to use an AM radio working on medium/long wavebands.

When conditions are poor, interference can arise, and some of the suppression devices described previously fall off in performance at very high frequencies unless specifically designed for the VHF band. Available suppression devices include reactive HT cable, resistive distributor caps, screened plug caps, screened leads and resistive spark plugs.

For VHF/FM receiver installation the following points should be particularly noted:

(a) Earthing of the receiver chassis and the aerial mounting is important. Use a separate earthing wire at the radio, and scrape paint away at the aerial mounting.

(b) If possible, use a good quality roof aerial to obtain maximum height and distance from interference generating devices on the vehicle.

(c) Use of a high quality aerial download is important, since losses in cheap cable can be significant.

(d) The polarisation of FM transmissions may be horizontal, vertical, circular or slanted. Because of this the optimum mounting angle is at 45° to the vehicle roof.

Citizens' Band radio (CB)

In the UK, CB transmitter/receivers work within the 27 MHz and 934 MHz bands, using the FM mode. At present interest is concentrated on 27 MHz where the design and manufacture of equipment is less difficult. Maximum transmitted power is 4 watts, and 40 channels spaced 10 kHz apart within the range 27.60125 to 27.99125 MHz are available.

Aerials are the key to effective transmission and reception. Regulations limit the aerial length to 1.65 metres including the loading coil and any associated circuitry, so tuning the aerial is necessary to obtain optimum results. The choice of a CB aerial is dependent on whether it is to be permanently installed or removable, and the performance will hinge on correct tuning and the location point on the vehicle. Common practice is to clip the aerial to the roof gutter or to employ wing mounting where the aerial can be rapidly unscrewed. An alternative is to use the boot rim to render the aerial theftproof, but a popular solution is to use the 'magmount' – a type of mounting having a strong magnetic base clamping to the vehicle at any point, usually the roof.

Aerial location determines the signal distribution for both trans-mission and reception, but it is wise to choose a point away from the engine compartment to minimise interference from vehicle electrical equipment.

The aerial is subject to considerable wind and acceleration forces. Cheaper units will whip backwards and forwards and in so doing will alter the relationship with the metal surface of the vehicle with which it forms a ground plane aerial system. The radiation pattern will change correspondingly, giving rise to break-up of both incoming and outgoing signals.

Interference problems on the vehicle carrying CB equipment fall into two categories:

(a) Interference to nearby TV and radio receivers when transmit-ting.

(b) Interference to CB set reception due to electrical equipment on the vehicle.

Problems of break-through to TV and radio are not frequent, but can be difficult to solve. Mostly trouble is not detected or reported because the vehicle is moving and the symptoms rapidly disappear at the TV/radio receiver, but when the CB set is used as a base station any trouble with nearby receivers will soon result in a complaint.

It must not be assumed by the CB operator that his equipment is faultless, for much depends upon the design. Harmonics (that is, multiples) of 27 MHz may be transmitted unknowingly and these can fall into other user's bands. Where trouble of this nature occurs, low pass filters in the aerial or supply leads can help, and should be fitted in base station aerials as a matter of course. In stubborn cases it may be necessary to call for assistance from the licensing authority, or, if possible, to have the equipment checked by the manufacturers.

Interference received on the CB set from the vehicle equipment is, fortunately, not usually a severe problem. The precautions outlined previously for radio/cassette units apply, but there are some extra points worth noting.

It is common practice to use a slide-mount on CB equipment enabling the set to be easily removed for use as a base station, for example. Care must be taken that the slide mount fittings are properly earthed and that first class connection occurs between the set and slide-mount.

Vehicle manufacturers in the UK are required to provide suppression of electrical equipment to cover 40 to 250 MHz to protect TV and VHF radio bands. Such suppression appears to be adequately effective at 27 MHz, but suppression of individual items such as alternators, clocks, stabilisers, flashers, wiper motors, etc, may still be necessary. The suppression capacitors and chokes available from auto-electrical suppliers for entertainment receivers will usually give the required results with CB equipment.

Other vehicle radio transmitters

Besides CB radio already mentioned, a considerable increase in the use of transceivers (ie combined transmitter and receiver units) has taken place in the last decade. Previously this type of equipment was fitted mainly to military, fire, ambulance and police vehicles, but a large business radio and radio telephone usage has developed.

Generally the suppression techniques described previously will suffice, with only a few difficult cases arising. Suppression is carried out to satisfy the 'receive mode', but care must be taken to use heavy duty chokes in the equipment supply cables since the loading on 'transmit' is relatively high.

Glass-fibre bodied vehicles

Such vehicles do not have the advantage of a metal box surrounding the engine as is the case, in effect, of conventional vehicles. It is usually necessary to line the bonnet, bulkhead and wing valances with metal foil, which could well be the aluminium foil available from builders merchants. Bonding of sheets one to another and the whole down to the chassis is essential.

Wiring harness may have to be wrapped in metal foil which again should be earthed to the vehicle chassis. The aerial base and radio chassis must be taken to the vehicle chassis by heavy metal braid. VHF radio suppression in glass-fibre cars may not be a feasible operation.

In addition to all the above, normal suppression components should be employed, but special attention paid to earth bonding. A screen enclosing the entire ignition system usually gives good im-provement, and fabrication from fine mesh perforated metal is convenient. Good bonding of the screening boxes to several chassis points is essential.

12 Bodywork and fittings

Radiator grille — removal and refitting

1   The radiator grille on later models is designed to be quickly detachable. The new grille is made of plastic, so do not use excessive force. Note: the grille will be damaged by any contact with oil.
2   Open the bonnet and support it securely.
3   Rotate the fasteners (Fig. 13.61) through 45° and remove them from the grille.
4   Lift the grille and remove it from the car.
5   Refitting is a reversal of removal.

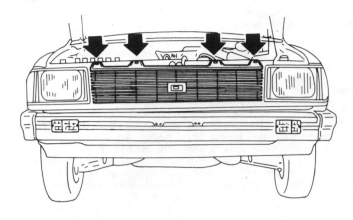

Fig. 13.61 Radiator grille fastener locations (Sec 12)

Instrument panel – removal and refitting

6   The instrument panel has been facelifted for later models. Removal is as follows.

7   Disconnect the battery earth lead.

8   Remove the manual choke knob.

9   Pull out the heater control knob and remove the heater control finisher.

10   Remove the screw(s) attaching the heater control assembly to the instrument panel.

11   Remove the ashtray and unscrew the panel securing screws now exposed.

12   Remove the screws securing the package tray to the instrument panel and remove the package tray.

13   Remove the steering column shroud.

14   Remove the side defroster duct.

15   Disconnect the speedometer cable from behind the speedometer.

16   Disconnect the radio aerial.

17   Disconnect all electrical wiring at their connectors. Be sure to label any which may be confused during refitting.

18   Remove the instrument panel securing bolts and lift the panel free.

19   Refitting is a reversal of removal.

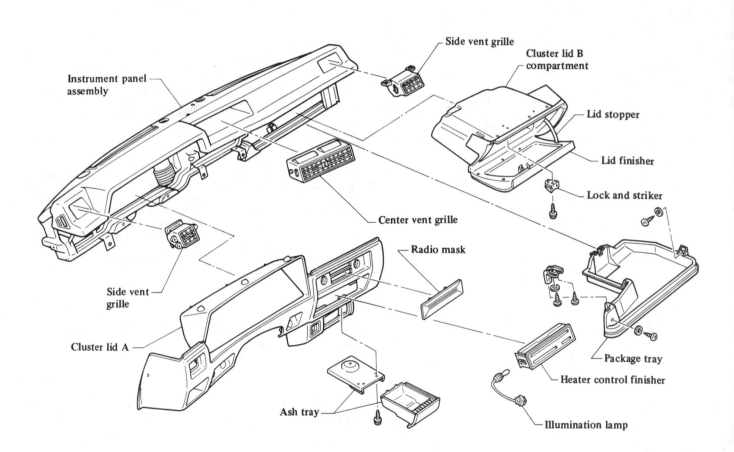

Fig. 13.62 Instrument panel assembly – later models (Sec 12)

General repair procedures

Whenever servicing, repair or overhaul work is carried out on the car or its components, it is necessary to observe the following procedures and instructions. This will assist in carrying out the operation efficiently and to a professional standard of workmanship.

Joint mating faces and gaskets

Where a gasket is used between the mating faces of two components, ensure that it is renewed on reassembly, and fit it dry unless otherwise stated in the repair procedure. Make sure that the mating faces are clean and dry with all traces of old gasket removed. When cleaning a joint face, use a tool which is not likely to score or damage the face, and remove any burrs or nicks with an oilstone or fine file.

Make sure that tapped holes are cleaned, and keep them free of jointing compound if this is being used unless specifically instructed otherwise.

Ensure that all orifices, channels or pipes are clear and blow through them, preferably using compressed air.

Oil seals

Whenever an oil seal is removed from its working location, either individually or as part of an assembly, it should be renewed.

The very fine sealing lip of the seal is easily damaged and will not seal if the surface it contacts is not completely clean and free from scratches, nicks or grooves. If the original sealing surface of the component cannot be restored, the component should be renewed.

Protect the lips of the seal from any surface which may damage them in the course of fitting. Use tape or a conical sleeve where possible. Lubricate the seal lips with oil before fitting and, on dual lipped seals, fill the space between the lips with grease.

Unless otherwise stated, oil seals must be fitted with their sealing lips toward the lubricant to be sealed.

Use a tubular drift or block of wood of the appropriate size to install the seal and, if the seal housing is shouldered, drive the seal down to the shoulder. If the seal housing is unshouldered, the seal should be fitted with its face flush with the housing top face.

Screw threads and fastenings

Always ensure that a blind tapped hole is completely free from oil, grease, water or other fluid before installing the bolt or stud. Failure to do this could cause the housing to crack due to the hydraulic action of the bolt or stud as it is screwed in.

When tightening a castellated nut to accept a split pin, tighten the nut to the specified torque, where applicable, and then tighten further to the next split pin hole. Never slacken the nut to align a split pin hole unless stated in the repair procedure.

When checking or retightening a nut or bolt to a specified torque setting, slacken the nut or bolt by a quarter of a turn, and then retighten to the specified setting.

Locknuts, locktabs and washers

Any fastening which will rotate against a component or housing in the course of tightening should always have a washer between it and the relevant component or housing.

Spring or split washers should always be renewed when they are used to lock a critical component such as a big-end bearing retaining nut or bolt.

Locktabs which are folded over to retain a nut or bolt should always be renewed.

Self-locking nuts can be reused in non-critical areas, providing resistance can be felt when the locking portion passes over the bolt or stud thread.

Split pins must always be replaced with new ones of the correct size for the hole.

Special tools

Some repair procedures in this manual entail the use of special tools such as a press, two or three-legged pullers, spring compressors etc. Wherever possible, suitable readily available alternatives to the manufacturer's special tools are described, and are shown in use. In some instances, where no alternative is possible, it has been necessary to resort to the use of a manufacturer's tool and this has been done for reasons of safety as well as the efficient completion of the repair operation. Unless you are highly skilled and have a thorough understanding of the procedure described, never attempt to bypass the use of any special tool when the procedure described specifies its use. Not only is there a very great risk of personal injury, but expensive damage could be caused to the components involved.

Safety first!

Professional motor mechanics are trained in safe working procedures. However enthusiastic you may be about getting on with the job in hand, do take the time to ensure that your safety is not put at risk. A moment's lack of attention can result in an accident, as can failure to observe certain elementary precautions.

There will always be new ways of having accidents, and the following points do not pretend to be a comprehensive list of all dangers; they are intended rather to make you aware of the risks and to encourage a safety-conscious approach to all work you carry out on your vehicle.

Essential DOs and DON'Ts

DON'T rely on a single jack when working underneath the vehicle. Always use reliable additional means of support, such as axle stands, securely placed under a part of the vehicle that you know will not give way.

DON'T attempt to loosen or tighten high-torque nuts (e.g. wheel hub nuts) while the vehicle is on a jack; it may be pulled off.

DON'T start the engine without first ascertaining that the transmission is in neutral and the parking brake applied.

DON'T suddenly remove the filler cap from a hot cooling system — cover it with a cloth and release the pressure gradually first, or you may get scalded by escaping coolant.

DON'T attempt to drain oil until you are sure it has cooled sufficiently to avoid scalding you.

DON'T grasp any part of the engine or exhaust without first ascertaining that it is sufficiently cool to avoid burning you.

DON'T syphon toxic liquids such as fuel, brake fluid or antifreeze by mouth, or allow them to remain on your skin.

DON'T inhale brake lining dust — it is injurious to health.

DON'T allow any spilt oil or grease to remain on the floor — wipe it up straight away, before someone slips on it.

DON'T use ill-fitting spanners or other tools which may slip and cause injury.

DON'T attempt to lift a heavy component which may be beyond your capability — get assistance.

DON'T rush to finish a job, or take unverified short cuts.

DON'T allow children or animals in or around an unattended vehicle.

DO wear eye protection when using power tools such as drill, sander, bench grinder etc, and when working under the vehicle.

DO use a barrier cream on your hands prior to undertaking dirty jobs — it will protect your skin from infection as well as making the dirt easier to remove afterwards; but make sure your hands aren't left slippery.

DO keep loose clothing (cuffs, tie etc) and long hair well out of the way of moving mechanical parts.

DO remove rings, wristwatch etc, before working on the vehicle — especially the electrical system.

DO ensure that any lifting tackle used has a safe working load rating adequate for the job.

DO keep your work area tidy — it is only too easy to fall over articles left lying around.

DO get someone to check periodically that all is well, when working alone on the vehicle.

DO carry out work in a logical sequence and check that everything is correctly assembled and tightened afterwards.

DO remember that your vehicle's safety affects that of yourself and others. If in doubt on any point, get specialist advice.

IF, in spite of following these precautions, you are unfortunate enough to injure yourself, seek medical attention as soon as possible.

Fire

Remember at all times that petrol (gasoline) is highly flammable. Never smoke, or have any kind of naked flame around, when working on the vehicle. But the risk does not end there — a spark caused by an electrical short-circuit, by two metal surfaces contacting each other, or even by static electricity built up in your body under certain conditions, can ignite petrol vapour, which in a confined space is highly explosive.

Always disconnect the battery earth (ground) terminal before working on any part of the fuel system, and never risk spilling fuel on to a hot engine or exhaust.

It is recommended that a fire extinguisher of a type suitable for fuel and electrical fires is kept handy in the garage or workplace at all times. Never try to extinguish a fuel or electrical fire with water.

Fumes

Certain fumes are highly toxic and can quickly cause unconsciousness and even death if inhaled to any extent. Petrol (gasoline) vapour comes into this category, as do the vapours from certain solvents such as trichloroethylene. Any draining or pouring of such volatile fluids should be done in a well ventilated area.

When using cleaning fluids and solvents, read the instructions carefully. Never use materials from unmarked containers — they may give off poisonous vapours.

Never run the engine of a motor vehicle in an enclosed space such as a garage. Exhaust fumes contain carbon monoxide which is extremely poisonous; if you need to run the engine, always do so in the open air or at least have the rear of the vehicle outside the workplace.

If you are fortunate enough to have the use of an inspection pit, never drain or pour petrol, and never run the engine, while the vehicle is standing over it; the fumes, being heavier than air, will concentrate in the pit with possibly lethal results.

The battery

Never cause a spark, or allow a naked light, near the vehicle's battery. It will normally be giving off a certain amount of hydrogen gas, which is highly explosive.

Always disconnect the battery earth (ground) terminal before working on the fuel or electrical systems.

If possible, loosen the filler plugs or cover when charging the battery from an external source. Do not charge at an excessive rate or the battery may burst.

Take care when topping up and when carrying the battery. The acid electrolyte, even when diluted, is very corrosive and should not be allowed to contact the eyes or skin.

If you ever need to prepare electrolyte yourself, always add the acid slowly to the water, and never the other way round. Protect against splashes by wearing rubber gloves and goggles.

When jump starting a car using a booster battery, for negative earth (ground) vehicles, connect the jump leads in the following sequence: First connect one jump lead between the positive (+) terminals of the two batteries. Then connect the other jump lead first to the negative (−) terminal of the booster battery, and then to a good earthing (ground) point on the vehicle to be started, at least 18 in (45 cm) from the battery if possible. Ensure that hands and jump leads are clear of any moving parts, and that the two vehicles do not touch. Disconnect the leads in the reverse order.

Mains electricity

When using an electric power tool, inspection light etc, which works from the mains, always ensure that the appliance is correctly connected to its plug and that, where necessary, it is properly earthed (grounded). Do not use such appliances in damp conditions and, again, beware of creating a spark or applying excessive heat in the vicinity of fuel or fuel vapour.

Ignition HT voltage

A severe electric shock can result from touching certain parts of the ignition system, such as the HT leads, when the engine is running or being cranked, particularly if components are damp or the insulation is defective. Where an electronic ignition system is fitted, the HT voltage is much higher and could prove fatal.

Fault diagnosis

Introduction

The vehicle owner who does his or her own maintenance according to the recommended schedules should not have to use this section of the manual very often. Modern component reliability is such that, provided those items subject to wear or deterioration are inspected or renewed at the specified intervals, sudden failure is comparatively rare. Faults do not usually just happen as a result of sudden failure, but develop over a period of time. Major mechanical failures in particular are usually preceded by characteristic symptoms over hundreds or even thousands of miles. Those components which do occasionally fail without warning are often small and easily carried in the vehicle.

With any fault finding, the first step is to decide where to begin investigations. Sometimes this is obvious, but on other occasions a little detective work will be necessary. The owner who makes half a dozen haphazard adjustments or replacements may be successful in curing a fault (or its symptoms), but he will be none the wiser if the fault recurs and he may well have spent more time and money than was necessary. A calm and logical approach will be found to be more satisfactory in the long run. Always take into account any warning signs or abnormalities that may have been noticed in the period preceding the fault – power loss, high or low gauge readings, unusual noises or smells, etc – and remember that failure of components such as fuses or spark plugs may only be pointers to some underlying fault.

The pages which follow here are intended to help in cases of failure to start or breakdown on the road. There is also a Fault Diagnosis Section at the end of each Chapter which should be consulted if the preliminary checks prove unfruitful. Whatever the fault, certain basic principles apply. These are as follows:

Verify the fault. This is simply a matter of being sure that you know what the symptoms are before starting work. This is particularly important if you are investigating a fault for someone else who may not have described it very accurately.

Don't overlook the obvious. For example, if the vehicle won't start, is there petrol in the tank? (Don't take anyone else's word on this particular point, and don't trust the fuel gauge either!) If an electrical fault is indicated, look for loose or broken wires before digging out the test gear.

Cure the disease, not the symptom. Substituting a flat battery with a fully charged one will get you off the hard shoulder, but if the underlying cause is not attended to, the new battery will go the same way. Similarly, changing oil-fouled spark plugs for a new set will get you moving again, but remember that the reason for the fouling (if it wasn't simply an incorrect grade of plug) will have to be established and corrected.

Don't take anything for granted. Particularly, don't forget that a 'new' component may itself be defective (especially if it's been rattling round in the boot for months), and don't leave components out of a fault diagnosis sequence just because they are new or recently fitted. When you do finally diagnose a difficult fault, you'll probably realise that all the evidence was there from the start.

Electrical faults

Electrical faults can be more puzzling than straightforward mechanical failures, but they are no less susceptible to logical analysis if the basic principles of operation are understood. Vehicle electrical wiring exists in extremely unfavourable conditions – heat, vibration and chemical attack – and the first things to look for are loose or corroded connections and broken or chafed wires, especially where the wires pass through holes in the bodywork or are subject to vibration.

All metal-bodied vehicles in current production have one pole of the battery 'earthed', ie connected to the vehicle bodywork, and in nearly all modern vehicles it is the negative (–) terminal. The various electrical components – motors, bulb holders etc – are also connected to earth, either by means of a lead or directly by their mountings. Electric current flows through the component and then back to the battery via the bodywork. If the component mounting is loose or corroded, or if a good path back to the battery is not available, the circuit will be incomplete and malfunction will result. The engine and/or gearbox are also earthed by means of flexible metal straps to the body or subframe; if these straps are loose or missing, starter motor, generator and ignition trouble may result.

Assuming the earth return to be satisfactory, electrical faults will be due either to component malfunction or to defects in the current supply. Individual components are dealt with in Chapter 10. If supply wires are broken or cracked internally this results in an open-circuit, and the easiest way to check for this is to bypass the suspect wire temporarily with a length of wire having a crocodile clip or suitable connector at each end. Alternatively, a 12V test lamp can be used to verify the presence of supply voltage at various points along the wire and the break can be thus isolated.

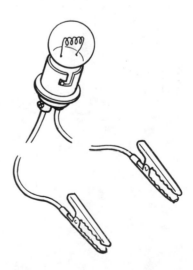

Simple test lamp is useful for tracing electrical faults

If a bare portion of a live wire touches the bodywork or other earthed metal part, the electricity will take the low-resistance path thus formed back to the battery: this is known as a short-circuit. Hopefully a short-circuit will blow a fuse, but otherwise it may cause burning of the insulation (and possibly further short-circuits) or even a fire. This is why it is inadvisable to bypass persistently blowing fuses with silver foil or wire.

Spares and tool kit

Most vehicles are supplied only with sufficient tools for wheel changing; the *Maintenance and minor repair* tool kit detailed in *Tools and working facilities,* with the addition of a hammer, is probably sufficient for those repairs that most motorists would consider attempting at the roadside. In addition a few items which can be fitted without too much trouble in the event of a breakdown should be carried. Experience and available space will modify the list below, but the following may save having to call on professional assistance:

Spark plugs, clean and correctly gapped
HT lead and plug cap – long enough to reach the plug furthest from the distributor
Distributor rotor, condenser and contact breaker points
Drivebelt(s) – emergency type may suffice
Spare fuses
Set of principal light bulbs
Tin of radiator sealer and hose bandage
Exhaust bandage
Roll of insulating tape

Length of soft iron wire
Length of electrical flex
Torch or inspection lamp (can double as test lamp)
Battery jump leads
Tow-rope
Ignition waterproofing aerosol
Litre of engine oil
Sealed can of hydraulic fluid
Emergency windscreen
Worm drive clips
Tube of filler paste

If spare fuel is carried, a can designed for the purpose should be used to minimise risks of leakage and collision damage. A first aid kit and a warning triangle, whilst not at present compulsory in the UK, are obviously sensible items to carry in addition to the above.

When touring abroad it may be advisable to carry additional spares which, even if you cannot fit them yourself, could save having to wait while parts are obtained. The items below may be worth considering:

Clutch and throttle cables
Cylinder head gasket
Alternator brushes
Fuel pump repair kit
Tyre valve core

One of the motoring organisations will be able to advise on availability of fuel etc in foreign countries.

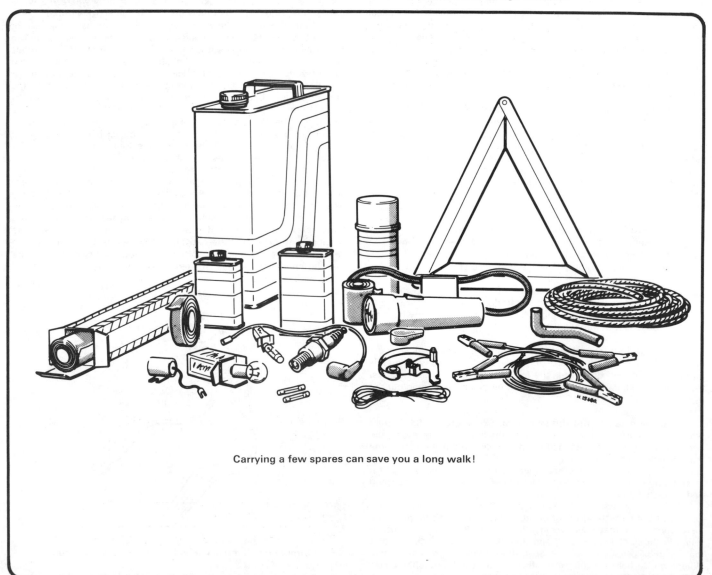

Carrying a few spares can save you a long walk!

Engine will not start

Engine fails to turn when starter operated
Flat battery (recharge, use jump leads, or push start)
Battery terminals loose or corroded
Battery earth to body defective
Engine earth strap loose or broken
Starter motor (or solenoid) wiring loose or broken
Automatic transmission selector in wrong position, or inhibitor switch faulty
Ignition/starter switch faulty
Major mechanical failure (seizure)
Starter or solenoid internal fault (see Chapter 10)

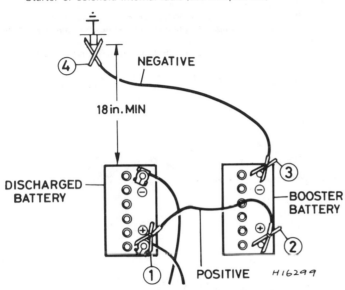

Jump start lead connections for negative earth vehicles – connect leads in order shown

Starter motor turns engine slowly
Partially discharged battery (recharge, use jump leads, or push start)
Battery terminals loose or corroded
Battery earth to body defective
Engine earth strap loose
Starter motor (or solenoid) wiring loose
Starter motor internal fault (see Chapter 10)

Starter motor spins without turning engine
Flat battery
Starter motor pinion sticking on sleeve
Flywheel gear teeth damaged or worn
Starter motor mounting bolts loose

Engine turns normally but fails to start
Damp or dirty HT leads and distributor cap (crank engine and check for spark)
Dirty or incorrectly gapped distributor points (if applicable)
No fuel in tank (check for delivery at carburettor)
Excessive choke (hot engine) or insufficient choke (cold engine)
Fouled or incorrectly gapped spark plugs (remove, clean and regap)
Other ignition system fault (see Chapter 4)
Other fuel system fault (see Chapter 3)
Poor compression
Major mechanical failure (eg camshaft drive)

Engine fires but will not run
Insufficient choke (cold engine)
Air leaks at carburettor or inlet manifold
Fuel starvation (see Chapter 3)
Ballast resistor defective, or other ignition fault (see Chapter 4)

Engine cuts out and will not restart

Engine cuts out suddenly – ignition fault
Loose or disconnected LT wires
Wet HT leads or distributor cap (after traversing water splash)
Coil or condenser failure (check for spark)
Other ignition fault (see Chapter 4)

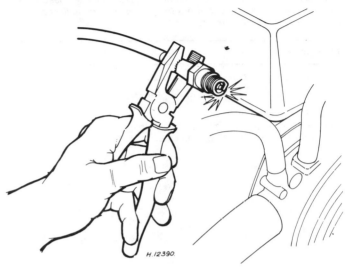

Crank engine and check for spark. Note use of insulated tool to hold plug lead

Engine misfires before cutting out – fuel fault
Fuel tank empty
Fuel pump defective or filter blocked (check for delivery)
Fuel tank filler vent blocked (suction will be evident on releasing cap)
Carburettor needle valve sticking
Carburettor jets blocked (fuel contaminated)
Other fuel system fault (see Chapter 3)

Engine cuts out – other causes
Serious overheating
Major mechanical failure (eg camshaft drive)

Engine overheats

Ignition (no-charge) warning light illuminated
Slack or broken drivebelt – retension or renew (Chapter 2)

Ignition warning light not illuminated
Coolant loss due to internal or external leakage (see Chapter 2)
Thermostat defective
Low oil level
Brakes binding
Radiator clogged externally or internally
Engine waterways clogged
Ignition timing incorrect or automatic advance malfunctioning
Mixture too weak

Note: *Do not add cold water to an overheated engine or damage may result*

Low engine oil pressure

Gauge reads low or warning light illuminated with engine running
Oil level low or incorrect grade
Defective gauge or sender unit

Wire to sender unit earthed
Engine overheating
Oil filter clogged or bypass valve defective
Oil pressure relief valve defective
Oil pick-up strainer clogged
Oil pump worn or mountings loose
Worn main or big-end bearings

Note: *Low oil pressure in a high-mileage engine at tickover is not necessarily a cause for concern. Sudden pressure loss at speed is far more significant. In any event, check the gauge or warning light sender before condemning the engine.*

Engine noises

Pre-ignition (pinking) on acceleration
Incorrect grade of fuel
Ignition timing incorrect
Distributor faulty or worn
Worn or maladjusted carburettor
Excessive carbon build-up in engine

Whistling or wheezing noises
Leaking vacuum hose
Leaking carburettor or manifold gasket
Blowing head gasket

Tapping or rattling
Incorrect valve clearances
Worn valve gear
Worn timing chain
Broken piston ring (ticking noise)

Knocking or thumping
Unintentional mechanical contact (eg fan blades)
Worn fanbelt
Peripheral component fault (generator, water pump etc)
Worn big-end bearings (regular heavy knocking, perhaps less under load)
Worn main bearings (rumbling and knocking, perhaps worsening under load)
Piston slap (most noticeable when cold)

Conversion factors

Length (distance)
Inches (in)	X	25.4	= Millimetres (mm)	X 0.0394	= Inches (in)
Feet (ft)	X	0.305	= Metres (m)	X 3.281	= Feet (ft)
Miles	X	1.609	= Kilometres (km)	X 0.621	= Miles

Volume (capacity)
Cubic inches (cu in; in^3)	X	16.387	= Cubic centimetres (cc; cm^3)	X 0.061	= Cubic inches (cu in; in^3)
Imperial pints (Imp pt)	X	0.568	= Litres (l)	X 1.76	= Imperial pints (Imp pt)
Imperial quarts (Imp qt)	X	1.137	= Litres (l)	X 0.88	= Imperial quarts (Imp qt)
Imperial quarts (Imp qt)	X	1.201	= US quarts (US qt)	X 0.833	= Imperial quarts (Imp qt)
US quarts (US qt)	X	0.946	= Litres (l)	X 1.057	= US quarts (US qt)
Imperial gallons (Imp gal)	X	4.546	= Litres (l)	X 0.22	= Imperial gallons (Imp gal)
Imperial gallons (Imp gal)	X	1.201	= US gallons (US gal)	X 0.833	= Imperial gallons (Imp gal)
US gallons (US gal)	X	3.785	= Litres (l)	X 0.264	= US gallons (US gal)

Mass (weight)
Ounces (oz)	X	28.35	= Grams (g)	X 0.035	= Ounces (oz)
Pounds (lb)	X	0.454	= Kilograms (kg)	X 2.205	= Pounds (lb)

Force
Ounces-force (ozf; oz)	X	0.278	= Newtons (N)	X 3.6	= Ounces-force (ozf; oz)
Pounds-force (lbf; lb)	X	4.448	= Newtons (N)	X 0.225	= Pounds-force (lbf; lb)
Newtons (N)	X	0.1	= Kilograms-force (kgf; kg)	X 9.81	= Newtons (N)

Pressure
Pounds-force per square inch (psi; lbf/in^2; lb/in^2)	X	0.070	= Kilograms-force per square centimetre (kgf/cm^2; kg/cm^2)	X 14.223	= Pounds-force per square inch (psi; lbf/in^2; lb/in^2)
Pounds-force per square inch (psi; lbf/in^2; lb/in^2)	X	0.068	= Atmospheres (atm)	X 14.696	= Pounds-force per square inch (psi; lbf/in^2; lb/in^2)
Pounds-force per square inch (psi; lbf/in^2; lb/in^2)	X	0.069	= Bars	X 14.5	= Pounds-force per square inch (psi; lbf/in^2; lb/in^2)
Pounds-force per square inch (psi; lbf/in^2; lb/in^2)	X	6.895	= Kilopascals (kPa)	X 0.145	= Pounds-force per square inch (psi; lbf/in^2; lb/in^2)
Kilopascals (kPa)	X	0.01	= Kilograms-force per square centimetre (kgf/cm^2; kg/cm^2)	X 98.1	= Kilopascals (kPa)

Torque (moment of force)
Pounds-force inches (lbf in; lb in)	X	1.152	= Kilograms-force centimetre (kgf cm; kg cm)	X 0.868	= Pounds-force inches (lbf in; lb in)
Pounds-force inches (lbf in; lb in)	X	0.113	= Newton metres (Nm)	X 8.85	= Pounds-force inches (lbf in; lb in)
Pounds-force inches (lbf in; lb in)	X	0.083	= Pounds-force feet (lbf ft; lb ft)	X 12	= Pounds-force inches (lbf in; lb in)
Pounds-force feet (lbf ft; lb ft)	X	0.138	= Kilograms-force metres (kgf m; kg m)	X 7.233	= Pounds-force feet (lbf ft; lb ft)
Pounds-force feet (lbf ft; lb ft)	X	1.356	= Newton metres (Nm)	X 0.738	= Pounds-force feet (lbf ft; lb ft)
Newton metres (Nm)	X	0.102	= Kilograms-force metres (kgf m; kg m)	X 9.804	= Newton metres (Nm)

Power
Horsepower (hp)	X	745.7	= Watts (W)	X 0.0013	= Horsepower (hp)

Velocity (speed)
Miles per hour (miles/hr; mph)	X	1.609	= Kilometres per hour (km/hr; kph)	X 0.621	= Miles per hour (miles/hr; mph)

Fuel consumption*
Miles per gallon, Imperial (mpg)	X	0.354	= Kilometres per litre (km/l)	X 2.825	= Miles per gallon, Imperial (mpg)
Miles per gallon, US (mpg)	X	0.425	= Kilometres per litre (km/l)	X 2.352	= Miles per gallon, US (mpg)

Temperature
Degrees Fahrenheit $= (°C \times 1.8) + 32$ Degrees Celsius (Degrees Centigrade; °C) $= (°F - 32) \times 0.56$

*It is common practice to convert from miles per gallon (mpg) to litres/100 kilometres (l/100km), where mpg (Imperial) x l/100 km = 282 and mpg (US) x l/100 km = 235

Index

Printed by
J H Haynes & Co Ltd
Sparkford Nr Yeovil
Somerset BA22 7JJ England